BILL ZIMMERMAN

TROUBLEMAKER

Bill Zimmerman, who holds a doctorate in psychology from the University of Chicago, is one of the nation's most experienced political consultants. As cofounder of the leading consulting firm Zimmerman & Markman, whose work for ballot initiatives and for organizations such as the ACLU, NRDC, and MoveOn.org has won multiple awards, he continues to advocate for social justice.

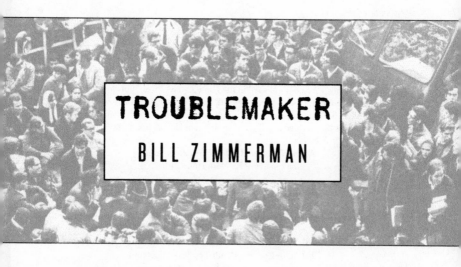

TROUBLEMAKER
BILL ZIMMERMAN

A MEMOIR FROM THE FRONT LINES OF THE SIXTIES

Anchor Books
A Division of Random House, Inc.
New York

For Joan, Nico, and Emma,

My past, present, and future

♦

FIRST ANCHOR BOOKS EDITION, JUNE 2012

Copyright © 2011 by Bill Zimmerman

The Library of Congress has cataloged the Doubleday edition as follows:
Zimmerman, Bill, 1940–
Troublemaker : a memoir from the front lines of the sixties / Bill Zimmerman. —1st ed.
p. cm.
1. Zimmerman, Bill, 1940– 2. Political activists—United States—Biography.
3. Civil rights workers—United States—Biography.
4. Civil rights movements—United States—History—20th century.
5. Vietnam War, 1961–1975—Protest movements.
6. Peace movements—United States—History—20th century.
7. United States—Politics and government—1963–1969.
8. United States—Politics and government—1969–1974.
9. United States—Social conditions—1960–1980.
10. Nineteen sixties. I. Title.
CT275.Z557A3 2011
973.92092—dc22
[B] 2010042787

Anchor ISBN: 978-0-307-73950-6

Author photograph © Markus Goerg
Map on page 334 by Mapping Specialists, Ltd.

Printed in the United States of America
10 9 8 7 6 5 4 3 2 1

One such wave (and not the least) I raised and rolled before the breath of an idea, till it reached its crest, and toppled over and fell at Damascus. The wash of that wave, thrown back by the resistance of vested things, will provide the matter of the following wave, when in fullness of time the sea shall be raised once more.

T. E. Lawrence, *Seven Pillars of Wisdom* (1926)

The events and occurrences in this book all happened as I describe them. To the extent possible, I have used real names, and when a person is initially identified by first and last names, the reader can assume it is a real name. When the initial identification is by first name only, that name is fictitious.

THE SOUND, BIG AND DEEP LIKE THE ROAR OF A GREAT BEAST, ROLLED UP FROM THE street below and spilled into our attic room in the little hotel. We bolted to the window to peer down on Boulevard St. Michel, the grand avenue of the Latin Quarter. No vehicles moved. Across the wide street French gendarmes were lined up shoulder to shoulder and three deep. Poised to charge, they held their lead-weighted batons at the ready. Arrayed opposite were the students of Paris, tens of thousands of them, also shoulder to shoulder across the boulevard but stretching back for blocks. Their defiant chant, "*Paix en Algérie . . . Paix en Algérie*," echoed repeatedly. It was the fall of 1960. We were three twenty-year-old dropouts from the University of Chicago living in a cheap hotel in Paris, and we had never seen anything like this.

We pounded down five flights of stairs as the chants continued. We had heard about student demonstrations, but here was a real one, and we were about to see it. We knew these student protests had influenced European political affairs and provoked political upheavals. We knew the students chanting for peace in Algeria were protesting the French government's war against an independence movement in their North African colony. But demonstrations like this were entirely unknown in the United States. The marches and freedom rides of the civil rights movement had not yet occurred, and the massive demonstrations to protest the U.S. war in Viet Nam were far in the future. It was the first year of the new

decade, but America remained firmly anchored in the 1950s, when political dissent was either ignored or suppressed.

Being young and curious, we ran out of the hotel and fell in with the
protesters. Before we could get our bearings, the phalanx of gendarmes
charged the crowd. People panicked. I saw one gendarme over the heads
of the crowd just as he swung his club across the face of a young student.
The blow was so vicious it made me wince. Protesters fought back briefly
but were no match for trained policemen inflicting great bodily harm.
Confused and fearful for our own heads, we fled the swinging batons and
with a group of students ran into the maze of side streets bordering the
grand boulevard.

The gendarmes followed. They chased us for two blocks. I was scared
and struggling for breath, but they finally gave up and turned back toward
the boulevard. I was then surprised to see the twenty students in the group
turn and head back as well. Instead of taking advantage of their escape,
they were returning to the fray. I did not understand why, but the three of
us were sufficiently interested and reckless enough to find out, so we
tagged along. Meanwhile, similar scenes must have happened elsewhere
because once back on St. Michel, I saw other groups of students emerge
from the side streets and rush the cops. Directly in front of us, gendarmes
pursued a band of students, so our group attacked them from behind. The
gendarmes, off balance because they had to change direction, could not
form a larger group. Frustrated, they became more vicious. I saw protesters thrown to the ground and beaten mercilessly.

The three of us were not sure what we were doing or why, but we continued to run with the demonstrators and elude the police. Twice our
movements took us near the river Seine. There I saw soldiers standing in
formations of about one hundred under or near the bridges. They had
rifles at the ready with fixed bayonets, but they did not move. They were a
reserve force waiting to crush the protesters if the police were unable to do
so. I realized that the demonstration had been futile. If troops like these
were ready to intervene, troops who could not be stopped by mere protesters, of what use was all the action on the street?

In the end, the troops were not needed. The gendarmes eventually
made it impossible for the protesters to move in packs. Groups of any size

were attacked. As we walked back to our hotel, two gendarmes ordered us to stop. One carried a tommy gun that looked as if it had been a prop in a 1930s gangster movie. I had never seen an automatic weapon on a city street. Instead of slinging it over his shoulder, the gendarme had the strap around his neck with the rifle held horizontally and pointed at one of my friends. With his finger resting on the trigger, even an inadvertent sneeze could set it off. In a belligerent tone, they demanded our "papers." We knew the drill and dutifully produced our precious U.S. passports. The gendarmes, ready to take us down, saw the U.S. documentation and waved us off.

Back at the hotel, students were crowded into the small bar and in the midst of a heated discussion. We tried to listen. Their French came too fast to understand, but a friendly student from the University of Grenoble translated for us. When the crowd dispersed, we offered to buy him a meal in exchange for a thorough account of what had happened on the streets. What I learned in that conversation turned everything I had just seen on its head. It was my first lesson in political strategy.

Daniel, the French student, claimed that what had looked like a defeat in which the police ran the students off the streets had actually almost toppled the French government of President Charles de Gaulle, which had been its objective all along. I was incredulous. Topple the government? Are you kidding? It was a rout! But Daniel stuck to his story and explained that French students had supported the Algerian war for independence for several years, and that student groups across France, acting in concert, had planned this demonstration for months. They believed the de Gaulle government would not relinquish its colony in Algeria no matter the lives lost, and that the only way to end the war was to overturn the government itself.

The strategy behind the demonstration, as Daniel explained it, was far from what a politically unsophisticated person like me could have seen. The students had good reason to risk fighting the police. If the police failed to control them, the army troops waiting patiently under the bridges would be deployed, which was exactly what the students wanted. They believed that if the government used the army against its own people on the streets of Paris, the resulting injuries and possible deaths would outrage the citizens of France, who would then demand their parliament form a new government. In classical jujitsu fashion, the purpose of the demonstration was not to win the street fight but to lose it, not to the police but to the army. If the military power of the army was used against the protesters, the students believed they could redirect the reaction into sufficient political power to achieve their ultimate objective, a new government ready to accept the inevitability of Algerian independence. (While the students lost to the police in the demonstration I witnessed, their continued protests, in combination with events in Algeria, eventually did force de Gaulle to acknowledge Algerian independence in 1962, which allowed him to survive in office until 1969.)

Daniel's strategy swept me off my feet. His line of reasoning sounded farfetched, but it revealed a way of thinking about politics and political struggle I knew nothing about. It was my first exposure to the rules of guerrilla warfare and how those rules could be applied to politics. Later I would learn more from the writings of Sun Tzu and others, and would come to understand that guerrilla tactics were actually a systematic method by which the weak can effectively fight the strong. I was a long way from such knowledge as I listened to Daniel that October night in Paris in 1960, but a window opened for me, a window that would grow wider in the years to come.

The notion that a political movement could win political victories by losing physical battles was one I saw in wide application only a few years later during the southern civil rights movement. As friends and I tried to stop the U.S. war in Viet Nam — just as Daniel and his comrades had tried to stop the French war in Algeria — we saw that principle repeated time and again. We lost dramatic and highly publicized street battles to various police departments but in so doing created enough political force to limit and then end the war in Viet Nam. I had been in awe of Daniel's comrades and their audacious strategy to bring down a French president, yet in less than a decade our efforts in the United States would help bring down one president and six years later a second.

We had no way to predict it, but with astounding speed the fifteen years that followed my encounter in Paris upended the United States, shook it loose from its cultural and political moorings, and fundamentally redefined it as a nation and society. I was part of that upending. I spent those fifteen years, 1960 to 1975, as a radical political activist. I witnessed or participated in many of the seminal events of those times and worked with many of the people who became famous during them.

I began as a volunteer in the southern civil rights movement, then joined and organized protests during the early years of the war. Along the way, I earned a Ph.D. and became a brain scientist, but quickly discovered that the military would be first to actually use my research, and not for humanitarian purposes. Renouncing my scientific career, I became one of the national leaders of the antiwar movement and helped spread it into new sectors of society. When our massive and militant demonstrations ran up against the limits of guerrilla tactics, we shifted to more traditional methods and eventually helped end the war by organizing citizens to effectively pressure their elected representatives in Washington.

Like other radical activists at that time, I often broke the law. I took chances with my physical safety, and on several occasions put my life on the line. I was arrested, indicted, or jailed for violating state and federal laws; some were serious felonies, like "conspiracy to commit offenses against the United States," that came with long prison sentences, yet I spent little time behind bars. I did join unlawful political conspiracies and did carry out illegal acts, but always in the belief that the authorities were abusing their power and acting unlawfully themselves. I never hurt anyone or intentionally jeopardized anyone's safety. I had no money, limited physical comfort, and no prospects for the future. But like others who had rejected society's conventional benefits and rewards, I became immune to the threat of their withdrawal.

The lives of a vast number of young people like me were turned upside down by the intense political struggles of the sixties and the moral imperatives they imposed. We gave up friendships, marriages, careers, financial security, and personal safety to join a movement that fundamentally altered our country and our culture. But these sacrifices were not motivated by guilt or asceticism. On the contrary, we loved a good time. We enshrined spontaneity, loved exuberance, and enthusiastically embraced all manner of stimulation and inspiration. Yet in spite of our wildness and the determined opposition of our elders, we built the largest mass movement in the modern history of the United States and contributed to a cultural transformation of unprecedented scope and speed.

Unlike Daniel and his friends, we were a student movement isolated from our past. While student activism had been a virtual institution in Paris and other European capitals for decades, U.S. students had never been significant actors on the political stage. Worse, we were cut off from older progressives by the witch hunts and loyalty oaths of the McCarthy era in the 1950s. As a result, we rose up not as a class but as a generation, the first in American history to do so. Cut off from those who might have given us guidance, and distrustful of almost everyone older than ourselves, we casually assumed that the previous generation was the enemy.

Alone, we navigated without compass or chart through new crosscurrents of political and social turmoil: assassination, youth rebellion, cultural upheaval, urban rioting, drug use, and sexual liberation. When the prospect of fighting, and possibly dying, in a pointless and criminal war in Viet Nam was added to this mix, the result was predictably chaotic.

We became a loose-knit army of young protesters who rejected economic exploitation and insisted on making love, not war. At times, we benefited from strategic leadership; at others, nimble individuals thrust suddenly to the forefront in the midst of spontaneous eruptions of protest provided spur-of-the-moment tactical leadership that allowed us to succeed. Our movement had but a few years to live through its childhood before the demands of maturity were thrust upon it. In many ways, we failed to meet those demands. In others, we performed with a brilliance and creativity never before seen in political combat.

Too many Americans now see the sixties as a spasm of reckless sexual and political abandon fueled by mind-altering drugs and hypnotic music, a temporary hiccup in the march toward American prosperity snuffed out by the conservative era that followed. They are mistaken. Sex, drugs, and rock and roll played their part, as did selfishness and self-interest, but the political movements of the period were built not by hedonists but by patriots. Our crime, if any, was in taking seriously the ideals of freedom and equality we had learned in school, so much so that we willingly sacrificed personal advantage and passionately fought back when those ideals were violated.

This book is a memoir of a life lived in the midst of that fascinating maelstrom, when millions of American youth were swept into political activism, and millions more were altered and shaped by new values and perspectives. The sixties exert a profound influence on us today, as they echo through much of our culture and politics. How remarkable that we were only kids when it all started, inexperienced college students, but that before it was over we had managed to build the astonishing, exuberant, reckless, effective, and inspiring marvel that roiled America between 1960 and 1975.

CHAPTER 1

WE HAD A CHOICE BETWEEN GRAVEL AND GRASS AND ALWAYS CHOSE GRAVEL. TWO blocks away, Garfield Park beckoned with a vast ocean of grass and trees, but we rarely went there. We were city kids, street kids, and the park was out of our element. We favored the Delano Elementary School playground with its odd mixture of hard-packed gravel and sand. My childhood friends and I hung out there, playing ball in the afternoons and into the night. We lived in a gritty working-class neighborhood on Chicago's West Side, but it was safe. The fifties were a safe decade. Few people questioned authority, and fewer still broke the rules.

On the east side of the park, everyone was black. On the west side, where I lived, we were all white. Italians dominated the neighborhood, but there were also Irish, Poles, and Jews. People stuck to their own kind. Race prejudice was the rule. Once, a black family moved across the park into an apartment a block from ours. Italian vigilantes made short work of them: rocks through their windows, racist slogans painted on their wall, insults shouted late into the night. The black family resisted until the first shotgun blast, then moved back across the park. Some of the rules were strictly enforced.

I was born the day after Christmas 1940, and despite my family's relative poverty I enjoyed a happy childhood with my parents and younger sister in a third-floor apartment across from the school. At times I had to pay a nickel toll to the little Italian gang leader for safe passage into the play-

ground; at others I used my fists to resist. I had friends, plenty to do after
school, and loving parents. Yet I knew from an early age that I didn't want
the lives my parents and relatives had so cautiously built. The 1950s were
the first period of calm after the twin traumas of the Great Depression and
World War II. The grown-ups around me worked hard to protect secure
but essentially boring lives. I wanted adventure and discovery.

My parents had been Jewish refugees as children. My mother came to
America in 1912 at age three, fleeing pogroms in Latvia. My father landed
at Ellis Island in 1910 at eighteen, in flight from the draft for the Austro-
Hungarian army. They had but one year of college between them but
were smart, well-informed, and respectful of learning. They were kind
and loving to my younger sister and me, and my father worked hard running a small wholesale novelty business as he strived to give us a middle-
class upbringing.

My carefree childhood ended at twelve when my mother required
extensive surgery to remove a malignant tumor on her spine. The tumor
led to a case of syringomyelia, a treatable condition today but one that
then left her a semi-invalid in chronic debilitating pain. This was before
families like ours had health insurance, so my father had to spend his life
savings on her care. I resolved at that point, just as I entered high school,
to earn what I could to ease his burden. I got after-school, Saturday, and
summer jobs, and remained employed in that fashion for the next twelve
years, until I completed my lengthy education.

Austin High School, which I attended with five thousand others
between 1954 and 1958, was an academic joke. In 1957, the Russians
launched *Sputnik*, the world's first space satellite, and shocked Americans
into the painful realization that we were no longer winning the race to
space. *Life* magazine picked Austin High to represent the sad state of
American education. In a photo-laden article that contrasted a friend of
mine from the varsity swimming team with a typical Russian high school
student, *Life* slammed American scientific teaching. The hardworking
Russian student was seen in various Moscow science laboratories, while
my friend was depicted in pursuit of fun and games. One picture, shot
from the back of an Austin classroom, showed students looking through
racy magazines shielded inside textbooks and invisible to the teacher in

front. *Life* achieved its purpose. Many of us were pushed into science curriculums to help overcome the widening "missile gap" with the Soviet Union that John Kennedy later used as the rationale for his 1960 presidential campaign.

But for me high school was a lark. I rarely worked hard, yet consistently got top grades. After school, I swam with the varsity team and won the city championship in the backstroke. During my first two years, I worked as a bicycle delivery boy for a local drugstore two nights a week and all day Saturday. Later, after getting my driver's license, I had a similar schedule delivering pizza. At fifteen, I worked full-time during the summer as a warehouseman loading trucks. At sixteen, the summer employment picture dramatically improved. Thanks to my swimming ability, I landed a job as a Chicago Park District lifeguard.

Being slightly nearsighted, I was assigned to a park pool rather than a Lake Michigan beach. The girls were at the beach, so I was crestfallen. When I told my father, he offered to "pull some strings." Several nights later, we sat in the storefront office of our local alderman waiting with the

Morse Avenue Beach lifeguard crew, summer 1959. I am in the middle row, second from the left. *Chicago Park District/Author's collection*

other supplicants who sought his favor. When it was our turn, my father explained the situation. The alderman turned to the precinct captain, who lived on our block and coordinated affairs between our neighbors and the city government, and asked if my parents were good Democrats. Yes, he answered, they always vote Democratic. Well, then, let's see if we can do something for their boy. Three days later I was assigned to the beach. It was my first taste of politics, Chicago-style. It would not be my last.

That summer was marvelous. I was paid $2 an hour, a princely sum at the time. With no concern for the future, I bought an old Pontiac for $150 and used it to learn to fly. Two years before, at fourteen, after building a lot of model planes, I had coaxed my father into paying for a ride in a single-engine airplane. When we lifted off Meigs Field, Chicago's old lakefront airport, I was in the co-pilot's seat of a Beechcraft. Floating over the downtown skyscrapers, we turned south toward Comiskey Park, home of the White Sox. The pilot then banked north, flew past the downtown skyscrapers and on to Wrigley Field, home of the Cubs, before returning to land. Only twenty-five minutes had passed, but I was hooked for life.

Pilots were the most glamorous of the celebrated warriors of World War II, and with the recent introduction of jet fighters they were more glamorous still. I thought being a military pilot could be the door to an adventurous life, even to the ultimate goal of space flight. So, whenever I could, I drove the old Pontiac northwest of the city to Palwaukee Airport, a small field with two grass strips and a short paved runway, to take flying lessons. My parents didn't like what I was doing, but it was my money and I would not be deterred. By summer's end I had twenty hours of solo flight time in a Piper J-3 Cub. It was enough to legitimately call myself a pilot, but not yet enough for a license to carry passengers.

Back in high school for my senior year, I thought of college for the first time. I knew nothing about higher education and assumed I would attend a two-year community college (they were called junior colleges then). My homeroom teacher, Virginia Heyse, noticed that I was curious and articulate and had gotten good grades with ease. She insisted I apply to the better schools, and when I objected that my family lacked the money for me to do so, she offered to help me apply for scholarships. Her intervention utterly changed my life.

The University of Chicago offered me full tuition. No doubt, I was a charity case, a poor kid with good grades and test scores from a culturally deprived environment. I knew nothing of the university's high academic stature, or why such stature was important. I was focused on the cost, and the scholarship meant that UC would cost no more than the local junior college. I was disappointed that UC didn't have a varsity football team or a Reserve Officers' Training Corps program to fast-track students into the military, two elements I had thought essential to college life, but neither did the junior college. My father was unable to help with expenses, but by living at home, getting a job at night, and commuting on public transportation, I could manage. On the basis of such primitive reasoning, I accepted the scholarship and unknowingly embarked upon a profound transformation. Three months later I would be a different person.

During Orientation Week in the fall of 1958, all UC students had to live in dorms, even the few commuters like me. I arrived on the sprawling and distinguished campus with its ivy-covered walls and gray stone buildings wearing blue jeans and a T-shirt. Over my shoulder I had a blue drawstring laundry bag with a few changes of underwear and some extra shirts. My classmates arrived with steamer trunks. They were the cream of the national high school crop. I was the token kid from Chicago's down-and-dirty West Side. Many of them had been educated at elite private schools in New York and New England and had studied subjects like psychology and calculus. I had never heard of calculus. They were conversant with art and literature. I had never been in a museum of art, never attended a concert, and never read a work of literature other than the three (A Tale of Two Cities, Wuthering Heights, and The Good Earth) I had been forced to study in what passed for a high school English class.

All of a sudden I was looking up from the bottom. I had hoped my education would be a stepping-stone to flight school and the space program, and I had naively thought that majoring in physics was the best way to get there. I should have been counseled to select another major, but was not. At UC there were Nobel laureates teaching the physical science classes. I could barely understand the lectures, and I became so confused and left behind I felt as if I had landed on another planet. How could school be so difficult when up to that point it had been so easy? Slowly, I began to realize that I had indeed landed in a parallel universe and that, in fact, my humanities and social science courses revealed another world I had never known, a world of books and ideas and critical thinking and intellectual curiosity.

My academic performance was dismal. I came close to failing all of my physical science courses. I was provoked by the humanities and social science classes, but felt completely at sea in them as well, having never known those fields even existed. Yet ideas began to stir, nurtured especially by the social science classes and new friends in the cafeteria and the campus poolroom, the one arena in which my West Side roots gave me a rare advantage. These new friends questioned traditional American culture and chafed at social constraints that seemed arbitrarily conformist and conservative. That, I could understand.

By the fall of 1958, a tiny beatnik subculture had emerged on the nation's elite college campuses. Its few adherents read the new Beat poets and ostentatiously rejected various social norms, especially dress codes, the girls making themselves visible with a new style, black tights under their skirts. Initially, I was enough of a jock to hold them in disdain, but then I succeeded in taking one to bed. There I learned that rebelling against society included rebelling against its sexual restraints, and the girls with black tights were leading the way. The beatnik perspective began to make sense.

I entered UC with a naive belief in god and country. Unaware of other cultures and ways of life, I had assumed that the United States was first in everything good and last in everything bad. Within months, my worldview changed dramatically. The humanities and social sciences classes at the university relied on the Socratic method, so I was forced to take part in the intellectual back-and-forth. UC had no graduate student teaching assistants, and the professors who led the classes taught critical thinking, no matter what the course content. Since I had to read voluminously in the classics and study both history and human behavior, my views soon exploded beyond the narrow American horizon in which they had been confined.

I wanted to participate more fully in campus life. My commute took over two hours a day. I swam with the varsity team in the afternoon and worked as a telephone solicitor at night. All of that, on top of my increasingly incomprehensible science and math classes, overwhelmed me. I left high school friends behind to spend time with new friends interested in books and ideas instead of sports and fast cars. But after one quarter I could no longer take the stress. I used my status as a varsity swimmer to get a cushy job doing minor maintenance in the field house. The higher salary, plus meager savings, allowed me to move to a dorm on campus. Then, in a stumbling and disjointed way, I embraced opinions that previously had been anathema to me.

Soon I too was in rebellion against the rigid conformity of the 1950s, a rebellion that was enhanced when Jack Kerouac, Allen Ginsberg, and Gregory Corso swept through Chicago. They were the most visible stars of the notorious Beat Generation, come to town to read their wild poetry. They set up in a small downtown ballroom. When my friends and I arrived, it looked as if all the bohemians from Bughouse Square, the local venue for soapbox oratory, had come too. The poets railed against the prevailing culture and were raucously applauded at every attack on conventional society. The Beats didn't wait for people to come gradually to their own conclusions, as our professors did, but instead hit them upside the head with their radical critique of contemporary American culture and social mores. Their poetry was laced with profanity never heard in public, and they took special pleasure in attacking the sacred cows of our conformist culture. My friends and I were smitten. We had never experienced anything like them, and we realized that if they could get away with that kind of behavior, so could we.

I doubt my friends and I could have clearly articulated it, but somehow we understood that much of society's moral authority had been undermined by the nuclear arms race and the Holocaust, two facts that deeply colored our perception of the world. The two most powerful nations on earth were poised to annihilate the human species, their nuclear weapons on hair triggers. Our government had already used those weapons against unarmed civilians, so it wasn't hard to imagine it doing so again. As schoolchildren we had been forced to hide under our desks and participate in useless air raid drills, which only reminded us that our death, indeed our actual vaporization, could occur in the next second and with no warning.

I was nine years old when the fifties began. The Nazi concentration camps had been shut down only five years before I was first made aware of them. One of my father's sisters, both of their husbands with several children, and numerous distant relatives had perished at Dachau and Buchenwald. It did not take an especially sensitive soul to understand that human beings were capable of unimaginable acts of horror and cruelty against other human beings.

My generation grew up under these twin clouds: that the end of the world might come in the next instant, and that human cruelty knew no limits, even in the most advanced civilizations. In the late 1950s, most students reluctantly agreed that these two horrors were a necessary part of living in society. A few of us rebelled and claimed that no society capable of giving rise to concentration camps and nuclear weapons had the moral authority to govern anyone's behavior. We sat then on the cusp of a new decade. Friends who accepted the social order later remained anchored to the culture of the fifties. The others, like me, who rejected it, did so unaware that another culture lay just over the horizon.

The confusion, questioning, and uncertainty that characterized my first year in college ended, and I returned to my summer job as a beach lifeguard. I had long since given up thoughts of flying lessons and saved my salary for campus expenses. I still wanted to fly, but military regimentation had become the opposite of what I wanted from life.

Late one summer night as I drove home along Lake Shore Drive, a car sped past me going far too fast to make the next curve. In a spectacular crash, it rolled over six or seven times, then tumbled end over end three times and came to rest upside down. As a lifeguard, I was trained in first aid, so I pulled over and ran to the wreck, which had started to burn. Seven teenage boys were packed inside. I pulled out two with severe injuries. Three others crawled out through windows without assistance. Two remained inside and unconscious. I got one out but had to put a tourniquet around his upper arm. By the time I finished, the front of the car was engulfed in flames, and I barely got the last victim out. A large crowd had gathered, but they all stood watching, not lifting a finger to help. When paramedics arrived, I told them what I knew about each victim and then walked off through the crowd of emergency vehicles and onlookers. People pointed at me, but I ignored them and drove away.

I knew I had performed heroically, and if I remained at the scene, I would be the subject of a news story the next day. But walking away had greater appeal. Maybe I had listened too often to *Lone Ranger* radio programs as a little boy, each of which ended with the nameless hero riding off as a bystander invariably asked, "Who was that masked man?" Or maybe I just wanted to believe I had helped for the right reasons rather than to draw attention to myself. In any case, a wave of satisfaction washed over me as I drove home. I liked being the Lone Ranger. It was a pure act, unpolluted by ego, and it made me feel more like a man.

When I returned to UC in the fall of 1959, I changed majors. Physics had been a disaster. During my first year I had not gotten a single A or B, only Cs and Ds. I put aside adolescent dreams of space flight, and based on what had interested me the year before, I declared myself a social science major. I liked the readings for my new classes: Gibbon on the fall of the Roman Empire, with obvious lessons for post–World War II America; Thucydides and Trotsky writing histories of wars they had personally commanded. It was my good fortune that the University of Chicago used no textbooks in their social science and humanities courses, only original sources. Because of those readings, the ideal of the scholar-activist seeped into my consciousness, and I realized one could be committed to ideas and still have an impact on the world.

It was a fascinating year, intellectually and socially. I made lasting friendships, enjoyed late-night rap sessions about remarkable books, and experimented with alcohol and marijuana. In 1959, gender-segregated dormitories prohibited women not only from men's rooms but even from the lobbies and common areas. The mixed-gender dormitories of today were not only unknown but unthinkable. However, at UC we were confined to dormitories only during our first year. For my second, a roommate and I shared a low-rent apartment in the Hyde Park neighborhood surrounding the campus. Living without supervision, we developed our first mature relationships with young women.

But there was a lot missing that year. My friends and I had no sense of direction and no ambition for work after college. We felt alienated from the larger society we were preparing to join. We emulated the Beat writers and poets, became outsiders, beatniks, and embraced that role. We grew beards at a time when no one else did, wore scruffy clothes to protest conformist styles, and in general questioned every conventional opinion we could. Yet beneath our arrogant and rebellious attitude, we were lost. We didn't know why we were in college. It was often fun and intellectually stimulating, but we had no idea where it was leading or where we wanted to go.

At UC then, class attendance was optional; we had only to pass our final exams. Taking full advantage, we made frequent weekend trips to New York, either hitchhiking or taking drive-away cars. Owners paid to have these cars delivered to another city so they could make the trip more comfortably by air. Students often drove them to get free transportation. Once in New York, we went to jazz clubs and hung out in Greenwich Village, then drove nonstop back to Chicago. Jack Kerouac's *On the Road* was our bible, but like that of its characters much of our wandering was aimless, moving for the sake of moving, rather than actually having a destination. Our intellectual alienation gradually provoked a deeper distancing that led us to question many aspects of conventional life.

At the end of that second school year, I suggested to two friends, Scott Van Leuven and Ron Chutter, that we save what we could over the summer and use our money to go to Europe in the fall. The university allowed students to drop out if they returned within a year. In Europe, we could live cheaply and stay until our money ran out. I moved back into my parents' home and spent my fourth summer as a lifeguard. Then, in September 1960, the three of us gathered in Chicago, took a drive-away car to New York, and from there hitchhiked to Canada, where cattle boats offered passage to England for only $50. Being bearded and looking as scruffy as we did, it was remarkable we were offered any rides at all, but late one night we walked across the border at Calais, Maine.

A tall, very proper, and very stiff Canadian immigration officer waved us into a shack and gave us forms to fill out. We could see he viewed us as pollutants about to soil his native land. Where the immigration form asked for national origin, I entered "U.S.," but the officer pushed me for a different answer. You're Hebrew, aren't you? I already knew all I needed to about anti-Semitism, and I strongly objected. He crossed off "U.S." and entered "Hebrew" on my form. Insults were hurled, and the Mounties soon had us in handcuffs. They "escorted" us across the bridge back to Maine. I doubt many others enjoy the distinction of having been deported from Canada for being Jewish.

We were forced to hitchhike back to New York, where we bought tickets on a French Line steamship, the SS *Flandre*, for $150. It was a big bite out of the $1,000 we had each brought with us, but there was no alternative. Five days later, we disembarked in Le Havre and made our way to Paris. We rented a cheap hotel room in the Latin Quarter, the neighborhood surrounding the Sorbonne on the city's Left Bank. After a few days, we enrolled in a French-language class at the Alliance Française and settled into a routine of morning classes and afternoon and evening exploration of Paris and all it had to offer. A month later, we first heard the roar of the student demonstration on Boulevard St. Michel.

CHAPTER 2

WE WERE TYPICAL AMERICAN STUDENTS IN PARIS. SCOTT, SHORT AND SOLID, TRAMPED around in a big navy blue duffle coat with a hood. Ron, taller and very thin, sported a wispy goatee and dressed as unattractively as possible. We saw cathedrals in and around Paris, the architecture and history of which we had studied at UC. We visited sites of the French Revolution, also a topic of study. We had coffee in the cafés that Jean-Paul Sartre and Simone de Beauvoir had made famous in their existential novels. We loitered in Henry Miller's old bookstore, having already read his previously banned books. We bumped into Gregory Corso, the Beat poet, on the street and spent an afternoon with him. And always we read voraciously.

Too soon, our money ran out. Scott and I went to London to find work. Ron went south to Spain to escape the cold. London was a bust. With dwindling cash reserves, there was only one way Scott and I could stay overseas—a kibbutz. The collective farms in Israel offered room and board in exchange for labor. I was not a Zionist, and Scott was not even Jewish, but it was too soon to go home. We learned of a Greek steamship that sailed from the southern tip of Italy through the Greek islands to Israel. Steerage passage was dirt cheap. We headed south.

Scott gave me a new perspective on the world. His father had been a left-wing writer blacklisted in the fifties. Until then, I had identified somewhat unthinkingly with the Beats' blanket rejection of conventional society. Scott showed me that there were political and moral reasons for that rejection. He introduced me to class politics and added to what little I knew of Marxism. We became close friends. At five feet seven inches, he was three inches shorter than I was. I was thinner and more agile, but his square build suggested hidden strength. A large Z-shaped scar on his forehead was the souvenir of a teenage traffic accident. While we looked nothing alike—I had black hair, and he was fair—we were equally cynical and shared a black sense of humor.

On the way south, with only a few dollars more than what we needed for the Greek ship, we slept in train stations and public parks. We lived on bread and cheese and bummed rides through France and into Italy. It may sound romantic. It was not. We were so hungry we often shoplifted food. We were "on the road," but all I remember is being cold and hungry, not once in a while, but all day and all night. It took us two weeks to get to Brindisi, the small port on the heel of the Italian peninsula.

The Greek ship was a rusting tramp steamer in need of new paint and fittings. Belowdecks in the hold were three or four truckloads of cargo and wooden benches for about thirty steerage passengers. Steerage meant no room, no bunk, no food, and no windows. Like the other steerage passengers, we boarded with a small supply of food and a few bottles filled with water or cheap wine. It was two days to Piraeus, the port of Athens, then another two through the Greek isles to Haifa, the main port in Israel. Steaming east across the Adriatic into the Gulf of Corinth, which separates the Greek mainland from the Peloponnesus, was not unfamiliar— the year before I had read Thucydides' *History of the Peloponnesian War.*

We restocked our food in Piraeus and got back aboard as the ship sailed for Haifa. The weather was bad and getting worse. Steerage passengers had slept little since leaving Italy. Wind and rain pounded the ship, and many got seasick. As night fell, the storm became more ferocious. Huge waves tossed the ship in the darkness. The smell of vomit filled the hold, while the waves crashing into the ship left us in fear for our lives. The storm continued through the night and into the next day. Crew members said it was the worst weather they had ever seen in the east Mediterranean. At noon the captain said the ship could no longer proceed in the high seas. He turned toward Rhodes and found a cove on the leeward side of the island. Finally anchored in its temporary shelter, we felt safe for the first time in twenty-four hours.

At dawn, the third day out of Piraeus, the storm still raged. We remained at anchor. All of us in steerage had consumed what little food we had brought aboard, but when we asked the crew for a few loaves of bread, they turned us down. By noon, we were very hungry. Scott and I climbed up to the bridge to make a polite request of the captain. Unshaven, the stub of an unlit cigar clamped to his mouth, he had a large potbelly that protruded from a torn and dirty T-shirt. Gruff and belligerent, he reminded us that food was not included in the cost of our passage. We persisted until he threatened to use force to remove us from the bridge.

We were still anchored and less than halfway to Haifa. I was unwilling to take no for an answer. There were thirty hungry people in steerage, while the ship had a crew of ten. Short of using their weapons, they could do little in the face of a passenger revolt, a mutiny of sorts. Scott and I gathered the able-bodied men in steerage. With several languages to contend with, we needed two of them to translate. I proposed a simple plan. When the ship's officers sat down for their evening meal, we would storm their dining room and take their food. The men looked surprised, but on reflection nodded in agreement.

At the appointed hour, Scott and I led the way. We pushed into the mess room. The captain and the officers shouted for us to leave. We shouted back, demanding that steerage passengers be fed. Two officers started to push me out the door. I pushed back, and several passengers came to my aid. The officers got angrier; we did, too. Our job was to convince the captain that he could not intimidate us. Once we did, his resolve weakened, and he offered us some bread. I demanded more and said that if we didn't get it, no one else was going to eat either. The captain relented and supplied the steerage passengers with food for the rest of the voyage. We had the power to get the food all along. It just took a little leadership.

Disembarking in Haifa, I was shocked to see that we had left not only Europe but Western civilization itself. At the beginning of 1961, Israel was

not yet the westernized country it is today. Signs of Arab and Middle Eastern life were everywhere. The language on the street was Hebrew, of
which we spoke not a word, but many people also spoke English or
French. We found the office of an organization that placed newcomers
into kibbutzim, or collective farms, and learned we were eligible for a sub-
sidized program in which we could take Hebrew-language courses in the
morning and work only in the afternoon. After minimal paperwork, we
boarded a bus for our new home, Kibbutz Ramat Ha-Shofet.

Israel was less than thirteen years old, and its citizens displayed a
remarkable solidarity. The Holocaust and the external threat from neighboring Arab countries played a role, but the solidarity came from their
shared sense of building a new country and a new way of life. It was evident in many ways, but most vividly in their hitchhiking. Everyone hitchhiked: old ladies, teenage girls, kids, farmers, soldiers. If a thumb went out
on a street or highway, the first car to go by almost invariably stopped.
There was no thought of crime. There was no hesitation to talk to a
stranger. It was the most open display of collective generosity I had ever
experienced. All the people acted as if they were connected to one
another.

Several hundred people lived on a typical kibbutz. Individually, they
received food, health care, clothing, housing, and schooling but earned
only a meager allowance for incidentals. Together, they owned the kibbutz's farmland and buildings. After studying Hebrew in the morning,
Scott and I worked the fields and barns every afternoon, and often wound
up in the *zevel*, the dreaded shit pile where cow manure was stacked for
use as fertilizer. We slept in four-person cabins and had a day and a half off
every weekend. Our kibbutz was so far to the left politically that instead of
religious services on Saturday mornings, people gathered to study Chinese and learn about Mao Tse-tung. After struggling with Hebrew during
the week, Scott and I had little appetite for the even more opaque Chinese, but it still beat religious instruction.

One day I was given a wheelbarrow full of pine tree seedlings and
told to plant them along a dirt road bordering some outlying acreage. As
a Jewish child of nine or ten, I had gone door-to-door raising money to
plant trees in Israel. The trees were a powerful symbol of the new nation's

success in turning desert into fertile farmland. While planting the little trees, I saw a dot in the sky just over the horizon. Soon, I could see a low-flying airplane coming directly at me. Then, hearing a jet engine, I realized it was a fighter maneuvering down the same road on which I was planting the trees. The jet was barely thirty feet up, and as it zoomed by, I could see the pilot's face. I raised my shovel and waved. He passed me and rocked his wings to wave back. It was a moment of pure inspiration. He was the sword and I was the plowshare, and together we were building a new land. Given my alienation from U.S. society, this experience was very seductive, and it occurred to me that I should consider remaining in Israel permanently.

At that time, there were frequent incidents on Israel's national borders, and in many places United Nations peacekeeping troops had been deployed. Kibbutz Ramat Ha-Shofet, south of the Sea of Galilee, was seven miles from the border with Jordan. One weekend, I borrowed a bike and pedaled off to see it. I rode in sunshine through farmland and rolling hills on a narrow country road. At last, I came to a small sign: "Danger. Frontier Ahead." I could see no people or buildings. The road sloped down a hill and continued into Jordan. A line of iron antitank pylons blocked vehicular traffic. I coasted down toward the pylons. This was foolhardy. The area was deserted, but this was a hostile border, a combat zone. When I got to the line of pylons, I got off the bike and laid it down. Still seeing no one, I took a few steps into Jordan, just to say I had.

Suddenly I heard shouts from a hilltop four hundred yards to my right and farther into Jordan. I looked up and saw two uniformed soldiers yelling at me as they moved down the hillside in my direction. I shouted back in Hebrew that I did not speak Arabic, which was all I could do. The soldiers stopped. They were still 350 yards away. One yelled back as the other dropped to one knee, raised his rifle, and aimed it at me. I understood that dialogue was not going to save me, so I slowly turned back toward Israel, keeping my eyes fixed on that rifle. Halfway through my turn, a circle of white smoke appeared in front of it.

The soldier had fired. In a split second, I had a vision of the bullet hurtling into my eye as I tried to see it, knowing it would kill me. I saw my essence swirling down a drain in the ground between my legs and disappearing forever. Without thinking, I dived into the ditch on the side of the road. The bullet struck the ground nearby. I poked my head above the ditch to see if the soldiers were still advancing. They were. Thoughts came and went in milliseconds. I remembered arguments about religion and god. I had always argued that god was Santa Claus for grown-ups, and in response often heard there is never an atheist in a foxhole. There I was, actually in a foxhole, knowing I had only myself to rely upon.

I crawled on my belly back toward Israel. The ditch was lined with thornbushes, which stabbed me repeatedly. I hardly noticed because of the adrenaline flooding my body. After ten feet, the ditch flattened out, exposing me to the soldiers. Six feet farther, it deepened again. I stuck my head out and saw them only 250 yards away. One fired as soon as he saw me, but white smoke in front of his barrel revealed the shot before I heard the sound. I ducked back into the ditch as the bullet hit close by. I knew they would fire again as soon as they saw me, so I poked my head out once more, intentionally drawing another shot, then ducked back to avoid it. After the bullet hit, I crawled rapidly across the exposed area knowing it would take a second or two before they could fire again. Just as I got past the flat area, they did.

By then, I was back across the border. The road and the ditch beside it gently rose with the slope I had coasted down on the bike. I crawled fast, still not noticing the sharp thorns tearing up my face and arms. The soldiers continued to advance and fired another shot. If I left the ditch and ran in a low crouch across the field to my right, the slope of the hill would prevent the soldiers, who were on my left, from seeing me. I bent over and ran as fast as I could, then, safely away, stood in a field catching my breath.

Abruptly, three jeeps bristling with Israeli soldiers roared up. They surrounded me with guns drawn. The Jordanian soldiers must have assumed I was an Israeli spy entering Jordan illegally. The Israeli soldiers assumed I was a Jordanian spy entering Israel illegally because when they asked for my papers, I didn't have them. They were in the pocket of my jacket tied to the bike lying by the road. Methodically, the Israelis set up two machine-gun emplacements pointed back toward Jordan, but would not risk a confrontation by retrieving my passport. Instead, they called the United Nations.

When the white UN vehicle arrived, my belongings were secured without incident. Realizing I was not a spy, the Israelis took me to a local police station to be bandaged and debriefed. I was mortified. I had nearly lost my life, but I had also put the lives of others in jeopardy, and I had involved dozens of soldiers, police, and UN personnel because of a childish and unthinking escapade. They dealt with the reality of that hostile border every day, risking their lives to maintain it, while I was just a kid playing at having an adventure. Someone from the kibbutz came to get me, but shame and embarrassment were my only punishment.

On later weekends, Scott and I explored the country in more sensible fashion. Easy hitchhiking and some spare change allowed us to go wherever we pleased. One weekend, it was south to the desert city of Beersheba. Israeli military bases in the Negev Desert surrounded the city, and when we arrived at dusk, off-duty soldiers roamed the streets on weekend passes. A movie theater advertised a Yugoslavian film with Hebrew and English subtitles. We hadn't seen a movie in a long time, so the English subtitles were a welcome attraction. We entered a dark theater two minutes after the show had started.

The film depicted a group of Jewish teenagers fighting Nazis with makeshift weapons. It was engaging and emotional, but inevitably ended with all of the teenagers shot dead. As the closing credits rolled, I tried to imagine what I would have done had I lived then. Cousins I had never known had fought back, and I hoped that like them I would have, too. The houselights interrupted my reverie, and I saw for the first time that the theater was packed with Israeli soldiers, men and women, in uniform and carrying their trademark Uzi submachine guns. We, the defenseless Jews portrayed in the film, were victims no longer. We had an army and all the guns we needed. We had a country and would never again have to beg to get into others. We were feared and respected by our enemies, and I felt proud and strong.

Then, suddenly, I felt stupid. My thoughts were pure militarism. More guns do not bring peace. That night I started to ask myself the hard questions about Israel I had overlooked earlier. Why had the Israelis not integrated themselves more effectively into the Middle East community? Why had they not given economic and technical assistance to the displaced

Palestinians to keep them from allying with external Arab enemies? Why did their Arab citizens live in urban ghettos and suffer employment discrimination? Why did the kibbutz I lived on hire cheap Arab labor when doing so was in violation of their socialist principles?

I realized that the military strength all around me could not secure a peaceful future, despite the fact that it made people feel more secure, and even proud, in the present. The surrounding Arab nations did want to overrun Israel. But holding them off with guns would be effective only as long as it took them to acquire an equal number of guns themselves. The Israelis were building their defenses to survive in the present, but they had failed to develop a strategy for the future. I feared the country would always be an armed camp and peace might never come.

That night in Beersheba ended my infatuation with Israel. It was March, and I was ready to go home. Scott and I wrote to friends begging to borrow money. Neither of our families was in a position to help. We scraped together $200, and instead of sightseeing on the weekends, we hitchhiked to Haifa and roamed the docks looking for ships headed back to the States that might hire us. On our third visit we found one leaving the same night for New Orleans. A crew member had fallen ill, and the captain offered to hire one of us as a replacement. We knew of freighters that sailed out of Casablanca for New York and took passengers for only $100. If one of us took the ship job and used his salary to get home from New Orleans, the other would have to get to Casablanca, two thousand miles away, on $100 and use the remaining $100 for passage.

Scott had always wanted to work on a ship. Years before, his father had been a merchant seaman who had used his spare time to pursue his writing. Scott thought he might one day do the same. I told him if he wanted the job, it was his. We went back to the kibbutz and got his gear, and later that night I watched his ship sail into the dark waters of the Mediterranean.

A few days later, I boarded the same Greek vessel I had traveled on two months before. With my cap pulled low over my eyes, no one in the crew recognized me. I disembarked at Athens and hitchhiked north. When I couldn't get a ride, I took second-class trains and buses. I crossed Greece and what was then Yugoslavia, passed through Trieste into Italy, and made my way west across northern Italy and southern France to

Spain. It was late April. Europe was warm and beautiful. Sleeping outside and traveling with limited funds was much easier than it had been in the winter.

Scott had encouraged me to visit a cousin of his in Seville on my way to Casablanca. When I arrived, I learned his cousin lived with John Fulton Short, the only American bullfighter then active in Spain. They were part of an expatriate community that included the prolific American author James Michener. I stayed a week with them, the highlight of which was a festival in a small Spanish village. Bullfighters practiced before the summer season by fighting exhibitions at these festivals, and Short was on a card with Antonio Ordóñez, the leading bullfighter in Spain and a living legend to his fans. I was invited to go along.

We arrived at the village several hours before the exhibition and joined a luncheon hosted by the mayor. The appearance of the great bullfighter in this simple country village would be remembered for a lifetime. At the luncheon, Ordóñez was interested in my travels, and we talked at length. Later, before the bullfight, I wandered around the village. I had a beard at a time when no one else did, so as I wandered, I was followed by clumps of children shouting, *"El Diablo. El Diablo."* The village bullring was tiny with only three rows of seats, but every seat was occupied. Short did well, but Ordóñez's extraordinary performance lived up to everyone's expectations. He was awarded two ears. As he strutted around the arena holding up his prize, he threw one to the mayor and the other to me.

The day after the bullfight, I headed south to Gibraltar and made the long ferry crossing to Tangier in Morocco. I was in Africa. Today, the stark contrast between Western civilization and the rest of the world has been muted by the global economy. Back then, it was much in evidence. The sights, smells, and sounds of the old Kasbah in Tangier were fascinating, and thanks to the low prices I was able to remain there for several days. I then took a primitive but very cheap bus to Casablanca, and two days later climbed aboard a freighter for the ten-day voyage to New York. The crossing was uneventful. I walked off the ship at the dismal Red Hook shipyards in Brooklyn, my duffel bag over my shoulder. Disoriented by the culture shock, I took a subway to the Holland Tunnel and started hitchhiking back to Chicago.

It was May 1961. I had been away eight months, and I had changed. For better or worse, I was an American and wanted to remain one. That meant I had to reconcile myself to the culture and values I had previously rejected. I realized that college was preferable to living on the road. I understood that the many books I had enjoyed during my travels meant that I might find topics of interest back at the university. I also recognized that I was not immortal, that there was no fun or glory in dodging bullets. And, deep in the back of my mind, behind those new thoughts, the student demonstration in Paris remained a lingering and vivid memory.

CHAPTER 3

WHILE OVERSEAS, SCOTT AND I HAD FREQUENTLY DEBATED ARTICLES IN THE *International Herald Tribune,* an English-language newspaper published in Paris and readily available across Europe. Scott's point of view was Marxist. Mine was not, but in discussions with him I became familiar with a few useful Marxist ideas, especially the importance of class in understanding politics, and the need to look beneath ideologies and culture in order to examine the material and particularly economic factors driving history.

Back home after our trip I began to read newspapers and take an interest in national and world affairs. The southern civil rights movement was still in its infancy, but it was occasionally covered in the press. I watched for news about the French war in Algeria, the Middle East, and the hostility between the United States and the U.S.S.R. However, reenrolling at UC meant I needed money for living expenses the following year, so I went back to work at the beach. They made me a mate, a junior officer just below captain who supervised a shift of lifeguards on a beach.

That summer, 1961, weather in Chicago was especially severe. We had to make more than the usual number of rescues. One night I almost drowned in a storm. A lifeboat had to be rowed in through towering waves. I asked Alan Alderman, a lifeguard and the only friend I still had from high school, where we had both been varsity swimmers, to accompany me. It was a mistake in judgment. The boat capsized far offshore, and we barely made it back in.

At the end of the summer, I looked death in the face once again. At 10:00 p.m. over the Labor Day weekend, a single-engine Beechcraft airplane caught fire and crashed into Lake Michigan while on approach to Meigs Field, the same lakefront airport where I had taken my first ride in a similar plane. I was trained that summer to use scuba equipment, which had just been introduced outside the military, because the Chicago Park District wanted an underwater recovery team. Ralph Erickson, who would become nationally known for popularizing scuba diving, trained us. Decades later, when I rented scuba equipment and showed my certification with his signature, I was treated like a pilot whose license had been signed by one of the Wright brothers.

The morning after the plane crash the new underwater recovery team was ordered to bring up the bodies. There were five: the pilot, his wife, and their three children. We thought the wreckage would be easy to find since thousands of people sitting or strolling on the lakefront the night before saw the plane go down. Unfortunately, by morning, they all pointed in different directions—so much for eyewitness testimony. The visibility on the murky lake bottom was only a foot or two. We knew then it would not be easy to find the plane.

In fact, it took two days of painstaking work. We operated off two police boats with U.S. Coast Guard and city fire department vessels nearby. The water temperature at the bottom was about fifty degrees, too cold for extended dives in wet suits, so we used more cumbersome dry suits instead. Given the limited visibility, we searched the lake bottom in fixed grids. During those hours underwater I could not help but ponder my own mortality.

On the afternoon of the second day, I saw a bright white seashell on the sandy bottom. Seashells are uncommon in Lake Michigan, so I reached down for it. It was a newly minted quarter, and there was only one way it could have gotten there. I marked the spot with a pop-up balloon and swam circles around it. In a few minutes I saw the body of a seven-year-old boy lying facedown on the bottom. I sent up another balloon to mark that spot. Next, I saw the plane. The pilot was sitting behind the controls. Swimming around to get a better look, I saw a hole in his forehead the size of a baseball, probably made by the control wheel on impact. I had little more than a matter-of-fact reaction to this horrifying sight. The pilot's wife and other children were in the rear seats or lying just outside the cabin. I marked the spot and surfaced.

Half a dozen other divers then followed my marker balloons down to the wreck. I had had enough and stripped off my gear. The bodies and the wreckage were brought up in the next two hours and loaded onto the police boats. Back at the harbor, reporters waited to cover the story, and the next day my picture appeared on the front page. It looked heroic, but that night I got sick with dizziness and nausea. It was a delayed reaction to the horror I had seen earlier. I had suppressed my feelings to get the job done, but once the adrenaline rush had ended, they swept over me like a dark wave.

The sight of so much death, of a pilot with a hole in his head, and a woman and three children dead because they had gone along for the ride, brought home how quickly and how arbitrarily life can end. I was a fledgling pilot myself. It could have been me up there fighting a fire at night with my entire family in the plane. How suddenly death comes, I thought, and how unpredictably it can sweep us away. How important, therefore, to find the right balance between caution and risk. Too much of the former would render life meaningless; too much of the latter could mean no life at all.

In September, I changed my UC major to psychology. Of the nonfiction reading I had done while traveling, I had found psychology and philosophy the most interesting. The in-depth analysis of human behavior in the writings of Freud and the neo-Freudians was new to me, and fascinating, as was the even deeper thinking of the classic European philosophers. But psychology seemed more practical than philosophy, and since my limited financial resources were always a concern, I chose psychology.

That 1961–62 academic year, my third, was more enjoyable than my first two. I studied harder than I had before, and my grades dramatically improved. I got A's and B's, and felt less like the class dunce I had been as a physics major. I even quit the swimming team to have more time to study. That cost me my cushy part-time job in the athletics department, so I looked for another with the psychology faculty. Shortly, I was hired by Professor Shep White to run experiments using the galvanic skin response, one of the basic measures in a lie detector test. I liked White a great deal; he became my informal adviser.

Since I had fallen back a year from my entering college class, I developed a new circle of friends. They were serious students, but they also enjoyed partying and listening to the emerging rock-and-roll music. With them, I experimented with marijuana, read avant-garde novels, and maintained my interest in the Beat poets and writers. The year passed uneventfully. I worked another summer at the beach and returned to UC in the fall of 1962 for my final year in college, which proved to be anything but uneventful.

On a grim October night, I filed into an auditorium to hear a hastily arranged lecture by Hans Morgenthau, a famous University of Chicago political science professor and close adviser to President Kennedy. It was the height of the Cuban missile crisis. Aerial recon photos had revealed Soviet nuclear missiles in Cuba, and Kennedy had threatened war if they were not removed. The confrontation escalated, and like Americans everywhere I feared a nuclear attack. Morgenthau gave us no comfort. He said we would be lucky to live through the night.

How do you spend the last night of your life? I was anxious and afraid. A nuclear holocaust had never felt so immediate. How could U.S. and Soviet leaders be so incompetent as to have allowed this to happen? Of course, Soviet missiles had no place on our borders, but didn't we have missiles in Turkey even closer to theirs? It was a childish game of chicken while the fate of the world hung in the balance. I was furious at those responsible, including Jack Kennedy, the youthful president who had promised a new direction. After that harrowing night, I took more interest in nuclear disarmament. So did others, though we remained a tiny minority.

Kennedy had campaigned by falsely claiming a "missile gap" with the Russians, yet his belligerence seemed balanced by his growing alarm over the size of the nuclear arsenal. On other issues he appeared open to new ideas. He read good books and had a sense of humor. His youthful vigor, even his wealth and glamour, suggested an enlightened attitude toward government and a loosening of the rigid culture that still dominated the times. Yet the massive nuclear arsenal made me wonder, and like some others I took interest in the activities of the Committee for a Sane Nuclear Policy and other groups working to limit the arms race. The most interesting among them was the Union of Concerned Scientists, founded by some of the same people who had unleashed the destructive technology they now realized world leaders could neither understand nor control.

Shortly after the missile crisis, I saw *Operation Abolition*, a documentary film made by right-wing supporters of the House Un-American Activities Committee (HUAC). Claiming to ferret out communists, this congressional committee was used to suppress political dissent and persecute advocates of civil liberties. The film showed HUAC hearings in San Francisco, where student, labor, and church activists had staged a peaceful protest. Police beat them with batons and used high-pressure fire hoses to push them down a long marble staircase: proper treatment according to the film's producers, who knew right-wing sympathizers would applaud those tactics. But the film was so heavy-handed that reasonable viewers became outraged by HUAC. As a result, left-wing groups screened the film in hopes those viewers would urge the House of Representatives to shut down the committee.

While I became increasingly interested in politics, I had to be practical about what to do after graduation. In 1962, there were no alternative lifestyles, or hippies, or public interest jobs. I had to make a living. Professor White encouraged me to pursue an advanced degree in psychology. With his guidance I applied to five graduate schools. But I had also read about lawyers assisting the southern civil rights movement, and I wondered if I could make a living doing that. I wasn't sure I was qualified, but to find out, I took the aptitude test required for law school admission. The results surprised me. I scored above the ninety-ninth percentile, which meant a chance at a good law school despite my poor grades the first two years of college. Having already applied to the top five doctoral programs in psychology, I also applied to the top five law schools.

News stories about the southern civil rights movement had captured my attention and that of many of my friends. With the national culture moving slowly in the direction of racial integration, the outrageous and rampant discrimination in the South violated our sense of basic American principles. But however extreme the injustice, the spectacle of young black students using nonviolent tactics to stand up to such racism and the violence that accompanied it was an inspiration. The situation was not close to what I had seen in Paris, but an entirely new phenomenon, and I found it fascinating.

My circle of UC friends had expanded to include several with an interest in English motorcycles. With them, I occasionally rode out to the Indiana countryside on weekends, either to watch races or to simply get out of the city. One of the motorcycle riders was Danny Lyon, a new friend who was an amateur photographer. The previous summer, 1962, Danny had had an extraordinary experience. He traveled to the South and took pictures of young blacks marching in civil rights protests. He was the first to make me aware that while most civil rights workers in the South were black, a few whites like him had also gotten deeply involved.

The first lunch counter sit-in had occurred in Greensboro, North Carolina, in February 1960. By fall 1961, black students were using sit-ins across the South to try to repeal the discriminatory Jim Crow laws, the basis of racial segregation. The older civil rights organizations were energized, but Danny worked with a new and more militant group. The Student Nonviolent Coordinating Committee (SNCC, pronounced "snick") came to be seen as the shock troops of "the movement." They organized in the toughest places, had the fewest resources, and acted fearlessly in the face of the worst segregationist violence.

After the summer, Danny made two more short trips for SNCC. His dramatic black-and-white pictures, shot in the midst of violent police attacks on demonstrators, or at crowded church meetings or courthouse protests, soon appeared in newsmagazines. SNCC then created inspirational posters from the photos, which became increasingly popular on dormitory walls. Inadvertently, Danny had become an accomplished photojournalist and a minor celebrity within the movement. Along with other friends, I was fascinated by his experiences and the dramatic struggles in the South. Whenever civil rights workers traveled north to raise money and recruit volunteers, I went to listen.

SNCC was headquartered in Atlanta but worked primarily in the small towns of the Black Belt, a swath of counties running through Georgia, Alabama, and Mississippi where blacks had the majority and discrimination against them was the most severe. Winning voting rights in those counties meant blacks could win local office, including law-enforcement positions like sheriff. SNCC "field secretaries" organized voter registration drives in some of these towns. The registration drives usually began with a months-long attempt to find a single potential black voter willing to risk going to the county courthouse to register. Throughout the South such attempts had been met with beatings, house burnings, jail sentences, shootings, and even lynch mobs. But if one person took the risk, others might be similarly inspired. If more tried to register and were refused, the stage could be set for boycotts, strikes, publicity, lawsuits, and other attempts to beat back the white powers controlling the county.

This effort was entirely new to the American experience. Civil rights protesters had adopted the tactics of nonviolent resistance first used by Gandhi in India. They sat silently in segregated areas and were beaten by white civilians. They marched down public streets in the face of attacks by police dogs and swinging batons. They allowed themselves to be arrested in such large numbers that they filled up the local jails and clogged the courts. And every time people in the rest of the country saw these outrages and witnessed the courage of the activists, public opposition to segregation grew. The young black activists in the South had successfully called forth a great nonviolent moral crusade.

Just before the 1963 spring break, Danny asked me to accompany him on a trip to Mississippi and Arkansas. He was going to take more pictures, and if I went along, I could get a firsthand look at the movement in the South. I immediately agreed, but I was nervous, too. Mississippi was the worst of the worst, the place where racist violence was most commonplace and where it enjoyed the greatest protection from local law enforcement. But to right wrongs, one had to take risks, and my curiosity about the civil rights movement was intense.

Driving south with Danny, I remembered a fourteen-year-old Chicago boy named Emmett Till who had been killed in Mississippi eight years before. I was a high school student about the same age, and his murder had been widely reported in the Chicago press. Till was visiting his uncle and was accused of whistling at a white woman in a general store. That night the woman's husband and an accomplice dragged Till from his uncle's home and tortured and killed him. Later, they were arrested and tried by an all-white jury. Despite the eyewitness account of Till's uncle, the jury took only an hour to acquit both defendants. Mississippi was notorious for such acquittals, but repression of this sort also inspired others to act. Only one hundred days after Till's murder, Rosa Parks refused to move to the back of the bus in Montgomery, Alabama, sparking a bus boycott there that lasted over a year. The boycott boosted the civil rights movement and inspired the future crusades of a young local minister named Martin Luther King Jr.

Danny and I stopped for the night in Cairo, a town at the southern tip of Illinois closer to Mississippi than Chicago, both in distance and in culture. Cairo prepared me for what was to come in Mississippi. Black activists Danny knew there suffered frequent arrests and beatings for nonviolent protests. When we moved with them that night, I could feel their paranoia. They were often followed. Their phones were tapped. Yet their quiet courage in the face of such risks inspired me. That night, college life seemed a world away.

Danny took pictures the next morning. Back on the road, we drove through the heaviest rainstorm either of us had ever experienced, finally crossing from Tennessee into Mississippi late that afternoon. The rain stopped as we rolled through the northern Mississippi countryside en route to Greenwood in the Delta, the old plantation region bordering the great river. There, black majorities, many of whom were dirt-poor sharecroppers, populated the white-controlled counties.

We had planned to arrive in daylight, but the rain slowed us down. As night fell, our thoughts turned to Jimmy Travis, a SNCC field secretary. Three days before, on a road near Greenwood, a car full of local whites pulled alongside Jimmy's car and fired on him with an automatic weapon. He was hit in the neck and seriously wounded. SNCC's response was to redouble its efforts in Greenwood. SNCC workers came from other areas to show their determination. Driving on that dark two-lane highway, Danny and I were often passed by other cars. Each time, trying to throw off the aim of a potential shooter, I tapped the brakes just as the other car sped past. It was silly, since we were still unknown to the locals, but it was a measure of the fear we both felt.

We arrived at the SNCC office at 10:00 p.m. There were a dozen people there, including the SNCC field secretaries Charlie Cobb, Frank Smith, and Willie Peacock. Recognizing Danny, they welcomed us as brothers, but said we would have to sleep in the office. It was too dangerous to stay in a motel if we were later seen walking into or out of the SNCC office. The local whites didn't like "Yankees" trying to agitate "their" black folk and would react violently. Nor could we stay with a black family, as black volunteers were doing, without attracting undue attention. Patrols around the office would give us a few minutes' warning if a mob of whites with baseball bats and chains attacked, as had recently happened in a nearby town. Sleeping on the office floor that night, I bolted upright ready to run every time I heard an unfamiliar noise.

The next morning Danny and I slipped out the back door and strolled away from the segregated black side of town to get breakfast and quietly look around. Danny was my height, somewhat heavier, with thick curly black hair and an open and friendly demeanor. We were dressed in jeans and work shirts and were disheveled from our night on the floor. As we walked single file down a narrow sidewalk on Greenwood's main street, a tall, stocky black man in bib overalls, about thirty-five, approached from the other direction. The sidewalk was not wide enough for us to pass. Given his size, my first reaction was to give way, but before I could, the man, who towered over me, stepped off the sidewalk into the mud in the gutter and said, "Yes, sir. Good mornin', sir." He tipped his straw hat and made room for me, a kid barely twenty-two years old. It was an instant lesson in what the Jim Crow laws really meant. This man, despite his age and stature, was not a man but a "boy," useful for physical labor but not a citizen with the same rights I enjoyed. I realized I could have gone so far as to strike him and my white-skin privilege would have saved me from any consequences. That was Mississippi in 1963.

Later, Danny and I tagged along as SNCC field workers went door-to-door in the black part of town. The streets were unpaved; open ditches carried off wastewater. Many of the houses were unpainted and ramshackle.

Standing in front of the Greenwood, Mississippi, Student Nonviolent Coordinating Committee office, talking to field secretary Frank Smith (center) and other voter registration workers. March 1963. © *Danny Lyon/Magnum Photos*

The SNCC workers talked to people about voting, but no one had signed up yet. Still, they maintained their contacts, patiently explained the law, and assured people that they would not leave Greenwood. As Danny snapped pictures, I got an occasional look inside the houses. The poverty was appalling. There were no closets, little furniture, and the walls and floors were made of unfinished wood. Outhouses stood in the backyards. It was a sight I had seen overseas, not one I thought I would encounter in the United States.

Yet the lack of physical security was more unnerving than the grinding poverty. As we walked around, I considered what we would do if white vigilantes attacked us. No help was available. Normally, I would call the police if violently attacked. In Greenwood, I would be lucky if the police merely looked the other way instead of joining the attack. The utter lack of recourse was frightening. I could not fathom how corrosive it must be for black citizens to live with such fear every moment of their lives, from early childhood to old age.

Greenwood was a city of twenty-five thousand, but it was so severely segregated that after walking through the black part of town all afternoon, Danny and I had not seen a single white person on foot or in a car. After dark, we went to a one-room church to see a SNCC-sponsored community meeting. The black pastor had bravely allowed SNCC to use the facility. He knew, as did his congregation, that the penalty might be a fire that burned his church to the ground. Danny and I were the only white people in the room that night.

With encouragement from the SNCC organizers, black folk stood and haltingly gave testimony about discrimination they had suffered in Greenwood. I heard heart-wrenching stories of rights denied, of needless cruelty at the hands of the police or other authorities, of arbitrary violence, of gratuitous insults and abuse. Some insisted they were no better or worse than white folk but, unlike whites, had no way to redress grievances. The SNCC workers told of other communities where blacks had organized to demand their rights, stories about the bus boycott in Montgomery and school integration in Arkansas. They celebrated the heroic men and women who had resisted white power throughout the South and worked for equal justice. These two points of view, the people's and the organizers', would have to merge to fuel the slow buildup of anger and energy required for the movement to succeed in Greenwood.

At the end of the meeting, I stood with everyone else and sang "We Shall Overcome," the stirring new anthem of the civil rights movement. We crossed arms and held hands with those on either side. As the hopeful song was triumphantly sung, I swayed from side to side with the others in time to the rhythm. At appropriate moments I optimistically squeezed the two hands I held, and as I looked around, I saw many eyes staring back at me, especially when someone called out a verse about blacks and whites together. I could see our mere presence gave people a small measure of hope that the larger world had not forgotten them, that they were not alone.

The elders in the room had known grandparents born into slavery. Less than a century had passed since their emancipation. They were no longer slaves but not yet free. They had waited almost a hundred years, asking only for the right to vote, the right to work, the right to walk down the sidewalk without having to step into the mud to accommodate another. I was moved to tears. The purity of their simple demands, and their naive and unwarranted optimism in the face of such oppression, somehow raised an infectious optimism in me as well.

In the morning, SNCC's principal leaders in Mississippi asked to meet with Danny and me. Bob Moses was the head of SNCC's Mississippi Project, and James Forman was SNCC's national coordinator based in Atlanta. Forman had come to Greenwood in response to the shooting of Jimmy Travis. Both were inspiring people, soft-spoken and intense, but with a determination and clarity of purpose that made one welcome their leadership. Moses was in his late twenties, slim, bespectacled, of average height, and very academic. Forman, somewhat older and taller, carried more weight and had a tougher exterior. They had an assignment for me.

The City of Greenwood needed to attract new business, but to maintain segregation, new businesses had to embrace the Jim Crow laws. If they did, it was widely rumored that the city government and leaders of the chamber of commerce would bend local zoning laws and provide favorable tax breaks. Moses and Forman wanted specifics so SNCC could expose the tax-breaks-for-racism practices in the press. They asked if I would spend a couple of days posing as a reporter and interview local leaders to get the full story.

Glad to be useful instead of a mere bystander, I agreed. I could claim to be a reporter for the *Chicago Maroon*, a weekly that served the small business community in Chicago. In fact, the *Maroon* was the campus newspaper at the university. I called the editor and asked him to cover for me if anyone called to verify my employment. The SNCC staff identified the leaders of the chamber of commerce and the city council, all of whom were prosperous local businessmen. Holding office was not a full-time job, so the political leadership and the business leadership were identical. To work undercover, I would have to keep my distance from the SNCC people during the day and enter and leave their office only through the back door at night.

Over the next few days, I interviewed most of the targeted businessmen. It was not difficult. I had to feign sympathy for their racism, but once I did, they were only too happy to open up to an approving Yankee. The trade-offs they described were straightforward. New businesses migrating to Greenwood had to operate the southern way, which meant no labor unions; no black workers supervising whites; separate toilets, drinking fountains, and dressing rooms; and all black employees confined to menial jobs. In exchange, compliant businesses got exemptions from taxes and zoning restrictions. The city fathers needed new jobs, and the more jobs the new businesses could promise, the more benefits they could claim.

The open racism was startling. Several otherwise polite and congenial businessmen told me with genuine sincerity that it was unfair to give a black man more than a menial job, because he could not be taught the skills required and in the end would only be frustrated and unhappy. It was more humane, they argued, to confine him to menial tasks and agricultural work, both better suited to his limited ability. Neither would it make sense, they claimed, to allow a black man to own the land he worked, because he would mismanage and lose it. They seemed convinced that the southern way meant more happiness and stability for blacks.

As I conducted these interviews, I saw that this extraordinary racism served a deeper purpose. The racism of the business owners had as much to do with controlling white workers as black. The owners' prosperity depended on skilled white workers accepting less than what would be considered a fair wage in other parts of the country. To get white workers to do so, employers had to first keep labor unions out and then make the white workers feel their jobs were in constant danger of being lost to blacks who would work for even less.

The Ku Klux Klan, together with the more mainstream White Citizens' Councils and other groups financed by the employers, encouraged racism among white workers. In turn, the white workers enforced the second-class citizenship of the blacks. Trade unions were rare in the South because local police were used like storm troopers to prevent union organizing. The police were white workers, too, but were firmly under the command of business leaders doubling as city officials. As long as working whites had more than poor blacks and were permitted to take out their frustrations on a group lower in the pecking order, a certain oppressive stability was achieved.

This was the basis of economic power in the South, whether on the level of a single town like Greenwood or an entire state like Mississippi. Poor whites believed they had more in common with wealthy whites than with poor blacks. Racism was not an end in itself but a tactic in the class war. The poor whites were allowed to flaunt their superiority over the blacks and view them as subhuman. But by casting blacks as a constant threat to white economic well-being, to white women, and to white-skin privilege, the white employers diverted the attention of their poorer cousins from class politics to race politics. However, this system required enough jobs to keep the white population employed, despite limited economic development in the South. Without those jobs, whites would be open to union organizers and might see the benefit of common struggle with blacks. Tax breaks and other inducements were simply the price paid for the new jobs.

I came to understand what Moses and Forman no doubt already knew, that the racism of the South was tied to politics and economics in a complex web designed to maintain the prosperity of those already prosperous. I wrote up an account of the specific arrangements I had uncovered and delivered it to them at the SNCC office. They welcomed the information. Since both appeared unusually relaxed, I took the opportunity to ask about strategy. Why was voter registration, rather than ending the Jim Crow laws, the focus of their work? If blacks did register and eventually win local office, how would that change the economic oppression at the heart of the problem? Even if SNCC won in Greenwood, how could the massive effort required be duplicated in the hundreds of other towns across the South? And, finally, was it worth risking the lives of people to achieve the limited goals they pursued?

Tough questions, but both Moses and Forman took them seriously. To my surprise, they did have a grand strategy not apparent to a novice like me. Their goals went beyond winning the right to vote, or to swim in municipal pools, or to eat at integrated lunch counters. Their focus was the U.S. Congress. They explained how the real power in Congress lay in the committee structure. Individual members did not submit bills on the floor of the House or Senate. Rather, new bills were first heard in the appropriate committee, and only if the committee approved could they then be sent to the entire body for a vote. The chairmen of these committees (there were no chairwomen then) exercised dictatorial control over the bills first accepted for consideration and whether or not they moved to the floor for a full vote.

Committee chairmen were chosen on the basis of seniority. It didn't matter how capable they were, only how long they had served. Ever since Lincoln's Republicans won the Civil War, the white-only electorate in the South viewed them with unmitigated hatred; Democrats were the only viable party in the region. One-party rule meant Southerners in the House and Senate were reelected without opposition and built seniority faster than officials from other regions. As a result, power in Congress rested disproportionately in the hands of backward, racist, conservative officials from the South. SNCC wanted to end racist practices in places like Greenwood, but also had a larger purpose: lifting the stranglehold these backward officials had on the entire country.

The leaders of SNCC had a long view. They knew there was a huge reservoir of political energy that could be harnessed to ultimately end the oppression of black people in the South, and they were determined to do just that. However, they also saw that winning voting rights could lead to a more progressive government for the rest of the country. Given such high stakes, the energy and sacrifice that SNCC had committed to voter registration suddenly made sense to me.

Regarding the risk to lives, Moses and Forman were less confident. They recognized that some would die but felt they were in a struggle for immense power, and in any battle of that magnitude there would be inevitable casualties. They were prepared, and ready as well to sacrifice themselves, as anyone who fights such battles must be. Yet they were confident they would ultimately win. They believed that by exposing racial injustice in the South, they would eventually raise a tidal wave of moral outrage that would transform American society. The United States, they said, could not continue to profess the democratic ideals and beliefs that are our national heritage and simultaneously tolerate the racist remnants of human slavery that remained within our borders.

I viewed these two brave and idealistic men with the same combination of incredulity and respect as I had Daniel after the student uprising in Paris three years before. They were older, more serious and experienced, but like Daniel's their eyes were focused over the horizon. As in Paris, I saw once more that in political struggle small things could be used to leverage very big things. In my old neighborhood in Chicago the watchword was "You can't fight city hall." In fact, I could see there were workable strategies for changing the world, and the thought that I might one day be part of such an effort awakened in me a sense of purpose I had not experienced before.

Danny and I left Greenwood and drove to the SNCC field office in Pine Bluff, Arkansas. On the way, we passed a chain gang working at the side of the highway. Black men in white work clothes were chained together at the ankles. They swung pickaxes and shovels, while white and

One of the photographs taken by Danny Lyon on our trip to Mississippi. This was on the road between Greenwood, Mississippi, and Pine Bluff, Arkansas.
© *Danny Lyon/Magnum Photos*

black prison guards sporting sunglasses and cowboy hats surrounded them, shotguns and rifles held butt-first on their hips. We pulled over. Danny took pictures until the guards pointed their guns in our direction and told us to move on. The pictures were later published in several books that chronicled the civil rights movement.

We spent a few days in Pine Bluff, a town not unlike Greenwood, and then left for Chicago. I did not fully understand it then, but the trip had changed my life. I had been inside a domestic U.S. colony and had watched as its oppressed people considered their first acts of resistance. I had seen gifted and determined leaders step bravely into the breach, draw down their courage, and risk everything in the pursuit of justice. Three days after we left Greenwood, the SNCC office that Danny and I had slept in was firebombed at 3:00 a.m. Everyone inside got out, but the office burned to the ground.

The pursuit of justice required risk, not the macho risks I had taken earlier, but risk that gives meaning and purpose to life. I realized that one day I would have a choice to make, a choice between a predictable life of safety and security and an unpredictable life, less safe and less secure, but more vibrant, more important, a life in which something meaningful could be achieved. I wondered how I would respond when the time came. During the long drive back to Chicago, it occurred to me that perhaps the time had already come and I was traveling in the wrong direction. Perhaps I should drop out of school, go south, and join SNCC.

If those thoughts were the first test of my commitment, I failed. The obstacle was money. I had none. I had no savings, no help from parents, no skills with which to earn a living. Education was the one opportunity I did have. I was willing to stand up to racists, but I realized I was not ready to risk my future. Not yet, anyway.

CHAPTER 4

SHORTLY AFTER I RETURNED FROM MISSISSIPPI, EDUCATIONAL OPPORTUNITIES WERE laid out before me like a banquet. I was accepted at all five of the doctoral programs in psychology. More surprising, I had also been invited to four of the five law schools. I was pleased, but I still had no idea what to do. My experience in Mississippi had dramatically increased my interest in working as a civil rights lawyer, so I called the American Civil Liberties Union and requested a meeting with a lawyer who had civil rights experience. I needed some career counseling.

I was referred to a young attorney, and when we met, I asked him if I would be able to make a living doing civil rights work. He looked incredulous and said no, of course not. Civil rights lawyers, he said, joking, earn their money on bankruptcies and divorces, then do civil rights work at night and on weekends. Even as a joke, bankruptcies and divorces were not my idea of a life's work. We had this talk in 1963. If it had been only two years later, in 1965, his answer would have been entirely different. By then, civil rights litigation in the United States had mushroomed, and many studied law confident they could support themselves in this new field.

Of necessity, my attention swung back to psychology. Professor White set up a meeting for me with one of his colleagues who was looking for a research assistant for the following year to help him in a fascinating new area of research. When I first sat down with Professor Allan Rechtschaffen,

I thought he was too young to hold joint appointments in the Departments of Psychology and Psychiatry, but he was the new director of the fabled UC Sleep Laboratory. Two monumental discoveries had been made there just prior to his arrival: the discovery of rapid-eye-movement, or REM, sleep, and the discovery that this physiologically distinct stage of sleep coincided with dreaming.

Rechtschaffen's enthusiasm for his research was infectious. Still in his thirties, he had dark hair and a trim athletic build. His intensity suggested a person who got things done, yet he was informal and unorthodox and seemed like a regular guy rather than a nerdy academic. The scientific study of dreaming, he explained, might one day tell us more about schizophrenia, since hallucinations, like dreams, were a form of vivid and convincing mental activity generated entirely within the brain. Also, dreaming was a unique psychological state that co-occurred with the REM period, a unique physiological state. Understanding their relationship might reveal much about the mind/body problem, that is, how the physical brain, part of the body, gives rise to consciousness and what we commonly refer to as the mind. Philosophers had grappled with this mystery since religion invented the disembodied soul. I was fascinated.

At the end of our long meeting, Rechtschaffen offered me a job as his research assistant. Along with gaining admittance to UC's graduate school, and the ability to bypass a master's degree and work directly for a doctorate, I had won a fellowship with the National Institute of Mental Health covering tuition and $3,000 a year for living expenses. The after-school job as a research assistant in the Sleep Lab would boost my annual income to $6,000, all that was needed in those days. In addition, Rechtschaffen offered to sponsor the research I was required to perform and said I could complete it in his lab. I had hit the academic jackpot. It was an offer I could not refuse. I had wanted to leave Chicago and explore alternatives, but my time in the Windy City was going to be extended.

With that settled, and given my new interest in the southern civil rights movement, I joined Chicago Area Friends of SNCC, an off-campus group supporting SNCC's work in the South. We sponsored educational events, raised money, collected food and clothing, and demonstrated when specific actions in the South needed support. Occasionally, SNCC leaders and field secretaries came to Chicago to report on their progress and raise money to sustain their work. Bob Moses came several times, as did John Lewis, later a distinguished and long-serving member of Congress himself.

Al Raby and Lawrence Landry, black civil rights activists and community leaders in Chicago, led Friends of SNCC with financial support from black businessmen, elected officials, and progressive unions, in particular the meatpackers' local. Years later, Friends of SNCC worked to improve education and housing for blacks in Chicago. Through the organization I learned the importance of labor unions and progressive churches in movements for social change. With large memberships they are able to raise money and deliver people to polling booths, protests, and parades. They were as critical to the civil rights movement as the evangelical churches would be decades later to right-wing conservatives.

The work I did for Friends of SNCC was minimal, but I started to soak up political information at a faster pace and take more interest in the news and public affairs. White student activists outside the South had launched Students for a Democratic Society (SDS). In their manifesto, the Port Huron Statement, they condemned U.S. aggression abroad and poverty and racism at home. I sympathized with them but did not join. Suddenly I was overcommitted. Between classes, part-time employment, and my volunteer work, I could only make time for another meeting if I sacrificed what little time I had left for fun. That was more than I was willing to give, so I watched SDS from the sidelines.

That spring was a turning point for me, just as larger events would soon make 1963 a turning point for the country. The Beat Generation had become passé. Influenced by the protests of the civil rights movement, I no longer felt like rejecting society; instead, I wanted to change it. But despite my new interest in reform, I had no overarching ideology or even a clear point of view about what kind of society I thought should be built. I could feel that change was in the air, and I applauded the modest dissent that began to bubble up through the hard crust of the fifties. Even the movies were changing. I was a pool player, so I had loved seeing *The Hustler*, an unusually dark film in which the good guy didn't win; in fact, there were no good guys. Two other films would soon harshly criticize

U.S. foreign policy. *Seven Days in May* revealed how we had put our-selves in danger of nuclear annihilation, while *Dr. Strangelove* openly ridiculed the leaders responsible.

But more than anything else, it was the music that helped put the 1950s behind us. Pete Seeger, Joan Baez, Phil Ochs, and many others, most prominently Bob Dylan, moved traditional folk music into a sharper and more explicit critique of society and politics. When I first heard Dylan's second album, *The Freewheelin' Bob Dylan*, released in May 1963, I almost wept with joy. "A Hard Rain's A-Gonna Fall," "Masters of War," and "Blowin' in the Wind" all spoke to the madness of our nuclear policy and resonated with the growing antinuclear movement sparked by the Cuban missile crisis only months before. A fourth song, "Oxford Town," told the story of James Meredith, the first black student to inte-grate the University of Mississippi. When a new group, Peter, Paul & Mary, recorded "Blowin' in the Wind" in July, it sold over a million copies.

Dylan's protest songs were a new art form. Combining brilliant metaphors and poetic juxtapositions with simple yet haunting music, he created intense emotion—anger, pathos, irony—often missing from polit-ical speech. For many of us, the new protest music, and Dylan in particu-lar, captured our attitudes so ingeniously that we were happy to have him speak for us. We pushed him to the forefront because his talent made us stronger, and we thought he could help us reform America. He hadn't asked for that role, and in a few years would abandon it, but for a brief interval he was the reluctant Pied Piper of our generation.

In addition to the changing culture, there were political reasons to be optimistic. In June, Kennedy delivered a landmark speech at American University. For the first time, a U.S. president called for peaceful coexis-tence with the Soviet Union and an end to the rapidly increasing nuclear arms race. As someone afraid that the spiraling arms race would make war inevitable, I was relieved and heartened by his words. But for all his good qualities, Kennedy was a contradictory figure. He would not forcefully intervene on behalf of civil rights in the South. I was confused. So were a lot of people.

Darker events then tore away my optimism. Two days after Kennedy's speech, Medgar Evers, leader of the Mississippi chapter of the National Association for the Advancement of Colored People, was assassinated by a rifle shot as he pulled in to his driveway. He was a World War II combat veteran who had spent years working against segregation in Mississippi. His Ku Klux Klan killer was quickly arrested and tried. Two successive all-white juries failed to reach a verdict; the killer was freed. It was hard to reconcile America's changing culture and loosening political restraints with the hard reality of its violence, racism, and poverty.

More bad news arrived from Viet Nam, an obscure country in Southeast Asia I had only recently heard about. I knew it was a former French colony lost to communist revolutionaries in 1954, and that afterward the United States had installed a puppet regime in the south and pushed the communists north. I had also seen press reports that southerners allied with the northern government were attacking the puppet army and trying to reunify the country, and that the United States had sent thousands of military advisers to shore up its client regime. In June, a horrifying picture from that little-known country shocked the world. A Buddhist monk in Viet Nam, protesting ongoing religious suppression by the puppet regime, committed suicide in public by pouring gasoline over his body and burning himself alive.

No one in America had ever seen anything like that. I asked myself what we were doing in Viet Nam and how conditions had become so intolerable that this monk and others who soon followed felt justified in burning themselves to death. The answers I found did not ease my concerns. When he canceled the Vietnamese election in 1956, President Eisenhower installed Ngo Dinh Diem, a resident of New Jersey, as president of South Viet Nam. Diem was a devout Catholic and a disciple of New York's Cardinal Spellman, a right-wing zealot. He suppressed Buddhist practices even though Viet Nam was 90 percent Buddhist. Their monks had been protesting ever since. Why was the United States so invested in this out-of-the-way place? Were our Cold War blinders so narrow we would prop up a Catholic autocrat in a country of Buddhists just because communists were on the other side?

As this took place, I graduated from college with a B.S. degree, major in psychology. Since I would be back at UC in the fall as a graduate student, I returned to work at the beach. I thought it would be a quiet summer. For the first time, nonconformists like me felt a little cultural and political wind at our backs, so we became more publicly assertive, both in our dress and in our opinions. The Chicago lifeguard corps was not prepared for these changes. At the beach that summer, I wasn't shy about my opposition to racism, and I let my hair grow a little longer than the customary crew cut. My superiors thought it was un-American to have long hair, so they ordered me to cut it. I told them I would not.

I didn't have shoulder-length hair or a ponytail. Those styles, associated with the hippies, were still a few years away. As in early pictures of the Beatles, my hair came down a little over my collar and a bit over my ears. That was it. My bosses were reluctant to fire a highly trained lifeguard supervisor, so they dealt with my insubordination by transferring me to a beach on the city's Near North Side. It was hardly punishment. Oak Street Beach, opposite Chicago's Gold Coast, was a favorite of airline stewardesses and single women drawn to the nightlife in the area.

I enjoyed my new assignment immensely, but unfortunately Oak Street was even more intolerant than the beach I had left. Blacks were informally banned. They were not forcibly removed, but they were informed, if not by lifeguards, then by police, that the beach was not safe for them. Most of the lifeguards referred to blacks as "niggers," and any fraternization, like interracial dating, was seen as an attack on god and country. I couldn't stop myself from objecting to the racism, so within a few weeks I was no longer welcome at that beach either.

I was transferred again, no doubt in hopes I would quit. My next assignment was to an all-black beach on the South Side staffed by black lifeguards and black police officers. I was the only white person there. Luckily, the lifeguard captain at Sixty-third Street Beach was an unusually smart and capable guy who was less militaristic than others I had worked under. I was judicious in dealing with the black lifeguards and beach patrons under my supervision, and with a little effort I got along fine and made new friends. Yet I understood how much I had changed. Once happy to embrace the lifeguard culture, I realized I was no longer able to fit in except on a black beach.

The cramped beach office had a small TV, and during the last week of the summer I used it to watch the March on Washington for Jobs and Freedom and saw Dr. Martin Luther King Jr. give his famous "I have a dream" speech. John Lewis, the new head of SNCC, spoke at his side. Civil rights leaders had gambled that a huge outpouring, not only of black support, but of white as well, would elevate the movement, extend its influence, and make civil rights a national priority. It worked. Over a quarter million people came, even some whites from the South, and Dr. King was catapulted onto the world stage. It was the largest demonstration in the country's history. For me, the motivation of the demonstrators was as important as their numbers. Not since pre–Civil War abolitionists had so many Americans joined a political movement based not on self-interest but on morality, on the interests of others.

I celebrated this remarkable new spirit, but segregationist violence quickly intruded. Three weeks after the march, on a Sunday morning in Birmingham, Alabama, a bomb went off in the Sixteenth Street Baptist Church. It was placed beneath a bathroom used by girls attending Sunday school and timed to explode during classes. Three fourteen-year-old girls and one eleven-year-old girl were killed. The bombing sickened me and was a shock to the nation and the world. Forced to choose between protesting blacks and racists killing black children, most Americans made the right decision. Support for the movement grew. But opposition hardened as well.

My graduate school obligations began in September. The class work was intense, and I put in long hours of study. My job at the Sleep Lab also required a lot of time. There I learned to operate and troubleshoot the complex instruments needed to monitor various stages of sleep, including electroencephalographs, or brain wave recorders. Often, as well, I had to work all night watching sleeping subjects in our experiments.

In early November, more bad news came from South Viet Nam. President Diem was overthrown in a military coup engineered by the CIA. When appeals to President Kennedy went unanswered, the coup leaders took it as a sign and killed Diem and his brother. Kennedy was furious. Their murders had not been part of the plan. I hoped I was not the only one asking myself why we had supported a government whose leader we then had to remove by force.

Three weeks later, before that question could be answered, another killing, not over civil rights, and not in Viet Nam, rocked the world and changed the course of American history. The assassination of President Kennedy on November 22 traumatized the nation. America had not experienced political violence for a long time. President McKinley had been assassinated in 1901, and the three wars we had fought since were all on the other side of an ocean. The gunshots in Dallas came as a profound shock, so much so that most people in my generation remember exactly where they were when they first heard the news.

I was in a basement pool hall in Woodlawn, the black neighborhood just south of Hyde Park. Most white students felt too intimidated to play there, but a few of us preferred the gritty atmosphere to the more antiseptic poolroom on campus. We played well, so the regular patrons accepted us. When the first news from Dallas came over the wall-mounted TV, it was reported that Vice President Lyndon Johnson had been shot. There was little reaction. Moments later, it became clear that Kennedy was the victim. Play stopped instantly and everyone gathered around the TV set. There wasn't a sound in the room. Some minutes later, among gasps and cries of disbelief, it was announced that Jack Kennedy, America's golden son, was dead.

Live TV news coverage, relatively new then, allowed millions to see the assassination, and see it again and again as the videotape was continually repeated. More shocking, we saw the alleged assassin killed in front of our eyes, shot by a lone assailant while in police custody. For the first time, television turned these faraway events into communal and personal experiences. The country was briefly a single electronic village, as we all simultaneously watched the same events and shared the same searing emotions. For several days, America was united in grief and in horror, while the constant repetition of the news footage drove those emotions ever deeper into our collective psyche.

Kennedy had been both the youngest man ever elected president and the youngest to die in office. His killing stripped the country of its optimism—mine along with it. I no longer believed the progressive change I had hoped for would come to pass. Successful movements for social change, like those advanced by suffragettes or labor organizers, had inspired Americans to believe such problems could be solved, that the country could adjust to new circumstances. Kennedy's death killed that hope and made us wonder if the rule of law, the cornerstone of democracy, would be replaced by rules written with bullets and bombs.

The assassination provoked a hard look at the United States. No longer could Americans hide behind the convenient dodge that we were the best country in the world, or end every conversation critical of the United States by asserting that claim. We had real problems, domestic and foreign, and they had come into sharper focus. Those of us who had worked for civil rights were forced to admit that it was not merely a southern problem. Jim Crow laws were confined to the South, but de facto, if not de jure, segregation existed everywhere else. Beyond race, poverty was crushing both whites and blacks across the country. American students had never organized to confront these issues, but some wanted to try and membership in SDS grew.

Meanwhile, several military coups destabilized South Viet Nam. The number of U.S. military advisers there had grown to sixteen thousand. What were so many soldiers doing in the middle of that mess? Just before his death, Kennedy had discussed a gradual withdrawal and signed an order to bring a thousand of them out. Four days after his death, Johnson reversed that order. We were giving $2 million a day to an inept and corrupt government, while the rebels rapidly captured new terrain. Yet Johnson and Defense Secretary Robert McNamara kept saying that South Viet Nam would not be lost to the communists.

In the midst of this political turmoil, my life continued to move in a very different direction, toward science and scientific research. I embraced the new skills Al Rechtschaffen taught me in the Sleep Lab. In addition to troubleshooting our electroencephalographs, they included wiring and operating a variety of other electronic devices, handling our lab animals, surgically implanting recording electrodes in specific parts of their brains, hand drawing graphs and charts for publication, performing statistical analyses, and numerous other tasks.

Most exciting for me were the experiments. In one we put people to sleep with their eyes taped open. Huge humidifiers in the Sleep Lab's bedrooms kept their corneas moist, and most fell soundly asleep in thirty to forty-five minutes. During REM periods, we held objects in front of their open eyes to see if the objects were incorporated into their dreams. They were not, which led us to the hypothesis that humans are functionally blind during REM sleep and, presumably, functionally deaf as well. Neurophysiological research confirmed our theory years later by showing that certain neurons in mammalian brains suppress external sensory input during REM sleep. (The common dream in which the alarm clock turns into a train whistle or a doorbell is not a REM dream, but rather a reverie that occurs in the transition between sleep and wakefulness.)

Allan Rechtschaffen was utterly committed to the pursuit of new knowledge. He was a rigorous and dedicated researcher, as interested in surgically probing the brains of our animals as in dissecting the dreams and psychological phenomena reported by our human subjects. He initiated me into the most difficult scientific problem on the planet: uncovering the workings of the human brain. In the process, Al gave me an extraordinary gift. By guiding me into scientific research, he fulfilled my desire for a "calling," a life's work. I knew how far I still had to go, but in his lab I got a glimpse of what my life might become, and for the first time I liked what I saw. I made a commitment to scientific research stronger than any commitment I had ever made before. Al became a friend, too. I could beat him at pool, but he crushed me in gin rummy games as we sat watching experimental subjects sleep through the night.

Al and I were both fans of the Beatles, still new to the United States and revolutionizing rock and roll. Every time they issued a new album, one of us would buy it on the first day. We were not alone. By April 1964, Beatles songs occupied the top five slots on the charts, an unprecedented feat never repeated. With other friends, some of whom were musicians themselves, I occasionally went to black bars on the South Side to hear Muddy Waters, Howlin' Wolf, Junior Wells, and other great Chicago blues artists. At the time, I also played a little poker, and that spring I found a game in a fraternity house where some serious money could be made. Another player, Sly, had found the same game, and we became friends.

Sly lived on the fringe of the university community. He was a professional gambler, but with a well-developed intellectual streak. His legs had been paralyzed by childhood polio, so he got around on two canes, which left his upper body and arms massively muscled. Dark haired, still short when standing with his canes, he was one hell of a poker player. He also had a murky involvement with bookies and horse racing in northern Indiana. One day he startled me with the news that he had just made $250,000 on a fixed horse race.

Sly wasn't one to keep his money in the bank. He bought an orange four-door Lincoln convertible, which became the most visible car in the neighborhood, and purchased a large town house on the North Side opposite Lincoln Park. Sly asked a few of us involved with SNCC to tell civil rights workers in the South that any of them were welcome to come to Chicago for a month of rest and relaxation at his house and at his expense. He would provide a car and food. Several accepted his hospitality and enjoyed a welcome relief from the violence that hung over them every day in the South.

There was a large attic in the house, and Sly made it available to two of our friends, Paul and Elvin, amateur musicians fascinated by the blues bands we had all heard on the South Side. They had started a band themselves and needed a place to rehearse. Soon, their band got a gig at a nearby bar, Big John's, and became a local sensation. When they recorded their first album, which wedded the sound of Chicago blues to the new folk and rock music sweeping the country, the Paul Butterfield Blues Band became a national sensation. With Paul playing harmonica and Elvin Bishop, a UC physics student, on guitar, they went on to record more albums that topped the national charts and transformed rock music in America.

At the end of the school year in May, I went to San Francisco to visit Scott Van Leuven, my traveling buddy in Europe four years before. He had just graduated from UCLA, where the Shah of Iran had been the commencement speaker. It was an outrageous choice. In 1951, the newly elected prime minister of Iran, Mohammad Mossadeq, had nationalized the country's oil industry and used the profits to improve the lives of his people. That upset the American and British owners who thought the profits were rightfully theirs, so the CIA engineered a coup that put the Shah back on his throne. Scott organized a walkout at graduation, but when he stood to leave, only two other people stood with him, neither of whom he knew. Mortified at the dismal response, typical of the then sorry state of student activism, the three bravely turned and left. Many years later, in a remarkable coincidence, one of the other two became my wife.

Scott and I explored San Francisco and spent several days in Palo Alto visiting friends from Chicago doing graduate work at Stanford. Our Chicago friends lived with half a dozen others in a large communal house. It was my first exposure to this exotic new lifestyle. Amazingly, men and women shared quarters with little regard for social convention. The women openly took the new birth control pill and casually discussed their sex lives. Marijuana was smoked all day long. Folk music, especially Dylan's, and rock and roll played like a constant soundtrack. We met their musician friends who, like Paul Butterfield in Chicago, were trying to wed rock and roll to folk music and the blues.

One afternoon, well lubricated on marijuana, our friends took us to visit a group of their friends about to leave on a cross-country trip in a converted school bus. As we pulled onto their property, I saw a bus hand-painted in a dizzying rainbow of Day-Glo colors. Above the front windshield, where the bus's destination usually appears, was one misspelled word: "Furthur." We were introduced, and from their looks I thought they were in costume preparing for a festival or a circus. They were not. They were busy getting the bus ready for the trip, and their clothes, like the bus, were as brightly colored as possible. Many of the men wore necklaces and bracelets made from beads. A few had hair as long as a girl's. Some of the women had painted bright colors on their faces and arms and put feathers or flowers in their hair. A few of the guys wore brightly colored pants. Was this some sort of put-on? Did these guys simply not understand the rules of masculinity that governed the rest of us? Colored pants? Necklaces? I was put off.

They called themselves the Merry Pranksters. Their leader, Ken Kesey, was the best-selling author of *One Flew over the Cuckoo's Nest.* He was so busy coordinating work on the bus that aside from a handshake, I had no other contact with him. The group left a few days later. Tom Wolfe described their trip in his novel *The Electric Kool-Aid Acid Test,* which made them famous. The "acid" in the title referred to lysergic acid diethylamide, LSD, the new hallucinatory drug attracting attention because of the proselytizing work of two Harvard psychologists, Tim Leary and Dick Alpert, who enthusiastically touted its psychological and spiritual benefits. Inevitably, Harvard lost patience with their enthusiasm, and both were fired, which focused more attention on the new drug.

The Pranksters were advocates and connoisseurs of LSD, and no doubt had benefited from its pleasures the day of my visit. Our friends from Chicago had also dropped acid and, while not part of the Pranksters, traveled in the same orbit. In the typical anything-goes spirit we had stumbled upon, the Chicagoans had formed a rock band but had not yet learned to play their instruments. It was no coincidence that Dick Alpert was also a guest of the Pranksters that day.

Alpert, later known as Ram Dass, asked about my work on dreaming, and we fell into a long conversation. Dreams, like drug-induced hallucinations, were a creation of the unconscious mind, and as psychologists we traded notes on their underlying similarities. Alpert encouraged me to try LSD. From my studies, I knew the pain and discomfort of anxiety attacks, which had been associated with LSD. If this drug could trigger reactions like that, I wanted to approach it more cautiously, so I declined. Nevertheless, all the talk about the drug's ability to provoke personal insights, vivid hallucinations, and intriguing out-of-body experiences sounded interesting. My reluctance evaporated two years later.

I could not know it at the time, but the Pranksters would become the model for the new hippie lifestyle about to seduce America's youth. My experiences around them, the rampant drug use, the sexual freedom, the bizarre but colorful styles of dress and grooming, the men with very long hair and beads, were all early signs of what was to come. In less than a year, the musical experimentation I saw on that trip led to the formation of the Jefferson Airplane, the Grateful Dead, and other San Francisco rock bands who created the ubiquitous background beat of the coming era. I had an unexpected preview of "sex, drugs, and rock and roll," the misleading cliché that would soon symbolize my generation's search for alternative lifestyles.

Back in Chicago, having successfully completed my first year of graduate study, I returned to Sixty-third Street Beach for one last summer. It was on the edge of Hyde Park, so I was able to live on campus and keep up my work in the Sleep Lab. I enjoyed the beach and found it amusing to be the only white person there. But the beach was contested turf between two rival street gangs, the Vice Lords and the Blackstone Rangers. Twice a week, I was the supervisor in charge until 10:00 p.m., when the beach closed. At 8:30 p.m., a police sergeant checked on the two cops assigned to the beach. Once he did, the cops took off for coffee and doughnuts, leaving me, the lone white guy, to handle any trouble, backed up only by a handful of lifeguards. I felt too vulnerable, so I bought a .32 automatic pistol in lawless northern Indiana. It was big enough to stop someone but small enough to easily conceal. For an hour and a half on the nights the two cops deserted me, I nervously patrolled the sand or sat in the beach office with the .32 in my jacket pocket, desperately hoping I would never have to use it. Thankfully, I never did.

That summer more murders traumatized the nation. SNCC sponsored Freedom Summer to allow college students to work for civil rights in Mississippi. In training sessions in Ohio, they winnowed the many volunteers down to a group of seven hundred. Their job was to run voter registration drives and set up summer schools for black children to compensate for substandard instruction in their segregated schools. On June 21, the volunteers' first day in Mississippi, a Neshoba County deputy arrested three of them: James Chaney, a black activist from Mississippi; Michael Schwerner, a white activist from New York; and Andrew Goodman, a white volunteer from New York. The deputy was in the Ku Klux Klan. He kept them in jail until a gang of Klansmen assembled and took them away.

The other volunteers were terrified as weeks went by with no word about the victims. The story was widely covered in the national press, and people everywhere looked on in horror. Meanwhile, thirty-five black churches were burned, sixty black homes and safe houses were destroyed, volunteers were beaten and arrested on false charges and often followed by pickup trucks bristling with guns and drunken men. Search parties combed the countryside for six weeks until the bodies of the tortured victims of the kidnapping were found. It was a season of terror in Mississippi.

Greenwood, where I had been the year before, was only eighty-five miles from Neshoba County. Bob Moses and Jim Forman had been right. Sadly, people did die. The three Freedom Summer deaths were only the most recent. But as Moses and Forman had predicted, the brutality and the many killings in the South did raise a tidal wave of moral outrage that washed across the rest of the country. American public opinion lined up firmly behind civil rights for blacks. In July, President Johnson skillfully used that support to push the 1964 Civil Rights Act through Congress. It made the Jim Crow laws in the South illegal.

It would take more murder and much more violence over the following years before blacks in the South could enjoy their hard-won civil rights, but eventually the new federal law was pushed down the unwilling throats of the last racist holdouts, and legal segregation in America came to an end. The transformation of law made me more optimistic. Slavery had lasted three hundred years. It had befuddled the founding geniuses who wrote our Constitution, and it had precipitated the most brutal war in our country's history. One hundred years after slavery was abolished, it still corroded the lives of black citizens like an invisible acid. Finally, after all the marches and all the demonstrations, after all the beatings, the lynch mobs, the burnings, and the killings, citizens of all races had to be given equal treatment under the law. Most surprising and inspirational to me and to so many others, this monumental and historic achievement had been won at long last by a grassroots movement of ordinary citizens using the tactics of nonviolence.

CHAPTER 5

VIET NAM WAS SLIDING INTO CHAOS. IN JULY 1964, JOHNSON APPOINTED A NEW U.S. ambassador and a new military commander. North Vietnamese troops were backing up rebels in the South, and the United States was complaining it was an invasion. An invasion? Wasn't it a civil war between two parts of the same country? The Republicans nominated Barry Goldwater for president, an archconservative and virulent anticommunist. His selection moved Republicans far to the right just as the rest of the country moved slightly left. Would that force Johnson, his opponent in November, to try to look tougher in comparison? Was war in Viet Nam part of his strategy?

The answer came on August 4, when the United States claimed that North Vietnamese vessels had attacked an American destroyer on patrol in international waters in the Gulf of Tonkin between Viet Nam and China. I immediately thought it was a hoax. So did most people I knew. Why would a nation of rice farmers with no advanced weaponry use small boats in an unprovoked attack against a heavily armed destroyer? Johnson asked Congress for the power to respond militarily. He did not ask for a declaration of war, only an authorization to use force.

I was amazed. There was little dispute and no attempt to substantiate the facts. Yet without a single dissenting vote in the House and only two in the Senate, Congress was stampeded into passing the Gulf of Tonkin Resolution. It gave Johnson the authority to "take all necessary steps" to protect U.S. interests in the region. Years later, we learned the attack in the Gulf of Tonkin was indeed a fabrication perpetrated to start a war. Johnson had Navy jets bomb targets on the North Vietnamese coast, but surprisingly he made no wider use of his war-making authority.

A month later, I began my second year of graduate study and was back at my job in the Sleep Lab. I also had to work as an extern at a local mental health hospital. The Ph.D. program was grooming me to be a clinical psychologist, while in the Sleep Lab I was being trained as a research scientist. Despite these obligations, however, my attention swung back to politics in October. The Berkeley campus of the University of California erupted in the first large-scale student demonstration of the 1960s. Surprisingly, the issue that set off the conflict was not Viet Nam and not civil rights for blacks. It was civil rights for students.

The Berkeley campus had a long-standing ban on political activity. Civil rights activists, some just back from Freedom Summer, criticized the ban. A former student then defied it by setting up a table to recruit civil rights supporters. University officials called the police. They arrested the former student and put him in a police car. A crowd of three thousand students gathered, surrounded the car, and refused to move. In effect, they captured the police car that had captured the activist, and they did it nonviolently. Mario Savio, a member of the campus Friends of SNCC chapter, rose to lead them. They used the roof of the squad car as a speakers' platform to debate the civil and political rights of students. It went on for thirty-six hours until the police gave up, released the arrested man, and dropped charges against him.

That small but stunning victory reverberated across the country. For the first time students had stood up for their own rights. More remarkably, they had found a nonviolent way to save a comrade from arrest and neutralize the authority of the police. This victory captured the imagination of activist students nationwide, myself included. Police had superior physical power, as I had seen in Paris, but Berkeley showed us that their power could be limited. Interestingly, the Berkeley protests had not been planned. Success came when creative leadership stepped in and took advantage of a purely spontaneous uprising.

A month later, Berkeley officials filed charges against the protest leaders. Angry students, led by a new group called the Free Speech Move-ment, organized a massive sit-in at the campus administration building. This time officials were reluctant to call the police. The spectacle of white middle- and upper-class students being beaten up by cops would not help the university, and while an attack on a few student protesters could be buried in local news coverage, a battle with thousands could not. The students, however, were tenacious, and eventually officials felt forced to have the cops clear the building. Over eight hundred were arrested. Predictably, the show of force backfired. The public was outraged, and officials were forced to drop charges. More important, the university had to repeal its ban on campus political activity.

The success at Berkeley was a revelation to me. I realized that the kind of moral outrage driving the civil rights movement in the South might also be harnessed for other issues. None of us could see it then, but the political and public relations factors that had first limited the police and protected the students at Berkeley were destined to change the bal-ance of forces in future protests and give birth to a range of tactics that empowered the movements of the 1960s. Even though the full implica-tions were not yet apparent, people like me understood that a corner had been turned at Berkeley and that there was much to learn from what had happened there.

That November was my first opportunity to vote in a presidential elec-tion. When Kennedy faced Nixon in 1960, the minimum voting age was still twenty-one, so I was not eligible. In 1964, the election was polarized around the issue of nuclear war. Johnson skillfully positioned himself as the peace candidate. He made Goldwater appear even more extreme than he was. In spite of my skepticism about the Gulf of Tonkin, I voted for Johnson because of the nuclear issue. He won the largest presidential vic-tory in history, a victory that dramatically underscored the nation's hunger for peace.

After the election, my externship and graduate courses led me to question clinical psychology. It was hardly an exact science. I had spent a quarter learning to administer the Rorschach test, then discovered it was valid only 40 percent of the time. Other graduate students in the clinical program seemed disproportionately neurotic, socially inept, or otherwise maladjusted. I wondered if they were planning to surround themselves with people more disturbed than they were so they could feel healthy in comparison. I knew that highly empathic people could be effective psychotherapists, but the field was not for me. I planned to stick to research.

That decision was reinforced by the thrill of an actual scientific discovery. Rechtschaffen thought the heightened electrical activity in the brain during REM sleep was an indication that the brain was producing more energy, that it was working harder metabolically. In those days, we had no way to measure metabolic activity in the brain, so Al invented one using a thermistor, a tiny electrical resistor the size of a caraway seed with two protruding miniature wires. When low-amplitude current goes down one wire, resistance in the thermistor fluctuates with temperature, so the current coming out the other wire can serve as a thermometer.

I assisted Al in a surgery on one of our cats. We used precision equipment to place recording electrodes in specific sites in its brain. These electrodes were attached to a small twenty-four-pin socket so that after the cat recovered from surgery, we could detect electrical activity at various points in its brain. I had assisted in many such operations, but this time we also inserted a thermistor into the cat's internal jugular vein and ran the wires out to the twenty-four-pin socket. That gave us a measure of blood temperature leaving the brain. Al reasoned that if brain metabolism increased during REM sleep, blood temperature leaving the brain would also increase.

It took eight hours to complete the surgery. The anesthetic had to wear off before the cat experienced the normal alternation between REM and non-REM sleep. Only then would we see if brain temperature increased during its first REM period. We set up an around-the-clock watch. I drew the night shift. By the second day, the cat had not revived and we grew concerned. That night, I sat alone nervously watching the eight ink pens on our recorder as they scratched out the cat's brain waves on the graph paper passing underneath. At 3:00 a.m., the cat came out of the anesthesia and fell asleep. Somewhat later, the recording pens indicated the classic brain wave pattern of REM sleep. This was the moment of truth. I stared at the ink pen showing jugular vein temperature. Nothing happened. A minute passed. Still nothing. Another minute. Then the flat line started to slowly arc up. I wasn't sure at first, but soon it was unmistakable. Jugular vein temperature dramatically increased. When the REM period ended, it immediately fell back.

I was astounded! It was a genuine scientific discovery. Brain metabolism increased during REM sleep. I picked up the phone to call Al, but then stopped to relish the moment. I was the only person in all of history who knew this simple fact. It was a moment of pure egotism, but it was an egotism that grew out of something meaningful rather than something selfish. I savored the feeling, hoping that eventually, as a scientist myself, I would experience it again, and that such experiences would satisfy the longing for meaning and honor in my life. In the following months, Al confirmed the discovery and described our findings in a paper published by a leading scientific journal. He was kind enough to include me as a co-author, which gave me my first credential as a published scientist. I couldn't have been more proud.

Soon, I had other such experiences. I assisted in research on narcolepsy and bruxism. We discovered that narcoleptics, rather than simply falling asleep, suddenly and at inappropriate times were actually falling immediately into REM sleep, which never occurs at sleep onset in normal people. "Bruxism" is the scientific name for nocturnal teeth grinding, and we found that it too occurs during REM sleep. Later, our findings had important implications for the treatment of both disorders.

The research was fascinating, but my attention kept getting pulled back to politics, usually because of some new outrage. The previous year, Malcolm X had drawn the attention of many of us concerned about civil rights. First a criminal, then a black separatist, Malcolm had matured into a leader who could speak convincingly to blacks from all walks of life. To those of us who cared about the economic as well as political rights of blacks and poor whites, he seemed irreplaceable, but in February Malcolm was killed by a shotgun blast as he addressed an audience in Washington Heights. After Kennedy's assassination, I couldn't believe that another political leader had been cut down at the height of his potential. Were they going to kill every leader capable of bringing the country together and moving it in a progressive direction?

Two weeks later, there was more racist violence. The Reverend James Bevel, whom I had met in Greenwood, worked on voter registration in Selma, Alabama. He called for a march from there to Montgomery, the state capital. John Lewis of SNCC came to help, but six blocks into the march state troopers and deputies, some on horseback, blocked their path. The cops assaulted the marchers using batons, tear gas, and even bullwhips. Many were severely injured. The images I saw on TV and in the papers disgusted me. Martin Luther King Jr. joined two subsequent marches, which finally made it to Montgomery, but three more people were killed. This extreme violence won more support for civil rights. Johnson called a joint session of Congress to advocate for a national voting rights act to finally end the southern practices that had kept blacks from registering to vote.

After several quiet months, U.S. military activity in Viet Nam dramatically increased. In February, South Vietnamese rebels attacked an American Army camp. In retaliation, Johnson bombed a North Vietnamese Army camp. Because he appeared to be defending American lives, or avenging their loss, a public opinion poll showed 80 percent approval for the U.S. military presence in Viet Nam. In March, confident of public support and frustrated by the lack of progress, Johnson ordered U.S. jets to bomb a range of North Vietnamese targets. Operation Rolling Thunder was supposed to last eight weeks. It would go on for three and a half years. Johnson also ordered thirty-five hundred combat Marines to Viet Nam to back up the twenty-three thousand American military advisers already there.

Opposition to the war grew on the elite college campuses, despite widespread support in the population at large. Yet few of us knew enough to be effective opponents. A new format was developed to solve that problem: the teach-in. (We added the suffix "-in" to various events to honor the sit-ins in the South; later the hippies would host love-ins and human be-ins.) The teach-ins I attended at UC featured experts on Viet Nam's history and politics, and people who had firsthand experience there. Some spoke at other teach-ins as part of a national effort to stop the war. The teach-ins were raucous affairs. Lecture halls often overflowed with people sitting on the floor or standing in the aisles. Skeptical questions were hurled at the speakers, and lively exchanges took place. Some sessions went on for hours or lasted into the night.

The teach-ins gave me a crash course in Southeast Asian history. For hundreds of years, the Vietnamese had fought off Chinese invaders. In the nineteenth century, they succumbed to France and became its colony. By the 1920s, Ho Chi Minh, a young patriot who would become the father of his country, founded the Vietnamese Communist Party to fight for national independence. European colonists imposed a high degree of economic exploitation on their Asian victims, so I wasn't surprised that the revolutionaries planned to recapture that wealth, and had adopted a socialist or communist ideology.

Prior to World War II, the Japanese seized Viet Nam and cut off Ho Chi Minh's movement. He joined forces with the Americans to fight them. When the war ended, Ho wrote a declaration of independence that heavily borrowed from our own and declared Viet Nam a new nation. The French objected. They still craved Viet Nam's ample tungsten and rubber, nor would they willingly relinquish a former colony at the junction of the Indian and Pacific oceans, a strategic location for an imperial power operating far from home. Ho Chi Minh had to launch another anticolonial war. In 1954, the military genius in command of his forces, General Vo Nguyen Giap, finally surrounded the French army at Dien Bien Phu and won a decisive victory.

That should have ended it, but that's when we got involved. The United States brokered a peace agreement that allowed Ho's forces to regroup in the North while anticommunist Vietnamese who had fought with the French gathered in the South. In a 1954 peace treaty signed in Geneva, the United States guaranteed the reunification of the country in 1956 following an election in which voters could choose between Ho's Communist Party and a noncommunist alternative.

That sounded like a good deal, but before the election the CIA informed Eisenhower that Ho Chi Minh was likely to win 80 percent of the vote. The United States canceled the election and set up a puppet regime in the South, permanently dividing the country in two, as was done in Korea. South Viet Nam wasn't a country at all. The United States had created it and was pretending to protect its national integrity. Pure hypocrisy. Johnson was not in pursuit of strategic interests in Viet Nam. Like Eisenhower, he just wanted to stop another country from joining the communist bloc, even if it had limited geopolitical significance and the price was American lives and treasure. Still unwilling to believe the worst about my country, I was shocked that the United States would stoop to such manipulation and duplicity.

The teach-ins led me to the works of Bernard Fall, a Howard University professor and the leading expert on Viet Nam in the West. He had published several books and numerous articles on Viet Nam and the other two countries in Indochina, Laos and Cambodia. Fall was anticommunist, but also highly critical of U.S. actions. He explained that after the canceled election in 1956, Ho Chi Minh built the Democratic Republic of Viet Nam in the North and was still the head of state. Meanwhile, revolutionaries in the South formed the National Liberation Front (NLF). Their plan was to overthrow the U.S. puppet regime and unify the country.

Fall argued persuasively that Vietnamese independence fighters had demonstrated their skill against the modern armies of France and Japan for over thirty years and would likely do just as well against the Americans. They were patriots who enjoyed the support and fierce loyalty of their people, which in the long run would mean more than the vast resources of the Americans. Fall convinced me that Johnson would never get the quick and easy victory he sought. But if I had this information, why didn't the CIA? And if they did have it, what did they know that the rest of us did not? Was there really anything at stake in Viet Nam beyond Cold War politics? I couldn't be sure.

The last straw for me came when Johnson authorized the use of napalm. Napalm is an incendiary weapon dropped in canisters from aircraft. It is basically gasoline mixed with an additive that turns the mixture into a sticky jellylike compound. The dropped canisters ignite in a massive fireball that throws the sticky gasoline in all directions. It adheres to the surfaces it touches, including human skin. If victims are not instantly burned alive, they die of suffocation because the fireball sucks all the oxygen out of the surrounding air.

In the aftermath of World War II, the Holocaust had cast a long shadow over Western morality, for Christians and Jews alike. The idea that citizens might once again remain passive while their governments committed unspeakable atrocities, that such citizens might become the "good Germans" of the future, horrified me and other students my age. The lesson burned into our psyches by World War II was that if a government commits atrocities, its citizens are obligated to resist. The Nazis had burned members of my father's family alive. Four years before in Israel, I had wondered what I would have done had I been in Germany then. Now it was my government burning people alive in Viet Nam. I had no choice but to act.

Dow Chemical manufactured the napalm. SDS members at UC planned a protest in front of a Dow facility in suburban Chicago. I joined them. We leafleted on campus to encourage others to attend, but only forty of us showed up. We picketed with signs blasting Dow, but given the small turnout, I thought we had failed. Later, though, I would point to that little protest and use it to prove that great projects can spring from small beginnings. Before the antiwar movement was done, hundreds of thousands demonstrated against Dow Chemical in a sustained campaign that lasted for years and made the company the embodiment of corporate evil.

While I picketed Dow in Chicago, SDS also sponsored the first mass antiwar demonstration in Washington, D.C. Previously, some SDS members had resisted shifting their focus from poverty and political reform, embodied in their signature call for "participatory democracy," to work against the expanding war in Viet Nam. Some of their leaders, including Tom Hayden, author of the stirring Port Huron Statement that had launched SDS, argued for this shift. Their efforts paid off. A surprising twenty-five thousand people attended the SDS demonstration. There was much to protest: new troop deployments, aerial bombardment of civilians, a corrupt regime in the South, and napalm. Speeches were made and songs were sung. Joan Baez did Dylan's "The Times They Are A-Changin' " and led the crowd in the civil rights anthem, "We Shall Overcome."

The success of the Washington protest convinced me that a genuine antiwar movement had been born. I identified with it even though I didn't attend SDS meetings. Like others, I saw the civil rights movement as the model for what we had to do: raise a great moral crusade that would expose the injustice of the war. I was convinced that once Americans knew the truth, they would turn against the war, just as so many had finally turned against racism in the South. The truth was simple enough. The United States was killing people in a poor agricultural country because their leaders were communists, and because our president saw them only as pawns on the Cold War chessboard. Never mind the unsettling parade of military dictators in South Viet Nam (by June 1965, there had been ten in the preceding twenty months), each of whom our government touted in his turn as the next great savior of the country.

Americans had no sympathy for communists. But for me, the hysteria over the "communist threat" had lost its punch after the collapse of Senator Joe McCarthy's witch hunts in the 1950s and my own exposure to right-wing propaganda like *Operation Abolition*. I was not a communist and was repulsed by what I knew of life in the U.S.S.R., but I was open to socialist ideas, the more so for poor countries struggling to modernize. Ho Chi Minh's communism seemed to me to grow out of a desire to move Viet Nam beyond its colonial past, not a decision to join the U.S.S.R. and China in a cold war against the United States.

Despite the escalating American military presence, North Vietnamese Army troops and NLF guerrillas kept up their attacks that spring. Johnson and his advisers found it difficult to believe their superior firepower had not prevailed, so they escalated to full-scale war, announcing in July 1965 that U.S. troop strength would be increased to 125,000 men. Johnson was fighting the French war all over again. Simultaneously, the Pentagon raised the monthly draft call to 35,000 men. The draft had been in place since World War II, but the peacetime quota had been low enough to allow young men unwilling to serve to find a way out. Marriage or college attendance was sufficient for a draft deferment. At 35,000 a month, that would change, and tens of thousands of young men would have to fight in Viet Nam against their will.

Irate about developments in Viet Nam, I still didn't think the war would distort my own life. I wanted to be part of the movement to stop it, but science remained at the center of my plans. My own draft deferment was secure. In March, I had started dating Charlotte Weissberg, and soon we became seriously involved. She was a brilliant, vivacious, dark-haired beauty, with the poise and graceful movement of a serious dance student. She came from the highbrow private school culture in Manhattan, the daughter of a Viennese physician who had fled the Nazis, but she knew how to have fun. Three years my junior, she was graduating from UC's college and beginning its Ph.D. program in sociology in the fall.

Charlotte had volunteered to spend June in a remote jungle village in Mexico's Yucatán Peninsula where UC maintained a social psychology field station. We planned to meet afterward and hitchhike through Central America. When the time came, I met her in Mérida, the Yucatán's delightful capital city, and she told me about her month with a family of Mayan Indians. We explored the nearby Mayan ruin sites at Chichén Itzá and Uxmal. I had no idea that pre-Columbian civilizations had been so advanced. Prior to the European conquest, one million Aztecs lived where Mexico City now stands and had the organizational ability to move food in and waste out every day.

Charlotte had learned of a sleepy island nearby in the Mexican Caribbean with a perfect climate and very low prices. A bus and a fishing boat got us to Cozumel, which was virtually undeveloped at the time. There was a single cheap hotel in the island's one small village and another on the beach to the north that rented screened-in beach cottages. We rented a cottage for a week, and there I learned an amazing fact: water in the Caribbean was transparent!

I had dived only in Lake Michigan, where on a good day the visibility is three feet. When I first put on a mask and snorkel and went underwater in Cozumel, I thought I could see to the ends of the earth. The visibility was close to a hundred feet. Instead of a flat sand bottom, there was a veritable garden of underwater life: coral reefs, brightly colored reef fish by the thousands, lobsters walking on the bottom, sea fans, anemones, eels, rays, even larger fish like barracuda and mackerel. I was in another world, and I was buoyant, so I could fly through the transparent water and glide to whatever caught my eye. And the water was warm! I stayed in it for hours. I thought this warm Caribbean island, cooled by the soft breezes of the trade winds, was an earthly paradise, and I promised myself that some-day I would find my way back.

From Cozumel we hitchhiked through British Honduras, which is now Belize, then through Honduras, El Salvador, Guatemala, and back into Mexico. Such a trip today might be dangerous, but then, before the revolutions and the drug trade that came later, we had no trouble. In early August, we traveled up the west coast of Mexico and crossed into Nogales, Arizona, with plans to see Los Angeles before returning to Chicago. Somewhere west of Nogales, we got a ride from a truck going all the way to L.A.

Crossing the border was a shock. After six weeks, we heard English on the radio for the first time, but when the trucker tuned in a Top 40 station and the music started, the shock was far greater. Instead of the usual pop music, the DJ was playing protest songs popular among activists and col-lege students but unknown to the AM radio audience. What had hap-pened? As the truck continued west, we learned that Bob Dylan, not at all a Top 40 artist up to that point, had the number one, two, and four songs on the chart. The number three song, "Eve of Destruction," while not Dylan's, was directly critical of the war in Viet Nam.

During the month we were away, the newly escalated war and the vastly enlarged draft quotas had created a cultural earthquake across the United States. Viet Nam was the center of attention for young men and their families, who for the first time faced the reality of being killed in a war. An uncertain and as yet undifferentiated subculture of opposition was in formation. I was amazed at how rapidly it had come about. We talked about it for several hours before an even bigger bombshell burst out of the radio. It was a news bulletin unlike any we had ever heard.

Massive rioting had just broken out in Watts, L.A.'s black ghetto. Fires were burning and looters were cleaning out stores as rooftop snipers shot at firemen and police. What?! Looters?! People shooting at the police?! Armed National Guard troops were on the way. Charlotte and I looked at each other in amazement. War in an American city, the city we would drive into in a matter of hours. We kept the radio tuned to the news, and as we approached L.A. from the south, I could see military trucks bristling with troops moving toward Watts. At the apartment of the friends hosting us, I suggested we drive to Watts to see what was happening, but everyone was too frightened to go out, afraid the riot would spread or that snipers would shoot at cars on the freeways.

The insurrection, as some came to call it, lasted six days. Before police regained control, thirty-four people were killed and a thousand wounded. Property losses were enormous. I had felt a little fear being so close to a war zone, but I was confused. Some of the rioters must have been motivated by poverty and a lack of opportunity. For the first time, cheap TV sets had brought programs that vividly depicted middle-class life into the living rooms of the poor, who then wished for a bigger share of the country's wealth. The sociologists called it a "revolution of rising expectations," but whatever the label the demand for equal opportunity had increased among the black poor, and their anger could no longer be contained.

The civil rights movement had been nonviolent and directed at political goals like voter registration. Addressing economic inequality would be far more complicated, and urban riots, accompanied by murder and arson, would not help. I did not know then that violent urban riots would engulf many northern cities over the next few years, but I could see the obvious, that a threshold had been crossed, and that America, its people, and its politics would never be the same. If any doubt remained that the fifties were over and a new period in American history had begun, that doubt ended in August 1965. Viet Nam was a full-scale shooting war, and Watts had drained nonviolence out of the struggle for black equality.

Ironically, Watts came only weeks after Johnson signed the National Voting Rights Act of 1965, a historic victory for everyone who had sacrificed to register black voters in the South. I celebrated that victory despite the escalating war in Viet Nam. The civil rights movement had changed the laws of the land. In the face of all the violence used against it, the movement had accomplished social change of enormous magnitude entirely through nonviolent means. It reinforced my belief that another moral crusade could be waged against the war.

But I was torn about Johnson. He had pushed hard for a progressive domestic agenda that included new civil rights laws, antipoverty programs, and Medicare, the first massive expansion of Social Security. Yet his foreign policy agenda was reactionary and backward. After passage of the Voting Rights Act, blacks in the South did vote and did elect blacks to law-enforcement and other offices. The rigid seniority system in Congress did change, just as the SNCC leaders had predicted it would. Unfortunately, they could not have predicted Viet Nam, and because of the war there was no happy ending.

In signing the Voting Rights Act, Johnson had famously said that it would drive the South out of the Democratic Party for a generation. It did. But his blunder in Viet Nam kept them out even longer. As the war dragged on, the inability of the antiwar movement to stop it led to our frustration and an ever-increasing militancy. As a result, we eventually used extreme tactics that alienated cultural conservatives in the southern states and turned their new relationship with the Republican Party into a permanent alliance. Regrettably, instead of the Voting Rights Act ushering in a more progressive era, the war in Viet Nam and our militant antiwar tactics amplified its impact in the South, which then led to a long period of national conservative domination. We could not know that in advance, but given the desperate urgency with which we tried to stop the war, I doubt that any long-term considerations would have stopped us.

CHAPTER 6

THE WAR BECAME MY CONSTANT PREOCCUPATION. I HAD OBLIGATIONS AS A GRADUATE student and research assistant in the Sleep Lab, but I was determined to be part of the effort to stop it. My only confusion was about the soldiers. I was certain the war was wrong, but my peers, maybe some people I knew, would be on the battlefield. Didn't I have to be on their side, too? Would that be possible? Was it even correct?

Antiwar tactics had escalated in Berkeley. While I was traveling with Charlotte, Berkeley students discovered that napalm was being manufactured next door in Oakland and shipped from there to Viet Nam. They got a pickup truck, painted it government gray, installed flashing yellow lights, and mounted a large sign on the rear that read, "Danger. Napalm Bombs Ahead." With their pickup, they followed the napalm trucks on the freeway. The stunt got great press coverage and provoked public opposition to the local manufacture of napalm.

The Berkeley activists also tried to block troop trains. Soldiers arrived at the Oakland Navy yards by train and boarded ships there for Viet Nam. Activists got the train schedules, and protesters sat on the tracks. For reasons of "national security," the government ordered the trains not to stop or slow down. Four times activists scrambled off the tracks as speeding trains bore down on them. That made for dramatic news footage. No trains were actually stopped, but the coverage amplified the power of the protesters by making opposition to the war appear more common and forceful than was actually the case. Later, manipulation of the news media using unusual tactics like these would become a hallmark of the antiwar movement.

Despite these isolated protests, society at large reacted to the war with knee-jerk patriotism. The news media and elected officials from both parties endorsed Johnson's war policies. The labor unions had already compromised their progressive ideals to support the Cold War, so they found it easy to applaud the new hot war in Viet Nam. My friends and I had not been bashful about rejecting society's values and traditions, but we were surprised by and ill prepared for the scorn heaped on us by America's mainstream institutions. For speaking out against the war, students were labeled unpatriotic, even traitors, which left us more determined to stand up for our beliefs. Scorn was a two-way street. Antiwar students, themselves still a minority within the national student population, ridiculed those institutions that uncritically accepted the official story from Washington. Like them, I thought the pigheadedness of our Viet Nam policy was so obvious it was hard to believe otherwise intelligent people had accepted it and were justifying a blunder of such magnitude.

In September and October, I had to put politics aside to prepare for doctoral exams. Over the previous two years, I had completed the course work required for a Ph.D. Next came the exams, a grueling three-day test covering everything a "doctor" of psychology should know. A University of Chicago Ph.D. came with enormous prestige. To preserve it, the faculty only granted Ph.D.'s to candidates demonstrating a high level of competence. Less than half usually passed. My more nervous classmates prepared for an entire year, doing nothing else. Others did much less. I put in six weeks, studying day and night.

While I crammed for the exams, antiwar opposition spread beyond the campuses. The War Resisters League, Women Strike for Peace, the Committee for a Sane Nuclear Policy, and other groups working together as the Fifth Avenue Peace Parade Committee drew twenty-five thousand to an antiwar march in New York on October 15. That weekend, antiwar protests in other cities drew another hundred thousand between them. In November, thirty-five thousand protesters circled the White House and marched to the Washington Monument.

Elements of the old socialist and communist parties active in the 1930s who had survived the witch hunts of the 1950s joined these protests. Younger activists were anxious to distance themselves from these parties because they were still beholden to the U.S.S.R. or China. We did not want to be captives of an ideology born in another place or time, so we called ourselves the New Left to underscore our differences with the old left. Nevertheless, the old left parties began to play a small role in expanding antiwar efforts, even though they were suspected of participating in part to build their own memberships.

I was barely aware of these events as I prepared for the doctoral exams, but Charlotte occasionally pointed to TV footage from Saigon, the capital of South Viet Nam, that showed a lone Buddhist monk in saffron robes sitting calmly in a lotus position at a busy intersection. The monk doused himself with gasoline and set himself ablaze. Engulfed in flames, he sat still until falling over dead. These new protests against the government happened several times and were so grotesque they riveted my attention and had a huge impact. Meanwhile, our president was asking our soldiers to willingly die in defense of the puppet regime these monks were protesting.

By the end of October, I was unable to focus on anything except the psychology I had stuffed into my head. I took the doctoral exams, and as predicted, they were tough. Being responsible for so much information and not knowing what parts of it would be included was nerve-racking, and with so much at stake I couldn't help but be anxious. When the three days were over, I had no idea how I had done. Results would not be available for three weeks.

On November 2, I saw footage on the news that further taxed my comprehension. Norman Morrison, a devout Quaker and father of three, walked onto the Pentagon grounds and sat down just below the window of Defense Secretary Robert McNamara, the architect and manager of the war. Morrison carried his baby daughter. He calmly put the infant aside, poured kerosene over his body, and set himself aflame. He was acting in sympathy with the Buddhist monks in Saigon and trying to awaken Americans to the crimes being committed in their name.

Morrison stunned me. On the one hand, his senseless act would leave three children fatherless. On the other, he died as a patriot, sacrificing himself to awaken a slumbering nation and save the lives of those on both sides of the war who would die and be maimed in the coming years. He was the first fatality of the antiwar movement. I knew there would be others, as there had been in the struggle for civil rights in the South, but Morrison raised the stakes and forced all of us to ask ourselves how far we were willing to go.

Just before Thanksgiving 1965, results of the doctoral exams were announced. Of thirty-three students taking the exam, eight passed, less than a quarter and much lower than usual. To my surprise, I was one of the eight. I would not have guessed it, but the facts argued otherwise. Never again would I doubt having the mental horsepower to keep up with my peers.

The next step was to design the research for my doctoral dissertation. But with the four-day Thanksgiving weekend just ahead, I thought I had earned a short vacation. Remembering the crystal clear waters in the Caribbean, and thinking the Florida Keys might be a more accessible substitute, I called Alan Alderman, my old lifeguard buddy, and proposed we take a drive-away car to Miami, dive off the keys for three days, and fly home. He readily agreed.

Several days later, on a moonless night, we drove across the Florida Everglades. There was no light at all in the swamp. The two-lane highway was virtually deserted. Suddenly the road swung sharply left, and our headlights revealed a car that had missed the turn and gone into the water. We pulled over as the car slowly sank. An arm was thrust out of the driver's window. As lifeguards, we reacted instantly, jumped in, swam to the car, opened the door, and pulled the driver out. He was an older black man, small in stature and quite thin. He complained of back pain, so we floated him to the bank and lifted him out of the water by his clothes.

He was barely coherent. Then he muttered, "Did she get out?" Alan and I looked at each other. She? Without a word we whirled around and dived back into the black water. The car had settled on the bottom with the roof a foot or two beneath the surface. We dived underwater and felt our way to the car. I found the front door handle; Alan got the rear. We swam into and through the car, exiting the doors on the other side. There was no one inside. The man was confused. We did not yet know how badly.

Eventually, a Florida state trooper arrived. With a pronounced southern accent, he asked the driver lying on the ground what had happened. "These boys here run me off the road." The trooper looked up at me as I shook my head, silently denying his accusation. The trooper said, "You know who you talkin' to, boy?" The driver replied, "Yes, sir, mister officer white man, sir. I know." The trooper motioned us out of the man's earshot, and we explained what had actually happened. He said an ambulance was on the way and we were free to go.

I was relieved, but shocked once again at the spectacle of southern racism. The trooper casually addressing the older, relatively well-dressed black man as "boy," dismissing his account of what had happened in favor of one given by actual boys scruffier than he but with white skin, releasing us so easily after our claim of innocence, all made it clear that even if we had forced the man off the road, the trooper would have let us go because the victim was only a black "boy." I had been so wrapped up with Viet Nam I had forgotten that while new civil rights legislation was on the books, it would take years to stop southern behavior and prejudices from inflicting more pain on black citizens.

Alan and I made it to the keys. They were a big disappointment. The water was neither as clear nor as warm as the Caribbean, and the underwater life far more limited.

Back in Chicago, I learned about new forms of antiwar protest that had been used while I was studying for my exams. Protesters in Wisconsin went to an Air Force base to make a citizen's arrest of the commander. Berkeley students gave leaflets to military personnel urging them to refuse duty in Viet Nam. These were isolated incidents involving only small groups, but such events were newsworthy. In Michigan, students held a sit-in at the local draft board. The head of the Selective Service System, General Lewis Hershey, revoked the deferments of some and said he would have them inducted. Many commentators condemned his overreaction, realizing that the country could not encourage military service as an act of patriotism and at the same time use it as a form of punishment.

As antiwar rhetoric escalated, so did that of our opponents. The FBI chief, J. Edgar Hoover, condemned antiwar students as part of a communist plot that threatened the American way of life. He was such a right-wing extremist his remarks surprised no one, but otherwise reasonable voices joined this chorus, including former president Eisenhower, various university presidents, senators, leading authors, columnists, business leaders, and educators. In their sputtering outrage, they saw disruptive students not just as a threat to U.S. war policy but as a repudiation of all things American. Their repugnance suggested that they felt their own morality to be under attack. They were right. If that morality led them to support the war, we would condemn it and all of them along with it.

During this time, the first draft card was burned. At protests, a few students had chanted, "Hell no, we won't go!" The chant was an effective organizing tool, but I thought asking eighteen- and nineteen-year-olds to burn their draft cards and refuse induction was asking a great deal. They would face up to five years in prison and a felony conviction, or they would have to renounce their citizenship and permanently leave the United States, assuming they found another country willing to grant them residency.

My dissertation loomed before me, but I wanted to use some of my time to help stop the war. My limited experience in the civil rights movement had taught me that if people were exposed to a terrible injustice, many would respond morally. To stop the war, we had to first prove to the American people that it was wrong. And because so many were dying in Viet Nam, we had to do it fast. The news media portrayed us as disloyal, distorted our antiwar message, and refused to give us fair coverage. That meant protests alone would not deliver the public education that could turn the tide.

We needed to get on TV with an educational campaign of our own, one that delivered accurate information directly to millions of voters. The previous summer, the Beatles had performed in the first large-scale outdoor rock concert at Shea Stadium in New York. Over fifty thousand attendees had generated huge profits. I knew that several entertainers had supported civil rights work and assumed some might also oppose the war.

I gathered a few civil rights activists and proposed we form a group to recruit entertainers, stage large concerts, and use the profits to buy TV airtime for an educational antiwar film.

One of the activists knew Harry Belafonte, the singer and actor who had first popularized West Indian calypso music in the United States. He had raised a great deal of money for the civil rights movement and was close to Martin Luther King and other leaders. Harry was performing in Chicago a few weeks later, so we arranged a meeting. When we sat down together, I found him personable and well-informed about Viet Nam. He liked our idea and agreed to help. Harry told us the heavyweight champ was coming to Chicago for a benefit the next day and we should try to recruit him, too. Cassius Clay had recently won the title and changed his name to Muhammad Ali, signaling that he was prepared to be as controversial out of the ring as he was in it.

Belafonte took me backstage at the benefit. Ali was the star attraction. When we shook hands, his swallowed mine. I had big hands, part of the reason I was a good swimmer, but his were enormous. I tried to imagine being hit by one of his fists. Ali, too, opposed the war and asked for more details about our plans. Years before, he had thrown his Olympic gold medal into a river to protest discriminatory laws and practices in his home state of Kentucky. And while I could not know it then, two years later he would be stripped of his heavyweight title for refusing induction into the military, justifying his action by saying, "No Viet Cong ever called me nigger." ("Viet Cong" was used by Americans to describe the NLF fighters in the South.)

Ali joined our project and offered to appear at any concerts we were able to stage. Harry promised to recruit other entertainers. For two months, our little group assisted him, but it became clear that while many performers wanted to participate, their promoters, lawyers, agents, and managers refused to cooperate because of concerns about diminished profits. Bad news also came after Harry spoke to his contacts at the TV networks. They would not sell us airtime for the kind of programming we wanted to run.

The civil rights movement had raised a lot of money from concerts, and the news media had provided sympathetic coverage that educated millions about the need for reform. If the antiwar movement was cut off from similar funding, and if our message about Viet Nam was kept off the nation's TV screens, the civil rights movement was no longer an appropriate model for the task ahead. Unlike the movement in the South, we didn't have financial resources or the support of any significant sector of society. We were illegitimate, outside the mainstream, but we were trying to save lives, so we were desperate, too. We had no time to patiently explain ourselves. Every day more lives were lost. Would we have to become outlaws to get our message across? We thanked Harry for his time and effort and shut down our project.

The war was going badly for Johnson. American casualties rapidly mounted. The U.S. military made weekly boasts about the enemy "body count," the number killed the previous week. It was always higher than the Americans killed, but American deaths were far too high. Johnson tried to wrest concessions from the North Vietnamese with a bombing halt, but after a thirty-seven-day pause had elicited nothing, he resumed the attacks. Only a few officials raised any questions. Bobby Kennedy, Jack's younger brother and a senator from New York, criticized Johnson for restarting the bombing, fueling an already bitter rivalry. Senator J. William Fulbright, chair of the Foreign Relations Committee, held hearings that found no rationale for the war and numerous strategic and tactical obstacles that would prevent a U.S. victory. The hearings led some officials and reporters to question U.S. policy, but they had little impact on broader public opinion.

In the cities of South Viet Nam, the Buddhists rose up again. They criticized the U.S.-backed regime and staged widespread street protests. The current head of state, a fighter pilot named Nguyen Cao Ky, used the military to crush these protests. That sparked a new wave of public suicides by fire. Watching this on TV, I wondered if other viewers were asking themselves why the people we were trying to protect in South Viet Nam were in revolt against the government we had installed to protect them, which was exactly what the Buddhists were trying to communicate.

In my view, the United States was guilty of war crimes in Viet Nam. We were bombing civilians, propping up a dictatorship that tortured its citizens, forcing peasants from their villages to prevent them from supporting the guerrillas, and burning people alive with napalm. In March, the military admitted spraying highly poisonous herbicides over Vietnamese farmland and forests to reduce NLF food supplies and deprive them of the cover afforded by the thick jungles. No thought had been given to the impact these potent toxic substances would have on civilians, especially children, nor to the horrifying genetic abnormalities that future generations would suffer. Agent Orange ultimately caused untold thousands of Vietnamese civilians, and thousands of American soldiers, to suffer a range of autoimmune diseases.

These tactics provoked opposition. A few academic and humanitarian organizations condemned the use of herbicides even though they stopped short of a call for U.S. withdrawal. In late March, over fifty thousand antiwar protesters did advocate immediate withdrawal at a march in New York City. It was twice the number protesting the previous fall. I attended a rally the same day in Chicago with fewer people, but small events were also staged in many cities new to such protests. The marchers were no longer just students but a somewhat broader cross-section of society. But we remained a tiny minority. Most Americans stubbornly and unthinkingly refused to believe their government would wage an unjust war. With such anemic opposition, a vote to repeal the Gulf of Tonkin Resolution in the U.S. Senate failed 92–5.

In the spring a new controversy engulfed the UC campus. With so many Americans dying in Viet Nam, the Selective Service System could not maintain the increased monthly draft quota. It announced an end to automatic student deferments and said it would draft students directly out of college based on academic performance. Colleges were asked to submit the class rank of every male student. The thresholds differed for each year in college, but if males ranked below a certain cutoff, their deferments were canceled. Many would become casualties in Viet Nam.

The UC chapter of Students for a Democratic Society argued that poor grades could be a death sentence, and if professors thought low grades might lead to forced military service, they could not grade fairly. SDS called on the university to refuse to deliver the rankings. To avoid accusations that the students merely wanted to protect themselves, they also called on the draft boards to end all student deferments. They believed that if more middle-class kids were drafted, instead of the burden falling disproportionately on the working class, the government would come under greater pressure to end the war. The demand that UC refuse a request to help in the war effort was no longer protest; it was a call for active resistance.

The issue was hotly debated on campus, but well-publicized meetings with UC officials had gained nothing. On Wednesday, May 11, at a pre-appointed time, two hundred students filtered into the campus Administration Building. They sat down in the offices and hallways and refused to move. Only twenty or so were members of SDS, but because of the controversy they had generated, many other students joined them. I heard about the sit-in that afternoon and walked from the Sleep Lab to the Ad Building to have a look.

It was a madhouse. Students who had commandeered typewriters and mimeograph machines cranked out leaflets, while others collected money to purchase supplies. At 5:00 p.m., everyone was ordered to leave. Most refused, fully aware that the police might be on their way. I assumed that the biggest risk I faced was a trespassing arrest, so I stayed. I saw friends arrive, check out the scene, and make the same decision.

By 7:00 p.m., more students appeared carrying food, drinks, and sleeping bags. Everyone gathered in a large lobby on the first floor to debate how long we would hold the building and what we would do when the police came. It quickly degenerated into a shouting match. We were united in opposing university complicity with the draft, but we were at loggerheads about how to proceed. A forceful young woman asked to speak. Jackie Goldberg, a graduate student in education, had been one of the top five leaders of the Free Speech Movement (FSM) at Berkeley two years before. She was tall, solidly built, and self-possessed. Of all of us in the building, she was the only one with any relevant experience.

Jackie pointed out that people in FSM had no idea their actions would impact students across the country. She advised we might be in a similar position. Our seizure of the Ad Building could spark other militant actions against the draft. As a result, we had a responsibility to function efficiently. We had to issue a press statement and be ready to counter statements made by the university and the Selective Service System. We had to decide under what circumstances we would leave the building, how long we would stay if our demands were not met, and what we would do when university employees returned to work in the morning.

Jackie explained that at mass meetings at Berkeley a single chairperson directed debates until a consensus was reached. All present had to respect the views of others and listen patiently until they finished speaking. If anyone tried to monopolize the debate, a consensus of the larger group could limit his or her time. However, as Jackie made clear, we were in no rush. We would be there all night, or we would be in jail. Watching her, I marveled at how effective leadership can rescue a bad situation and turn it toward success. Years later, Jackie became the first open lesbian elected to both the Los Angeles Board of Education and the City Council. Later, she served as the voice of progressive politics in California during three terms in the legislature.

We asked Jackie to chair the meeting, and she quickly summarized the questions at hand. If the cops came, we agreed we would all go limp and passively resist arrest. If they did not, how would we handle the employees in the morning? Sit-ins had occurred on many campuses after FSM, but there had never been a building seizure in which entry was denied to those not participating, including employees. Some argued that we had to escalate beyond a simple sit-in to get the national press coverage that could inspire more actions against the draft. After a lengthy and surprisingly mature discussion, given the earlier chaos, we decided to seize the building. Volunteers secured the doors and screened everyone entering and leaving.

I was impressed with the way the decision had been made. Most of the people in the building were college students. I was a little older and concerned that I had more to lose. As a graduate student, I had a draft deferment. As long as deferments were being given, I wanted to keep mine, but I agreed with SDS that all student deferments should be abolished. Poor and working-class kids were fighting the war, while the middle-class parents of students with deferments cheered the war effort as a patriotic duty. If the children of these hypocrites were forced to fight, more would oppose the war. That meant more to me than my own draft status.

I did not fear arrest. Nor did I think it was constitutional for the authorities to take away my draft deferment. But I could not afford to jeopardize my research, my job, or my status at UC. I didn't believe the university would be so vindictive as to take all that away from me, and if that did become a possibility, I assumed there would be some advance warning. The balance between caution and risk seemed favorable, so I decided to stay and do what I could. I called Professor Rechtschaffen and told him. He tried to talk me out of it, but I persisted, and he had the decency to wish me luck.

By midnight, the cops had failed to materialize. About four hundred students were in the building. Jackie chaired the mass meeting until 3:00 a.m., calmly and patiently imposing discipline and periodically summarizing how the discussion had progressed, the decisions that remained to be made, and the alternative solutions available. Her demeanor set the tone for all of us. Apart from a few ideologues pushing narrow agendas, we listened to each other, and the more we listened, the more we came to appreciate valid points on all sides of the arguments. It was participatory democracy in action, an ideal that had earlier been the abstract rallying cry of SDS but which suddenly seemed more concrete and perhaps even attainable.

The next morning, UC officials surprised us. Mindful of the disastrous events at Berkeley, they stated that a massive police presence was inappropriate on campus and that the conflict would have to be resolved within the academic community. Knowing the seizure would continue, the press descended on the campus. Our designated spokespeople stood in front of the cameras for the first time, while others, me included, wrote press statements explaining our actions. We called ourselves Students Against the Rank.

With Charlotte and a few other graduate student friends, I approached Jeff Blum, a first-year college student who was one of the SDS leaders, and explained that just as graduate students at Berkeley had formed the Graduate Student Coordinating Committee to back up FSM, we should do the same. It would underscore the fact that we were not just irresponsible college kids trying to escape the draft. Jeff, who decades later would head USAction, a massive national consumer group, agreed.

Peter Nagourney and I co-chaired the new committee. Along with Charlotte and Jackie, we recruited others. We organized food purchases, trash pickups, sleeping bags, fund-raising, and security. We also put together a medical unit. Meanwhile, in the first-floor lobby, mass meetings remained in session as we tested our commitment to participatory democracy. That afternoon, UC officials agreed to negotiate. Peter and I were asked to represent the students. We met with Edward Levi, the former law school dean and current UC provost, and George Beadle, the UC president. Beadle said little; Levi did the talking.

Both men deserved respect. Beadle had won the Nobel Prize in Physiology or Medicine eight years before. Levi was one of the foremost legal scholars in the nation. I politely explained our demands. Levi wanted to debate their merits, so we listened patiently to his views. He argued that we were asking UC to break the law. I responded that no law forced the university to send student rankings to the draft board; it was merely a request that could be turned down, and if a prestigious campus like ours turned them down, other universities would follow. Levi admitted I was correct, but claimed that the federal government could punish the university by withholding research grants. I agreed, arguing that was precisely what was wrong with the current relationship between government and the universities. How can academic independence be maintained when private universities become financially dependent on government grants?

We kept it polite, but we reached an impasse. Levi insisted we leave the building before our demands could be considered. Our respect for people who supported the war had its limits. We told him that no one was leaving until the university changed its policy. He bristled. His tactics changed as he tried to assert his authority and intimidate us. I had to show him we were negotiating as equals and that we had some leverage. UC's payroll checks, due out the next day, were issued from the Ad Building. I pointed out that if thousands of employees were not paid on Friday, he would have more than a few hundred protesting students on his hands. To drive home our point, Peter and I got up and walked out. At the door, I turned and said, if you change your minds, call us; we're working out of President Beadle's office.

Thursday evening we saw our actions covered on local and national news programs. We were portrayed in the context of spreading student resistance to the war. Later, Richard Flacks, a young sociology professor who had been a founder of SDS six years before, joined us, the first faculty member to do so. Charlotte was his student, so I already knew him. Flacks delivered a moving speech, saying that whether we had intended it or not, the media would cast us as national antidraft spokespeople and that students across the country would look to us for leadership. Thanks to him, other young faculty members appeared in the building, too.

It was my first experience in the middle of a national news story, and I soon saw the power that came with the coverage. Levi called early the next morning. He wanted to resume negotiations. Somewhat later, students from the conservative business school staged a raid and tried to force their way into the Ad Building. We barred the doors, and after a lengthy pushing match they backed off. When Peter and I joined Levi, he was more conciliatory. He didn't like the national press, and he wanted the seizure to end.

Peter and I were bluffing about the paychecks. The previous night, after we had made the threat, radical students argued that it was unfair to deprive UC's employees of their paychecks. These students were militant about the draft and the war, but their politics led them to identify with the poorest among the workers, the janitors, maintenance men, secretaries, waitresses, and clerks whose work enabled the campus to function. With their opposition, I was not sure we could continue the seizure into the weekend.

Levi offered to schedule a two-day conference open to all UC students, faculty, and employees. Evidence could be presented by both sides, after which he would put the question of further cooperation with the draft before the Faculty Senate and be bound by its decision. We insisted he make this commitment public before we left the building, and he agreed. I thought it was the best deal we could get. We called a mass meeting in the Ad Building to decide what to do. Some students, flush with their newfound power, wanted to stay until our demands were met. Others argued that it was unclear what would happen if we stayed, and that to our credit we had both forced the university to reevaluate its relationship to the draft and forced the issue of the draft onto the national stage. Not bad for three days' work. A large majority accepted the terms. We cleaned up the premises and all walked out together.

On Monday, hundreds of students at the University of Wisconsin occupied their administration building and issued demands similar to ours. The same day a large demonstration at City University of New York also demanded an end to university complicity with the draft. But it was late May. Final exams limited students' options everywhere, so the antidraft crusade temporarily fizzled. In September, it would roar back with a vengeance.

For the first time, I had played a leadership role in a major political event, and I was delighted with the experience. The tactical maneuvering, the camaraderie, our connection to national issues and to others across the country working for the same goals, were electrifying. I had done something meaningful against the war, and, I confess, I had enjoyed having an army of activists at my back. In the past, I had shunned leadership roles. It was time for that to change.

CHAPTER 7

I SPENT THE SUMMER OF 1966 WATCHING OTHER PEOPLE SLEEP. DESPITE MY COMMIT-
ment to antiwar work, I was determined to let nothing stand in the way of
completing my Ph.D. and building a career as a research scientist. The
previous spring I had discussed dissertation research projects with Al
Rechtschaffen. I wanted to do research that was at the cutting edge. John
Lilly's work had revealed higher intelligence and advanced communication in dolphins, but no one had yet studied their sleep patterns. I contacted him and suggested a collaboration, but he was unresponsive.

Rechtschaffen favored a different topic. While there was anecdotal
knowledge about human sleep patterns, no systematic data had been collected on the differences between light and deep sleepers, or how factors
in their physiology or psychology correlated with each condition. Such
knowledge could generate clues about improving sleep, and might also
reveal more about its origin and function. I accepted Al's advice, and
together we laid out a plan. I would test a large number of people in the
lab, select sixteen very light sleepers and sixteen very deep sleepers,
administer a battery of psychological and physiological tests to each, and
analyze the differences between the two groups. First, I read what was
available in the scientific literature. Then, to find sixteen very light sleepers and sixteen very deep sleepers, I developed criteria based on auditory
awakening thresholds, the precise decibel level of a standard tone needed
to awaken the subject. I tested dozens of volunteers. They slept in the lab

overnight, and I periodically awakened them with my gradually increasing tones. Selecting people at both ends of the normal distribution, I had found the thirty-two subjects I needed by early September.

Martin Luther King Jr. briefly interrupted this work. He had gained great stature after winning the Nobel Peace Prize two years before. Over the summer, he brought the civil rights movement north to address the economic exploitation of blacks. Chicago was his first target, and to work in the city, he formed an alliance with Al Raby and other veterans of Chicago Area Friends of SNCC. Their objective was to end segregated housing, because, despite Chicago's liberal veneer, sociologists viewed it as the most segregated city in America. About 40 percent of the city was black and boxed into two huge ghettos on the South Side and the West Side.

King launched the open housing campaign in July using tactics that had worked in the South. He scheduled a march August 5 into Marquette Park, an all-white working-class area. I knew it to be a racist enclave on the Southwest Side. Since I thought violence was likely, I didn't think many blacks would participate. That put added responsibility on white supporters like me. I had stood with the civil rights movement in the South, so I was damn well going to stand with them in my own backyard.

When I got to the staging area on the edge of the park with Charlotte and two friends, I saw thousands of people. Most were angry counterdemonstrators kept apart from the few marchers by hundreds of police. We joined the marchers. There were only five hundred of us, mostly black but with a number of white priests and nuns and supporters like us. The racists were a howling mob. They shouted obscenities, waved Confederate flags, and flaunted Nazi symbols. The police barely held them back. Rocks occasionally came flying toward us, after which a few cops would wade into the crowd in a futile attempt to arrest the throwers. The racists, believing their homes and way of life under attack, had come prepared to fight.

I was nervous. It was a situation that could get out of control very quickly. Suddenly it did. Groups of young toughs ran toward a corner of the park. Counterdemonstrators had six policemen surrounded, and more were running to join the attack. Soon the six cops were inside a mob of a hundred waving their fists and throwing rocks. The mob was so threatening that when other cops came on the run to rescue the first six, they actually fired their revolvers in the air to disperse the rioters. I had never seen that, nor had I ever experienced such chaos.

A three-car caravan came through the police lines. It pulled up in front of us. Dr. King got out as bodyguards rushed to surround him. The racists surged forward, and the police pushed them back. King began the march down the center of an adjacent street, and we fell in behind him. The police accompanied us and provided protection from people standing three deep on both sidewalks. Rocks flew past me. One struck a man directly in front of King. The cops pushed the crowd back, but another rock hit King on the side of his head. I saw him drop to his knees, stunned and in pain. His head was bleeding, but he got to his feet and marched on.

King's courage and defiance energized us all. We had three miles to go. The police took up positions in front of us, on either side, and in the rear. It was a riot in motion. They carried their clubs at the ready and repeatedly brought them down on the heads of white racists. I nervously searched for new threats as we marched. For the next two hours, I dodged the rocks and bottles that rained down on us, and tried to keep an eye out for my friends, as they were doing for me. Occasionally, a cherry bomb exploded overhead.

Unable to get at us, the rioters turned on parked cars, local stores, and passing buses. They threw rocks and bottles and broke windows. When the cops tried to club the rioters into submission, it provoked more violence. Young men were responsible for the worst of it, but many of the obscene shouts and curses came from gray-haired ladies and men in business suits. That surprised me, even though it had often occurred in the South. In fact, all that separated this scene from one in Mississippi or Alabama was that the cops were on our side. Good thing the racists had gone after them first.

Most of the counterdemonstrators attacking us were ethnic Catholics—Polish, Irish, some Italian. Nevertheless, I saw middle-aged and older people shouting venomous insults at the few white priests and nuns who marched with us. Their racism was so much a part of their psyches that it drove them to attack people to whom they might otherwise be

confessing their sins or seeking solace in tragedy—a vivid sign of the prejudice still to be overcome.

During the two-hour ordeal, several marchers were injured, but were
it not for the police, I am certain there would have been fatalities. As it
happened, the racists suffered more injuries at the hands of the police
than they were able to inflict on us. Nevertheless, the violence and the
depth of the hatred shocked everyone. Later, looking back on that day, Dr.
King said, "I've been in many demonstrations all across the South, but I
can say that I had never seen, even in Mississippi, mobs as hostile and as
hate-filled as in Chicago."

Two weeks later, the Nazi Party and the Ku Klux Klan held a rally of
their own in Marquette Park. The four of us who had marched with King
decided to go. We had been so astounded by the hatred we had witnessed
we wanted to have another look. Since we were all white, we thought we
could blend in and go unnoticed. We arrived at the park and saw a
crowded spectacle of racism and paranoia, with rows of Nazi flags and
men dressed in the white robes of the KKK. We stood to the side and listened to the speakers.

But we were not as inconspicuous as we thought. Four hostile young
guys approached us. One asked what four Jews were doing at a Nazi rally.
I looked around nervously. I knew that we could not defend ourselves and
that any confrontation might trigger a riot in which we could be severely
beaten. Frightened, I encouraged the others to turn and calmly walk back
to our car. As we did, I knew we might be attacked from behind, but I was
afraid to turn around and further provoke the four racists. It was a long
walk. They shouted anti-Semitic insults but otherwise stayed put. We
were lucky to get out in one piece.

The difficulty King had in addressing black economic exploitation in
Chicago was repeated wherever such protests occurred. As a result, some
civil rights leaders questioned nonviolence. Stokely Carmichael, the new
leader of SNCC, was advancing "black power" and more militant forms
of advocacy. He would soon ask all whites to leave SNCC. In October,
Huey Newton and Bobby Seale would form the Black Panther Party in
Oakland. Initially, they organized neighborhood self-defense units to stop
police brutality, but later would advocate the transformation of capitalist

society. Nonviolence had been effective in winning political rights in the South. Many were skeptical it could advance economic rights elsewhere.

In September, the 1966–67 academic year began. I watched as widespread opposition to the draft evolved into outright resistance. Provoked by our sit-in the previous spring and similar events on other campuses, the new antidraft crusade gained strength as draft calls increased and students realized that many draftees would be killed. Antiwar students were reluctant to face jail or exile, but the possibility of dying helped some find the courage to resist. These students were patriots. They rejected the jingoistic cry "My country, right or wrong" and sought a deeper patriotism, one that brought the country back to the ideals of the founders. Who wanted to die for jingoism?

Every American male was required to register with a local draft board on his eighteenth birthday and carry a draft card at all times. The military preferred young recruits, eighteen or nineteen, because it was easier to break them psychologically. Many still believed they were immortal, which helped convince them to face enemy fire. A few brave souls defied the draft laws and burned their draft cards, a federal felony. They usually did so at demonstrations and were cheered by everyone present. Hundreds of protesters would surround these young men to protect them from arrest, chanting the now-common "Hell no, we won't go!"

I could not participate in most of this, because I spent the fall and winter months administering hundreds of psychological and physiological tests to each of the thirty-two light and deep sleepers I had identified. I was looking for patterns of correlation. But despite not joining in, I remained fully aware of the antiwar activity happening around me.

My attitude about Viet Nam had changed. The government continued to fight the war despite increasing public criticism, mounting U.S. casualties, battlefield failures, and rampant corruption in South Viet Nam. Two years had passed since the Gulf of Tonkin, and well over a year since the big troop buildup and the bombing of North Viet Nam. Yet Washington fought on, and at great cost. Worse, they were expanding the war. This was not a mistake. It was deliberate. With others, I reluctantly concluded that the war had been not a blunder but a necessary expression of American policy. That meant we could never convince Johnson the war was wrong. Strategically, we were left with no choice but to refuse to cooperate and to disrupt his plans wherever possible. Understanding that pushed us further out of the mainstream and left me feeling as alienated from society as I had felt during the beatnik years.

Young people who opposed the war shared a certain kinship, a community of opposition. But two tendencies began to split us apart. Some, like me, haunted by the stereotype of the good German who fails to protest government atrocities, were determined to stop the war. Others thought such effort hopeless. Their rejection of traditional society was more profound, and they talked of building a counterculture. In late 1966, activists and hippies still cross-pollinated each other: we all dressed unconventionally and wore our hair long; they came to our protests, and we went to their concerts. Hippie men did not yet wear ponytails and beads, but a few had gone that far, and an alienated multitude was moving in their direction. We were siblings just beginning to drift apart.

In the fall of 1966, antiwar demonstrations in several cities failed. In New York, only fifteen thousand marched. Yet the war was debated with increasing bitterness. Protesters were called traitors and, in return, bitterly heckled government leaders who supported the war. Nor was the antagonism confined to protesters. Johnson could not attend church services for fear of antiwar sermons, of which there were many. Defense Secretary McNamara was publicly ridiculed on the ski slopes in Colorado. He was also subjected to withering criticism from within his own family. Whenever either man spoke in public, he was picketed and shouted down.

By the end of the year, after only a year and a half of fully engaged ground combat, five thousand Americans had been killed and thirty thousand wounded. The United States had close to 400,000 troops in Viet Nam. They fought an elusive insurgency, not an organized army. Snipers, small-arms fire, handmade bombs, mines, and booby traps caused fully half the American casualties. It was a guerrilla war, and it put the Pentagon on unfamiliar terrain. Because the enemy did not wear uniforms and were indistinguishable from civilians, U.S. soldiers routinely killed innocent bystanders. The soldiers, afraid that death could come from any quarter, shot first and asked questions afterward. The innocent deaths inflamed and further embittered the Vietnamese.

Instead of "winning hearts and minds," the professed U.S. strategy, American actions pushed Vietnamese civilians into the enemy camp. Our soldiers, inured to casual death and murder, committed more acts of violence. Captured guerrillas were tortured either for revenge or for intelligence. Prisoners were commonly executed in front of others to induce them to reveal information. Some captured NLF guerrillas were taken up in helicopters, two by two. One was thrown out the door at altitude to terrify the other into revealing military intelligence. These acts brutalized everyone exposed to them.

In Saigon, the South Vietnamese government, run by officers from the puppet army, was so riddled with corruption, the *New York Times* reported in November, that 40 percent of U.S. economic aid to the country had been stolen or had ended up on the black market. The city's ancient culture was overrun by a massive number of Americans who created a distasteful background of strip joints and prostitutes that outraged the tradition-bound Vietnamese.

These facts convinced some prominent spokesmen to turn against the war. Harrison Salisbury, a senior editor at the *New York Times* and a respected journalist neither pro- nor antiwar, obtained permission to visit Hanoi, the capital of North Viet Nam. Over Christmas, he wrote that American bombs had indeed inflicted massive civilian casualties, and that talk of "surgical bombing strikes" was pure mythology. Senator J. William Fulbright, powerful chairman of the Foreign Relations Committee, continued to criticize the war effort and was no longer on speaking terms with Johnson. Senator Bobby Kennedy also continued his criticism.

Draft resistance spread. Young men in small but increasing numbers gave up their citizenship and went abroad. Others refused induction and were jailed. Antiwar lawyers offered draft-counseling services to young men or free legal representation if they were resisters. Church groups helped fugitives get to Canada in a modern version of the Underground Railroad that had spirited escaped slaves north before the Civil War. The culture of resistance became more commonplace. Young men were encouraged to defy the draft by religious leaders, popular songs, and celebrities like Muhammad Ali, who had defied it himself. Campus posters trumpeted the tongue-in-cheek line "Girls say yes to boys who say no." And, a year after our seizure of the UC Ad Building, the Selective Service System stopped using class rank to draft students.

But draft resistance had a polarizing effect on society. During World War II, military service had been universal. To older veterans, young resisters were cowardly, unpatriotic, and unappreciative of the sacrifices made to protect their freedoms. Many imagined the Vietnamese communists simplistically as a threat to our security. Burdened by that misunderstanding, they could not get past the question "I served, so why shouldn't you?" In their fury, they saw us as traitors undermining the country from within. We reacted with our own anger, and the chasm between us grew wider. The so-called culture wars that would divide our nation in the decades ahead, and that still divide us today, have deep roots in this draft resistance.

During the early months of 1967, I became even more disillusioned. Having already concluded that the war was not a mistake but a necessary aspect of U.S. foreign policy, I looked more closely at our other policies. The more I read, the more it seemed that the American government was intentionally organized to protect the prerogatives of those already privileged. If such protections required policy detours into areas of injustice and war, the government made ready accommodation. In fact, our government no longer represented the majority of our people, if it ever had, but operated instead on behalf of an elite. It would never be possible to stop the war by convincing such a government that it was morally wrong.

Nor would average Americans rise up to oppose the war on the basis of morality, as so many had in support of civil rights. Sadly, most Americans still had racist attitudes and blind faith in the correctness of U.S. policy. The people of Viet Nam, for whom antiwar activists sought sympathy, were Asian, half a world away, and communists to boot. But war was not an issue to be decided by majority rule, especially a war based on lies about its origin and lies about how it was being conducted. The U.S. Constitution places many issues beyond the reach of majority rule: discrimination, abridging free speech, limiting religious practices, and so forth. I was sure that protesting such a war belonged on that list. But with a majority in support of the war, I grudgingly understood we would have to stop it through disruption, not persuasion, and that we had to be ready for the inevitable anger that would result.

The same conclusions gained currency across the antiwar movement and the wider student population. Conventional social mores became associated with the war, so we migrated with our hippie cousins to an increasingly vibrant counterculture. The new music filled our heads. We rejected alcohol for marijuana, seeing it as a healthier and safer choice. Because it was illegal, it made outlaws of us all, and that outlaw status further undermined our respect for other laws. We flaunted sexual morality by open sexual relations and cohabitation, virtually unknown before. For us, mainstream culture had outlived its usefulness, so we widened our agenda to not only stop the war but also fundamentally reorganize government and society. We were not lacking in audacity.

The developing counterculture got a boost in January. I heard reports from friends in San Francisco about the "human be-in" held in the city's Golden Gate Park. Some twenty-five thousand came that Saturday afternoon, hippies from San Francisco and activists from Berkeley. It was a free festival. Food was given away, marijuana was openly smoked, and, some said, acts of love were freely performed. The new rock bands played: the Grateful Dead, Jefferson Airplane, and others that had gained popularity at Bill Graham's Fillmore Auditorium. Allen Ginsberg, the Beat poet, chanted mantras as part of his transformation into a hippie guru. There were speakers, too, including Tim Leary, the LSD advocate. The drug had just been banned under California law, and Leary, in endorsing its continued use, advised the crowd to "turn on, tune in, drop out." The human be-in was only a single San Francisco event, but Leary's words became hippie dogma, and in future years millions followed his advice.

Winter turned into spring, always a great relief in Chicago. I had finished the experimental phase of my doctoral research and had analyzed most of the mountain of data I had collected. At first, I was lost in a sea of computer printouts, but I quickly recovered and began to write up my findings. I was determined to complete my dissertation in four years despite the average Ph.D. at the University of Chicago taking seven.

I had discovered a constellation of psychological and physiological characteristics correlated with light and deep sleep, and I was developing a theoretical construct about brain function to explain them. Writing the two-hundred-page dissertation, and teasing out the theoretical implications of my findings, took long hours and total concentration. The research was solid, so I was confident the dissertation would be approved. That meant I would get my Ph.D. in a matter of months and before the fall term, so as I wrote, I also looked for a job. I hated watching the unfolding political events from the outside, but I had no choice.

To do scientific research and get the grants needed to fund it, I looked for an appointment as an assistant professor of psychology. I was tired of the Midwest, where seeing an ocean or a mountain required an eight-hundred-mile drive. I wanted a place on the East or West Coast, but knew my choices would be limited. Universities looking for new professors did their recruiting in the spring. Typically, the prospect was invited to visit for two days, present research to a faculty seminar, and sit for interviews by its members.

I made three such trips, to Washington University in St. Louis, Dalhousie University in Halifax, and Brooklyn College, a part of the City University of New York. Each school wanted a sleep lab, and each offered me an assistant professorship and the chance to build one. At Brooklyn College, a young professor named Bart Meyers was doing research in psychopharmacology and was open to a joint project on brain chemistry during sleep. That was the direction I wanted to move in, too. But Bart made an additional offer.

He was the faculty adviser to the campus SDS chapter and a committed antiwar activist. When he attended the University of Michigan for graduate work, he had befriended Dick Flacks, the faculty member who first joined us during the seizure of the UC Ad Building. Bart was plainspoken, unassuming, and iconoclastic. Only a few years my senior, he fit comfortably into the emerging counterculture and was cut from the same activist mold as Flacks, a mold I wanted to fit into as well. Bart offered to collaborate on politics as well as brain chemistry. With Rechtschaffen's blessing, I chose Brooklyn College.

In the past I had not let politics interfere with my pursuit of a scientific career. This time I did. Had career been my only consideration, I would have chosen Washington University, a more prestigious school with a deeper commitment to research. My dedication to science was still strong, but I was seeking more than just the best research opportunity. I was determined to oppose the war and work for political change. Teaching at Brooklyn College and living in the political epicenter of New York City would give me the best chance to do that, so for the first time I compromised my scientific ambitions in the interests of politics. I wanted to escape the Midwest, so personal factors played a role, too.

On April 15, 1967, the antiwar movement achieved a significant milestone. Charlotte and I went to New York to attend what became the biggest demonstration in U.S. history. When we got to the rallying point in Central Park, we could hardly believe our eyes. It was a vast throng, larger than any we had ever seen. Different groups prepared to march behind colorful banners advertising who they were and why they opposed the war. People distributed free food and drink, marshals formed up the march, and legal volunteers passed out flyers about what to do if arrested. It was remarkably well organized! And best of all, people of all ages and races were participating. Parents had brought children, and some young people had brought grandparents.

That afternoon we numbered over 400,000, far more than had attended the March on Washington in 1963. Among us was the star of that event, Dr. Martin Luther King Jr. Charlotte and I, jubilant over the turnout, marched with the crowd from Central Park to the United Nations building. We filled the wide avenues from sidewalk to sidewalk and were actually cheered by bystanders. The line of march stretched the entire distance from the park to the UN. The crowd, the colorful banners, and the goodwill among the marchers allowed us to briefly feel like the majority we knew we were not.

At the UN building, many prominent people spoke, most importantly King. Eleven days before, at the Riverside Church in New York, he had finally said what many of us had been waiting to hear. At the UN, he reiterated his remarks. The war, he argued, would jeopardize the critically important social reforms and antipoverty programs advanced by President Johnson. Further, in the absence of a total mobilization of society, the burden of fighting the war had fallen disproportionately on minority blacks and Latinos, and the children of the white working class. Middle-class kids either escaped the draft by attending college or got more of the noncombatant assignments in Viet Nam as a consequence of their education. Black soldiers in particular suffered the highest fatality rates and generally drew the most dangerous assignments. King concluded by saying, "The pursuit of this widened war has narrowed the promised dimensions of the domestic welfare programs, making the poor white and the Negro bear the heaviest burdens both at the front and at home."

I knew that King's overt opposition to the war would be a turning point, and that our best strategy was to bring the antiwar movement together with the expanding fight for black equality. That approach would have the greatest impact if King led the way. He seemed ready to do so. The size of the demonstration, the degree to which it included a cross section of America, and the hand of partnership King had extended transformed the antiwar movement that day from a campus phenomenon at the fringe of society into a genuine political force.

In early May, the movement got an additional boost from Bertrand Russell, the world-renowned British philosopher, who sponsored an independent war crimes tribunal in Stockholm. The tribunal did not limit itself to isolated acts committed by individual soldiers, but also looked at military tactics designed to terrorize the Vietnamese population and undermine their will to fight. The United States denied its bombing purposely targeted villages, schools, hospitals, and other nonmilitary facilities, but testimony in Stockholm made it clear that such attacks, which had also been verified by Salisbury in the *New York Times*, were too widespread to be accidents.

In politics, as in physics, every action produces a reaction. On May 13, a large pro-war demonstration was held in New York. It attracted seventy thousand, and, sadly, many came from labor unions, especially the construction trades. That demonstration, widely covered in the press, locked in the perception, and soon the reality, that antiwar "radicals" and union "hard hats" were on opposite sides of the war. The otherwise progressive trade union movement had long before been convinced that the Cold War was the controlling dynamic of U.S. foreign policy. If the Russians and the Chinese were on one side, we had to be on the other. There was dissension within the unions, and some did work against the war, but the antiwar movement failed to reach out and prevent this disagreement from hardening into an enduring break.

By early June, I had finished writing my dissertation and had begun to meticulously review it with Rechtschaffen. He was an exacting mentor, so I had to painstakingly substantiate every claim I made about my methods and findings. Al had taught me everything I knew about the scientific method, so in addition to verifying the quality of my work, he was putting the finishing touches on my training. The following year I would have to not only function on my own as a scientist but also help train others. My four-year association with Al Rechtschaffen had been the most fruitful in my life and had created a deep bond between us.

I was required to defend the dissertation before a faculty committee looking for holes in my methods or reasoning and judging if the overall work met the high standards of the university. Normally, such a rigorous defense might have been a cause for anxiety, but because my research had already met Rechtschaffen's exacting standards, I knew it was solid and would be approved. In mid-July, it was.

That left me time for a vacation before moving to Brooklyn in the fall. I flew to San Francisco to visit Scott. For three years, since my last visit, when we met the Merry Pranksters, he had been in law school and driving a cab to earn money. Two months before his graduation, he called to tell me he had decided to quit. He didn't want to be a lawyer and saw no point in finishing. I told him he was being unduly influenced by the antimaterialist hippie subculture all around him, and that it was silly not to graduate. I failed to change his mind, so in July I went to see him and have a look at the hippies who had taken over the Haight-Ashbury neighborhood in San Francisco.

It was the summer of 1967, and it came to be called the Summer of Love. When I first saw it on the streets of the Haight, as the neighborhood was called, it felt as if I had passed into another world. Scott and I walked down sidewalks teeming with young people in bizarre and colorful costumes. The men had long hair or ponytails and wore tie-dyed shirts and beaded necklaces and bracelets. The women had painted faces, feathers, and equally colorful costumes. For the first time in the United States, we saw street musicians and performers on all the commercial streets. People

we didn't know talked to us, offered us food, and casually passed marijuana joints. They were all young and happy, and their expressive socia-
bility was infectious.

The Haight was adjacent to the Panhandle portion of Golden Gate
Park. There, we passed clusters of people playing musical instruments,
throwing Frisbees, sunbathing, fully clothed or otherwise, and cooking
food we were welcome to share. The previous January, at the human be-
in, the rock band the Mamas & the Papas had sung a song with the lyrics:
"If you're going to San Francisco, be sure to wear some flowers in your
hair . . . If you come to San Francisco, summertime will be a love-in
there." A record of the song, released in May, rose to the top of the charts
and provoked one of the greatest mass migrations of young people in history. Hundreds of thousands came to the Haight, straining the city's infra-
structure. Many did put flowers in their hair, and the press called them
"flower children." The label stuck.

Hippie rejection of materialistic culture had exploded over the previous
six months. Fueled by the more open sexuality that followed the discovery
of oral contraception, and by widespread revulsion at the violence in Viet
Nam, the hippies lived by and made famous the ubiquitous 1960s slogan
"Make love, not war." They embraced altered states of consciousness, regularly using marijuana and hallucinogens: LSD, psilocybin (found in "magic
mushrooms"), and mescaline (found in peyote buds). Opiates and cocaine
were not part of the scene. The new rock bands identified with the hippies
and promoted the notion of a dropout culture. Not believing they could
alter the juggernaut of American capitalism through politics, the hippies
tried culture instead, starting with Leary's slogan, "Turn on, tune in, drop
out." And drop out they did, from schools, from jobs, from families. Their
alternative counterculture rejected money and conventional lifestyles, pro-
moting instead shared property and life in the moment. Ram Dass said it
best with the title of his popular book, *Be Here Now.*

The political people in the antiwar movement agreed with much of
this thinking, but had real differences with the hippies. We thought that
disciplined organizational action was necessary to change society. The
hippies thought organizations were pointless and that society would only
change if individuals first changed themselves. We thought leadership

and structure were necessary. They wanted every act to be spontaneous, every person to "do his own thing." While we all accepted a subsistence lifestyle without expensive clothes, cars, or other luxuries, they were about enjoyment, friendship, shared experience, and whatever transcendence could be achieved through mind-altering drugs, music, and sex.

The week I spent with Scott in the Haight amazed me. "Free" was the hippie ideology, because "free" was the way they wanted to undermine capitalism. Young doctors established free health clinics. Young lawyers dispensed free legal advice and draft counseling. Free food was available wherever we went. There was even a "free store" where anyone could walk in and pick up clothing or furniture. People raised money elsewhere and collected surplus merchandise to make it all work. However naive it seems in retrospect, it was in fact a new culture under construction, a culture of sharing and sensitivity and nonviolence.

I was tempted by it, but I was no hippie. Scott had dropped out. I had mastered the establishment game and become successful. We were on different paths. In a month I could put a "Dr." before my name and claim my pedigree from one of the nation's leading universities. A month later, I would even be called "Professor." No way I was going to trade all of that for a life of sex, drugs, and rock and roll. Still, the temptation was there. What was wrong with living more spontaneously and with less emphasis on money and ambition and status?

When the flower children left San Francisco, they returned home with the new culture they had created. Remarkably, their eventual impact was enormous, both in the United States and around the world. Their ideas about spontaneity, life, and love spread like wildfire, first among middle-class kids, but in later years universally. The intergenerational conflicts that resulted widened the gap between youth and their elders. Sex, drugs, and rock and roll did not fit easily into the outdated worldview or morality of the previous generation. The hippies did spark a new culture, and in its own way it did take over the world.

However, the culture in the Haight rapidly collapsed. Within months, sensationalist reports of drug-crazed hippies and girls dancing bare breasted in the park drew hordes of gawking tourists. Commercialism seeped in to capture the tourist dollars. Hard drugs arrived with the usual human calamities. Even the hippie rock bands eventually turned commercial. They got rich and fell under the influence of managers and lawyers interested primarily in money. The Summer of Love was but a brief flicker, yet its fading echo still reverberates today.

While the hippie kids were having fun in San Francisco, urban blacks were suffering. Cries of "black power" had rung through the northern ghettos, and a new black culture had emerged based on the notion that "black is beautiful." Black pride encouraged people to grow their hair naturally into large Afros, dress in African garb, and embrace their history. Integration was devalued as blacks stood up for their own heritage. Police brutality intensified and again and again provided the flash point for rioting.

What I had seen in Watts two years before was only the beginning. The following summer, in 1966, riots in Cleveland and Omaha required National Guard intervention. In July 1967, a riot in Newark left twenty-six dead and 725 injured. Only a few days after guardsmen put it down, another erupted in Detroit. There, forty-three were killed and two thousand buildings destroyed. Even the Guard couldn't handle it. Johnson called in regular Army troops. Whether they were riots or open rebellions, this level of violence alienated the white community. So did the sudden emphasis on black power and the new black separatism. Overall sympathy for black rights dropped like a stone.

At the end of the summer, I went to New York and found a rent-controlled apartment in Brooklyn Heights, just across the bridge from Manhattan. It was a fifth-floor walk-up but only a block from the river and convenient to Brooklyn College. Looking forward to my new life, I returned to Chicago to attend commencement exercises at the university's Rockefeller Memorial Chapel. Edward Levi, who would be appointed president the following year, distributed the degrees. I stood in a line of graduate students, ready to get mine. As I approached my old opponent from the negotiations that ended the seizure of the Ad Building, Levi smiled and said, "I'm very pleased to see you up here." The negotiations the previous year had left us with a grudging respect for each other. That was fortunate because our paths would cross once more, eight years later, when President Ford appointed Levi his attorney general, and I was awaiting trial on federal criminal charges that could put me in prison for fifteen years.

CHAPTER 8

ONE DAY I WAS A STUDENT, A KID IN CHICAGO, AND THE NEXT, OR SO IT SEEMED, I WOKE up a professor and a grown-up in Brooklyn. I had a two-room apartment in the Heights, and if I leaned far enough out my front window, I could actually see the Statue of Liberty. My new colleagues in the psychology department asked me to teach two courses, personality theory and abnormal psychology. Having never taught before, I went to work writing course outlines, selecting textbooks, deciding on term papers and exams, and preparing lectures. The campus sat in a gritty urban neighborhood with a high population density. It wasn't pretty. A number of buildings faced each other across a large grassy area intersected by paved walkways.

Despite enjoying a certain prestige, Brooklyn College (BC) was a commuter school. The students lived off campus, usually at home with parents. In 1967, only a few had embraced the new culture of the sixties. Most of the rest were curious and would soon follow. I liked them, and once past my initial nervousness, I had fun teaching. But I was busy. I also started writing an article for a peer-reviewed professional journal describing my dissertation research. In the academic and scientific community, "publish or perish" is no exaggeration. To advance, one must continually produce books or articles on original research. It was too much all at once, so I decided to delay building a new lab and launching a research project.

I was not willing to delay work against the war. Antiwar outrage had reached new levels. Draft resistance was commonplace. Thousands of

Taken by one of my psychology students at Brooklyn College. *Author's collection*

angry young men had fled to Canada, while a smaller number went to jail rather than serve, their lives and families engulfed in chaos. Vets in wheelchairs were becoming a common sight. Most people only a few years younger than I was knew someone from high school who was already a casualty. There were tens of thousands of them.

In September, after presidential elections in South Viet Nam, two corrupt military officers, Nguyen Van Thieu and Nguyen Cao Ky, became president and vice president with only 35 percent of the vote. They would remain in place for the duration of the war. Meanwhile, hundreds of thousands of Vietnamese were already dead, most innocent noncombatants. Americans saw them killed every night on TV when they watched wartime news footage beamed into their living rooms. It had a tremendous impact. Some cheered the slaughter. Many, like me, were horrified and seethed with anger. I was desperate to find a way to stop it. Johnson had turned me into a "good German" in spite of myself. My impotence turned to rage, as it did for so many others.

Public opinion shifted slightly in our direction. An October poll showed that 46 percent of Americans thought the war was "a mistake."

But when asked about immediate withdrawal, a large majority opposed. Their reasons seemed to me to be contradictory and illogical: Viet Nam would be left in a mess; the dead would have died in vain.

Many of us in the antiwar movement were determined to take action, so we decided to symbolically attack the Pentagon. Peaceful demonstrators had already obtained permits for a rally at the Lincoln Memorial in Washington, D.C., on October 21. We would piggyback on their event and march illegally from the memorial to the Pentagon. Opponents of this plan argued that angry protesters outside the Pentagon would inevitably become violent and that the government would respond with greater violence. We countered that more protests in Central Park and more marches down Fifth Avenue were not enough. We had to escalate, too.

I dived into organizing for the Pentagon march with Bart Meyers, my antiwar colleague in the psychology department. Together, we gave speeches to justify the action, raised money to cover expenses, and arranged charter buses for the trip to Washington. Since Bart was the faculty adviser to the campus SDS chapter, I offered to play the same role for the W. E. B. DuBois Club, a rival student antiwar group that despite its name appealed primarily to white students. But the activist students needed little help from us, so we focused on educating the faculty about the war and recruiting more of them into opposition.

The third week in October, immediately prior to the march, protest actions took place to build momentum for the confrontation at the Pentagon. Tactics included sit-ins at recruiting facilities, anti-napalm protests at Dow Chemical plants, attempts to get city councils to pass antiwar resolutions, and numerous teach-ins. On Thursday, October 19, two days before the protest at the Pentagon, U.S. Navy recruiters appeared at BC and set up a recruiting table in the administration building. With forty students, Bart and I walked a picket line demanding they leave.

When they didn't, a dozen student protesters left the picket line, went inside, and set up a table to distribute antiwar literature across from the Navy recruiters. A college dean refused to allow it. That seemed grossly unfair, so Bart and I went inside and argued that if the Navy could distribute literature, our students should be able to as well. The dean knew how to push students around, but was not used to arguing with angry faculty. He became agitated, upset that his authority was being challenged, and he refused to budge. Students heard this angry exchange and sat down in front of the Navy recruiters, blocking access to their table. The nervous dean, new to such confrontations, threatened to call the police. Bart and I insisted the problem be handled by college disciplinary procedures. The dean disagreed—and then made the call.

The cops appeared and started to arrest the sitting students. Bart and I grabbed the dean and told him that if he didn't stop the cops, we would sit down, too. He could then explain to the press and to college officials why he had ordered faculty members arrested for exercising their free speech rights. To show him we weren't bluffing, we sat down in front so we would be the next arrested. He immediately called off the cops. The students already in custody were cordoned off. Bart argued for their release. I went to the nearest pay phone and called the city newspapers and the three TV network affiliates, realizing that the student protest had become news-

"Direct democracy, direct action": At the urging of Bart Meyers, Brooklyn College students block a police van during a 1967 protest against Navy recruitment on campus. *Author's collection*

worthy and hoping the attention of the press would inhibit the worst instincts of both the police and the dean.

When I returned, a paddy wagon had pulled onto the grass quadrangle in front of the building, ready to haul away those arrested inside. A curious crowd gathered around it. Bart was handed a bullhorn, and we both mounted a pedestal at the side of the building to face the crowd. Bart explained that students had been arrested and that they would soon be put in the paddy wagon and taken away. He said it was a dangerous situation and more police were on their way. To avoid provoking them, Bart urged the students to demonstrate their peaceful intent by sitting down on the grass where they were and staying put.

He had stolen a page from the Free Speech Movement at Berkeley, where a crowd of students had surrounded a police car with an arrested student inside and refused to move until he was released. The paddy wagon at BC was similarly hemmed in, but no one could accuse Bart of inciting students when he had simply urged calm and restraint. I thought it was brilliant. Bart passed the bullhorn to me, and I explained that more students were in the building and had sat down to support the students already arrested. The Navy recruiters were surrounded. As I spoke, additional police arrived. They pushed their way through the students on the grass, grabbed those inside the building, and started to drag them out.

They were brutal. The arrested students sat passively, but the cops hit and kicked many of them. I saw several students dragged out by their clothing, and then bounced down the concrete steps. One girl was dragged out by her hair. It was shocking. Bart and I took back the bullhorn, remounted the pedestal, and angrily condemned the police violence. BC students, new to antiwar protests, found it hard to believe that police would beat them so viciously.

Howard Moltz, a distinguished professor of psychology, learned that one of his female graduate students had been arrested. He naively approached the arresting officer asking for her release and promising to take responsibility for her. The cop slapped handcuffs on Moltz and charged him with interfering with a police officer and resisting arrest.

Students streamed toward the building from every direction. Soon, so many blocked the entrance the cops could no longer drag out arrested students. With the bullhorn, Bart and I rallied the crowd. It was no longer an antiwar action but a protest against police brutality. Reinforcements arrived, including the city's feared tactical squad, about two hundred cops in all. They parked paddy wagons behind the building. A psychology graduate student ran up to me and said they planned to use the back door to remove the arrested students. Bart explained this to the crowd and suggested that all the students on his left continue to sit around the trapped paddy wagon, and all the students on his right follow me to the rear of the building.

I led about five hundred students around to the back doors. We sat down and packed ourselves in tightly between the building and the parked paddy wagons. I was afraid of being hit, as was everyone else. The police tactics had shaken us, and we did not know what to expect. Suddenly the back doors burst open. A phalanx of cops charged out of the building, swinging their clubs to clear a path to the wagons. A girl near me was hit and started bleeding, and as I helped her, I saw nightsticks come down with full force on the heads of other students around me. Worse, I could hear the impact of the clubs on their heads. Blood flowed. People screamed. I was terrified, but knew I could not resist or fight back. I just tried to avoid being hit.

With a path cleared, the cops dragged the arrested students out of the building and into the paddy wagons. They did not arrest any of the students outside, just beat them bloody and left them lying where they fell. I was angry and confused and didn't know what to do. Students lined the sidewalks on both sides of the street as the wagons pulled away. They extended their arms in the Nazi salute and shouted, "*Sieg Heil*," as Hitler had been cheered. In all, sixty students were arrested, many for the ridiculous charge of felonious assault on a police officer.

While this melee went on behind the building, a thousand students had assembled in front. Bart called for a strike to shut down the campus. I announced a bail fund to get the arrested students out of jail and began to pass buckets for contributions. Meanwhile, reporters and cameramen arrived and interviewed witnesses.

I was livid. These cops had not been subject to any threats, real or imagined. Why had they become so violent? Their victims were middle-class college students, not hoodlums. The students had not destroyed property or committed violence. Did these cops support the war and see us as traitors? Or did they just vent their own frustration by beating up others? That night, I watched TV news footage of the confrontation, which fully justified student claims of police brutality. The next morning, headlines in the *New York Times* and the *Daily News* also told of the battle and the brutality.

Friday morning, when I arrived on campus, I saw student picket lines at every entrance. The news coverage had helped make the strike a success. College officials were forced to admit that 90 percent of the student body boycotted classes that day. Over a hundred members of the faculty signed a supporting petition. Like Professor Moltz, some had heard of police brutality elsewhere but routinely dismissed reports of it as exaggeration. Seeing it in the flesh made all the difference.

Student leaders called a mass meeting on the grass. Bart and I remained on the sidelines, quietly offering advice to a few students we were close to but otherwise not taking a leadership role. After much debate, a set of demands was cobbled together to present to the college. If they were not met over the weekend, the strike would resume on Monday. Bart and I took stock. We had turned a physical defeat by the police into a political victory with the strike. For the first time, most of the students and many of the faculty were making common cause with campus antiwar activists.

Early Saturday morning, thanks to the action on campus, we had an overflow crowd ready to board our chartered buses for the trip to the Pentagon. There were a few experienced antiwar activists among us, but most were attending their first protest. We used the four-hour drive as a mobile teach-in. I lectured the riders on my bus about the war and how to handle arrests. I told them about undercover agents who might advocate violence in order to give police an excuse to attack. Bart and others did likewise on the other buses. I had no idea what to expect, except that the local authorities had promised to prevent us from getting to the Pentagon.

Our bus parked near the Lincoln Memorial. There were demonstrators everywhere, more than a hundred thousand, and from afar I could see an ocean of banners and picket signs. The crowd was a mix of pacifists, students, anarchists, minority people, senior citizens, revolutionaries, and contingents from various antiwar groups. We all gathered at the Lincoln Memorial. Several speeches were made, most notably by Dave Dellinger, a well-known pacifist who had helped organize the event, and Dr. Benjamin Spock, the nation's foremost pediatrician.

Then, over the heads of the crowd, I saw the first group break away and walk toward the Potomac River bridge that led to the Pentagon. Our group from BC joined others falling in behind them, including a banner-carrying delegation from the Abraham Lincoln Brigade, the American volunteers who had fought fascism during the Spanish Civil War. As those aging heroes passed, thousands cheered them, me included, eager to pick up the torch they had once carried. Eventually, our march stretched almost the entire distance from the Lincoln Memorial to the Pentagon, fifty thousand people. It was the culmination of months of organizing. That number of people ready to commit civil disobedience was unprecedented—and unstoppable.

We marched unimpeded toward what we saw as the enemy. Never mind that the enemy was a respected American institution. To us, the Pentagon was the brain of an evil monster, and we burned with the need to confront it. Nevertheless, we had no idea what to do when we got to the building. Most of us intended to simply stand in front of it in silent protest and defiance. A few were determined to get inside and ransack it. Others wanted to deface its outer walls. The more whimsical spoke of "levitating" the building and "exorcising" the evil spirits inside.

At the edge of the huge parking lot, we were stopped by hundreds of uniformed police and U.S. marshals. In the distance, I saw paratroopers standing shoulder to shoulder directly in front of the building, a human wall ready to serve as a last line of defense. They held rifles, some with fixed bayonets. The cops and marshals tried to keep us boxed into the parking lot. The pacifists among us figured they had gotten as far as they could and gathered a rally so their leaders could make more speeches condemning the war. I joined others looking for a way past the cops so we could get closer to the building.

We knew we were playing to the press, and that much of the country would see and read about our actions. Politically, we had the government in a no-win position, even though we were certain to lose any physical confrontations. If they let us alone, the world would witness the spectacle of fifty thousand protesting Americans surrounding their own military headquarters in a time of war. Except for French students protesting the war in Algeria, nothing like that had ever happened, anywhere. If they attacked us, not with guns and bullets, but with nightsticks and rifle butts, a damaging picture of the U.S. military suppressing its own citizens would be the story. Either way, government authority would be undercut.

While I searched for an opening, spontaneous skirmishes broke out between cops and demonstrators. It looked chaotic until a few hundred militants ran out of the parking lot and took a circuitous route toward the building. I saw them carrying long poles for self-protection. As the militants turned toward the building, they ran into the first of two lines of temporary fencing erected to keep protesters at bay. They tore down a section, which separated the parking lot from the grounds of the Pentagon itself. Marshals rushed over and forced them back.

That action set the stage for the rest of us. We formed into small groups and ripped down fencing until squads of cops and marshals ran over to stop us. When they did, we fled to regroup elsewhere and start on another section of fence. Beyond the first fence, I could see the second and beyond it the paratroopers. Like other protesters, I was willing to engage the police and the marshals. The soldiers were another story. At first glance, they were as intimidating as they were supposed to be. But as I talked with others, we realized they could only be a symbolic deterrent. The cops and marshals did the crowd control. The soldiers never moved. We came to doubt they had live ammunition. The government would not risk having troops open fire on American citizens. A bigger public relations disaster could not be imagined.

Protesters continued to pour into the parking lot. Our numbers and our determination had been underestimated. There were too few cops and marshals to control us. When they rushed to secure one section of fencing, they inevitably left another unguarded, and with so many of us milling around, the unguarded section was soon pulled down. After two hours, our hit-and-run tactics had destroyed the outermost ring of temporary fences. Our entire horde then advanced out of the massive parking lot and onto the grounds of the Pentagon itself. We pushed up to the second line of fencing, which was only a hundred yards from the building.

Off to the side, I caught a glimpse of a few dozen protesters making a wide flanking maneuver. They had spotted an unguarded door for reporters and cameramen at the side of the Pentagon. Marshals rushed in to block their access, leading to a short skirmish, but not before ten of them got past the marshals and made it inside. They were quickly apprehended and thrown out. In the meantime, others got around or over the second line of fencing. They were met with tear gas and the rifle butts of military police (MPs) who had emerged from behind the paratroopers. I watched the battle from afar along with thousands of others. We all stopped where we were and sang "America the Beautiful."

I moved through the chaotic scene, picking my battles carefully. I wanted to fight back, but also avoid arrest or injury. Thanks to the fight with police at BC two days before, I was determined to stand up to police brutality. I could see that others from BC had been similarly affected. We pushed back against the cops wherever we could and helped others under attack. In the general confusion, people ran in all directions but kept tearing down sections of fencing whenever there was an opening.

These skirmishes lasted another two hours. Little by little, in groups of eight or ten, hundreds of protesters were arrested and hauled away in police vans. Among them was the author Norman Mailer, whose account of the day, published under the title *The Armies of the Night*, would win both the Pulitzer Prize and the National Book Award. Ironically, the most peaceful protesters were the ones arrested. They were the easiest targets. Those of us pulling down the fences were mobile and did not stand around waiting to be apprehended.

By late afternoon, the arrests had not yet made a dent in our numbers, and after prolonged skirmishing we had breached the second line of fencing. The crowd pushed up to the paratroopers, only twenty or thirty yards from the building. The soldiers stood shoulder to shoulder, and as we stopped in front of them, cops and marshals wandered through the crowd making random arrests. Every time they got close to my group, we were able to dodge them. There were still some twenty thousand of us, but we were reluctant to move against the soldiers. They had not attacked us,

This iconic photo, from the October 1967 march on the Pentagon, inspired the press to coin the term "flower power." *Bernie Boston/The Washington Post via Getty Images*

and, ultimately, we were there to save their lives. We also had some concern for their bayonets.

Marshals and MPs gathered behind the paratroopers. We sat down on the grass or pavement a few feet in front of them. I was in the first row, and like others I talked to the soldiers immediately in front of me about the war and why we were there to protest it. Some of the young soldiers were hostile, but many were ill at ease, unaccustomed to what they were experiencing, and ambivalent about those of us confronting them. A short distance away on my right protesters had stood up and moved closer to the troops. Some MPs emerged from behind the paratroopers to push them back. Their rifles had no bayonets but were held at their waists pointed slightly up, directly at the heads of the demonstrators standing face-to-face in front of them. No one backed off. It looked like trouble.

Suddenly a long-haired protester wearing a bulky sweater and carrying a bunch of flowers stepped forward. He pulled out a single flower and stuck the stem into the barrel of a rifle pointed at him. He then calmly moved down the line of MPs and put each of his flowers into a different rifle barrel. A photographer caught this symbolic act on film, and the resulting photo appeared across the country the next day. It became the visual story of the event, but the photo was destined to play a larger role as an enduring icon of the 1960s.

The press, having coined the term "flower children" only months before in San Francisco, used the picture to invent "flower power" to describe the new hippie/activist alliance opposed to the war. They used the term ironically, even derisively, as though "flower" and "power" were inherently antithetical. I liked the phrase, as did others, because it symbolized our ideas. Flower power meant freeing men from outdated norms of masculinity that sapped their sensitivity, their poetry, and their urge to share instead of dominate. We did want to "make love, not war," but we also wanted to use our long hair and flowers to redefine manhood. We embraced the iconic photo as an appropriate symbol of our new ethos.

After dark, our numbers dwindled. Many protesters had come from other cities and had to get back to their buses for the return trip. I wasn't leaving, so I gave up my ride. Thousands of others did, too. We made bonfires with the picket signs carried earlier. Impromptu speakers used bullhorns to urge the soldiers to switch sides. Many knew the history of the Russian Revolution and wanted to induce our soldiers to abandon the government and join the people, as Russian soldiers had in 1917. Around 9:00 p.m., one did. A single soldier dropped his rifle, threw down his helmet, and advanced toward the protesters. Before he got far, he was seized from behind and led away. We never found out what happened to him.

Soon, I saw draft cards being burned. Many young men in the crowd had not yet taken that step. In the eerie scene, with bonfires encircling the Pentagon, they were inspired to do so. Over two hundred draft cards went up in smoke. Food and blankets arrived, and I tried to settle in for the night. I no longer knew why I was there. It served no purpose to stay. It was too dark for news footage, and we had no realistic chance of getting to the building. But I could not bring myself to leave. I had a right to be there, and I was not going to be run off. It was only pride and egotism, but I clung to my determination.

As the bonfires died out and the night wore on, many protesters left. Around midnight, the marshals assumed our resolve had weakened. They moved the soldiers toward us. It was imprudent to resist, so we slowly fell back, trying to maintain discipline. Marshals pushed into the crowd and made more arrests. Again, they used their nightsticks with abandon and viciously attacked anyone who resisted. I went mobile with the tiny group that had stayed with me, and we avoided arrest, but I saw females being beaten mercilessly as I moved through the area. After the soldiers had pushed the crowd back some hundred feet, they stopped.

Outraged by the needless brutality, I resolved to stay the night. When the sun came up, I wanted the press to see that some of us had survived. At first light, only several hundred of us remained, but we had escaped arrest and injury and hopefully made our point. We got up, formed a line, and marched to the White House. Given the early hour, we wanted to wake up, or at least shake up, President Johnson. We paraded under his windows until motorcycle cops drove us off with nightsticks. But we were there long enough to make sure Johnson heard the chant that had become emblematic of the antiwar movement, "Hey, hey, LBJ, how many kids did you kill today?"

Monday morning, I was back at Brooklyn College ready to fight another battle. Roughly two-thirds of the student body remained out. The strike was holding. At Columbia and on other city campuses, demonstrations were under way to support us. Late in the morning, about three thousand BC students came to a rally on the grass. The college president offered modest concessions if the students ended the strike. I knew that presidents of publicly funded colleges who cannot control their campuses often get their budgets cut, if not worse. I felt he wasn't offering enough, and Bart agreed, so we both spoke and tried to help the students understand that they had more leverage than they realized . . . if they stuck together. A two-hour debate ensued. It was thorough and well considered, not unlike the mass meetings held at UC by Students Against the Rank. Eventually, students rejected the president's offer, and in response frustrated college officials went to court and got an injunction prohibiting outdoor gatherings on campus.

That was a foolish and desperate step. The next morning, Bart and I combined our classes and taught them together on the grass in defiance of the injunction. College officials ordered us to stop. We refused. Go ahead and arrest us for teaching, we said. But the officials realized we had them cornered. They had already learned that bringing cops on campus would only backfire. Our open defiance of the injunction was ample evidence of their impotence, and they backed off. At a rally later that day, college officials gave in to all the student demands.

They promised to never again bring police onto campus to resolve an internal dispute. They dropped all disciplinary action against students who had participated in the strike or the protest against the Navy recruiters. They dropped charges against students arrested for trespassing and promised to intercede on behalf of students charged with resisting arrest or assault. They agreed that no recruiters from the armed forces, the CIA, or weapons contractors like Dow Chemical could recruit anywhere on campus. Our students could see the power they had won by remaining united. They voted to accept the offer and return to classes.

With the strike over, my focus shifted back to teaching. I revised my abnormal psychology course because it seemed intellectually dishonest to lecture students about individual causes of insanity and neuroses when whole societies also acted in irrational, even insane ways. War was one example, but so too were class divisions, racism, ethnic prejudice, crushing poverty, religious intolerance, rampant competition, and needless scarcity. All were, I thought, irrational, maladaptive, even psychotic aspects of societal behavior that provoked individuals to act irrationally themselves. Shouldn't this irrational behavior also be part of studying abnormal psychology? If individual psyches were as far as psychology could reach, while irrational social behavior remained the purview of sociology and political science, were not the divisions between the social sciences artificial, even counterproductive?

Between teaching, writing my research article, and keeping up with the war, I was busy, but my life at BC was cushioned by newfound wealth. My $11,000 annual salary was almost twice what I had earned as a graduate student. To celebrate, I took flying lessons at Westchester County Airport, joyful at being able to finish what I had started ten years before. I also took advantage of my new status as a single male, since Charlotte and I had stopped dating when I left Chicago. From the standpoint of sexual liberation, these years were the happy interval between the repression of the 1950s and the self-imposed restraints necessitated later by HIV/AIDS.

Big news came in late November. Defense Secretary McNamara, the architect of the war, resigned in the face of its obvious failure. Previously, a few other administration officials had also quit because of the war. Senator Eugene McCarthy, an antiwar Democrat from Minnesota, made the surprise announcement that he would run against Johnson in the Democratic presidential primaries a few months later. By year's end, 460,000 American troops were in Viet Nam. A million had already rotated through, and sixteen thousand of them were dead.

Antiwar tactics escalated. During the strike at BC, Berkeley activists had sponsored Stop the Draft Week, an attempt to forcibly shut down the local draft board in neighboring Oakland. Making no pretense that it was a peaceful protest, a thousand of them came equipped with shields and motorcycle helmets to ward off blows from the police. They blocked access to the draft board office, and the cops went after them with clubs flying. Street fighting with cops had become another tactic in the protester arsenal. The Oakland police made frequent use of tear gas and Mace, and the battles raged on for a week.

At the University of Wisconsin, students tried to evict campus recruiters from Dow Chemical. Police were called, and they beat the protesters severely. When thousands of other students saw how badly the protesters had been hurt, they also raised their arms in the Nazi salute and chanted, "*Sieg Heil.*" The police fired tear gas, which touched off a riot. The crowd threw rocks and bricks at the cops and forced them to retreat. The local sheriff then sent in a riot squad with attack dogs. Episodes like this were no longer isolated events.

Also in November, Secretary of State Dean Rusk spoke in New York. The Fifth Avenue Peace Parade Committee organized a legal picket line, but SDS activists called for fighting in the streets. As dignitaries arrived, thousands of demonstrators tormented them with curses and insults. They threw eggs and red paint at the cops, overturned garbage cans, blocked streets, and set off fire alarms. The cops, responding with their usual violence, mistakenly attacked peaceful protesters and innocent bystanders.

Stop the Draft Week inspired an attempt to close down the Whitehall Induction Center in lower Manhattan the week of December 4. I was angry at the police brutality I had witnessed at BC and the Pentagon. I knew that street fighting entailed risk, but those who had opposed unjust wars in the past had to risk their lives. I only had to risk injury and arrest, so I joined the effort. My thinking about the war had evolved again. Our enemy wasn't just the Pentagon; it was the entire government. Since we lacked the power to fight the government, our only option was to make trouble for it, to throw monkey wrenches into its machinery. Regrettably, I knew that wasn't a strategy; it was a desperate tactic forced on us by the lack of an alternative.

At Whitehall, I wore protective gear and a helmet and carried wet rags for air filtration in case we were teargassed. To our surprise, mounted police were deployed, and in the maze of narrow streets in lower Manhattan their huge horses were intimidating. I was with the main group that first assembled in front of the induction center, but the horses immediately drove us off. I ran into a side street with a dozen others, chased by cops on foot. We fought back briefly and ran off to regroup farther away. With half a dozen big horses galloping toward me on a narrow street, fear was all I felt, but I learned to contain my fear and see the larger situation: where to retreat, when to run, how to move offensively.

Others came prepared for the horses. A new breed of gritty urban hippies had evolved in the East Village, and some had formed into small anarchist groups. They had pockets full of marbles. When the horses approached, the anarchists rolled marbles under their hooves, which made them lose traction on the pavement and trip. The mounted cops were furious, but had to back away from the marbles. Running skirmishes lasted for hours that day, but we failed to shut down the induction center. Later in the week, there was more street fighting, but also traditional picket lines and peaceful sit-ins. By Friday, six hundred had been arrested, including the writer Grace Paley and America's leading pediatrician, Dr. Benjamin Spock, whose book *Baby and Child Care* had been the bible upon which many in our generation were raised. Dr. Spock felt he had no alternative but to resist and be arrested. That was what we all felt.

Despite our desperate tactics at Whitehall, I knew that in the long run we had to win a political battle, not a street fight. We had made some progress. The number of Americans opposed to the war was up dramatically, and as a result military recruitment was more difficult, government options were diminished, and the war would likely be the central issue in the coming presidential election. In the process, many of us in the antiwar movement had also changed. Tempered by recent events, I no longer saw the United States as the benevolent giant of my youth, but rather as a malevolent force bullying other countries, exploiting the weakest of its own citizens, and using physical brutality against them if they chose to dissent. I was not yet ready to carry the NLF flag, as some friends were doing, but by the end of 1967 neither would I recite the Pledge of Allegiance nor stand when others sang "The Star-Spangled Banner."

CHAPTER 9

I HAD TO LEARN MORE ABOUT U.S. FOREIGN POLICY. IF I WAS GOING TO SPEAK PUBLICLY against the war, as I had started to, I needed a broader understanding. I began to read in earnest but was deeply disappointed. The United States had long used its military power to take economic advantage of other countries. Beyond simply pursuing our own national interests, our policies had been honed to serve the narrower interests of our businessmen and corporations. In Central and South America and parts of the Pacific, our only real concern was to protect markets and resources for American business. If the locals objected, they were swept aside with money or military might. We were imperialists, but unlike British or other imperial colonies, ours had a veneer of political independence and self-government that masked highly exploitative economic relations.

Even our desire to rescue friends in the two world wars had taken a backseat to our economic self-interest. We watched France and England suffer three years of deadly combat in World War I before we came to a consensus and sent the first troops. During the buildup to World War II, our conservative business leaders opposed attacking Hitler because they hoped he would march east and overthrow communism in the Soviet Union, to them a greater threat. When Hitler turned west instead, these conservatives forced us to sit on our hands for two years until he had conquered almost every country on the European continent. Only the bombing of Pearl Harbor broke the stalemate and forced us to enter the war in

Europe. After World War II, the powerful economic bloc that President Eisenhower called the "military-industrial complex" used America's great wealth and newly acquired weapons-manufacturing capacity to design an economic imperialism with worldwide reach—Iran in 1953 being but one of many examples.

As I digested this revisionist history, which was far different from what I had been taught in school, it pushed me further to the left and solidified my identification as a political radical. I came to view the liberal community, with which I had once identified, with disdain. I had seen them make too many compromises, especially in the fight against communism. Condoning the suppression of free speech and free assembly in order to ferret out domestic communists seemed to me to be too great a sacrifice of sacred principles, the more so since communists had never been a significant threat in the United States. When many leading liberals failed to support the struggle for civil rights in the South because they feared alienating allies they needed on other issues, I no longer wanted to be associated with them. Later, to protect their positions in society, these "Cold War liberals" supported the war in Viet Nam, and my disdain for them turned to disgust.

The word "radical" literally means "getting to the root of things," and as I read more about the history of U.S. foreign affairs, the root cause most often was economic. To maintain its expanding prosperity, our capitalist economic system required expanding markets and resources. After World War II, having the wealth and the military might to acquire them was too big a temptation to resist. It was clear to me that the larger problem was capitalism itself, even though I could see no other system that functioned better. I wanted to be part of the debate about how to solve fundamental problems in the United States, so I knew I had to learn more about our economic system and the Marxist theory that was its only alternative.

At the beginning of 1968, as I underwent these radical changes, I was unaware of how completely the world around me was about to be turned upside down. I read diligently as I graded term papers and exams for the first time. Antiwar protests happened with mounting frequency, especially those directed against President Johnson. Many of us in the antiwar movement had argued for ridiculing Johnson whenever and wherever he spoke publicly. He was the one person who could single-handedly stop the war, so he became the focal point of our anger. Wherever he appeared, antiwar activists mercilessly taunted him with "Hey, hey, LBJ, how many kids did you kill today?"

On January 21, North Vietnamese forces encircled an isolated mountain base at Khe Sanh in South Viet Nam and trapped five thousand U.S. Marines inside. The press compared it to the siege at Dien Bien Phu in 1954, when a French military base was similarly encircled and overrun by Vietnamese forces under the command of General Vo Nguyen Giap, who thereafter was widely admired as a military genius. That defeat led to the French withdrawal from Indochina. Fourteen years later, General Giap was in command at Khe Sanh. The Marines would fight for weeks with massive air support until a relief column finally broke through the siege in March.

Ten days after the first encirclement of Khe Sanh, on the night of January 31, the Vietnamese launched an offensive that became a turning point in the war. It began with seventeen NLF soldiers driving a truck and a taxi to the fortresslike U.S. embassy in Saigon. Five sappers among them blew a hole in the towering wall. They overpowered a Marine guard and destroyed the fortified doors of the building with an antitank round. A gun battle ensued, and after several hours the outnumbered Vietnamese were forced back. The fact that the embassy, one of the most fortified and heavily guarded targets in all of South Viet Nam, was breached at all came as a profound shock, yet similar incursions had simultaneously taken place at two other locations that were equally well protected, the South Vietnamese presidential palace and, unbelievably, U.S. military headquarters in Saigon.

But that wasn't the half of it. It was the night before the festival of Tet, the lunar New Year, and celebrations were under way throughout the country. Immediately following the Saigon attacks, NLF and North Vietnamese Army (NVA) soldiers numbering over a hundred thousand used the revelry to cover simultaneous attacks on more than one hundred cities and military installations throughout South Viet Nam. Despite this vast operation, and the logistics required to coordinate so many perfectly timed actions in secret, they achieved complete and total surprise. It was the worst U.S. intelligence failure since the Japanese bombed Pearl Harbor in 1941.

Unlike Pearl Harbor, however, TV film crews were present throughout South Viet Nam. They filmed the Tet Offensive as it happened. A TV crew captured the hand-to-hand fighting inside the embassy. I saw it the next day, along with other bloody scenes of firefights in which American soldiers were shot on camera or shown wounded or dead in the midst of battle. The public had seen battlefield footage before, but as the huge size of the Tet Offensive sank in, and as the scope of the surprise attacks began to register, many Americans stopped believing the war could be won. Johnson and the military had promised we would prevail, that our awesome power would bring inevitable victory. The footage of the Tet Offensive revealed that it had all been a lie.

There were more shocks. I saw TV footage of General Nguyen Ngoc Loan, the South Vietnamese police chief, walking up to an NLF prisoner standing handcuffed in the street. The general raised a pistol to the prisoner's ear and shot him at point-blank range. A fountain of blood spurted from the exit wound on the other side of the man's head before he fell to the ground dead. A photo of this distressing scene appeared the next morning on the front page of every newspaper in America. This was the South Vietnamese democracy American men were sacrificing their lives to protect.

Elsewhere, the little village of Ben Tre in the Mekong Delta near Saigon was leveled by a brutal U.S. bombardment. The Associated Press quoted an American Army officer as he made one of the most controversial public statements uttered during the war. In justifying the attack, the officer said of the village, "We had to destroy it in order to save it." For years afterward, I and other opponents of the war often referred to that statement, the quintessential proof of the futility of our effort in Viet Nam.

American forces gradually beat back the Tet Offensive and inflicted massive casualties on NLF and NVA forces. They prevented the general uprising that the offensive was designed to provoke. But despite this failure, the Tet Offensive was a stunning political defeat for Johnson. Public opinion shifted dramatically against him, and no matter how much he and his people tried to downplay the brilliantly executed but ultimately unsuccessful Tet Offensive, their words rang hollow and support for the war eroded.

Paradoxically, as the popularity of the war decreased, anger at the antiwar movement increased. Our disruptive actions outraged most Americans. A Harris poll showed them so alienated by our tactics that 40 percent were willing to suspend our constitutional right to protest. Pro- and antiwar forces were at loggerheads, and the country was more polarized than at any time since the Civil War. Yet actions by both sides increased the polarization.

Several street-theater troupes had sprung up to entertain and educate people at protests. They also performed surprise antiwar skits in random public spaces, like busy street corners. Two of the groups, the Pageant Players and the Bread and Puppet Theatre, were especially smart and amusing. Early one week, guerrilla-theater activists announced their intention to use napalm to burn a live dog the following Saturday in Central Park. Predictably, the city went berserk. The press covered the story, and animal lovers demanded police intervention. Right-wing and conservative commentators screamed about the depravity of the antiwar movement.

I knew a few people in the group, so on Saturday I went to Central Park to watch their performance. A large crowd had assembled, along with numerous camera crews. A cute little mutt on a leash was led around, which sparked howls of outrage. The performers let the anger build, then one stepped forward with a bullhorn and delivered an obscenity-laced attack on New Yorkers who looked the other way when the military used napalm on human beings but were outraged when the victim was a dog. He removed the leash and allowed the mutt to run off. The press, having hyped the story all week, had to report it on Saturday. As a result, they delivered the antiwar message for us. We were getting very good at manipulating the media in this way.

Inevitably, the negative reactions to the Tet Offensive spread. Walter Cronkite, the *CBS Evening News* anchor, traveled to Viet Nam himself to investigate. He was the most popular and influential newsman in America and had been neutral on the war. When he returned in late February, he discarded his neutrality and stated the obvious, that "the bloody experience in Viet Nam is to end in a stalemate." His statement surprised Johnson and jolted public opinion.

Shortly afterward, the first presidential primary took place in New Hampshire. The result was stunning. Senator Eugene McCarthy, running in opposition to the war, came within 230 votes of beating Johnson. Sensing the president's weakness, Senator Robert Kennedy of New York entered the race four days later. I remained wary of Kennedy. Years before, he had worked for Senator Joe McCarthy during the witch hunts in the 1950s and later, as his brother's attorney general, had given only tepid support to the civil rights movement. But I had to admit that under his brother's influence, and in his subsequent years in the Senate, he had moved sharply left and become a staunch liberal. His candidacy was instantly popular and at the top of the news.

Kennedy came to Brooklyn College shortly after entering the race. Antiwar students and activists remained skeptical. While he had condemned Johnson's policies in Viet Nam, he had not been clear about how to end the war. To his credit, he called on America to more equitably distribute the nation's wealth and resources, and his convincing and emotional speeches drew passionate crowds. Many yearned for the hopefulness that had died with his brother in Dallas. Not me. I was so blinded by my rage at the war, I only saw a waffling politician unable to support immediate withdrawal.

Bart and I walked a picket line with antiwar students in front of the BC auditorium in which Kennedy was to speak. Most of the signs urged him to support withdrawal. At the start of his speech, we went inside and stood at the rear, holding up those same signs. Mine said, "Bobby Bird." Johnson's wife was known as Lady Bird, and his two daughters were often referred to as Lynda Bird and Luci Bird. For me to refer to Kennedy as Bobby Bird meant that he had not sufficiently separated himself from the president. Kennedy saw my sign and joked from the podium about taking it back to Washington to show Johnson. He spoke with charm and good humor and did send an aide to ask me for the sign. Some weeks later, his position on ending the war hardened significantly. I hoped that our protest at BC had played some small role.

Both Kennedy and McCarthy campaigned vigorously against Johnson. Polls showed the president headed for defeat in Wisconsin and possible losses in other states. Johnson scheduled a televised speech for March 31 promising new developments in Viet Nam. Bart and I watched the speech together, afraid Johnson would escalate the war to draw more support. Instead, he rejected further escalation and said he had cut back the bombing in North Viet Nam. At the end of the very detailed speech, he raised his eyes, looked mournfully into the camera, and said, "I have concluded that I should not permit the Presidency to become involved in the partisan divisions that are developing in this political year . . . Accordingly, I shall not seek, and I will not accept, the nomination of my party for another term as your President."

We were speechless. Because of antiwar protests and chants, Johnson had become a hostage in the White House, unable to appear in public without provoking riots and damaging controversy. Bart and I sat in shocked silence as we tried to digest the news. The antiwar movement had made Johnson's presidency untenable. Gradually, it dawned on us: our actions had brought down the president of the United States.

In 1960, French student demonstrators in Paris had told me their plan to end the war in Algeria by bringing down President de Gaulle. I had been skeptical, yet I marveled at their audacity. I thought then that even if such a thing were possible in France, with its long tradition of student demonstrations, it was so alien to America that it would take a century before anything comparable could happen here. History had moved faster than my limited imagination. Instead of a hundred years, it had taken only seven and a half.

The news hit the papers the next morning, April Fools' Day, but those of us who had seen the speech on television knew it was no joke. The balance of power had shifted. Vice President Humphrey would run in the primaries against Kennedy and McCarthy. As his VP, Humphrey had to support Johnson on the war, but as a longtime liberal he might not be as ruthless. Any of the three would de-escalate, Kennedy and McCarthy faster than Humphrey, but an end to the war had suddenly become a possibility.

Johnson was a truly tragic figure. Because he lacked the courage or political will to get out of Viet Nam, hundreds of thousands of Vietnamese and tens of thousands of Americans died on his watch. The cultural and political divisions provoked by the war destroyed America's social cohesion for decades to come. Johnson is not remembered as a hero on a par with Franklin Delano Roosevelt, his own fond hope, but instead will always be associated with one of the most tragic and willful mistakes in American history.

It took only four days to crush our newfound optimism. On April 4, I taught a BC night school course as a volunteer, trying to help people who worked during the day earn a college degree. A young woman I dated was waiting for me when the class ended, but as I approached her, I saw she was crying. She looked up at me and said softly that Martin Luther King Jr. had just been shot and killed in Memphis. I sank to the floor of the corridor dizzy with shock. First it was Jack Kennedy, then Malcolm X, the most promising and inspirational black leader, and now King, the one man still able to bridge the gap between the races and provide the moral leadership needed to reshape America.

As a young student, I had been critical of King for being insufficiently militant during the early civil rights movement. But over the previous two years, King had made a more radical critique of American society. President Johnson's attempts to end racial discrimination and reduce the worst aspects of poverty through his Great Society programs did not go far enough for my taste, yet they were worthwhile. When Johnson became ensnared in Viet Nam, he had to divert more and more of the nation's treasury to the military. The poverty programs suffered, even though Johnson insisted we could afford both "guns and butter."

King knew we could not, and said so. When he tried to move the civil rights struggle into northern cities, he quickly concluded there could be no racial justice without economic justice. In 1964, when he became the youngest man to win the Nobel Peace Prize, he also won easy access to the national news media. He used it to explain the link between poverty and racism, and people listened. In recent months, he had gone further and argued that neither racial nor economic justice could be achieved without peace. His appeal had been moral as well as fiscal.

Blacks were the most loyal component of the Democratic Party vote.

King's analysis raised the possibility that black opposition to the war might change black voting patterns. More people had become aware that black men were disproportionately drafted and even more disproportionately killed and wounded. Many blacks and many of us in the antiwar movement came to the troubling conclusion that King had been assassinated because he had pointed to those links and jeopardized the fragile stability of class and race relations in America.

Millions in black neighborhoods across America came to the same conclusion. Black anger and dismay reached unprecedented levels. Simultaneous rebellions broke out in over one hundred American cities. Nothing on that scale had ever occurred. First the police were overwhelmed, then the National Guard. Regular Army troops were deployed. Running gun battles took place on city streets, and many were killed. There were reports of black Viet Nam veterans using skills acquired in the military to fight back. Massive property damage occurred, and fires were set that consumed whole neighborhoods and burned for days.

Brooklyn College suspended classes after the assassination and held memorial services on campus. I consoled students and discussed what might be done to advance King's work. But I also urged my students to get home before dark, and then took my own advice. That night, the impoverished Bedford-Stuyvesant ghetto in Brooklyn exploded. Parts of Flatbush Avenue, the main street between my apartment and the BC campus, were engulfed in flames. Whole sections of the city were cordoned off as I watched news footage from the safety of my apartment.

The widespread violence was antithetical to King's beliefs. He had always worked within the system and had opposed violence in any form. He had never given up trying to effect change through existing structures of society, whether religious, political, civic, or commercial. Yet, after he was killed, hundreds of thousands, perhaps millions, of blacks concluded that this approach had led only to his death, that social justice was no longer available within the system, and so insurrection and revolution were the only answer. Black power groups like the Black Panther Party and the newly transformed SNCC organization fed this perception as the riots continued over the next two weeks.

I was drawn to their point of view, if not yet their revolution. At that time, I viewed capitalism as a zero-sum game; that is, for any one person to get more, someone else had to have less, if not in this country, then in another we were exploiting. The only nonviolent way to redistribute wealth was through tax law or expanded entitlements, but those who already own the wealth inevitably resist. I didn't think elections were the answer, since the wealthy can more easily finance political campaigns. So I agreed with black power advocates that radical change could not be won within the system, but how could it be won? Members of the working class, whether they wore blue collars or white, would not risk a radical transformation given the big stake many had in home mortgages and retirement pensions, which conveniently also made money for bankers and financiers. And even if we could fundamentally change capitalism, what would we put in its place? Not the stultifying state communism of the Soviet Union or the People's Republic of China. Politically, I looked out on a bleak landscape.

A few days after the riots had subsided, I heard a news report that SDS members at Columbia University had seized five buildings on the Manhattan campus. On TV that night, I saw banners with incendiary antiwar slogans hanging from the upper windows. The students had unusual demands. Not surprisingly, they insisted Columbia halt scientific research in support of the war. However, they were equally insistent that the university halt construction of a gymnasium in a park near the campus that bordered Harlem because the gym would be off-limits to its black residents. For the first time, students simultaneously opposed the war and supported the interests of poor black neighbors. King's assassination had moved them, but they had also responded to a growing desire by antiwar activists to address domestic issues, especially racism.

The next afternoon I went to Columbia with a delegation of Brooklyn College students and two faculty members. Columbia students had come to BC to stand with our student strike the previous fall, so we wanted to support them and their attempt to treat war and racism as part of the same problem. We spoke to student leaders, visited the five occupied buildings, and made short speeches in each to encourage the protesters to hold out.

The day after our visit to Columbia, I spoke to a large rally on the BC campus and encouraged our students to support theirs. I also asked students to participate in a one-day strike on April 26 and one of the numerous antiwar protests set for the weekend of April 27. Lynn Rossman, a talented student leader, spoke after me. Several seemingly unfriendly young men had gathered in the first row in front of her. Fearing a physical attack, I walked back to the podium and stood next to her as she spoke. Several antiwar students realized what I was doing and inconspicuously moved up to join me. Our preemptive action worked. The young toughs in the first row realized we were onto them and evaporated into the crowd.

On April 26, the continuing strike at Columbia had forced the city's attention back to the war. Over 200,000 high school and college students in New York refused to attend classes. So did another million in other American cities. The next day, 150,000 people attended a protest in Central Park. I went with a large delegation from BC. Half of us marched down each side of the park and converged at Sheep Meadow, a large grassy field in the middle. We listened to speeches by national leaders and celebrities, but were moved most by Coretta Scott King, widowed less than a month before. Her willingness to appear at an antiwar demonstration so soon after her husband's murder was a signal she would continue his work against the war and help bring the races together to oppose it. Our protest had competition that day. New York's Roman Catholic community staged a simultaneous pro-war rally in midtown Manhattan. A mere 3,000 came.

The protest at Columbia continued. University officials had refused to negotiate with the students. On the night of April 30, they called the cops. Unlike our strike at BC, the national press, headquartered in midtown Manhattan only minutes from Columbia, arrived before the cops finished clearing the buildings. What we heard on the radio that night and saw the next day in the newspapers and on TV was the most vicious police violence anyone had witnessed outside the South. Dozens of students suffered severe injuries and were pictured bleeding profusely from head wounds. That the police did this to kids at one of the most elite universities in the country was shocking, but that they did it in full view of the press indicated a degree of arrogance, a sense that they were above the law, that outraged many New Yorkers. Some antiwar protesters said it was the last straw; there would be no more peaceful protests.

The brutality at Columbia boosted the drive to organize a major confrontation at the Democratic Party convention in Chicago that summer. Tom Hayden and Rennie Davis, two national antiwar leaders, had called for disrupting the convention if it failed to oppose the war. Abbie Hoffman and Jerry Rubin, the most visible leaders of the Youth International Party, or yippies, a hippie/activist wing of the antiwar movement, joined the call. The yippies wanted to stage a "festival of life," smoke dope in the streets, run wild in the city, and use humor and satire to expose the hypocrisy of those who supported the war.

Having worked with Chicago cops over the eight summers I had spent as a lifeguard, I knew such plans were more dangerous than the organizers realized. Mayor Richard J. Daley ran the city with an iron fist. His was the last of the big-city political machines, and he was in his fourth term as mayor (he would be elected to six). Daley was a hard man, the kind who would take pleasure in ordering an assault on long-haired hippie antiwar protesters, and I knew that the cops under his command would be only too happy to comply. He was proud to have brought the convention to Chicago and would resort to any level of violence to prevent its disruption.

Strategically, the action made little sense to me. As antiwar activists, we were furious with the Democratic president and the Democratic Party, but as of March 31 we had all but deposed the president. Of the three Democratic candidates in the race, two were openly critical of the war. Weren't they preferable to Richard Nixon, the likely Republican nominee? I failed to see what would be accomplished by a bloodbath in Chicago. Many others thought as I did, and organizing for the convention, while fueled to some extent by the violence at Columbia, remained anemic. I did not plan to join the organizing effort or go to the convention.

Neither was I interested in volunteering for one of the presidential candidates. My cynicism about work within the system was too deep. Those campaigning for McCarthy were pushing the slogan "Keep clean for Gene," trying to get long-haired activists like me to tone down their rhetoric, cut their hair, dress conventionally, and build support for their candidate. I was too alienated and bitter to feel comfortable making those compromises. I also thought Kennedy would make a better candidate against Nixon and that he had a deeper commitment to social justice than McCarthy. Nonetheless, having voted for Johnson in 1964, I remained too deeply suspicious of electoral politics to participate.

The academic year drew to a close. My students had responded well to my teaching, and I felt far more confident in front of them than I had at the beginning of the year. I also completed an article for a scientific journal based on my doctoral research, gone through the usual peer review, and seen it published. Finally, I had earned my private pilot's license and occasionally experienced the pure bliss of going to the airport to fly a rented plane whenever I felt like it. I took friends up and made short trips with them. The kaleidoscope of political events had kept me from research, but Bart and I intended to investigate the newly discovered neurotransmitters to see what effect they might have on the regulation of sleep and dreams—projects for the next academic year.

I developed an exotic plan. I was thirteen years old the last time I had a summer vacation. At fourteen, I worked part-time as a drugstore delivery boy. At fifteen, I had a full-time job loading trucks for a wholesale drug company. I then spent eight summers as a lifeguard, and three more in Al Rechtschaffen's Sleep Lab. The following year at BC, my annual salary would increase to the princely sum of $14,000. I could do whatever I wanted for the summer, a freedom I had never experienced.

Doctoral candidates at the University of Chicago had to read either French or German. I had chosen French, and while I did learn to read it efficiently, I had never been able to speak it well. A summer alone in a French-speaking country could correct that deficiency, and if there was a beautiful beach in the vicinity, so much the better. I was thinking of Corsica or North Africa. I had another interest. My pessimism about America, and my growing concern that it could not be reformed, had left me more open to the prospect of leaving it or of dropping out to join the hippies. I wanted a taste of living outside society, and I thought I could get it in a place where I knew no one and did not speak the local language.

Shortly after I made my plans, tumultuous events in Paris captured the attention of the world. Student strikes spread rapidly to a few French factories, then swept like wildfire through the entire French economy.

Within two weeks, a majority of the French workforce had joined a general strike. Their demands were unlike any the world had ever seen. They insisted on the usual improvements in working conditions and wages, but went much further, demanding new social and class relations that were humane, less competitive, more imaginative, and more uplifting than what existed under France's top-down bureaucratic state. They were, in effect, demanding a new culture. Unusual slogans gave voice to these unusual demands: "Be realistic, demand the impossible." "I am a Marxist of the Groucho tendency." "Workers of all countries, enjoy!" It was a strange brew of socialism, anarchism, and the new hippie thinking that in less than a year had migrated from the Summer of Love to the streets of Paris.

I devoured this news, and the more I learned, the more interested I became. Was this a viable attempt to reform capitalism? Had the French found a way to unite radical students and factory workers behind a common agenda? Was there a vision here for an alternative society? Could it last? I already had plans to fly to Paris on my way to a French beach farther south. I decided to stay there awhile and learn what I could. One of my BC faculty friends knew a woman in the French film industry, and in response to his request she agreed to show me around.

A few days before the school year ended, I listened to election returns come in from California, the last of the Democratic primaries. Bobby Kennedy had been surging in the polls and had made forceful statements about ending the combat in Viet Nam. Late that night, when his California victory was announced, I allowed myself a glimmer of optimism about the country and the war.

To many people, especially those who had supported his brother, Bobby was a second coming of hope, and despite my skepticism I knew he had evolved. With his frequent calls to end poverty and racism, he had redefined himself as a progressive. His potential was magnified because he was a Kennedy, which would allow him to effectively carry his progressive ideals into the mainstream. His leadership had been amplified by his remarkably charismatic speaking style, and his victory speech that night at the Ambassador Hotel in Los Angeles was suitably stirring. I instantly felt that his California triumph was tantamount to winning the presidency, as it would likely lead to his nomination and then a majority in November.

After the speech Kennedy turned from the podium and walked through the hotel kitchen toward the exit. Surrounded by bodyguards, well-wishers, and hotel staff, he moved slowly through the crowd. Shots rang out; confused shouts and a short scuffle followed. Kennedy went down and lay in a pool of blood on the kitchen floor, the only American leader still capable of unifying the nation. He died twenty-six hours later.

I did not fully appreciate then what the country had lost in Bobby Kennedy. His might have been a transformational presidency, one that could have moved the country and the world to new commitments against war, racism, and poverty. He was the last chance we had to harness the energy and turmoil of the 1960s and use them to build a progressive new America. Had he been elected, we might have escaped the coming conservative era, its excessive greed, and the widening class divisions that left America's workers with a decreasing standard of living. Perhaps our dependence on foreign oil might also have been avoided, along with the disastrous war in Iraq and the deep financial hole it left us in.

While I failed to understand the long-term implications of Kennedy's assassination, the short-term prospects were obvious: charismatic leaders would not be permitted to change the basic direction or structure of the country. The official story was that the assassination was the work of a lone gunman, as it was after the assassinations of Jack Kennedy and Martin Luther King Jr. I didn't buy it, nor did a growing number of skeptical Americans. I believed all three assassinations, and perhaps Malcolm's as well, were the result of conspiracies perpetrated by powerful forces determined to crush any attempt to fundamentally change the nation.

My head was spinning. In only four months, we had seen the surprise attacks of the Tet Offensive, brutal repression at Columbia, an unprecedented general strike in France, and the murder in quick succession of the two leading progressives in America. The war in Viet Nam had unleashed a nightmare of violence that had seeped into the nation's political system like a contagion. I feared there was no way to save the country, no way to stop the war, and no way to lead America to a humane civil society and government.

The United States was no longer the country I had read about in my history books. Since it wasn't, I was no longer sure I still owed it my loyalty. And for the first time since Mississippi in 1963, I questioned my political commitment. Was all the work and sacrifice worth the effort? We still hadn't stopped the war, yet recent events had forced an even larger agenda upon us. Of course, antiwar work had to be maintained, but we also had to take on the more difficult task of building a progressive America. If we didn't, there would be more wars and more unnecessary suffering because of poverty and racism at home.

The assassinations of King and Kennedy meant that leaders could not be relied upon to change America. Reform would have to come from the bottom and be driven by a popular movement organizing on its own behalf and not dependent on leaders to survive. It would be impossible to develop leaders more popular or credentialed than King and Kennedy, yet even their status had not been enough to save their lives.

Could we in the antiwar and civil rights movements organize a majority movement to reform America? I doubted it. Radical activists like us had been incapable of convincing a majority to support immediate withdrawal from Viet Nam. If that failure meant we had little chance of a larger success, why even try? Why be involved in politics at all? And if, in the end, the basic problem was capitalism, what chance did we have to convince working Americans to risk what they owned, and possibly their lives, in order to change the capitalist system? In late June, I boarded a plane for Paris, disillusioned but still hopeful that I might find some answers.

CHAPTER 10

THE HOTEL STELLA NEAR THE SORBONNE WAS AN ULTRACHEAP DESTINATION IN THE Latin Quarter, the epicenter of the May 1968 events. I checked in and rendezvoused with Anne-Marie, the young woman who had agreed to be my guide. She was slender, light haired, about twenty-five, with a slightly retreating chin that accentuated the facial pout so common to the French. She was smart, well-informed, a political activist, and a participant in the general strike and its aftermath.

We walked to Boulevard St. Michel, where the first student demonstrations had taken place. I wasn't surprised. It was only a block from where I had joined the 1960 protest against the war in Algeria. In 1960, protesters tried to bring down a president; in 1968, they tried to bring down the social order itself. The earlier demonstration had shown me my future. I wondered if the French would do me that favor again.

Anne-Marie explained that the situation in France had gradually normalized over the past week or two. Nevertheless, events were still fresh in everyone's mind. When the May events began, participants had no inkling of what was to come. Students at the Sorbonne staged a protest about mistreatment of students in Nanterre. The gendarmes were called, more Sorbonne students joined the protest, police vans were blocked, tear gas was fired, and by the end of the day hundreds of students had been arrested. Not unlike Brooklyn College the previous fall.

What happened next, however, was completely different. University and high school students across France called strikes to support the students at the Sorbonne. In response, police closed the university and sealed its buildings. For a week, running skirmishes took place in the Latin Quarter. The students had built barricades to thwart movement by the police. Anne-Marie showed me the locations. Many of the paving stones they had dug up to use had not yet been replaced. At the end of that first week, on a Friday, a huge demonstration gathered on the Left Bank. Protesters stayed the night and built more barricades. At 2:00 a.m., the gendarmes attacked with lead-weighted nightsticks. Protesters resisted and the battle raged for hours. The gendarmes thought they were operating under cover of darkness, but cameras were there, and when the press came out the next day, French citizens were outraged at their brutality.

On Monday, the largest labor federations in France called a one-day general strike to protest the police violence. Over one million angry people marched through Paris. The gendarmes wisely remained out of sight. In response to the massive turnout, the government reopened the Sorbonne and released all students previously arrested. It was too late. These concessions failed to stifle increasingly ambitious demands. When the students at the Sorbonne got back into their buildings, instead of business as usual, they took control and declared the Sorbonne a "people's university."

Remarkably, workers in several manufacturing plants followed the students' example and took over their factories. These were not minor facilities. Among them were a large aircraft plant and the Renault automobile factory. Instead of remaining at their stations, the workers made management decisions and discussed plans to share the company profits. This was unlike the famous sit-down strikes in Detroit in the late 1930s. The sit-down strikers made no plans to keep building and selling cars. The Renault workers did. They weren't striking for rights; they were taking over. Two days later, fifty factories were occupied. After another day, 200,000 workers were on strike. The next day, 2 million. By the following week, the strike had mushroomed to 10 million, two-thirds of the entire national workforce.

Nor did it stop there. Inspired by the factory takeovers, people took control of schools, workplaces, cultural centers, even government offices.

In each instance, they developed plans to run their businesses or institutions on the basis of humane considerations rather than profit or government agendas, and in an egalitarian anti-authoritarian fashion. With so many people in motion, the authorities were helpless. The state effectively vanished.

Anne-Marie worked in the film industry. She told me that she and her colleagues took control of a studio and worked out an egalitarian system for deciding what films to produce and with what budgets. One afternoon, she took me to the Odéon, one of the national theaters, where she introduced me to a collective still in control there. They were choosing plays to stage, and I was surprised that it was not just the actors and directors involved, but the stagehands, carpenters, and painters as well.

This was six weeks after the start of these tumultuous events, and the turmoil had subsided. Yet Paris was not quite back to normal. It looked the same, but for the people Anne-Marie introduced me to, the factory workers, artists, students, activists, and middle-management people who had lived through it, life was different. The monthlong experience had shown them that fundamental alternatives to the social order could at least be contemplated, if not yet enacted. Their reality had not changed, but their consciousness had.

It all sounded like participatory democracy to me. More interesting, however, was the near-universal claim that the underlying impetus for May 1968 had more to do with happiness, quality of life, and relations between people than with narrow economic concerns. People were sick of humdrum routines and the increasing personal isolation that broke down communities. They wanted more autonomy, involvement, gratification, friendship, meaning, creativity, beauty, and fun. If anything, rather than an episode of labor unrest, May 1968 had been a spiritual uprising, perhaps the first on such a large scale in an industrialized society.

Anne-Marie explained that during the uprising many services, like food distribution and transportation, were paralyzed. In response, neighbors formed self-help groups to get essential work done. Some Parisians were frightened by the disorder. Others embraced the disruption and chaos, marched in demonstrations, joined street parties and spontaneous celebrations, and generally had positive experiences working alongside total strangers. But it could not go on indefinitely. May 1968 had been spontaneous. No preparations for civil administration had been made. Eventually, the strikers relinquished control of the factories, the students gave up the Sorbonne, and the de Gaulle government survived another crisis.

But the Parisians had spread a subversive vision across the globe. Unsuccessful in the short run, they had pointed the way toward a nonviolent means of transforming society and modifying the capitalist order. Two facts stood out for me. First, when enough people decided it was time for a change, government was swept aside quickly and with relative ease. Second, if the problems of civil administration had been planned for in advance, there was sufficient energy and creativity to have sustained the situation much longer.

Did that mean revolutionary change was possible? In the United States, it could never happen through violent means, but if change as fundamental as what had briefly occurred in France could be brought about without violence, the situation in the United States might not be as hopeless as I had thought. I realized, of course, that we were decades away from being able to replicate their experience, but eight years before in Paris I had thought we were a century away from being able to depose a president. In the interval I had seen how rapidly history can move, and how unpredictable its moves can be. Perhaps it was too soon to give up on change.

Feeling slightly more optimistic, I thanked Anne-Marie for her time and her insights and boarded a southbound train. My plan was to disappear for two months, find a beach, live simply, read a lot, and pay no attention to the news. Anne-Marie's friends had recommended Tunisia in North Africa because the people there were especially friendly. This was a time when Westerners could still travel freely in Islamic countries without encountering the pervasive hostility that later became commonplace. Tunisia was inexpensive, and as an added bonus I would see the Sahara Desert, a region that had always fascinated me.

The trip was a vacation, but I did have an agenda. The most interesting slogan from the May 1968 uprising was *"Sous les pavés, la plage."* Literally translated, it meant "Under the paving stones, the beach."

Alliteration made it sound more elegant in French. The paving stones, similar to our cobblestones, were pried up during demonstrations and hurled at the gendarmes or made into barricades, so there was another layer of meaning not apparent in the translation. The slogan captured what I wanted to learn that summer. How much of our inherent humanity had civilization paved over, and at what cost to our nature and the manner in which we lived in the natural world? Could we still connect to what was underneath, and if so, how?

I had asked my students to read unorthodox books that provoked similar questions. R. D. Laing argued in *The Politics of Experience* that a society based on greed and competition so distorted natural human instincts that a kind of insanity was required to function within it. Those labeled insane by such a society were reflecting the collective insanity of the social order. Norman O. Brown, in *Life Against Death*, eloquently argued against the repression of spontaneity, joy, sex, fun, creativity, and adventure as our culture squeezes us into a common mold and trains us from first grade to sit still and follow orders.

In a third book, *Eros and Civilization*, which I planned to reread, Herbert Marcuse had taken Sigmund Freud's most insightful work, *Civilization and Its Discontents*, and fused it with Marxist thought. Instead of psychological constructs to explain how civilization repressed basic human instincts and redirected them into the greed and competition that drove society forward, Marcuse combined a hard-nosed economic analysis with Freud's psychology to discuss the same repression in more objective terms. Freud had tried to understand the phenomenon; Marcuse looked for a path to liberation, a way to bring our instincts for life and love and sex and procreation together with a revolutionary agenda for rebuilding civilization, not on the basis of greed and competition, but rather for the benefit and pleasure of all.

The hippies advocated escape from greed and competition by dropping out. Whatever might be lost materially would be gained through increased freedom. If friendship, community, creativity, and a natural lifestyle had more value than a new car or stylish clothes, one could step off the career track, discard the stress, get a simple job, pool expenses, and live a life organized around pleasure rather than ambition. Colin Turnbull's

Forest People described the happy social egalitarianism of the Pygmy people in Africa, and the writings of Margaret Mead and Ruth Benedict (not yet discredited as they were later) portrayed blissful living in various Polynesian cultures. Noncompetitive, cooperative societies free from psychological repression had survived and were theoretically possible.

The question for me was whether or not such a society could exist in the modern world, and if so, how to create it. The hippies believed that change happens one person at a time. I believed that change happened on a larger scale. But I was confused about the way forward, and I questioned my own beliefs. Having always been a person of strong opinions, I was no longer sure I had any answers. I intended to isolate myself from worldly concerns and use my free time over the summer to find some. I wanted to get under my own pavement, as well as civilization's, and see what beaches might lie beneath.

Two hours off the plane in Tunis, capital city of Tunisia, I was thrilled to have come to North Africa. I was outside Western civilization once again. The clothing was different, the architecture, the food, the stores, even the sounds and smells were unfamiliar. Years later, such places would acquire American fast-food restaurants and TV sets blaring Hollywood sitcoms. But in 1968, little of that was true. North Africa still retained its historically unique culture, which so captivated me that I spent three days just wandering around Tunis. I walked the winding streets of the Kasbah, bargained with the local merchants, ate Middle Eastern food, and learned about the rest of the country. Then I stuck out my thumb and hitchhiked south.

The Mediterranean coast, running west to east across the top of Africa, turns south at Tunis for some 250 miles before turning east again at the Libyan border and the city of Tripoli. At that turn in the coastline, a peninsula, Île de Djerba, juts into the Mediterranean. It's called an island, but it's connected to the mainland by a thin spit of land and a road bridge. I had learned that Djerba was inexpensive and had great beaches and friendly people. I hitchhiked toward it with the sea to my left and the edge of the great desert on my right.

I got a few rides from trucks deadheading back to the countryside after hauling produce to Tunis. On the morning of the second day, a VW bus stopped. Inside were a young Dutch couple, Luc and Vera, and their infant son. Like most Dutch, they spoke fluent English, and they told me they had sold what they owned to go off on an African adventure. Dutch hippies in Africa; the world had changed indeed. I told them about Djerba, and they were intrigued enough to want to look themselves. We arrived at night, got beds in a cheap rooming house, and spent the next day inspecting Houmt Souk, the little town in the center of the peninsula.

Houmt Souk was eight blocks long and built around a marketplace and central square. A few of the streets were paved, but most were sand. One-story houses covered with white plaster were the rule. We saw few cars but a great many camels. The men wore traditional Arab dress. Some women were veiled and covered head to toe; others were robed but not veiled. Half a mile away, the beaches along the coast were pristine, deserted, and beautiful. The remainder of the peninsula was empty desert, although some fifteen miles distant there was a resort that catered to German and Scandinavian tourists.

Luc, Vera, and I loved the place and wanted to stay, so I suggested we rent a house for two months. A couple of days later we found one. It had four almost windowless rooms built around a central open area, which itself was no bigger than another room. The open area was paved and sloped very slightly down to a drain in the center. It and the roofs of the rooms around it served as water collectors on the rare days when rain fell. The open area doubled as a roofless living room. The drain in the center fed a cistern below from which we drew our water.

We slept soundly the first night, but were rudely awakened by loud bells very early the next morning. They seemed to be directly outside our windows. We ran outside to investigate. Camels! Lots of them! Bedouins coming from the countryside to sell produce and other goods in the market rode into town every morning. Bells of various sizes and shapes hung from their camels. We had indeed left Western civilization! The bells became our alarm clock. We awoke to their sound every morning afterward.

That first day in the house, I volunteered to shop for food while Luc and Vera fixed a space for the baby. I strolled through the open-air market, bought vegetables, fruits, and some dairy, but I could not find meat. Using my limited French, I asked after the butcher and was directed to a folding table upon which lay several strips of what appeared to be burned meat, black all over. I asked the Bedouin behind the table if he had any fresh red meat, and he answered, "You want red meat? Of course, here is plenty." He then waved his hand over the black strips, which magically transformed to red as the innumerable flies perched on top rose and flew away. I swallowed hard, thanked the Bedouin for his effort, and walked on. The few other butcher tables in the market enjoyed the same arrangement with the flies. The meat was goat or camel, not very appetizing to begin with, so back at the house Luc, Vera, and I agreed to get our protein from dairy and be vegetarians for the summer.

My time in Houmt Souk was like a dream of paradise. The camels woke me in the morning. I ate breakfast with Luc and Vera and then walked alone to the beach. Inside my backpack I had water, food, a book, usually Marcuse's, and a bedspread to lie on. I walked three to five miles along the beach never seeing another human being. When I found a lone palm tree for protection from the summer sun, I settled in for several hours and read or snorkeled. I had brought a diving mask and snorkel and a folding Hawaiian sling for spearfishing, but unlike in the Caribbean there were no coral reefs or abundant fish. Nevertheless, the water was warm and clear, and I found enough fish to occasionally supplement our vegetarian diet. When I was ready, I hiked back in the still-blazing sun, stopping occasionally to cool off in the water.

During the six weeks I spent there, that routine was broken only once, by naked ladies. One afternoon, returning home along the beach, I saw far in front of me that Bedouins had walked their camels into the sea for a bath. As I got closer, I could see that the camels were not the only ones bathing. A group of women, from children to older matrons, were frolicking naked in the water. No men were in sight. I knew I had to get out of there, fast. Given how the Bedouins covered their women, I could not imagine offending them more than by eyeballing their wives, daughters, and mothers in the nude. I imagined desert warriors galloping down on me with curved swords flashing in the sun, intent on having my head. I turned ninety degrees and walked straight back into the desert away from the sea. I hoped my route would signal a lack of interest to anyone standing guard nearby. After a half mile, I turned parallel to the shore and continued, nervously looking over my shoulder until I was well clear of the naked ladies.

Typically, when I got back to the house, Luc, Vera, and I cooked a big meal, ate in the roofless central room, and, full and happy, lay back on floor cushions for a siesta. As the day ended and the temperature fell, I showered, dressed, and walked to the center of town. The Tunisians in Houmt Souk were gentle and friendly. I never encountered hostility or hustlers trying to sell me goods I did not want. At sunset, young boys appeared with little clusters of jasmine flowers tied together into a bundle the size of a carnation. The men strolling through town bought these little bundles for a penny, carried them at their sides, and occasionally held them up to smell the jasmine. I did the same. The intermittent whiff of the flower's perfume slowed me down and allowed me to appreciate the beauty around me. I was completely at peace.

Djerba was idyllic, but the questions I had come with were not answered. My life there, combined with the reading and thinking I had done, left me wondering if I could live that way permanently. I was not sure I wanted to, but I was tempted and was left with a nagging curiosity. I thought that at some point, I should try. Otherwise, I would never know if my attachment to civilization was real or just an arbitrary consequence of where I had been born and raised. In the meantime, I was ready to resume the life I had been living. I looked forward to research in the fall and the work of scientific inquiry that had so motivated me in graduate school.

There was a tiny travel office in Houmt Souk where I had seen a sign advertising a new airline link between Tunis and Prague, which was not far from my father's birthplace. I had always wanted to see it, so I decided to end my summer by spending a week there. The night before buying my ticket, I got a telegram from Chicago. My mother, who suffered from a chronic debilitating disease, had taken a turn for the worse. My father asked me to return immediately. The next day I left for Paris, where I had to spend the night before flying on. Taking advantage of being back in the West, I went to a restaurant and ordered the thickest steak on the menu. I cut the first piece with relish, but when I put it into my mouth, I found it repulsive. It would be months before I was comfortable eating meat again.

The next morning, as I boarded the Chicago-bound plane, I saw headlines in the Paris newspapers announcing the Soviet invasion of Czechoslovakia. Russian tanks were rolling into Prague and violently suppressing a new government that had tried to increase freedoms and loosen their more repressive Soviet-inspired policies. The glimmer of hope from behind the Iron Curtain known as the Prague Spring was dying under a hail of Soviet bullets. I had been saved from landing in the middle of it, but simultaneously condemned to be in Chicago during the Democratic convention.

My mother's illness, which affected the nerves in her spinal cord, had progressed and left her unable to walk. She required full-time nursing care, which my father at seventy-six was unable to provide. My father, my sister, Robin, and I spent several days looking for a decent nursing home. The suitable ones were too expensive, and given what we could afford, the remaining choices were only barely acceptable. These facilities were generally clean and able to care for basic needs, but little was done to provide patients with distraction, amusement, or recreation. Given my mother's grim prognosis, the nursing home we selected would likely be where she would die. I was frustrated and ashamed. My mother was going to be warehoused, not attended to with concern and consideration, and there was nothing I could do about it. I was relieved that her life was not yet in danger, but furious that proper care was financially beyond our reach.

During the week prior to the Democratic convention, I helped Robin and my father make arrangements and move my mother into the nursing home. It was a sad and trying time for all of us, and I paid little attention to the gathering storm at the center of the city. The convention would not formally open until Monday, August 26, but delegates and demonstrators assembled the previous weekend. The former went to their hotels, the latter to Grant Park. On the city's lakefront opposite the downtown skyscrapers, the park was the ideal campsite for the protesters. Mayor Daley, without justification, refused to give them a permit. They set up camp anyway.

I went to Grant Park several times over the weekend, drawn to the action like a moth to a flame. Protesters marched, held training sessions, and staged concerts. Some prepared for battle with the police. I moved in and out of these events as an observer only, which was all I wanted to be.

On Sunday night, for no apparent reason, police insisted that Grant Park be vacated at the 11:00 p.m. curfew. There were thousands present. I was not among them, but I heard later that the cops pushed them all onto a nearby street and, once cornered, waded into the crowd and viciously attacked them with clubs. Some protesters formed small groups, used hit-and-run tactics, and fought back. The cops, unused to people fighting back, became even more ferocious.

The police had been provoked, not on Sunday night, but earlier. The yippies had threatened to lace the city's water supply with LSD and engage in other exotic acts of sabotage. They had no capacity to carry out these threats, but they got the sensational publicity they wanted. Apparently, some cops took their preposterous threats seriously and rose to defend their families and neighbors. The politicians who controlled the cops, desperate to protect the convention and the city's image, happily allowed the police to use excessive force against the demonstrators, not understanding that this would destroy the city's image. Most of the pro-testers were battle hardened and ready to resist. It was a riot waiting to hap-pen, and the few pacifist groups who came simply to demonstrate were caught in the middle.

Very late Sunday night, a friend called. Ron Chutter was in jail in a North Side precinct and needed bail money. He had been one of those forced out of the park. Ron was the friend Scott and I had gone to Europe with in 1960. When I arrived at the station house, other protesters were being processed out. I got a good look at all the head injuries that had been inflicted. Bloodstained shirts were everywhere. The cops in the sta-tion house either laughed at the injured or tried to provoke them with insults and profanities.

When the convention opened on Monday, I could not bring myself to just sit and watch, so I reluctantly joined the demonstrations. First we marched on police headquarters to protest the previous night's arrests. Then we marched back to the park and gathered on a small hill under a statue of a soldier on horseback. The cops swarmed into the park to clear the hill. It was an unprovoked and brutal attack, as would be revealed later when pictures of the battle around the statue were published. I dodged the cops, avoided the front lines, and eventually fled.

Later that night, I went back. At the 11:00 p.m. curfew, a large number of demonstrators again refused to leave the park. The cops attacked. In addition to nightsticks, they used a lot of tear gas. It was another bloodbath. I fled with others into the city, but this time the cops chased us. Once on city streets, they couldn't tell the difference between protesters and nonparticipating citizens. Driven by their anger and outrage, they essentially declared war on anyone young who had long hair. As I moved around avoiding them, I saw cops attack innocent people on the street and pull others off their porches. Later I learned that reporters covering the action had received similar treatment.

The next day, I watched a variety of groups march and protest. Anarchists taunted the police, while civil rights activists, clergymen, and pacifists marched peacefully. Daley would not let anyone near the convention. Gradually, the focus of news coverage changed. Instead of the story being convention disputes about the war, or the contest for the presidential nomination, the coverage shifted to police tactics and Daley's dictatorial control. Reporters had rarely been the targets of indiscriminate police brutality. They reacted angrily, which turned public opinion against the cops. A few convention delegates joined the protesters, while others expressed outrage at the police tactics. The image of the United States was not enhanced, either at home or abroad, when pictures of street violence in Chicago were compared with pictures taken the previous week in Czechoslovakia.

On Tuesday there was less violence. Daley backed off that night and allowed protesters to sleep in the park. On Wednesday, I joined a crowd of about fifteen thousand for an antiwar rally addressed by several well-known speakers. Inside the convention, some delegates tried to insert a peace plank into the party platform. When it was voted down and the news reached us at the rally, a few protesters lowered a nearby American flag and replaced it with a bloodstained shirt. That set off the cops. They charged the crowd and beat people viciously. As we dispersed, National Guardsmen wielding machine guns blocked the streets. Many protesters were trapped near the Hilton hotel, where most of the press was headquartered. The police beatings there were filmed and shown repeatedly on the news. I had had enough street fighting and had fled to sit out the last day of the convention in my father's apartment. With Daley's support and that of the other traditional Democrats, Hubert Humphrey easily defeated Eugene McCarthy for the nomination and the privilege of running against Richard Nixon in November.

Roughly ten thousand demonstrators had come to Chicago, and perhaps ten thousand more joined them from the city itself. Over twenty-six thousand police and National Guardsmen confronted them. It was a relatively low turnout for the antiwar movement, but it elicited a massive police overreaction witnessed by the national press corps. The events in Chicago became a turning point in the fight to end the war. Images of armed troops and police in the streets of the United States, and the pitched and bloody battles between them and thousands of protesters, were seared into the American psyche and would remain there for some time. It was a turning point for me as well.

The rush of events since the Tet Offensive, the assassinations of King and Kennedy, the urban riots, and Paris, Prague, and Chicago convinced me that American society and government needed more than reform. Stopping the war was not enough; we needed to start over and build a new and equitable society. I didn't care who was in the White House. We had to overturn the social order, just as the French had tried to do. It may sound farfetched today, but many of us saw no alternative after Chicago but to commit ourselves to revolutionary change.

We had no choice: the society we wanted could only be achieved through a revolutionary transformation. But what kind of revolution? It would not be one in which industrial workers or landless peasants take up arms, as they had in Russia, China, and Cuba. Our industrial workers were too conservative and had too deeply bought into the current economic system. Some activists argued that students or youth could be the basis of a revolutionary movement; I thought that was wishful thinking.

Marx had provided a vocabulary for understanding revolution, but his aging analysis did not reveal how to create one in a modern industrial society. As I pondered these questions, others in the antiwar movement accepted Marxist doctrine with the uncritical enthusiasm of zealots. They embraced the communist label, called themselves Marxist revolutionaries, and met frequently to discuss theory and practice. I thought they were a little delusional. I also thought that the job of a revolutionary was to make a revolution, not merely join a debating club with the same name. I saw such people as posturing. Some of them tried to shame the rest of us into accepting their views by living among the poor workers they sought to organize and sacrificing more of their already limited creature comforts as a sign of their commitment. I thought rather than the renunciation of personal comforts, the object of a revolution was to provide them for everyone.

Nevertheless, a revolution of some sort seemed to me to be essential. I differed with others about its nature and practicality, but I viewed the priorities and power relationships in society to be so misconstrued that nothing short of a revolution would be an effective remedy. I knew we could not blindly follow past revolutionary models, in which starving and homeless workers or peasants with nothing left to lose take up arms against a dictatorial state. We had to invent a new model, the most crucial element of which was a nonviolent strategy. The power and surveillance capacity of the state had grown too large to even contemplate its violent overthrow. Revolutionary change in the United States would bring enormous conflict but could only be achieved through a general strike or other essentially nonviolent tactics, and only if an overwhelming majority supported the change. Otherwise, it would be merely suicidal.

I returned to Brooklyn College and watched the presidential election unfold. The turmoil around the Democratic convention left Humphrey with vastly reduced support. Nixon surged in the polls. Humphrey had an enviable record as a senator and a local official in Minnesota and had been one of the nation's strongest advocates for civil rights legislation. However, when Johnson offered him the vice presidency, he sold his soul to get it. For people who thought as I did, the sight of this liberal stalwart becoming a cheerleader for a war he must have known was wrong turned him into an object of ridicule and scorn.

Humphrey personified liberals who gave lip service to principle but turned their backs whenever the cost was too high or the risk too great. He helped turn the word "liberal" into an insult within the antiwar movement. We often expressed more contempt for liberals than for the die-hard conservatives who at least remained true to their values. For this reason, few hard-core antiwar activists like me could bring themselves to support or even vote for Humphrey. Admittedly, that was a strategic capitulation, not a strategy.

Troop strength in Viet Nam had increased to half a million. There were over thirty thousand U.S. dead. Not surprisingly, Nixon campaigned for "law and order." Humphrey was unwilling to oppose the war until days before the election, afraid that Johnson would contradict any peace proposals he put forward. Halloween weekend, Johnson announced a bombing halt. By then, the United States had dropped one million tons of bombs on North Viet Nam. The bombing halt gave a last-minute boost to Humphrey's candidacy, but it was too late. Nixon prevailed by a mere 0.7 percent of the vote, garnering only 43.4 percent to Humphrey's 42.7 percent.

The remaining vote went to a third-party segregationist candidate, former Democrat George Wallace, the past and future governor of Alabama. He actually carried five southern states. Wallace had gained fame by blocking racial integration in Alabama. White Southerners gave him their votes in droves, in part to repudiate Johnson's leadership on civil rights. Without those Wallace votes, and absent earlier opposition to the war, Humphrey faltered.

Wallace's vote deepened the cultural divide first created by the civil rights and antiwar movements. Whites in the South, and white working-class people elsewhere, were alienated from these movements but found it hard to support Republicans they knew to be the servants of big business. Wallace was an acceptable populist alternative and served as a political halfway house for these voters. Years later, many were gullible enough to be taken in by Ronald Reagan's superior communications skills. They shifted to the Republicans in the 1980 election and emerged as the so-called Reagan Democrats. Their support for Republican policies they had opposed since the Great Depression, policies counter to their economic interests, was based on the false hope that Reagan could resurrect their old way of life, before they lost their children to sex, drugs, and rock and roll. Cultural nostalgia trumped economic self-interest. A new conservative age was born; it would darken the American landscape for another three decades.

CHAPTER 11

THE MURDEROUS GROUND WAR IN VIET NAM CONTINUED. DURING THE 1968 PRESIDEN-
tial campaign, the antiwar movement scheduled no large-scale protests.
But while protest was temporarily diminished, resistance to the war
increased. Thousands of draft cards were burned or sent back to draft
boards. Thousands of young men refused induction to face exile in
Canada or jail in America. I was not part of this, as I was unwilling to urge
young men to resist the draft or desert; I had never endured the sacrifices
those choices required and thought it arrogant for me to do so.

For the first time since the Civil War, active-duty military personnel
deserted in large numbers. Sweden, especially, opened its borders to
deserters, and many soldiers and Marines unwilling to risk death and kill
innocents in Viet Nam reluctantly renounced their American citizenship
and went there. Desertion rates were hidden then, but in 1974, when
President Ford offered clemency to draft resisters and deserters, an incred-
ible 350,000 were declared eligible. Most were resisters. However, the
Army reported that it had 33,000 deserters in 1971 alone. During the first
two and a half years of the Iraq war, there were 8,000 desertions. The military was reluctant to allow new recruits to discover how often their comrades ran off.

At Brooklyn College, I continued teaching and prepared for the sleep
research I had put on hold the previous year. I still thought it intellectually dishonest to teach my psychology courses in the traditional fashion.

The world had gone a little crazy, and I thought the academic discipline of psychology should help students understand why. I continued to use unorthodox material in my lectures and often talked about world events and social, rather than individual, pathology in my classes. The students responded well. They knew they had much to learn about the topsy-turvy world they would soon have to join.

I also studied brain chemistry. Neurotransmitters, the chemicals that carry impulses across the synapses between neurons in the brain, had been discovered, and new findings in the field were being made with great frequency. I had no training in this discipline but thought it would be the key to understanding the brain's regulation of sleep and dreams, and eventually the larger question about the purpose of sleep itself. I overcame my lack of training first by reading and then by collaborating closely with Bart Meyers, who was an expert in the field.

As Bart and I planned our joint research, he got a troubling reprint request. In the days before e-mail and digital word processing, it was common for one scientist to ask another for a printed copy of published research. Scientists received stacks of reprints from journals that published their work. Other scientists who wanted a copy for their files requested these reprints. Before modern information technology, this slow system was all we had. What troubled us about the particular request Bart received was that it came from Fort Detrick, Maryland.

We knew that Fort Detrick was the center for U.S. Army research on chemical and biological weapons. Seymour Hersh, a young reporter who would become one of the country's leading investigative journalists, had described it in a recent book, *Chemical and Biological Warfare: America's Hidden Arsenal*. Hersh's book had caused a minor sensation merely by revealing that the United States still conducted such research. Most Americans thought it was, or should be, a war crime to do so.

We made some discreet inquiries. Why was a scientist at Fort Detrick interested in Bart's work? The study he requested had focused on a common brain chemical, an amine. Bart had manipulated the amine's concentration in the brains of monkeys and observed the impact on learning behavior. Unknown to him at the time, that particular amine could neutralize the Army's nerve gas. Scientists at Fort Detrick were developing a new nerve gas not so easily neutralized. They were collecting all available knowledge about the chemical Bart had studied. If they succeeded, we had no doubt the nerve gas would end up in Viet Nam.

Nerve gas! Bart's research was helping, however indirectly, to make nerve gas! And he could do nothing to stop it. The research had already been published and was in the public domain. The request for the reprint was merely a formality, since the library at Fort Detrick no doubt had a copy of the journal in which it appeared. Nerve gas! As scientists, we had naively assumed we could control our work and the uses to which it was put. Here was the first test. It was hard to imagine a more fundamental violation of what Bart and I thought we stood for.

Nerve gas was bad enough, but its potential use in Viet Nam made us crazy. We spent our time organizing against the war, at BC and elsewhere. How could we fight the war with one hand and contribute to it with the other? How could we allow our work to advance a war we both despised, and in a manner so inherently contemptible it was by any reasonable standard a war crime? The war had already turned us into good Germans. Now we were being set up as the modern equivalent of the nuclear physicists whose work had resulted in the atomic bomb.

My scientific training had not encouraged me to think about how the basic research I did might be applied by others. Neither had I been smart enough to consider the issue on my own. Scientific culture draws a sharp line between the work of scientists and the work of engineers. Scientists do "basic research" to discover how the natural world works, as Bart had done with the brain amine and learning behavior. This presumably pure pursuit of truth is done with no thought of future application. Engineers do "applied research" by taking the scientists' discoveries and figuring out how to use them, whether in medicine, communications, transportation . . . or weapons technology.

Bart and I were paralyzed. We had no idea what to do. We faced questions we should have thought about years before. What was the role of the scientist in society? What new knowledge could be entrusted to a society organized around greed and competition, and that still used war to solve its problems? What knowledge was too dangerous to entrust to them? Who decides? Was any institution in society able to make these judgments?

Would such decisions be governed by the right values? Should scientists themselves have a role?

We started reading, voraciously. Albert Einstein and the nuclear physicists of the early twentieth century were the first place we looked. Their discoveries enabled the engineers of the Manhattan Project in the 1940s to construct the nuclear weapons that had come to threaten the survival of the human species. Indeed, Einstein had written to President Roosevelt encouraging him to develop the atomic bomb before the Nazis did. But later Einstein and other nuclear pioneers pointed to the danger of nuclear proliferation and worked diligently to stop it, unfortunately to no avail. Would we, the biological scientists of the 1960s, suffer the same fate?

Evidence that our society could not be entrusted with the knowledge necessary to make nerve gas was right in front of us: it had already made nerve gas and was ready to use it on human beings. Should we withhold new knowledge that could be used to "improve" nerve gas and other weapons of mass destruction? Yes, certainly, from our point of view, but how? If we stopped or withheld our research, would not other scientists just pick up where we had left off?

Gradually, we zeroed in on the key question: Was the search for new knowledge truly a pure and noble pursuit, or was it polluted by the ostensible goals of the society in which the new knowledge was developed?

Bart and I knew that scientific research had always, by necessity, been an open book. From the beginnings of experimental science in Europe hundreds of years ago, the publication of research results was essential to progress. Wide-ranging contributions move science forward. No scientist wants to waste effort in pursuit of answers others already have, so it is to the advantage of all that results are freely published. Research done in secret is almost always on applications, not basic principles.

We discovered that some very famous scientists had indeed withheld their work in situations similar to ours. No less a figure than Leonardo da Vinci refused to publish plans for a submarine in the sixteenth century for fear it would be used as a weapon. In the seventeenth century, for the same reason, Robert Boyle, the father of modern chemistry, kept secret a poison he had developed. However, these were engineering projects, not basic research, because basic research does not allow for predictions about the applications that might flow from it. Witness the nuclear physicists who made their basic discoveries long before anyone could anticipate using them to manufacture world-killing weapons.

We thought about redirecting our research onto less dangerous terrain. Leo Szilard, one of the nuclear physicists who had developed the atomic bomb, provided an unfortunate example. He quit physics in disgust when he saw how recklessly governments had used the new weapon, and shifted to biology. Yet twenty years later biology had become a new source of weapons technology.

The eminent plant biologist Arthur Galston had discovered in the 1940s that a chemical capable of regulating plant growth could induce soybeans to grow more rapidly, thus increasing crop yields. He also found that if large amounts of this chemical were used, the plant would grow too fast, lose its leaves, and die. Other researchers then used this discovery to develop a powerful defoliant. After further refinements, including adding the highly toxic chemical dioxin, Dow Chemical and Monsanto marketed the defoliant to the U.S. military as Agent Orange. Galston, horrified at the damage Agent Orange did to humans and to the environment, campaigned vigorously against its continuing use in Viet Nam.

I had once wanted to research sleep in dolphins. Surely, dolphins were free from weapons applications. Not so. Our reading revealed that the U.S. Navy had trained dolphins to discriminate underwater between U.S. and Soviet submarines. In response to certain signals, they were trained to swim directly into the Soviet subs. Why? Because they had bombs strapped on their backs. If war broke out, the Navy would be ready with kamikaze dolphins.

In graduate school, Al Rechtschaffen and I had done a few small studies on how psychoactive drugs affected sleep and dreaming. Other scientists were investigating LSD and mescaline to promote psychotherapy, or to research the underlying causes of mental illness. Was this area safe from military application? No, again. Rumors among scientists, verified later by congressional investigators, indicated that the CIA had used these drugs in combination with sleep deprivation or water boarding to destabilize prisoners being tortured for information. The conclusion was inescapable. Scientists doing basic research could not anticipate how their work might later be used and had no ability to control it.

What was the alternative? If scientists simply halted research, progress would stop. I didn't want to stop doing research, not after finally finding a calling that had inspired me and that I had worked so diligently to prepare for over the previous five years. There had to be a middle ground, but neither Bart nor I could find it. We felt we had to at least temporarily suspend our own research and take some time assessing our next move.

Meanwhile, other troubling questions affected the antiwar movement. Nixon's election had been a depressing watershed. The war would go on indefinitely, and the movement had to resolve its many ideological and tactical disagreements to meet the challenge. Those who wanted to narrowly focus on the war gradually gave way to others determined to also work against racism and poverty. However, new struggles demanded our attention. Women in the movement emphasized gender oppression, outside *and* inside the left. Environmental concerns emerged. Gay rights were talked about. And other minorities organized alongside blacks and demanded their rights.

Sympathy grew for the troops. Some saw them as villains, while many of us argued that they, too, were victims of the war and potential allies against it. There were bitter disagreements about whether protests should remain within the law or violate it. Revolutionary ideology played a corrosive role. Political sects and small factions insisted they each were the true vanguard of the revolution and anyone failing to follow their leadership was irrelevant at best and a traitor at worst. Long-standing friendships were broken by abstract arguments and arcane disputes. The year 1968 had been momentous for our country and the world, but it had left the antiwar movement without unity or strategic direction. Our weakness was underscored in January. I went to Washington to protest Nixon's inauguration, but few were there to protest with me.

The twin anchors of my life, scientific research and antiwar activism, were in disarray. Not knowing where to turn, I fled from both. I flew rented airplanes whenever possible, dated frequently, and hung out in Greenwich Village. At the Fillmore East, which had opened the previous spring, I saw concerts by the Grateful Dead, the Jefferson Airplane, Janis Joplin, Jimi Hendrix, Country Joe and the Fish, and others. A college friend, David Steinberg, had become a successful stand-up comic, and I often went to nightclubs in the Village to see him perform. He opened once for Joni Mitchell, and we spent a night hanging out with her and a relatively unknown singer-songwriter named Leonard Cohen.

Despite the distractions, political and otherwise, nagging questions about scientific research followed me everywhere. Bart and I focused on Einstein and Szilard. They had tried for years to stuff the nuclear genie back into the bottle but with no success. How could they or anyone live with guilt of that magnitude? If the government already had facilities committed to chemical and biological warfare research, biological scientists would soon be victimized in the same way. We were determined not to be among them.

We soon realized, however, that basic research with weapons applications was only part of the problem. Starting in the 1950s, the massive Cold War expansion of the military-industrial complex had dramatically increased the influence big corporations exerted over government and the economy. Those corporations also benefited from scientific research. If science and society were inextricably linked, the products of science had to serve the larger goals of society. Under American capitalism, those larger goals were clear enough: the pursuit of corporate and individual profits and the acquisition of sufficient military power to protect them. Bart and I believed that corporate influence undermined democracy and increased class differences, which led to poverty and unnecessary suffering. Were we willing to do research that would increase corporate power by increasing corporate wealth?

The green crop revolution, instigated in part by Arthur Galston's discovery of a plant growth hormone, provides an illustration of this problem. Basic research in plant genetics and agronomy by Galston and others led to super strains of cereal crops capable of alleviating hunger in undeveloped countries. However, in many areas expensive fertilizers were required to grow the new crop strains. Few of the local farmers could afford them. Those who could were able to compete more effectively.

They drove the others deeper into poverty. In the end, the research led to more profit for global chemical companies and wider class differences for local farmers.

Another illustration came from psychology. A few years earlier, researchers had discovered that if an infant's environment were enriched with a variety of shapes, colors, and patterns, intelligence would increase. It was a wonderful discovery, and it led to all the stimulating mobiles that now adorn infant cribs around the world. But Bart and I knew that toy companies were marketing these items, and that the first parents to use them were those who could afford the toys. Poor people in the United States and elsewhere would lag behind, and the gap between them and the rich, this time of intelligence, would increase.

We understood that new discoveries often alleviate suffering and improve quality of life, but when they are marketed for profit within a capitalist system, the benefits are always distributed unequally. Did we want to be part of a system in which profit always took precedence over people? We imagined some disturbing scenarios. The first successful surgical heart transplant had occurred less than a year before. As transplant technology developed, we guessed that economic necessity would one day force the poor to sell their organs to the rich. We were right. Today it is commonplace for the poor in undeveloped countries to sell kidneys, parts of livers, and even corneas in order to survive.

These were not abstract musings. Our lives and careers depended upon the conclusions we reached. Aiding, however indirectly, the economic exploitation that resulted from corporate power disturbed us, but scientific research could not be isolated from that exploitation. The ability to engineer new discoveries into new products depends on money and resources. The institutions with the most resources inevitably are first to take advantage of new knowledge: the military, the government, the big corporations. We scientists are free to happily pursue truth and remain aloof from concerns about how our discoveries are applied, while others with very different values are likely to be first to use those discoveries for their own purposes.

Bart and I did not want to stop scientific research. We wanted to provoke an open discussion about the connections between science and society. Would it not make more sense to set outcome goals in advance and do the research necessary to reach them? Perhaps it was time to retire the noble fiction of "pure" or "basic" research, and focus on research needed to solve societal problems. We wanted to provoke more science for the people and less science for the corporations and the military.

I took a closer look at sleep research. I had thought its first application would be a cure for schizophrenia, but more likely it would lead to improved sleeping pills, giving pharmaceutical corporations huge profits. People with sleep disorders would benefit, but the drug companies were among the leading opponents of universal health care, which would drive down their profits. Giving them billions more in revenue meant they would spend a portion to block health-care reform. Sleep research might also help put astronauts into suspended animation on long space voyages, and in so doing prop up a government space program that I felt was diverting billions from more pressing needs at home. I realized that eventually even a cure for schizophrenia could have a similar outcome.

I had no religion or guiding ideology, but I wanted my life to have value and meaning. Fighting for justice had given me that, and the rewards were immediate and palpable. If I tried to get the same benefit from scientific research, I would be constantly looking over my shoulder and wondering what others might eventually do with my work.

It was the defining moral crisis of my life. Agonizing over it for months, Bart and I finally decided that we had to do what the nuclear physicists on both sides of World War II should have done—refuse to develop any new knowledge that could lead to weapons of mass destruction. Scientists had to put society before science, and if it had to start with us, so be it. We in the scientific community were obligated to first help build a more equitable and mature society. Only then could new knowledge be developed without risk. Reluctantly, with great anger and even greater fear, we understood that we not only had to give up our research careers but also had to do it publicly and urge other scientists to take the same step.

We announced our decision to our faculty colleagues in the psychology department. Some were mystified by our reasoning or stupefied by how far we had taken it. Not sharing our politics, they could not follow our logic, and not sharing our values, they could not understand our commitment. They reacted furiously, feeling with some justification that our decision was an attack on their own work. We knew that in their eyes we had taken a step from which there would be no return. We also knew that everyone in psychology and the larger community of science would condemn and punish us in the strongest possible way. We waited for the other shoe to drop, and we contacted other young scientists who had supported the antiwar movement to see if any agreed with us or were open to our point of view.

Meanwhile, one exception to the ideological bickering dragging down the antiwar movement was draft counseling. Across the country left-wing lawyers and legal workers were counseling young men about the draft laws. Some sought advice about conscientious objector status in order to work in medical facilities or other noncombat roles. Some wanted to know how to renounce their citizenship and flee the country, or refuse induction and face prison or exile. The lawyers did not advocate particular actions. They simply explained procedures and implications. I decided to help. Nonlegal people like me publicized the service and got enough training in draft law to steer individuals to the counselors best suited to their needs.

In late January, I invited a young woman I had been dating to move in with me. Janice was a firebrand, smart, dark haired, energetic, and fun loving. She shared my politics and quickly came to like Bart and my other friends. She put me to work redecorating my apartment. She also played guitar, and with it brought more music into my life.

One night, Janice came home distraught. Her close friend Jake was in trouble with the Army. He had seen a psychiatrist who for $50 gave him a letter stating that he was psychotically depressed and unfit for military service. Jake submitted the letter to the Army, but it wanted to verify the diagnosis before exempting him from military service. An Army psychiatrist would administer a Rorschach test the following Saturday. Janice was afraid Jake would end up dead in Viet Nam and asked if I could help.

The Rorschach, or inkblot, test was one of the reasons I had decided not to become a psychotherapist. Despite widespread use, it has no actual validity. Jake arrived at our apartment the next day. I pulled out my copy of the test and told him I would prepare a set of responses to the inkblots that would verify the diagnosis of psychotic depression. His job would be to memorize those responses, rehearse the dramatic emotional reactions that were expected to go with them, as an actor would do, and then play the whole rehearsed fraud back to the Army psychiatrist on Saturday. Jake, happy to learn the secrets of the Rorschach test, embraced the plan enthusiastically. We rehearsed that night and twice more the following week.

On Saturday, Janice and I anxiously awaited the post-physical phone call. Jake confirmed that our little scheme had gone exactly as planned. Rarely have I heard such joy and relief over the phone. Violating the confidentiality of the Rorschach test to help him gave me an opportunity to be a draft resister myself. In college and grad school, I had escaped the draft with a student deferment. By the time deferments were discontinued, I was a few years too old for the military. Helping Jake was the least I could do. Years later, he wrote a successful book, and on my copy he penned, "I owe you my life. Much love."

In addition to counseling potential draftees, I was often asked by students for informal personal counseling. I was young, single, and accessible, so they often came to my office hours pretending to have academic problems but actually seeking help with personal issues. Most lived at home, which meant that their problems generally revolved around relations with their parents. I was fascinated watching these problems evolve.

During my first semester at BC, the most frequent complaint was about parents upset that their children were sexually active. By the next semester, parents were ready to tolerate sex but screamed at their kids about drugs, believing that even casual use of marijuana would inevitably lead to heroin addiction and prison. The following year, the complaints evolved again. Parental fears about sex and marijuana were subsumed under a bigger fear: politics. Many parents, afraid of reprisals, forbade their children to become politically active. All this was typical of the rapid cultural evolution and generational warfare common in the late 1960s.

I had one student older than the others, about twenty-four. He had a dark and brooding presence and often sat silently in the back. When I criticized the war, he squirmed, and when I made the assumption that he had been there, he said I was right. In one class I discussed rumors about systematic murders carried out by the CIA in Viet Nam under the auspices of something called the Phoenix Program. Villages thought to support the NLF with food and cover were targeted. Military patrols under CIA command stole into these villages at night and murdered the elders and leaders. After class, the older student came into my office and confided that he had been part of such a team and had killed people in their sleep. He suffered nightmares, regretted his crimes, and sought redemption. I couldn't give him that, but I did help him find a counselor with relevant experience. Seeing his torment and understanding the violence he had caused left me anguished but more determined than ever to continue working against the war.

Bart and I understood that there would be an official reaction to the announcement that we would no longer do research, either from the BC Department of Psychology or the BC administration. While waiting for it, we scoured the country for other scientists who agreed with our analysis and who had also stopped doing research. We found two at the Massachusetts Institute of Technology and one at the University of California, Berkeley. We contacted them, discussed launching a newsletter, and agreed to stay in touch and continue recruiting.

In March, I was fired. Or, more precisely, and more politely, the psychology department chairman informed me that my two-year contract would not be renewed. Bart, who had been at BC four years longer than I had, already was tenured and could not be fired, but the chairman and the college administration made it clear to him that he would never get another promotion. His decision to renounce research meant he would be unable to get a comparable job at another university. With two kids to care for, he would have to remain at BC at his current rank indefinitely. I had naively thought that science and politics were the two poles of my life, widely separated and independent. I was wrong. Science, like most things, was fully entwined with politics and, if anything, fully subordinate to it.

The student response to my firing was immediate and dramatic. A large protest rally demanded my reinstatement. Over two thousand signatures were collected on a petition. Students tried to present the petition to a psychology department faculty meeting. They were turned away. In response, they busted in and presented the petition anyway. It did no good. Several days later, out of frustration, they seized the offices of the entire psychology department in protest. That didn't work either. Quitting research was a serious offense.

I appreciated the support of so many students, but was not certain I wanted them to succeed. I had joined the faculty to do research. Academic life has many advantages, and I had enjoyed teaching, but at that point I felt called to the larger political struggle off campus. I was furious that I had to relinquish the scientific research that had grounded me for five years, but I wanted to do more to stop the war than was possible on a single college campus. I was also afraid that I had to either channel my anger into activism or simply drop out.

But the academic year was not yet over. Bart and I worked with the antiwar students on campus to support Viet Nam veterans planning to march in New York in early April in an antiwar protest. They had asked others to join them. We sent a large contingent, but the overall turnout, about a hundred thousand, was somewhat disappointing.

Back on campus, minority students forcefully stood up for their own needs. Many had gravitated to the self-defense and self-help organizations emerging in their communities. The Black Panther Party had spread rapidly out of California. Following their lead, members of other ethnic groups created similar organizations: the Young Lords (Puerto Ricans in New York), the Brown Berets (Latinos in California), La Raza Unida (Hispanics in the Southwest), and the American Indian Movement (Indians on reservations and in urban ghettos).

Black and Puerto Rican students at BC invited white students to join them in presenting a set of demands to the college. On April 18, two hundred students marched into the college president's office. They wanted open admissions for all black and Puerto Rican high school graduates, academic programs in black and Puerto Rican history and culture, a say in the hiring of black and Puerto Rican faculty, and tutorial programs for anyone needing remedial help. They also demanded the college renew my contract.

The president promised to air the demands two days later at a Faculty Council meeting. These meetings were open, so several hundred students and some faculty not on the council, like me, attended. When the agenda dragged on and it became clear that the demands would not be discussed, black and Puerto Rican students took control of the podium, barred the doors, and said that no one was leaving until their demands were at least read. I watched their announcement reverberate through the room. Some faculty members panicked, thinking they had been taken hostage. Others took it in stride, realizing that all they were required to do was sit for a few minutes and hear the demands. Racial tension was palpable. All the panicked faculty members were white; the students blocking the doors were not. The demands were read, followed by the rapid departure of the nervous faculty members. The rest of us stayed to discuss the issues.

With their demands ignored, protesting students held rallies on campus and gradually drew support. The college hosted a forum to debate the issues. Over two thousand attended, and more students and faculty endorsed the minority effort. When college officials refused to consider open admissions, minority activists and their white allies shifted to a hit-and-run campaign. They occupied the president's office. The police were called despite the promise the previous year not to do so, but the students dispersed before the cops arrived. Then they barred the student union and set up blockades at the campus entrances, and dispersed again. The college president went to court and got an injunction banning further protests. By this time, Bart and I were helping the protesting students. We were confident that the injunction violated our free speech and assembly rights, so we defied it and continued to demonstrate.

Harrowing news arrived from the University of Chicago. Dick Flacks, the first professor to join our antidraft building seizure three years before, had been attacked and left for dead in his campus office. Flacks and Bart had been friends in graduate school, so the news was a shock to us both. Flacks's assailant had fractured his skull in two places with repeated blows from a ball-peen hammer. The sadist then tried to cut off his right hand and nearly succeeded before fleeing. Flacks was rushed to the university hospital. After months of rehabilitation, he recovered but has lived with a visible indentation on top of his head and only limited use of his right hand. Later, he joined the sociology faculty at the University of California,

Santa Barbara, and became its chairman and a leading American sociologist. His assailant was never identified.

Several months before the attack, UC students had again seized the Administration Building, this time to protest the firing of Marlene Dixon, a radical sociologist and colleague of Flacks's. They stayed for two weeks and then gave up. Edward Levi, the new president, did not call the police, but when the seizure ended, he suspended eighty-two students and permanently expelled a handful of their leaders, among them Jeff Blum, who as a first-year student had helped lead the 1966 seizure. It was much harsher treatment than we had received, but the conservative *Chicago Tribune* criticized Levi's "lax" response and editorialized against campus radicals, often singling Flacks out as an instigator. That publicity probably led to his being targeted.

Bart and I thought about our own security. Like Flacks, we shared an isolated office on the fifth floor. Our visibility in Brooklyn was not that different from what his had been in Chicago. Suddenly the stakes were higher. I considered the pistol I had bought to protect myself as a lifeguard supervisor, but realized it was neither safe to leave it in our office nor practical to carry it around campus. In the end, we stashed a tire iron and a hammer in our desk drawers, fully aware of how inadequate they would be in a real attack.

Five days later, on the morning of May 11, I saw the stakes being raised for others, too. In the predawn hours, police raided the homes of twenty-three of the protesting BC students, all of whom were black or Puerto Rican. It was unprecedented. Not only had the cops gone to their homes; they had broken down doors and come in wearing flak jackets and brandishing shotguns. The students were charged with felonies carrying a maximum sentence of 228 years. Nothing comparable had ever been done to white students.

Supporters organized a strike. The administration responded with a quasi-military occupation. Over a hundred city police were assigned to the campus full-time. Outraged students and faculty had to walk past uniformed cops as they moved in and out of their classrooms. Normally conservative groups like the student government, the campus newspaper, and the Jewish and Catholic religious organizations protested. The cops remained for a month, until the end of the semester. By then, I was no longer bashful about joining in when others chanted, "The only solution is revolution." Indeed, I believed it.

At the end of the school year, to protest the police occupation, I gave all my students As. So did many other professors. The following year, the fight with the university administration was won. The protest did not save my job, but it did win open admission for minority students at Brooklyn College and all other campuses of the City University of New York. Institutes for the study of African American and Puerto Rican history and culture were established. Tutorial programs and basic skills courses were developed for disadvantaged students. The Brooklyn district attorney, angry with the college president for denying he had instigated the home arrests when they had been carried out at his request, dropped all charges against the students. Once more, victory had come after initial setbacks because activists remained united, expanded their numbers through persistent organizing, and defiantly pursued their goals.

My time at Brooklyn College had come to an end. After two years, I was no longer a professor and no longer a scientist. I had no job and no future, but I did have some savings, and I was nursing a radical new idea about what to do next.

CHAPTER 12

THE PREVIOUS SUMMER IN NORTH AFRICA, I HAD TOYED WITH THE NOTION OF DROP-ping out to live an idyllic life on a warm beach. Giving up my research career and losing my professorship at Brooklyn gave me a chance to try. It was a big step, but I was tempted and began to consider it.

I had tried to change the country and, along with everyone else, had failed. The effort left me even more alienated from the politics and culture of the United States than I had been previously. American capitalism, the root of my alienation and the ultimate cause of the war, might be impossible to change. If it was, why not start over somewhere else, where money wouldn't matter? Dropout friends lived in hippie communes in the cities or on communal farms as part of a back-to-the-land movement. I had sometimes felt a tug in their direction, not strong enough to act upon, but there. If I acted now and failed, I was only twenty-eight. There would be time to rebuild.

I saw the islands of the Caribbean as the Garden of Eden. The climate is always warm yet because of the cooling trade winds never too hot. Fruits and vegetables grow easily and can be harvested year-round. Fish are easily caught (they were then; I know they are not now). Instead of creating a rural commune in Colorado as the friends who had introduced me to the Merry Pranksters did, why not start one on a tropical island? Instead of suffering through frigid, high-altitude winters shivering inside a geodesic dome, why not grow food, catch fish, and spread out on a beach in perpetual summer?

It was a momentous decision, and I was close but not quite ready to make it. I flew to Chicago to visit my family. By coincidence, SDS had scheduled a convention there. It promised to be a showdown between two warring factions. I had joined SDS as a national member several years before because I wanted to support their work and help swell their numbers, but I had never affiliated with a local chapter. At the Chicago Coliseum, I used my membership card to have a look around. It was heartbreaking.

The leaders of SDS had sunk into a swamp of sectarian bickering and dispute. Different factions insisted they were the authentic revolutionaries while their opponents were dangerous and deluded impostors. These so-called leaders relied on revolutionary sloganeering as a substitute for the real work of organizing. The convention was teeming with fanatical members of the Progressive Labor Party, a Stalinist organization that had raided SDS chapters for new members. They took control of those chapters when their recruitment gave them a majority. An opposing faction had published a theoretical tract that argued "youth" could be the driving force behind a revolutionary transformation of America. They titled their tract with a line lifted from a Bob Dylan song, "You Don't Need a Weatherman to Tell Which Way the Wind Is Blowing." They believed the wind was blowing toward immediate armed struggle against the U.S. government. These overgrown children, playing at being revolutionaries, came to be called Weatherman.

The other revolutionary pretenders, the Progressive Labor Party, thought only workers could make a revolution. They favored an armed revolution in the future. At present, they were so determined to preserve working-class loyalty that they opposed the separate ethnic struggles being waged by the Black Panther Party and other militant minority groups. They went so far as to accuse the North Vietnamese of being "sellouts" for agreeing to negotiate with the United States.

I watched the conflict between these fantasies play out in a cesspool of mutual hate and recrimination. It was hard to stomach. The irrelevant debates taking place on the podium were so far removed from the real political life of the country that SDS disintegrated on the spot. Once a million students would have acknowledged membership in the organization, but despite its remarkable size and early success, factionalism and revolutionary posturing had rendered it impotent. The Chicago Coliseum was its funeral.

While SDS had led the early antiwar movement, its time had passed. New groups not based on the campuses were organizing big protests for the fall. Nixon had increased the aerial bombardment of Viet Nam while simultaneously putting the country to sleep with promises of pending, but never quite realized, peace accords. *Life* magazine provided a wake-up call. As summer began, it published photo portraits of all 242 American soldiers killed the previous week in Viet Nam. The huge photo spread stunned readers as they gazed upon the smiling and hopeful young faces, knowing that each had died during a single week of combat. Yet the old paradox remained. Voters were dissatisfied with the war, but even more dissatisfied with the antiwar movement. The spectacle at the Chicago Coliseum, our militant tactics, and Nixon's diplomatic charade all conspired to keep us out of the mainstream.

I remained disoriented and confused after having renounced scientific research, yet I was determined to make the best of my situation. I was free to start over and redefine my life. I thought I had two choices. I could opt for full-time work as an antiwar organizer and live on a subsistence salary. I still desperately wanted to stop the war. And with the movement in disarray, people like me were needed to rebuild it. My commitment to political activism was strong and was also a calling, as science had been. My other choice was the Caribbean. I was still uncertain, but if I did go, I knew better than to try it alone. I wanted a chance to sort out my options, so Janice and I agreed to go with Bart and his family on a cross-country camping trip.

We camped for three weeks in upstate New York, Canada's North Woods, and then farther west in Quebec and Ontario. When we got to Minnesota, Bart, his wife, and their two young children continued west. Janice and I stayed with my friend Ron Chutter. Ron lived with his girl-friend, Eddie Ilustre, a dark and unusually beautiful Hawaiian girl with long flowing black hair and a soft Polynesian face. Ron had failed to graduate college after our European trip. To make a living, he and Eddie managed a small corner grocery store owned by his father in a poor white section of Minneapolis. They paid no rent for the store or the small apartment above it where they lived. However, they had to keep the store open from eight in the morning to eight at night six days a week. They were not happy.

I told Ron and Eddie what I was considering: that a bunch of friends sell their possessions, pool their money, and buy acreage on a Caribbean beach to plant a garden and build a few houses. The idea was to escape capitalism, have no need of money, and live a natural life. If it worked, other friends would join us, and a thriving community could be built. I knew it was a long shot, but not trying would lead to regrets about never having made the attempt. It might be a pipe dream, but there was only one way to find out. I told them that if I went, I would do it in September, and they would be welcome to join me.

Janice and I left Minneapolis in a drive-away car bound for San Francisco. We stopped to camp in the beautiful national parks on both sides of the U.S.-Canadian border. After exploring California, we spent a week with Scott Van Leuven, who, after dropping out of law school two years before, was still driving a cab in San Francisco. I gave him the same speech I had given Ron and Eddie, and like them he was interested.

In mid-August, Janice and I drove back east as the three-day rock festival at Woodstock got under way. Many friends, especially from the New York area, were among the half-million people there. It was an instant city. That many people celebrating the new rock music, and the new culture growing up around it, made us feel that our point of view was on the ascendancy, and that despite our differences with the larger society, history might be on our side. Unfortunately, that would be a short-lived fantasy. It didn't take long for greed and competition to corrupt the world of rock music and the industry that sprang up around it.

Back in New York in September, a revitalized antiwar movement showed some promise, but the American people remained so confused by Nixon's maneuvering I was convinced there was little we could do to actually stop the war. I was ready to leave. While frustrated and angry about losing my scientific career, I was also optimistic about the Caribbean. Our quest might work. If it did, what could be better? First Scott, then Ron and Eddie, signed on. Janice stayed behind, so the three of us who had gone to Europe together as twenty-year-olds, plus Eddie, pooled our funds, bought lightweight camping gear, and boarded a cheap flight to the U.S. Virgin Islands. Having finally made the decision, I was eager and ready for a great adventure.

We stopped first at the national park on St. John. For two weeks we tanned our skins, slept in tents, and cooked over a campfire. I taught the others what I knew about spearfishing and which fish were good to eat. At the end of our training exercise we struck out for the Leeward Islands to the east and south. We hitchhiked on sailboats and private planes, but had only limited success. For the most part, we sailed between the islands by paying small fares to fishing boats or local freighters.

Arriving at a new island was always fun. Typically, we found a place to camp and spent a few days reading in the sun, spearfishing, and enjoying ourselves. Then we talked to local residents and learned about local conditions before inquiring about land for sale. Unfortunately, we kept running into the same problem. All the resort hotels being built on Caribbean islands had driven up the price of real estate. Land speculators and agents who worked for hotel chains had already visited the main islands, and it was local folklore that one day such people would show up and offer an outrageous fortune for beachfront land that previously had not been very valuable. Prices had shot up to thousands of dollars an acre. The locals were holding out for a bonanza, so people like us with limited funds had no chance.

Disappointed, we headed for islands farther off the beaten path where the construction of a resort was less likely, smaller islands with limited populations and no tourism. I found these smaller islands more interesting. Lacking the tourist culture, they were friendlier to strangers and had a more relaxed atmosphere. I had a great time enjoying the freedom, the nurturing climate, and the spearfishing, but our problem persisted. People on these islands were well aware of the rampant real estate speculation around them and had raised their prices accordingly.

As we moved from island to island, we occasionally picked up news from the States. In November, Seymour Hersh, the investigative reporter who had written the book about Fort Detrick, revealed that a U.S. Army unit at My Lai, a small village in rural South Viet Nam, had wantonly shot and killed 504 people, all of them old men, women, and children. More would have died had a U.S. helicopter pilot not landed in the middle of the slaughter and ordered a halt. When officers on the ground refused, the pilot threatened to have his door-gunners machine-gun their troops. That ended it. A horrifying photograph of dead women, children, and babies sprawled along the sides of a ditch became one more iconic image of the war.

A few days after the My Lai story broke, a massive antiwar demonstration took place in Washington, D.C. The November Mobilization to End the Viet Nam War was the single largest demonstration in U.S. history, with reliable attendance figures ranging from 500,000 to 800,000. That turnout was remarkable considering that in mid-October another Washington protest, the Viet Nam Moratorium, had drawn 250,000. In other cities that same day, 2 million more attended religious protests, teach-ins, and street rallies or simply wore black armbands.

I was stunned by these massive numbers and happy that the larger antiwar movement had outgrown the sectarians in SDS. But I was not tempted to return. New polling had 71 percent of the American people still supporting Nixon on the war. If the antiwar movement continued to draw such big numbers in the face of that kind of support, polarization in the United States would only intensify. It would be no easier to stop the war. In any case, I remained determined to give my Caribbean fantasy a chance to succeed.

Having struck out on the Leeward Islands, relatively close to the United States, we went to the Windward Islands farther south. Our first stop was Dominica, a large island with little tourism or development. Its capital, Roseau, was an impoverished old port with houses on stilts and open ditches that carried sewage to the sea. We hoped the lack of development would mean lower real estate values. Instead of camping, we stayed in a cheap hostel, the kind where the walls don't go up to the ceiling so that guests are separated only by a partition. We spent a few weeks trekking out to remote locations on rented motorbikes and hired Land

Cruisers. Other than cliff sides dropping into the sea, there was no beach-front land we could afford.

While traveling across Dominica, we found a cheap rental house with electricity and running water. A house with a kitchen, beds, and a bath-room was a welcome luxury. We moved in for two weeks and relaxed. Despite our problems, we knew enough to enjoy ourselves when we could. Life remained slow and relatively carefree. I had fallen into the island rhythm: one day at a time, no planning, take everything as it comes. We read and swam, and when the two weeks were over, we pushed on to a group of very small islands farther south, hoping that hotel land specu-lators had not yet been there.

The island chain known as the Grenadines is one of the most beauti-ful places on earth. Innumerable tiny islands dot the warm blue water between St. Vincent and Grenada. Under sunny skies, the green islands can be seen in every direction, each one surrounded by beaches of pow-dery white sand and the aquamarine colors of the shallow sea around it. A few dozen are inhabited, while hundreds more are only sandbars with a few palm trees. We took a mail boat to the largest island, Carriacou, only six miles long and a mile wide.

There was good camping, so we set up on a beach and befriended two Peace Corps volunteers. Our hopes soared when they introduced us to local residents who offered to help us find land. It was truly a paradise, slow, friendly, and stunningly beautiful. However, a few of the nearby islands, like Petit St. Vincent, had resorts for the very rich and watering holes for wealthy yachtsmen sailing through the extraordinary waters. These facilities were too exclusive to proliferate, but to the surprise of the people helping us, they had proven to local landowners that their little parcels might have great value. These islanders lived comfortably. They were willing to wait for the inflated land prices in their dreams. Who could blame them?

Our exploration of the Grenadines failed, and we returned to Carria-cou to spend a few days in our camp on the beach. The snorkeling and spearfishing were exceptionally good. Of our many Caribbean adven-tures, the only one with political overtones began in that camp. The

Peace Corps workers suggested we check out a tiny uninhabited island two miles offshore. The coral and fish were especially plentiful and gorgeous. They lent us a small dinghy about to fall apart, and Scott and I rowed out to the little island. Our spearfishing gear and some freshwater sat on the floor of the rickety old boat.

The island was only big enough to support one palm tree and a few bushes, but it was surrounded by an abundant coral reef. As we crossed over it, the bottom of the dinghy struck its sharp edges. The flimsy boat immediately sprang a leak and sank. We were only fifty feet from the beach, so we grabbed the gear and swam in. The dinghy was a total loss, but there were numerous yachts in the vicinity, and since it was still morning, we decided to explore the reef before worrying about how to be rescued.

We speared a number of fish, ate some for lunch, and lay back on the sand for a little siesta. Awakening around 4:00 p.m., we were surprised to see that the yacht and sailboat traffic had decreased dramatically. The few boats still visible were out of hailing distance, so we stood on the beach and waved our arms and T-shirts. Nobody saw us. As the sun dropped farther toward the horizon, boat traffic disappeared. We were marooned. We gathered all the burnable driftwood, cooked our fish, and made beds for ourselves out of fallen palm fronds.

The next morning, the boat traffic was back. With no wood left to make a signal fire, we waved our shirts at the passing yachts. Still no luck. After two hours, an unusually large yacht passed about a half mile away. Just as we thought it too had failed to notice us, the yacht stopped and put a small motorboat into the water, which started up and headed toward us. The sailor at the helm avoided the coral, beached the boat, and invited us to climb in with our gear. He then pointed the boat back toward Carriacou. I half jokingly suggested that he take us to the big yacht for a hot breakfast, but he said that the owner had given him explicit instructions not to do so. Who's the owner? I asked. Roy Cohn, he answered.

Cohn had been Senator Joe McCarthy's henchman during the communist witch hunts of the 1950s. Since then, he had evolved into a mean, pompous, conniving lawyer who was a feared power broker in New York. He had gotten rich manipulating wealthy supporters and money-hungry

Republican politicians and had used his influence to support right-wing causes. Thankfully, he had also bought a big boat so that one day he could rescue two wayward lefties marooned on a desert island. The episode was particularly poignant for Scott. His father, Mick, and his uncle Ken had been political activists in the 1930s, close to or in the Communist Party, and as a result had suffered in the 1950s because of McCarthy and Cohn. Scott's own political activism had grown out of these experiences, yet there we were, indebted to Roy Cohn, a man reviled and detested by every left-wing person in America.

As we left Carriacou, I knew we were running out of options. Yet my relaxed tropical mentality kept me from thinking too far ahead. We boarded a fishing boat to Grenada, and despite knowing it would likely be our last chance, I remained half-confident that things would work out. The island was as big as Dominica but with some tourism and an econ-omy based on bananas and spices, primarily mace and nutmeg, which come from the same plant. We camped for a while but once again opted for a small hotel in St. George's, the capital. After days of looking at prop-erties for sale, we struck out. All the beachfront land was too expensive.

We could no longer deny the obvious: our original vision would never be realized. We had traveled for months investigating every possibility. As we struggled to accept our failure, a real estate agent told us about a mountainside property available for $700 an acre, cheap compared with what we had seen but situated in a thick forest far from the beach. Perfect land for growing bananas, he said. We looked at each other. Tell us about growing bananas, we replied. The agent explained that the first step was to clear the land with machetes since it was too remote for bulldozers. Farmhands could then be hired to plant and care for the banana trees. It was our only chance to stay in the Caribbean, so for the first time we con-sidered the unusual prospect of owning a small banana plantation.

Clearing thickly forested land with machetes was extreme work, so I asked what the men who did it would be paid. The agent said about $3 a day. I was shocked. Oh, you can't pay them less, he said, they have a union. Less was not what I had in mind. For work like that, we'd want to pay more. The agent thought I was crazy. If you pay more, he said, the other landowners would burn you out for fear their workers will also demand more. We were taken aback. We hadn't come to the Caribbean to make a living exploiting the labor of others. We left the agent's office defeated and out of ideas.

That night, the seriousness of our predicament finally overcame my laid-back tropical attitude. We were in a remote location with absolutely no prospects. While not my original vision, the profits from a small banana plantation might allow us to live comfortably on the beach. I thought it was a better option than going back to the States. Instead of doing it as little capitalists, I realized there might be a socialist solution. The next morning we told the agent that we would not pay slave wages, but we would make our workers part owners of a cooperative enterprise. We would put up the capital, and they would supply the labor. There would be no wages, only profits to share. Yes, the agent said, marveling at our generosity, that would work.

We asked all about operating a banana plantation, including how the harvested bananas would be sold. The agent said there was only one way. Once a week a ship owned by the United Fruit Company docked in the harbor and bought all the bananas available on the island. His answer dropped the bottom out of our plan. We excused ourselves and went outside to talk.

United Fruit was among the most exploitative corporations in the world. It was the symbol of American imperialism in Latin America. The company was the biggest single landowner in Honduras and was thought to be more powerful there than the government. In other countries, it was second only to the Catholic Church in landholdings. It underpaid workers, had them toil in terrible conditions, bribed officials to get favorable taxes and tariffs, and used its wealth to elect local officials who would protect its business interests. We were not about to form a business relationship with the United Fruit Company.

It was the end of the line. After six months of trying, I understood that my destiny was not going to be an idyllic, stress-free life on a tropical beach. Only those with capital could escape capitalism. I had no choice but to return to the States. Strangely, I was neither angry nor bitter but resigned to my fate, a fate that perhaps I had been drawn to all along. If I could not escape civilization, I had to go back and either passively accept it or work to change it. Politics drove me out of science, which I incorrectly thought existed in a separate sphere. In Grenada, politics prevented my escape. Its influence was more pervasive than I had thought. Perhaps my Caribbean dream had ended because politics was my destiny.

A few days later, we flew to Miami and got a drive-away car to San Francisco. It was March 1970. We stopped in southern Colorado to visit our friends' commune. Sitting in their huge geodesic dome, I saw that they too had trouble. Their original money had been drained by the purchase of several hundred acres of high-altitude pastureland. Their attempts to be self-sufficient had failed, and they were forced to seek part-time employment to stay afloat. It was a bleak scene. They had lost their joy. Ours was not the only dream that had crumbled.

In San Francisco, Ron and Eddie went off together. Scott and I moved into a communal house in Marin County inhabited by four women he knew, their babies, and various men who floated in and out. The women got welfare payments and took occasional work as waitresses. The first day there, I developed a burning itch in my crotch. Our hostesses treated me for diaper rash, but to no avail. They recommended a doctor who immediately said, "Poison oak." He cured me with a little cortisone. Being from the East, I knew poison ivy but had never heard of poison oak. A week before, hiking near the commune in Colorado, I had to answer a call of nature. When finished, I reached for the nearest leaves. Poison oak. Welcome to the West.

Life in Marin County was peaceful and relaxed. I read, listened to music, talked to the people around me, and, like them, smoked a lot of dope. After a month, I was bored out of my mind. The hippie life was not for me. Having gotten it out of my system, I knew what I had to do: work full-time against the war. My old girlfriend Charlotte had left the University of Chicago to finish her doctorate in sociology at Harvard. I called and asked if she would take me in until I figured out my next move. Two days later, I was at the San Francisco airport boarding a plane for Boston.

CHAPTER 13

I MOVED INTO CHARLOTTE'S APARTMENT IN THE BACK BAY NEIGHBORHOOD OF BOSTON in late April. She roomed with her lifelong friend, Janet Mendelsohn, and Janet's boyfriend, Walter Teller. Janet and Walter were fledgling filmmakers, and Walter was associated with Newsreel, a collective that made antiwar documentary films shown on college campuses or in art house theaters. All three welcomed me and took the time to explain events that had happened while I was away, including major escalations in antiwar tactics, like the burning of a branch of the Bank of America by University of California, Santa Barbara, students in February. But the biggest event I had missed was the infamous Chicago Seven trial.

Eight people were indicted on federal riot and conspiracy charges after the protests at the Democratic convention. One of the eight, Bobby Seale, a leader of the Black Panther Party and the only nonwhite defendant, was severed from the case and tried separately after being bound and gagged by the judge for his continued insistence on separate counsel. The remaining seven included Tom Hayden and Rennie Davis, who had been the most visible organizers of the protest, and Abbie Hoffman and Jerry Rubin, equally visible leaders of the mercurial yippies, sponsors of many hilarious stunts orchestrated to ridicule the war and those who supported it.

The humorless presiding judge, Julius Hoffman, was so obviously biased that the defendants turned the trial into a circus and questioned the government's right to prosecute them at all. Unconcerned about their own fate, they used the trial to criticize the war. Decorum collapsed in a frenzy of cross-accusations and satirical antics. The defendants mocked the judge and the prosecutor for their amoral support of the war and the racism behind it. The judge and the prosecutor showed open contempt for the defendants and their lawyers, Bill Kunstler and Leonard Weinglass.

The innumerable physical, ideological, and comedic confrontations in the courtroom, widely covered by the press, captivated people who had never before seen such a trial. Frequent and widespread protests in cities across the country supported the defendants. The legitimacy of the courts was undermined. In the end, even though an independent commission would call the convention violence a "police riot," five of the seven were found guilty and slapped with numerous contempt-of-court citations. They were then freed pending an appeal.

I spent my first several days in Boston quietly getting caught up and settling in, but on April 30, I was thrust back into the antiwar maelstrom. President Nixon announced that five days earlier he had secretly ordered three divisions of American troops in Viet Nam to cross the international boundary and invade neighboring Cambodia. The country was officially neutral in the war, but supply lines between North Viet Nam and its allied forces in the South passed through Cambodian territory, and Nixon wanted them cut off. In his announcement, he said that the invasion was "not for the purpose of expanding the war into Cambodia but for the purpose of ending the war in Viet Nam and winning the just peace we desire."

Whom was he kidding? The attack unleashed a torrent of protest. Editorials condemned it as an unwarranted expansion of the war. Clergy protested. Even a few conservative politicians and business leaders joined the opposition. The most vocal and furious reaction came from the campuses, and over the next four days student and faculty strikes shut down hundreds of them.

The invasion was particularly infuriating because of Nixon's previous posturing about ending the war. Token troop withdrawals had been publicized but offset by an increased reliance on airpower, which allowed Nixon to enlarge the war while claiming it was winding down. The invasion of

Cambodia made the painful truth all too clear: the war was not going to end; it was going to spread. Nixon's doublespeak about enlarging it in order to end it backfired. Instead of calming the nation's fears, it exposed his duplicity, at least for those willing to listen.

The day after Nixon's revelation, on May 1, I went to an antiwar rally at Harvard with Charlotte, Janet, and Walter. It was a Friday. That night Nixon labeled antiwar students "bums blowing up campuses." Over the weekend, we went to meetings at several colleges around Boston to help coordinate campus strikes for the following week. The fury against Nixon was rampant. On Monday, we marched with a group from Harvard. But as we marched in Boston, events spiraled out of control on a campus in Ohio.

Kent State University students had shut down the school on Friday and planned an outdoor protest for Monday, May 4. Campus officials banned the protest, and the Ohio governor put a few companies of National Guard on alert in case the police needed backup. They did. On Monday, the Kent State students refused police orders to disperse. They were fighting mad and chanted a slogan that had become commonplace among militants on other campuses: "Bring the war home." It meant that if the government didn't respond to or even allow peaceful protest, protesters would stop being peaceful. The warfare at the Chicago convention two years before had inspired this threat. National Guardsmen advanced on the students. They were met with a barrage of rocks. The guardsmen had received no training in riot control and had no body armor or shields. They regrouped and advanced again, this time using tear gas. Predictably, the students threw the tear-gas canisters back at them.

Untrained, the guardsmen panicked. For no understandable reason, they had been given live ammunition. Shots rang out, but not warning shots fired over the heads of the crowd. The frightened guardsmen actually shot directly at the students, some of whom could have been the children of their friends and neighbors. Thirteen were hit. Four were killed. Only two of the four had participated in the protest. The other two were simply walking between classes; one was even a member of the campus Reserve Officers' Training Corps (ROTC) unit. Of the four killed, all were shot from at least 250 feet away, proof that they were not a threat to the troops.

A Rubicon was crossed. The war had indeed come home. The killings, coming so soon after the invasion of Cambodia, led to a state of open rebellion the next morning. Over a thousand campuses were shut down. On no notice, a hundred thousand protested in Washington, D.C. High schools, even some elementary schools, saw mass student walkouts for the first time. Like everyone else, I was enraged. I went to Harvard with Walter. What we saw and did there was typical of what happened across the nation.

There were thousands milling around the ivy-covered campus. In their fury they looked for something to destroy. The ROTC program was being phased out in response to earlier student protests, but the ROTC building remained a potent symbol of the war. Walter and I joined the shouting and angry students who surrounded it. Those in front of us broke the windows and threw burning objects inside. A chant went up to "burn it down." Walter and I were too far back in the crowd to lend a hand, but had we been closer, I would have assisted in the arson. Instead, our part of the crowd surrounded the arsonists and protected them from police interference. We succeeded for only a short time. Cops with swinging batons cleared a path to the building, and the flames were extinguished.

For the rest of that week, there were protests at all the colleges in the Boston area. Simultaneously, thousands of demonstrations took place across the country and around the world. A week later, passions finally cooled, but when I awoke on May 15, it was to the news that more students had been shot and killed. The night before, at Jackson State College in Mississippi, police had gunned down fourteen black students. Two were dead.

The country split into warring camps. Pro-war forces made feeble attempts to justify the shootings at Kent State and Jackson State. Antiwar people recoiled in horror. But the activists and protesters, people like me and virtually everyone I knew, understood what those killings meant. It was not that we had reason to fear ourselves. We knew the odds of getting killed were low enough to justify the risk of continued protest. Rather, it was the sickening realization that American authorities had become so determined to wage war in Viet Nam that they were willing to kill American students to do so.

The divide between pro- and antiwar Americans had become so wide and so bitter that many could no longer tolerate even talking to people on the other side. Similar, even angrier divisions existed among military veterans. Many who had served in Viet Nam spoke out against the war after being discharged. When their opposition was expressed to veterans of previous wars, they were condemned and called traitors and cowards. After the horrifying experiences many of these vets had endured in the jungles of Viet Nam, the name-calling and hatred fueled additional outrage and led many vets to disengage from society.

Reports also reached us about unchecked demoralization among American troops in Viet Nam. Soldiers wore peace signs on their helmets as a signal to fighters on the other side that they would not initiate action. Others shirked their duties and sabotaged equipment whenever possible. Marijuana use was pervasive, and thousands of soldiers were addicted to cheap and readily available heroin, undermining their willingness to fight. In addition to combat wounds, U.S. military hospitals saw huge increases in drug overdose and abuse cases.

The invasion of Cambodia and the killings at Kent State and Jackson State pushed me over a line I had not yet crossed. I realized there was no way to force the government to change its policy in Viet Nam. That meant to me that the government had no legitimate call on my loyalty. I was sick of being a good German, and I was no longer able to simply oppose the war. I came to see the government of the United States as the enemy. It was then that I went over to the other side. I was not alone. My objective, and that of my friends, shifted from an American withdrawal to a Vietnamese victory. At demonstrations I joined others who chanted, "One side's right, one side's wrong. Victory to the Viet Cong."

That summer in Boston, I got acquainted with young scientists from Harvard and the Massachusetts Institute of Technology who were organizing under the banner of "Science for the People." In the year and a half since Bart and I had renounced our research, a few more young scientists had also concluded that science needed new priorities. They had formed a group in Boston that held meetings, published a newsletter, and recruited new members. Some would later become famous scientists, for example the biologist Stephen Jay Gould. Others, like Richard Lewontin, Richard

Levins, and Ethan Signer, also became national leaders in biology. Over the summer, I attended Science for the People meetings, wrote for its newsletter, and worked with its members to refine our understanding of the role of science in society.

I had to find a job, too. I wanted one that would allow me to contribute more to the antiwar movement than just my presence at a protest. Bart Meyers suggested I take a teaching job on a college campus, even if it was only for one year. That would give me a salary and a base from which to do antiwar work. During the year, I could look for a larger role in the movement. Bart called Howard Moltz, the senior psychology professor at Brooklyn College who had been arrested during the protest in 1967. He had also opposed my firing in 1969.

In a happy coincidence, Moltz had since become chairman of the psychology department at the University of Chicago. He graciously arranged for me to teach there, not in his department, but in the college. Chicago was one of the few universities that maintained a separate faculty for their college rather than rely on professors from the graduate departments to teach the undergraduate courses. Professors with college appointments were not under the same pressure to do research and publish, so I was an acceptable candidate. The fact that I had a Ph.D. from UC and had attended the college myself gave them added confidence in my ability. I became an assistant professorial lecturer and was assigned to teach a social science course to first- and second-year students that combined psychology, sociology, and anthropology.

Chicago was familiar terrain. Since I hoped to work for the antiwar movement the following year, and could expect only subsistence wages, I had to save as much of my salary as possible. Instead of renting my own apartment, I answered a bulletin board ad and moved in with three undergraduate women who shared a large three-bedroom apartment with a vacant "maid's room" on the other side of their kitchen. I just wanted a room with a door. This room had one and was separated from the rest of the apartment. It was an unusual arrangement, but throughout the year we respected each other's privacy and got along fine, although I did get a lot of questioning looks whenever I entertained female guests.

The antiwar movement floundered that fall. The various antiwar coalitions were reluctant to sponsor another national protest in Washington. Some feared being unable to top the unprecedented attendance the previous fall. Others felt that if we did succeed on such a massive scale and again had no impact on the war, the result would only be increased demoralization. But rampant fragmentation and sectarian bickering were the main impediment. Given the vacuum, the Socialist Workers Party, a Trotskyist organization with little popular support, called for a demonstration in October. Only a hundred thousand came. Meanwhile, returning veterans began to play a larger role in the antiwar movement. After being castigated by traditional veterans' organizations, they formed one of their own, Vietnam Veterans Against the War.

Antidraft organizing had decreased the previous winter after the government introduced a draft lottery. A random drawing assigned a number from 1 to 365 to each day of the year. Those born on days that drew low numbers were likely to be drafted; those with high numbers were not and could plan their lives accordingly. Like antiwar vets, antiwar students were split between those only opposing the war and those working for more fundamental change.

The larger student movement was undermined by the actions of former SDS leaders in Weatherman. In October 1969, they had sponsored their "Days of Rage" in Chicago. The action consisted of nothing more than a few hundred "revolutionaries" running through the streets breaking car and house windows, taunting pedestrians, and throwing rocks at police. Weatherman leaders assumed such actions would inspire "revolutionary youth" to join them. Instead, they just looked ridiculous.

In the year following that action, the small Weatherman faction staged similar events elsewhere. Like all true believers, they took each tactical failure as a sign of success. Finally, they revealed how truly repugnant they had become. At their convention, they spoke of "enemies"; among them, for some bizarre reason, was the actress Sharon Tate, who along with four friends had been murdered by Charles Manson and his cult of followers. In describing the murders, Bernardine Dohrn, a Weatherman leader, was quoted as saying, "Dig it: first they killed those pigs, then they ate dinner in the same room with them, then they even shoved a fork into pig Tate's stomach! Wild!" Sharon Tate was eight months pregnant at the time. Dohrn held up three outstretched fingers to symbolize the fork, and for a brief time that became the Weatherman salute.

Some Weatherman leaders were children of wealth and were used to getting what they wanted when they wanted it. They were too impatient and too arrogant to do the slow work of organizing. Unfortunately, the mainstream press eagerly covered their sensationalist actions, which discredited the rest of us and damaged the antiwar cause.

At the time, I too thought of myself as a revolutionary and was fully committed to the overthrow of capitalism. However, I thought the work of a revolutionary was to actually make a revolution, not just be in favor of one. That required a practical strategy, an understanding of the balance of forces, the marshaling of resources, and workable tactics. We had none of that. No plan, no relevant experience, and no idea how to build a revolutionary organization. Neither did I have a clear vision of a revolutionary future. Was it socialism? Perhaps, but it definitely was not the communism of the U.S.S.R. or the People's Republic of China. Was it some hybrid of social democracy with public ownership of large corporations? Again, I didn't know, but whatever it was, I knew it had to grow out of the American experience and not be imported from abroad.

One plan being floated that fall did seem to me to be a practical first step toward building a revolutionary movement. Rennie Davis, one of the Chicago Seven, called for massive civil disobedience designed to shut down the city of Washington, D.C., in early May. He wanted to recruit thousands of activists to physically block bridges and intersections, and in doing so bring Washington and the government to a standstill. I liked the plan. If it succeeded, we would have a new and effective nonviolent tactic, which would demonstrate to antiwar activists that we had more strength than we realized. That understanding might empower people to act even more forcefully in the future. In any case, if we wanted to build a real revolutionary movement, we had to figure out how to organize large numbers of people to take risks. We had no ability to acquire power in any other way.

I spent the first month in Chicago settling in and preparing my classes. While still at Brooklyn, I had wanted to expand my antiwar work beyond the campus. Antiwar students at UC were already well organized, so I decided to focus on the larger scientific community, where I hoped to have more impact. Veterans of the early SDS, appalled by its descent into factionalism and dogma, had formed another organization, the New University Conference (NUC), designed to give graduate students and young faculty a chance to support the progressive goals they had advocated years before as college students. I found the faculty members at UC who were involved to be decent, levelheaded, and committed activists. When Bart Meyers was elected one of their national leaders, I signed on.

Two of the NUC activists at UC were respected young professors, Len Radinsky, a paleontologist, and Mel Rothenberg, a mathematician. I told them about Science for the People in Boston and suggested that we three and Bart co-author a manifesto for them. With the exception of the nuclear physicists in World War II, there was little in the literature about scientists resisting an unjust war or renouncing their work to join a resistance movement. The American Association for the Advancement of Science (AAAS), the preeminent scientific organization in the United States and the publisher of *Science* magazine, had scheduled its annual convention in Chicago over the Christmas break. I suggested we use the manifesto at the convention to publicize our thinking and recruit new support.

I contacted AAAS officials and asked permission to present our views at a seminar we would sponsor. They refused. I then asked for table space so we could distribute literature and talk to attendees. They refused again. They didn't like what we were saying. How could they? But scientists in general prided themselves on free inquiry and openness to divergent points of view. Was ours too radical even to consider? If so, a radical response was appropriate.

I called Science for the People in Boston and proposed that we disrupt the AAAS convention, forcefully if necessary, until our analysis was heard. The publicity would garner national attention and deliver our message to a broader public and scientific audience. At the convention, we could expose the role science was playing in Viet Nam, discuss other abuses of scientific research, urge young scientists to join us, and advocate for new research priorities to help the Vietnamese and others struggling for justice. My proposal was discussed at length and adopted.

I took responsibility for organizing the AAAS protest. I worked with Radinsky and Rothenberg, and long-distance with Bart, to draft the lengthy manifesto. It discussed theory, reviewed history, cited examples, and suggested scientific research that would benefit people in need. We revised the document many times before we were satisfied. I also prepared for the convention. Working with the people in Boston and NUC members in Chicago, I reviewed the convention schedule and made plans to disrupt those seminars dealing with weapons research. I made arrangements to print and distribute our manifesto along with other literature we had developed, and I organized friends to find temporary housing for activists joining us from out of town who could not afford hotels.

While organizing for the convention, I had great fun teaching. My course dealt with the three social sciences—psychology, sociology, and anthropology—that study how we are shaped as individuals. Students had to read the classic books and articles in each field, but I added more contemporary and controversial material to their reading lists. I encouraged them to look beyond the psychological and societal factors that shape human life and also use Marxist tools like class analysis and economic determinism to understand behavior.

When the first quarter ended just before Christmas break, I gave my students a startling intellectual challenge. They had been fascinated by the hypothetical state of pure communism that Marx believed would be the final stage in the evolution of society. In the distant future, the state would wither away, and each person would work to the best of his or her ability and be rewarded according to his or her needs, regardless of the kind or amount of work performed. I pointed out that within our community, the university, grades were the equivalent of salary or wealth. With good grades students could maintain their standing, insure their survival, and secure future comfort. Since I had to give them end-of-quarter grades, to illustrate Marx's idealized system I intended to distribute the wealth, that is, the grades, on the basis of need. Students fidgeted in their chairs, wondering what I was talking about.

The idea, I explained, was to break the connection between how hard or how well one had worked, which under capitalism determined the reward one "deserved," and focus instead on what one "needed," regardless of past work. They looked at me in disbelief as I explained that they could choose whatever grade they "needed." If a student had a scholarship that required a certain grade point average, an A was "needed," but if wealthy parents were paying tuition, it was not. If a student majored in one of the biological or physical sciences, there was less "need" of a good grade in my social science class than if the student majored in a social science. I also laid out my needs. I had to submit a distribution of As, Bs, and Cs to look like I was doing my job. There would be no Ds or Fs.

Students would not believe I was serious. This is just an exercise, one said, you're not really going to do this, are you? I said that I was and that the grades would be official. (Grades then were less important for admission to graduate school.) I told them that they would all have the right to ask for and get any grade they legitimately needed, but they would have to publicly state their reasons in the society of the classroom, and the class as a whole would have to insure a distribution of all three grades, which was my need. They all sat wide-eyed around a large circular table. I asked them to begin.

Hesitantly, the first few students said they needed As or Bs. They couldn't help but justify their request by describing work they had or had not done. Other students correctly pointed out that these justifications were irrelevant given the ground rules I had established. I said nothing because I wanted all the responsibility to rest with the students. I simply wrote down the grades. After about ten of the twenty-two in class had made their requests, one well-spoken and well-to-do young white woman said that she needed an A. In justifying it, she spoke in a tone that suggested outrage at the prospect of receiving anything less.

The next student was a young black man in a special program for disadvantaged kids who got scholarships and remedial instruction for their course work. This particular young man was very likable. He still had a lot of the ghetto in him, but he spoke up during discussions and added a perspective that the other students had come to value. They all wanted him to succeed, but his lack of preparation was obvious. He said he needed a C. The last girl to speak looked over at him, shocked. Wait a minute, she said, you're on scholarship, you need an A.

He was embarrassed. You don't understand, he said, I didn't do all the work in this class, so I don't deserve an A. The white girl insisted, Bill just said the amount of work you did doesn't matter; it's not about what you deserve, it's about what you need. But the young man could not grasp her reasoning. It wouldn't be fair, he said, and besides, Bill needs some Cs, so I should take one. The girl was frustrated, and the two of them went back and forth several times. Others urged the black student to ask for an A. They got nowhere. He could not get past his own guilt at having taken advantage of my lax rules by not doing all the assigned work. Despite his disadvantaged background, or perhaps because of it, he had an ingrained sense of what he did or did not deserve. Finally, the young woman reached her breaking point. She burst out, this is ridiculous; you take my A and I'll take your C, that'll solve it.

For a moment, the room was silent. Then, surprised that she was serious, the other students began to nod their agreement. The young man finally understood the point his classmates had tried to make. I recorded the two grades. There was nothing more I needed to say. The young woman had reached out to a classmate with a deep concern and an insistent generosity that she could never have imagined beforehand. The young man had a social interaction unlike anything he had ever experienced. The class had learned a little bit about the distribution of wealth, the connection between work and reward, and the considerations that must be shown to fellow citizens when such issues are debated and decided. Their minds were bigger for it. I had done my job, but I had to ask for confidentiality because I knew I would be fired if the UC administration learned how I had determined grades. The students agreed and kept their word. I never had a moment in three years of teaching college that was as satisfying as that one.

With my grades submitted, I turned to the upcoming AAAS convention. Ironically, the site was the Hilton hotel where two years before, during the Democratic convention, some of the most violent police attacks had occurred. The five-day convention drew several thousand scientists. The main activities were keynote speeches during lunch and dinner, and dozens of simultaneous two-hour seminars held throughout the day attended by scientists with a specialized interest in the narrow area of research being discussed. We had ten committed Science for the People activists from Boston and Chicago and another dozen available part-time.

Several of us pooled our money and rented a hotel suite to use as a head-quarters. We distributed flyers inviting convention attendees to visit the suite and learn more about us, and we gave away copies of the manifesto four of us had written earlier.

On the first day, we targeted seminars reporting on research with clear weapons applications. Scientists normally expect friendly criticism about the accuracy of their findings, but only a few of the older nuclear physicists in attendance had ever faced public objections to the morality of their work. Scientists think of themselves as aloof from mundane considerations of politics and morality. They also have a strong sense of public decorum. People ruled out of order or asked to delay their remarks at a seminar were expected to comply. We did not. We attended these seminars alone or in small groups. While most of us were aggressive, others had some difficulty standing up to leaders in their fields, including a few with Nobel prizes.

Typically, at the start of a seminar, we stood up and raised questions about the use to which the research being described would eventually be put. When told we were out of order, we walked up to the podium and kept talking, essentially hijacking the meeting and insisting we be heard and our points debated. That often provoked heated reactions from scientists in the audience doing related work, which was our intent. We wanted all the people there to struggle with the implications of their research and consider how most applications were beyond their control and governed by priorities they might not respect. We succeeded because of our forceful tactics and our refusal to play by the rules. Nothing like this had ever before happened at a major scientific gathering.

After the first day, we attracted enough attention to hold our own seminars in our suite. We also held nightly meetings to openly plan actions for the following day. Chicago press covered our initial disruptions, which increased attendance. After two days, our actions were newsworthy enough to merit extensive local and some national coverage. By the third day, our unpredictable tactics had almost everyone at the convention either debating the substance of our critique or arguing about expelling us from the premises. We were unrelenting, both because we knew we were having an impact and because we remained outraged at the convention's attempt to exclude us in the first place.

On the third night, Dr. Philip Handler, president of the National Academy of Sciences, was scheduled to give a keynote speech in the huge hotel ballroom following an introduction by the famous anthropologist Margaret Mead. We thought that would be a good place to inject ourselves, so we planned to seize the stage as Mead began. I was selected to deliver a lengthy speech that described the thinking in our manifesto and explained that because we were excluded from the proceedings we had to disrupt the convention to be heard. I had written a draft that was later improved upon by others. We expected a frosty reception, so we placed a dozen people throughout the ballroom ready to shout "Let him speak" if the convention authorities tried to stop me before I finished.

Mead was a towering figure in academia. Virtually every college student for the previous three decades had read her *Coming of Age in Samoa*, published in 1928. She had once famously said, "A small group of thoughtful people could change the world. Indeed, it's the only thing that ever has." The quotation was singularly appropriate to the situation, but I lacked the presence of mind to include it in my speech. As Mead walked to the microphone, leaning as usual on her wooden staff, ten of us climbed onto the stage and surrounded her. I politely apologized for having to interrupt her and took the microphone. Surrounded by my young scientist friends, then cast in the unfamiliar role of bodyguards, I delivered a very angry and impolite fifteen-minute speech to the two thousand people in front of me. No one interrupted, although some walked out.

By the time the convention ended, our fledgling Science for the People organization had gained national press and some notoriety. In the coming months, membership grew rapidly as the controversy about our activities spread through the mass media and scientific publications. Our bimonthly newsletter became a magazine and began a publishing run that lasted for many years. Most important, we helped move the protest movement into the mainstream world of scientific research. Our actions provoked similar activities within other academic disciplines. Soon historians, literature professors, teachers, engineers, and others spoke up within their own professional societies to question their academic, professional, and organizational priorities.

In January, I returned to classroom teaching. A few weeks later, I found Abbie Hoffman asleep on my living room couch. One of my young roommates had invited the Chicago Seven defendant to stay with us while he was in town for court proceedings. Abbie was a whirling dervish, spewing a constant stream of ideas, some brilliant, some ridiculous, but under his wild head of hair he had a great sense of humor and was very entertaining. We liked each other, and over the next twenty years occasionally worked together on various projects.

Chicago was my hometown, so I renewed a few old friendships. One was with Sly, the gambler who had helped southern civil rights workers and the Paul Butterfield Blues Band. In the intervening years, Sly had lost everything and was $100,000 in debt. Unfortunately, his debt was to a Chicago bookie with a well-earned reputation for extracting a pound of flesh when cash was unavailable. Sly had a hot tip and asked me to stop by the converted bookstore where he lived. The Super Bowl was five days away, and Sly had learned, before it became public, that a star player was going to be out with an injury. Sly had placed a $100,000 bet on the other team and offered me a piece of the action. I declined.

Two days later the injured player made an unexpected recovery. Sly invited his friends to watch the game with him, promising that if he won his bet, he would sponsor a big celebration. On Sunday, before the game began, he asked each of us to claim a portion of his possessions. If he lost the bet, he planned to get in his car, drive off, and disappear. If that happened, he wanted friends to share his goods. I chose his ex-girlfriend's bicycle, which she had left behind. We settled around the TV set and prepared for the worst. It came. Sly gave each of us a heartfelt hug, used his two canes to walk out the door, and without a backward glance drove away on the snow-covered street.

For two years he hid in a tiny town in upstate New York. While there, someone who owed him a great deal of money went into partnership with the bookie to whom he was in debt. An arrangement was struck in which the two debts canceled each other out, and Sly returned to Chicago. He lived modestly in Hyde Park and eked out a meager living gambling and working whatever angles he could. When the time came, he would provide critical help to me on a difficult and dangerous mission.

CHAPTER 14

OUR SUCCESSFUL ACTIONS AT THE AAAS CONVENTION PROVOKED WIDESPREAD INTER-
est in Science for the People. Along with the other organizers, I wrote articles for our new magazine and spoke at meetings urging young scientists
to join us. The vast majority of the scientific community considered our
views to be heresy of the worst sort, but younger scientists, more affected
by the climate of protest and cultural change, were curious and open to
discussion. I planned to help organize for the attempt to shut down Washington in May, but before I got started, Vietnam Veterans Against the War
(VVAW) captured the attention of the antiwar movement.

In late January 1971, VVAW held its Winter Soldier hearings in
Detroit. Rumors about torture, atrocities, and war crimes in Viet Nam
would be the subject of an open investigation. "Winter Soldier" came
from a Revolutionary War pamphlet by Tom Paine. He decried the "summer soldiers and the sunshine patriots" who returned home before the terrible winter at Valley Forge. His heroes were the "winter soldiers" who
remained with Washington's army and eventually won our nation's independence.

The event was a partial response to the recent court-martial of Lieutenant William Calley, the lone man indicted for the My Lai massacre.
The leaders of VVAW, sensing a cover-up, wanted to place blame on the
generals and politicians who set war policy. Based on the experience of the
vets, atrocities like My Lai were common and the result of those policies.

The proceedings got a big publicity boost when Jane Fonda, a famous movie star increasingly visible as a participant in the antiwar movement, became a co-sponsor with VVAW and attended in person.

Ex-soldiers not only testified about wartime atrocities they had witnessed. They testified about atrocities they had committed, including horrifying tales of murder and brutality. None tried to justify his actions, only establish context. Most were draftees who had thought they were fighting to save the Vietnamese. Yet the same villagers who had run away when they approached later welcomed NLF guerrillas with food and water. In combat, these soldiers had seen friends blown apart by an enemy that was often invisible, disappearing into the thick jungle or down into an intricate network of tunnels. The guerrillas easily dissolved into the civilian population, which left U.S. forces unable to retaliate . . . other than to kill more civilians, as they had at My Lai. Their attacks drove more civilians into the enemy camp, while politicians in Washington deceitfully boasted about winning "the hearts and minds" of the Vietnamese people.

Information about these war crimes was expected, but quite unexpectedly the appalling testimony also created new sympathy for the soldiers from the antiwar activists who heard it. The men who testified at Winter Soldier were racked with guilt and ashamed of what they had done. They openly confessed in hopes of preventing others from committing similar crimes. In introducing himself, one soldier said, "My testimony concerns the leveling of villages for no valid reason, throwing Viet Cong suspects from the aircraft after binding them and gagging them with copper wire." Another began, "My testimony involves burning of villages with civilians in them, the cutting off of ears, cutting off of heads, torturing of prisoners, calling in of artillery on villages for games, corpsmen killing wounded prisoners."

I saw this on film clips rather than in person, but it had a powerful effect on me. Others who were there listened spellbound for several days as 109 combat veterans delivered their shocking accounts. Many openly cried or fought back tears. Their crimes and the courage they displayed in taking responsibility for their actions moved some in the audience to tears as well. These men, many of whom suffered recurring nightmares and incapacitating flashbacks, knew in their hearts that they could never be forgiven. The searing pain on their faces and the compassion they showed for each other broke my heart. Many activists had been ambivalent about the veterans, seeing them as willing instruments of death or pawns manipulated to kill. Their testimony in Detroit revealed their own pain and suffering and the extreme difficulty they experienced trying to reintegrate themselves into civilian life. Their stories redefined them as victims, too.

While the Winter Soldier hearings focused on war crimes, they also exposed a general breakdown of military discipline in Viet Nam. Many soldiers had tried to escape the war in the personal oblivion provided by heroin and marijuana. Others had resisted by refusing to go into battle. But by 1971 entire units had refused to fight. The threat of punishment didn't scare them; it was just another way to avoid combat. Their goal was to stay alive long enough to get home. They had seen too many comrades killed or crippled in a war they could neither understand nor justify.

To the troops, officers ordering them into combat were the greatest threat to their lives. Their response was mutiny. They warned their officers not to initiate attacks against the enemy. Officers who ignored such warnings might be awakened at night by a smoke grenade. If that weren't enough, tear gas might follow. The final step was permanent. Officers who kept ordering aggressive action were killed by fragmentation grenades rolled into their tents at night. The practice became so common it acquired its own name: "fragging." Gung ho officers not "fragged" had bounties put on their heads by soldiers pooling their money, and were shot in the back as they tried to lead troops into battle. The military suppressed this information, but there were certainly hundreds and more likely thousands killed this way.

Years later, a trusted friend who was a combat medic in Viet Nam told me that random autopsies on dead officers at his base in the spring of 1971 revealed 40 percent killed by M16 bullets. The United States used M16 rifles; the Vietnamese used AK-47s. The medic also told me of an incident in which hand grenades planted by enlisted men exploded inside a crowded but windowless officers' club made of concrete blocks. When my medic friend rushed in to give first aid, he found forty-one dead officers and over a hundred wounded. The incident was blamed on the Vietnamese.

As information spread about resistance inside the military, we in the antiwar movement realized that Nixon's troop reductions were not part of a peace plan. We concluded he was being forced to withdraw U.S. forces because so many soldiers were in open mutiny, a fact that could not be publicly revealed. No army can function unless it can convince young men to advance together into a hail of bullets. If some knew others had gotten away with holding back, they all would. The military was stuck. It could not discipline the tens of thousands of mutinous soldiers without revealing the truth to other soldiers and the public. Unpunished, the mutinous behavior quickly spread, and to other service branches as well. Sailors on aircraft carriers pushed planes into the sea, while airmen sabotaged firing mechanisms on bombs to prevent civilian casualties. Unable to discipline this behavior, military leaders had no alternative but to withdraw our ground forces.

Henry Kissinger packaged a new war policy for Nixon. The German-born national security adviser spoke with a thick accent and was often compared to the title character in the film *Dr. Strangelove*. He was a renowned egotist and was said to strut around the White House like a power-mad make-believe Bismarck. They called the plan "Vietnamization." Ground operations were shifted to the puppet army in the South, trained, supplied, and paid for by Washington. American ground forces were gradually withdrawn, making it look to the American public as if the war were winding down. Meanwhile, U.S. aerial bombardment, far less visible to the public, was dramatically increased. At that point, the United States had already dropped more bombs on Viet Nam, a country the size of England, than had been dropped by all nations fighting in World War II. Yet Nixon and Kissinger would more than double the bomb tonnage before the war ended. For them, "Vietnamization" had an added benefit: it would change the color of the corpses.

When opponents of the war realized that morale was collapsing inside the military, some farsighted activists set up coffeehouses near military bases and encouraged off-duty personnel to visit. They hosted dances and films to draw new recruits, then held discussion groups to give them an opportunity to learn more about the war. Combat veterans from VVAW described their experiences and their disillusionment. Antiwar protests were held near these bases and drew increasing numbers of young soldiers. Many of these coffeehouses published their own newspapers, which were clandestinely distributed on the bases. The seeds of rebellion were planted well before the soldiers got to the battlefield.

During the winter and spring of 1971, a new alliance formed to give leadership to the antiwar movement. The People's Coalition for Peace and Justice (PCPJ) agreed to sponsor the civil disobedience designed to shut down Washington in early May. The action was called Mayday for short, and Rennie Davis was put in charge of tactics and planning. Rennie was using his visibility as a Chicago Seven defendant to publicize the action. I called him in February to offer air support. If dropping leaflets from a plane would help, I said I would fly it. We discussed several aerial possibilities, but after a few calls we decided the added benefit was low. Instead, I agreed to help lead the Illinois contingent on the ground in Washington.

The PCPJ plan was to group protesters by state and assign each to block a specific intersection or bridge. The PCPJ office in Chicago asked me to recruit on nearby campuses. When I did, I argued that antiwar activists should no longer tolerate arrest, or simply stand silently listening to speeches. Demonstrations of that sort had not affected war policy. Instead, the lack of success demoralized participants and undermined belief in their own effectiveness. We had to change that, even if more risk was required. If we could amass the power to shut down the government, even for a day, it would instantly restore momentum to our movement.

While we organized for Mayday, VVAW planned a week of activities in Washington to start on April 19. Its members wanted to publicize the Winter Soldier testimony and visit senators and representatives in large groups to argue that the war could not be won. At the same time, Trotskyists in the Socialist Workers Party (SWP) called for their own national mobilization in Washington on April 24. They were trying to piggyback on the Mayday protest a week later and the VVAW events a week before. It was a smart move. Some people were unwilling to risk arrest during Mayday but wanted someplace to lodge a peaceful protest, even if it meant attending an event sponsored by the unpopular SWP.

In March, Arcadius Kahan, a distinguished professor of economics and the dean of social sciences in the University of Chicago college, called me into his office. He regretted to inform me that after the end of the academic year, UC would no longer require my services. The university was famous throughout the world as a center for scientific research. My activities at the AAAS convention and the press statements I made were unacceptable from a member of the UC faculty. The dean made no mention of my grading system the previous quarter. Nor did he know that I had assigned my current students to work for various community organizations and labor unions as part of their training in social science research methodology. One group needed help researching tax fraud by a local steel mill; another was investigating racial tracking in Chicago high schools.

Kahan was obviously conflicted and drew me into a conversation about his own history. He had been a Jewish student in the Communist Party when the Nazis marched into Poland in 1939. He joined an armed underground unit that sabotaged facilities but more often just struggled to stay alive. Kahan became a leader and survived the war. After the Soviets drove the Nazis out, he expected the Polish Communist Party and his battle-hardened comrades to establish the new government. Instead, Soviet officials confiscated their weapons and created a puppet state to serve their own security interests. Kahan's comrades who objected were imprisoned. Bitter and disillusioned, he fled the country.

Kahan was warning me about communists. I honored his bravery during World War II and sympathized with his experience, but told him that while the antiwar movement questioned the inequities and excesses of capitalism, we did not favor Soviet communism. In fact, we detested Soviet internal repression. That was why we called ourselves the New Left. Others might be divided between two Cold War extremes, but we advocated a third way. Kahan listened politely. He was clearly a man of courage and principle, but traumas suffered at Soviet hands left him little patience for my point of view.

My termination was expected. It meant little to me, since I had no intention of teaching again. The success of our activities at the AAAS convention had strengthened Science for the People. Enough money was coming in from an expanding membership to offer me a full-time job in Boston the following year. My plan had worked. I had used the one-year assignment at UC to springboard into a political job, which was what I had wanted all along. The pay would be only $50 a week, but I had some savings and little desire for what more money could buy. Meanwhile, I focused on Mayday.

Thanks to the PCPJ organizers, Mayday was unusually well planned. Starting months in advance, they had raised substantial funding from wealthy donors. Fourteen regional offices were established to recruit and train participants. A thirty-minute film, *Time Is Running Out*, narrated by the singer-songwriter Joni Mitchell, often accompanied speakers like me who recruited on college campuses. Leaders had a step-by-step guide for training people in nonviolent tactics. Volunteers got a multicolored training manual with a hundred pages of information and detailed maps of Washington. Traffic patterns had been thoroughly analyzed. Twenty-one choke points were selected, including the Potomac River bridges coming in from suburban Virginia and the major arteries from adjacent suburbs in Maryland. Also targeted were key traffic circles within the city where the main streets converged. Each choke point was assigned to a different state or region so people could work out effective lines of communication before coming to Washington.

Our tactics were simple. Two dozen people would sit down and block traffic at each of the twenty-one choke points. If they went limp and police had to carry them away, it would tie up the choke point for fifteen minutes. Meanwhile, another two dozen would be waiting nearby ready to replace them. With tens of thousands of activists and only twenty-one choke points, we could sustain that tactic all day. Old cars, bought for the purpose, would be abandoned on the bridges at irregular intervals. We expected the police would hate this and become violent, so we encouraged the use of helmets and protective gear. We also urged participants to form "affinity groups" of five to eight people who would stick together for mutual protection.

In the weeks before Mayday, the U.S. death toll in Viet Nam surpassed forty-five thousand, triggering new opposition. Antiwar clergymen (there were no clergywomen then) spoke out from their pulpits, appeared in media interviews, and led local marches. Protests targeted corporations profiting from the war. Nixon's approval rating dropped to 50 percent, and support for his Viet Nam strategy fell to only 34 percent. Roughly half of Americans polled finally concluded that the war was "morally wrong," yet they didn't know how to end it. Emotional but obviously contradictory arguments about those already dead having "died in vain" confused people. So did Nixon's claim that premature withdrawal would benefit our Cold War enemies.

On Monday, April 19, VVAW's week of protest began with over a thousand Viet Nam veterans marching to the gate of Arlington National Cemetery led by a group of Gold Star Mothers (those who had lost sons in the war). The gate was locked to prevent their entry. The outraged vets held a memorial service led by a military chaplain who had recently resigned his commission to protest the war. They then marched to the National Mall. Nixon's Justice Department had obtained an injunction to prevent them from camping there. They defied it and set up their tents. That afternoon the court of appeals overturned the injunction.

The next morning the vets marched back to Arlington. Again the gate was locked, but with so many reporters present, embarrassed officials were forced to let them in. That night the Supreme Court overruled the court of appeals and prohibited the vets from camping on the mall. Lawyers said it was the fastest reversal of an appellate decision in their history. The veterans were disappointed and hurt. They angrily refused to leave, and park police assured them that despite Supreme Court orders, they would not arrest combat veterans for camping on the mall. The next morning a typical headline read, "Vets Overrule Supreme Court."

The country was absolutely riveted by the spectacle of combat veterans opposing the war. Press coverage of their ongoing protests and lobbying in Congress was the lead story on TV news programs at night and on the nation's front pages in the morning. For the first time, Americans in large numbers saw how these once innocent young men had been so brutalized by their experiences in Viet Nam that even after physical wounds had healed, the psychological damage would cause them and their families to suffer for years to come. The intense press coverage of the vets changed the face of the antiwar movement. Instead of protesting students, the public saw battle-scarred veterans. I thought that was a step in the right direction.

On Wednesday, seventy-five vets marched to the Pentagon and turned themselves in as war criminals, a historic first. A Pentagon official recorded their names but would not do more. Groups of vets in fatigue jackets and military garb walked the halls of Congress to lay their case before members who supported the war. The next day, a VVAW spokesman named John Kerry testified before the Senate Foreign Relations Committee. Decades later he would chair it. News media overflowed into the corridors. Kerry, speaking as a young veteran, asked the question that came to haunt the nation, and then echoed down through the decades to be asked again when he ran for president as the Democratic nominee during the Iraq war in 2004: "How do you ask a man to be the last man to die for a mistake?"

On Friday, veterans gathered near the U.S. Capitol steps to return the combat medals they had won in Viet Nam, medals that no longer symbolized their valor, but their shame. It was the emotional high point of the week. Some vets came in wheelchairs, some on crutches or leaning on canes. They had planned to stuff all the medals into a body bag, but when they arrived at the Capitol, they found a temporary fence that blocked their access to the steps. They set up a microphone and formed a long line behind it. One by one they stepped up, gave their names, and described the medals they held aloft. Then, with gestures of anger and disgust, they hurled their medals over the fence.

Many of the vets were bearded or ponytailed. They wore scruffy clothes, saying with their appearance that they had rejected everything the military and conventional society expected of them. Some had sacrificed a limb or a portion of their sanity to "defend" their country. They shook their fists at the fence and cursed the politicians inside who had been brave enough to send them to war but were afraid to face their protest. Once, their medals had been treasured emblems of their bravery, their sacrifice, and their commitment to the nation. Once, their medals might have been passed down to children, as some of their fathers had passed medals from World War II to them. Now they wanted only to be rid of them.

"I'm not proud of these medals. I'm not proud of what I did to receive them. A whole year, we never took one prisoner alive. Just wasted them."

"I pray that time will forgive me and my brothers for what we did."

"Specialist Fourth Class, Army, retired. I'm taking nine Purple Hearts, a Distinguished Service Cross, a Silver Star, a Bronze Star, Army Commendation Medal, and a lot of other shit. This is from my brothers."

"I have a Vietnamese campaign ribbon, a Vietnamese service ribbon, a national defense ribbon, and Purple Heart."

"We're not going to fight anymore, but if we have to fight again, it will be to take these steps."

It went on for hours. Some eight hundred veterans threw back their medals. Bitter as they were toward those who had sent them to war, they were above reproach. Who could accuse *them* of being draft dodgers or cowards? Who could say that *they* were dupes of the communists or fault their patriotism? Their credibility was unquestioned, and their determination to redeem themselves for what they had done in Viet Nam delivered a profound shock to the country. For me, even having seen it only on television, nothing that occurred during the entire course of the war was as moving or as powerful.

The emotion unleashed by the VVAW protests led 200,000 to turn out for the April 24 demonstration sponsored by SWP. They marched from the White House to the Capitol. There, at a protest rally, antiwar senators, congressmen, and labor leaders pleaded with Congress to find a way to override Nixon and end the war. Coretta Scott King was among them. In San Francisco another 200,000 demonstrated.

Friday morning, April 30, I walked into the Mayday office near Farragut Square, a few blocks from the White House. I came to help the organizers get ready for the action on Monday. Their meticulous planning had paid off. The next day, forty thousand people set up camp in West Potomac Park, south of the Lincoln Memorial between the river and the Tidal Basin. It was an instant city. Walking around inside it, I saw thousands of tents with colorful protest banners flying above. NLF flags fluttered next to U.S. flags flown upside down in the international distress signal. There were larger tents that housed communal kitchens, medical facilities, security offices, and press and information services. Rock musicians played on a stage with a huge sound system. I sat in on several regional meetings where plans and tactics were reviewed, and I saw nonviolent training sessions being held. The turnout and the planning gave me confidence that on Monday we would succeed.

I helped convene the Illinois activists, several hundred strong, to review plans. Our assignment was to block Mount Vernon Square in the heart of the city where Massachusetts and New York avenues meet K Street between Seventh and Ninth streets. The square was two blocks long, which gave us many opportunities to block traffic. On the other hand, the police would be able to separate us and disrupt our coordination. We reviewed maps, designated positions we could retreat to, and encouraged everyone to form affinity groups. I coordinated with the national leadership group to insure that Illinois's plans meshed with all the others.

Meanwhile, Nixon was not happy with what he saw. His aides later revealed that he had been so upset by the possibility of our success, they thought he was on the verge of paranoia. He refused suggestions to give federal workers the day off since it might look as if he were unable to control the situation. When he saw the size of our encampment, he arranged for the revocation of our permit on the grounds of rampant drug use. Sunday morning at dawn, he had the U.S. Park Police and D.C. Metro cops raid our tent city in full riot gear. I awoke in my tent to police bullhorns ordering everyone out of the park. With no warning, they fired tear-gas grenades and knocked over tents as they pushed through the area. Day was just breaking, and like everyone else I was too disoriented to resist. We fled into the city.

Without cell phones and the Internet, still decades away, we could not communicate, so many activists went to the college campuses in the area. Phones at the Mayday office rang nonstop. We sent organizers to the campuses and posted notices on bulletin boards. By Sunday evening we had pulled people back together. Most slept that night on a campus or in a black church. Washington's black voters are among the most liberal in the country; their churches were opposed to the war and opened their doors to us. I remained confident. Our activists were well trained and briefed. They would know what to do on Monday. That night I slept in a church with others from Illinois and hastily organized an affinity group.

On the street early Monday morning, we were met by an overwhelming police presence. Besides fifty-one hundred Metro cops and two thousand National Guardsmen mobilized to stop us, there were thousands of federal troops. Nixon had left for his summer retreat in California, but not before ordering soldiers and Marines from all over the East Coast onto troop transport planes Sunday night. These aircraft landed at nearby Andrews Air Force Base at the rate of one every three minutes. Over ten thousand troops were mobilized, including four thousand from the 82nd Airborne Division.

The military lined the bridges from Virginia, which made it impossible for demonstrators to block traffic there. That was a significant setback, so activists assigned to abandon cars on the bridges during the day used them all during the morning rush hour instead. In the city, the troops were held in reserve while the cops cleared the streets. When I arrived at Mount Vernon Square with other Illinois affinity groups, I saw police everywhere. Our people sat down in the intersection, but there were enough cops to grab each of them immediately. Instead of taking names and processing those arrested, the cops simply threw them into paddy wagons and drove off. It took only a minute or two, not the fifteen minutes we had assumed in our planning. When the next group sat down, there were enough cops to handle them the same way.

My affinity group decided not to sit passively and await arrest. When our turn came, we sat down in the street with four other affinity groups in a section of the square with few cops. It took them a while to clear the other sections and turn toward us. When a large contingent moved aggressively in our direction, my group jumped up and fled into the surrounding streets. There I saw troops standing at the ready in the parks and around the monuments, just as I had seen troops hiding under the bridges in Paris in 1960 as gendarmes fought the street demonstrators.

We evaded the roaming bands of police. They swept down the streets, corralled people against buildings, and beat them with nightsticks. They were berserk men with guns, and they seemed out of control. They attacked anyone who looked like a protester but got many who were not. I was on the run, often breathless, and constantly looking out for cops, but my affinity group managed to dodge them and work our way through side streets back to Mount Vernon Square. We hid nearby and waited for an opportunity to block the square. The small transistor radios we carried told of indiscriminate arrests numbering in the thousands. We saw an opening and rushed in to block traffic. A squad of police came after us, but once again we fled and got away. Zigzagging through side streets, I saw police fire tear gas to keep other activists from forming groups. Much of the gas floated into cars and buses bringing commuters into the city. It was a war zone.

By dodging the gas, swallowing our fear, and keeping a sharp eye out for cops, my group managed to get back to Mount Vernon Square to block traffic a third time. We did not last long, but we got away again. By then, there were no longer enough Illinois affinity groups to block the square. We couldn't go back. Instead, we joined a few other affinity groups and roamed the city randomly disrupting traffic where there weren't enough police to respond. In one place a single cop managed to collar someone in my group. The cop marched him across the street to a phone box and called for a wagon. The rest of us watched helplessly. We were unable to assist our friend, and the lone cop was unable to arrest any more of us. It was a standoff.

Suddenly it occurred to me that we were not really helpless. The cop was in uniform, had a gun, and was an intimidating presence. Yet much of his power came from our accepting his aura of authority. What if we didn't? I thought we had a responsibility to rescue our friend, so I convinced the others to try. The cop was not likely to use his firearm against us. I laid out a plan. We all strolled across the street toward the cop with friendly smiles on our faces. The slow walk, as though we had a question, was meant to mentally disarm him. Ten feet away, two of us abruptly

charged at full speed and threw body blocks that knocked him over. The
others grabbed our friend, and we all ran around the corner before the
cop could react.

I knew he would call for backup and run after us. He had already
called in the bust. If a paddy wagon showed up and found him empty-
handed, he would look foolish. We had a one-block head start. Past the
corner, we cut into an alley and kept running. Up ahead, I saw an elderly
black woman leaning on a cane. As we approached, she waved us over
and said, "Quick, y'all, come in here. You can hide in my basement." I
was surprised. We were all white. But we hastily ducked inside. She welcomed us graciously, served milk and cookies, and said she fully supported what we were doing in her city that day.

We left her basement, but the streets had become more dangerous.
Traffic flowed, which freed the cops to make more street sweeps. I saw
them bust anyone who looked vaguely like a protester. My group realized
that if we stuck together, we would become a target. It was safer to separate. I worked my way back to Mayday headquarters off Farragut Square
and went to work fielding calls from reporters seeking new information. It
was still an hour before noon, but I learned that every available jail cell in
the city was full. A practice field at RFK Stadium had been converted into
an outdoor cell block with temporary barbed-wire fencing. New arrestees
were held there like prisoners of war. We called lawyers seeking an injunction to limit the police tactics, but the sweeps, the tear-gas assaults, and
the mass arrests continued.

We refused to be intimidated by all the arrests, but we had lost too
many people to block traffic the next morning. We had to modify our tactics. The arrests had been orchestrated by the Justice Department. If we
could no longer close down the government, we might be able to close
down the Justice Department if we concentrated all our forces there Tuesday morning. The activists who had escaped arrest Monday were once
again scattered across the city, so we called the campuses and black
churches and posted bulletins announcing the new plan.

Tuesday morning, I joined four thousand others in the small park
near the Mayday office. We marched to the Justice Department and sat
down on the streets and sidewalks adjacent to the block-square building. It

was a nose-to-nose confrontation. From where I sat on Tenth Street, I could see Attorney General John Mitchell, widely considered the ruthless hatchet man of the Nixon administration, standing on the roof. He was directing the police and federal forces under his command. We had the building surrounded. Normal vehicular and pedestrian traffic was stopped, but the cops were able to clear a path for special vehicles going in or out of the building's garage.

We were orderly and nonviolent. We knew we would be arrested. It was a change of strategy, but it was the best use of the resources we had. Every reporter and camera in town was there to watch. The huge number of arrests the day before had no precedent in the nation's history. We wanted to make clear through press coverage that arrests would not deter us. None of us wanted a criminal record, but the stakes were so high in the present that the risk of problems in the future seemed trivial. We wanted to ridicule the government's power. All the police could do was make more arrests, which meant little to us. To underscore the point, some in the crowd where I sat on Tenth Street got out musical instruments and played while others danced on the pavement. Arrest us! Who cares!

The stalemate lasted a few hours. Mitchell finally understood that he could not wait us out. He ordered arrests to begin. It was a highly choreographed operation. Everyone, including the cops, behaved reasonably, no doubt because of all the press and cameras. The cops set up two processing lines. I was escorted into one of them, fingerprinted, and put into a waiting paddy wagon. When it was full and pulled away, I expected we would go to the POW camp at the stadium. Instead, we drove out of the city. I saw rural countryside out the back window and wondered where we were going. An hour later, we drove into a small town in Virginia. Its jail had six two-person cells. They put all fourteen of us into one of them. The stadium was full, as was every jail cell in the city and all of its suburbs.

The overcrowding was amusing at first, fourteen people, male and female, stuffed into a very narrow two-person cell. We looked like commuters on a packed subway train. However, as the hours passed and new arrestees were crammed into the other cells, it was obvious that our situation was not temporary. We were given no food or water, and it took prolonged screams to get to a bathroom. That night we had to lie on top of each other on the floor to get any sleep. Every time one of us rolled over or moved, all fourteen people had to adjust their positions. All day Wednesday it continued. The only food we received was at noon, when we were given baloney sandwiches on white bread. We were kept jailed without charges so we would not return to Washington and continue demonstrating, which the authorities knew we would do immediately upon release.

While I sat in that tiny jail cell on Wednesday, the surviving protesters marched to the Capitol. Several senators and representatives spoke to the crowd endorsing their demand that Congress take action to stop the war. Even though the few thousand protesters in front of the Capitol did nothing but listen to these speeches, federal authorities saw them as a threat. Cops attacked with a vengeance and dragged off over a thousand. In a story I heard later, an aide to Ron Dellums was arrested as the congressman tried to intervene. "Hey," he said, "that's a member of my staff. Get your hands off of him. I'm a United States congressman." The cop replied, "I don't give a fuck who you are." He struck the distinguished black congressman with his nightstick and pushed him down the stairs.

That confrontation was the end of Mayday. Thousands remained in lockups throughout the area, including me. Conditions were terrible everywhere. In my little Virginia jail we never got another meal after the baloney sandwiches. Wednesday night was the same as the night before. I am lucky enough to be able to sleep well in uncomfortable conditions, so I spent much of the time unconscious. Others, especially those with claustrophobic tendencies, had a more difficult time. It lasted until Thursday morning, forty-six hours after we had arrived. We were then loaded back into paddy wagons and driven to the central lockup in Washington.

The city's main jail looked like a prison in an old movie. An open central area had metal stairways that connected five tiers of cells on all four sides. I was put in a cell for an hour and then brought to a processing area. For the first time since my arrest I was asked my name. Nobody was checking identification, so I spelled my last name with an S instead of a Z. Alphabetical order would distance it from my real name, but if caught, I could claim it was a clerical error. My falsified last name was recorded, and I was released.

Outside I learned that FBI agents had arrested Rennie Davis, Abbie Hoffman, and John Froines on riot and conspiracy charges. All three were notorious Chicago Seven defendants. Froines had worked closely with Rennie coordinating Mayday, and we had become acquainted in the process. Police agencies like to target well-known people because they assume it buttresses their reputation and demonstrates they are on the job. Since the news audience is drawn to people it already knows, the press gives enhanced coverage to those it has already made famous, which further enhances their fame. A self-perpetuating cycle results: the more famous people are, the more famous they become, and if they are on the wrong side of the law, the more likely they are to be arrested, which enhances their fame, or notoriety, once again. That's why the FBI sought out the three of them. Later, charges were dropped because the feds refused to reveal infiltrators in their employ. I concluded that it might be more effective to work in the shadows than in the limelight.

During the three days of the Mayday demonstrations, over fourteen thousand people were arrested, the largest mass arrest in the country's history. Some were beaten. Most were arrested illegally and held illegally, as I was, uncharged and stuffed into drastically overcrowded cells with little food and no toilets. Thousands were kept overnight in outdoor pens at the stadium and in the exercise yard at the main jail. Nighttime temperatures fell below forty degrees with no blankets provided. Lawful assemblies, like those in front of the Capitol, were arbitrarily attacked. The same federal authorities charged with protecting citizens from such mistreatment perpetrated these abuses. Years later, the courts expunged most of the arrests and forced the city and federal governments to pay compensation to protesters and innocent civilians.

I went to the airport and flew home to Chicago sad and disappointed. Our strategy and our tactics had both failed. We did not immobilize the government. The massive arrests and our mistreatment by the police did not provoke a huge public outcry. The suspension of our civil liberties went almost unnoticed. The workers did not rise up and support us as they had in Paris in 1968. Nobody did. We had miscalculated.

In the succeeding days, I realized we were guilty of a larger miscalculation. A majority of Americans were finally opposed to the war. Yet the militant tactics of the antiwar movement alienated those same people, most of whom were not activists but ordinary citizens. We who had been protesting for years could not help but be militant, but others, new to the cause, were not going to run in the streets or risk arrest to express their opposition. Nor could they easily sympathize with those of us who did. The tactic of mass antiwar demonstrations had not only outlived its usefulness; it had died on the streets of Washington.

I understood that a new antiwar movement had to be built using tactics that drew people in rather than pushed them away. We had to make it easy for people to join us, not require them to carry foreign flags, risk arrest, or adopt a militant posture toward a government many still considered their own. If we failed, the majority opposed to the war would be of no value. But until a new strategy and other tactics emerged, I vowed that Mayday would be the last time I labored in support of a large-scale antiwar demonstration. At Science for the People in the fall, I planned to build opposition to the war within the scientific community and help develop a new perspective on science that could have implications beyond Viet Nam. Mayday had failed, but the tide was turning against the war. It was no time to give up.

CHAPTER 15

IN JUNE, I FINISHED AT THE UNIVERSITY OF CHICAGO, AND THE PROTECTIVE COCOON OF academic life I had lived in for so long dissolved, this time for good. I stayed in the city over the summer to earn some extra money and upgrade my private pilot's license to commercial status. The upgrade was a personal challenge, but also insurance against future poverty. Someday I might need a real job, and since I liked to fly, I wanted the option.

I looked for a flight instructor at Midway Airport and was introduced to a tall, muscular fellow in his mid-thirties with close-cropped hair and a military bearing. He was anxious to get home. Since his apartment was directly across the street from the airport, he invited me along. Walking in, I saw the windowsill facing the street. It was lined with small marijuana plants.

Bob Talbot was a master pilot licensed to fly everything from gliders to seaplanes to multiengine transports. He gave freelance flight instruction and taught aviation courses at the local community college. He was just what I was looking for, but despite the rebellious streak revealed by the marijuana plants, he advertised himself as a patriotic Republican. I didn't want to begin our association on false pretenses, so I told him we had absolutely nothing in common—except flying and marijuana. On reflection, we each thought it would be a challenge to learn about the other, so we agreed to fly together.

Talbot was a harsh and demanding instructor. For weeks I suffered through precision maneuvers and simulated emergency drills. One day he told me to fly over Lake Michigan and descend to an altitude of two feet. He wasn't joking. I went down as low as I thought possible, but Talbot insisted I was still twenty feet up. I inched down farther, afraid the extended landing gear would hit the water and flip us over. It wasn't enough. When he was finally satisfied, I had to maintain that two-foot altitude for ten very long minutes. Any deviation and we were dead.

Now, he said, you're ready to fly under a bridge. We headed back over land to one he knew. When I saw how low it was, I was sure I was going to die, but as we got closer, I knew I had acquired the skill to do it. We flew together often, and had fun, too. By the end of the summer, I easily passed the flying and written tests for my commercial license. And despite our differences, we became good friends. Two years later I got him into so much trouble he swung all the way over to my end of the political spectrum.

By summer's end, I had increased my savings to $8,000. In the bank, that money gave me no immediate benefit, so I bought a thirteen-year-old airplane for $5,000. It was a Cessna 172 that had already depreciated enough for me to resell it a few years later for a comparable price. A farmer in Wisconsin had it in his barn. Talbot and I flew up to inspect it together. It was a single-engine four-seat aircraft that cruised at 120 miles per hour behind a 145-horsepower engine. It was small, but it was mine, and I was thrilled! My job with Science for the People required some travel, which I could do in the little Cessna. A week later, I flew it to Boston.

John Froines, whom I befriended during the preparations for Mayday, had earned a Ph.D. in chemistry at Yale in 1967, the same year I got mine. He, too, had rejected his scientific career to do antiwar work. On John's invitation, I moved into a big communal house on Dartmouth Street in Somerville, adjacent to Cambridge and Boston, which he shared with six other adults. Three stories tall, it sat on a corner lot surrounded by rosebushes. Each of us cooked one night a week, washed dishes another, and shared cleaning and yard work on the weekends. Four of the adults were coupled up so there were bedrooms for everyone, and three of the women had very young children. The rest of us tried to help the mothers with child care, but while our intentions were sound, our practice was not.

I liked everyone, and despite never having lived this way before, I found it congenial. I was already close to John, who lived with his wife, Ann, and their six-year-old daughter, and I soon formed lasting friendships with Danny Schechter and Marilyn Webb. Danny lived with Linda Gordon, a feminist historian, and was the newscaster on WBCN, one of the first FM radio stations to feature rock music and progressive politics. On the air, he was "Danny Schechter, the News Dissector." Marilyn was the divorced mother of a two-year-old daughter. She was an early leader of the new feminist movement and had helped start and edit one of the first feminist periodicals, *Off Our Backs*, in Washington, D.C.

It was the classic 1960s commune, despite most of us being in our early thirties and the calendar saying it was 1971. Unlike the hippie stereotype, however, we all worked long hours fulfilling what we understood to be our political responsibilities. Everyone in the house was an antiwar activist or organizer, even though some pursued academic careers or other endeavors. We all took part in antiwar work in the Boston area, and the house soon became a center of activism. My housemates had a well-established network of friends, which I easily joined.

By mid-fall I had integrated myself into the staff at the Science for the People office and was working productively. I had successfully jumped from a career in science and academia into full-time political work. I was happy to be part of a successful organization and gratified that I could contribute to it. I had smart and experienced colleagues who could teach me more of what I wanted to learn. And at the end of the day, I went home to a communal dinner with friends I respected and whose company I enjoyed.

Work against the war had gotten a big boost that summer because of the release of the Pentagon Papers, a top-secret history of the Viet Nam War prepared for the Defense Department. Daniel Ellsberg, a former Marine Corps officer and later a State Department officer in Viet Nam and defense analyst for the RAND Corporation, became a consultant to the project. Ellsberg saw that given the available resources, military lead-

ers had been pessimistic about victory in Viet Nam from the very beginning. Yet the Johnson and Nixon administrations had ordered hundreds of
thousands of Americans into combat and had hidden their skepticism
from Congress and the American people.

Ellsberg believed he had a moral obligation to publicize the truth,
even if it meant life in prison for espionage, theft, and conspiracy. He
secretly photocopied seven thousand classified pages with the help of
Tony Russo, a former colleague at RAND, and gave them to the *New York
Times*, then the *Washington Post* and other newspapers. Nixon stopped
the publication, but when lawsuits against him reached the Supreme
Court, he was overruled. In a landmark decision that expanded First
Amendment freedoms for the first time in the twentieth century, the
Supreme Court permitted publication. The contents were a bombshell.
An outraged press became even more critical of the war, and antiwar
members of Congress ramped up their opposition. Nixon and Kissinger
ignored the outcries and refused to alter their war strategy.

While these revelations affected the larger antiwar movement, I was
pursuing a more limited agenda. The previous spring I had written an article for *Science for the People* magazine encouraging American scientists
to do research that would help doctors and scientists in Viet Nam. When
I joined the organization in Boston, I launched a Science for Viet Nam
campaign to promote such work. The campaign suggested specific
research projects that were needed and publicized research already under
way to encourage more scientists to participate. I knew it was easier for scientists to redirect their work than to leave it behind as Bart and I had done.

Our greatest concern at the time was Agent Orange. The United
States sprayed this herbicide over Vietnamese jungles and rice fields to
deprive NLF guerrillas of cover and food. The herbicide was one of the
worst examples of the perversion of science.

Agent Orange has a half-life in the soil of decades. We could do little
about the genetic damage caused by dioxin, which would lead to tens of
thousands of Vietnamese babies born with horrifying birth defects, some
as many as forty years later. Nor could anything be done to prevent the
autoimmune diseases that would eventually disable thousands of Ameri-

can soldiers exposed to Agent Orange. However, Science for Viet Nam worked with one team of agronomists trying to find microorganisms capable of metabolizing dioxin out of the soil and another looking for rice strains resistant to dioxin so that contaminated fields could again be used for food production.

Beyond the horrors of Agent Orange, Vietnamese civilians suffered shrapnel-like wounds from plastic fragments in antipersonnel bombs. Unlike the more common metal shards, these plastic fragments could not be detected by X-rays and therefore could not be removed, adding to the already overwhelming burdens on Vietnamese clinics. We looked for bio-engineers to try to find ways to localize these plastic fragments in human flesh. We also helped American scientists assist Vietnamese colleagues working on reforestation. Saturation bombing had left large areas pock-marked with bomb craters. One solution, adopted in many areas, was to flood the craters for use as fish farms. Our researchers investigated using ants for pest control, and tried to synthesize pheromones (olfactory sex attractants) for the same purpose. Others looked for medicinal plants that might flourish in Indochina.

Unlike protests that fell on deaf ears in Washington, we wanted our work to benefit the Vietnamese and strengthen their ability to survive the American war. The Science for Viet Nam campaign also gathered up-to-date scientific journals from professors and students, which we shipped to Hanoi, the North Vietnamese capital. American physicists helped colleagues at the University of Hanoi with computer programs, while others scoured their departments for surplus equipment, like mass spectrometers, that could be donated.

From my perch coordinating the Science for Viet Nam project, I could recruit other scientists not only to oppose the war but also to take the side of the so-called enemy and possibly engage in useful and important work. It had been three years since Bart received the reprint request from Fort Detrick, and in that interval I had found my way back to science, not as a researcher, but as an organizer.

However, the Science for Viet Nam project was only a small part of my work. I had numerous responsibilities, and within the larger community of young scientists with whom I worked, three individuals became my closest colleagues. Herb Fox, Al Weinrub, and I were in charge of expanding the Science for the People membership, coordinating its communications, and publishing its magazine. We were often invited to speak on university campuses about science and society, and to recruit new members. When it was my turn and the weather permitted, I traveled in my little airplane. Flying was cheap then. Gasoline for cars cost thirty-five cents a gallon and avgas for aircraft was only slightly more. My plane covered 120 miles in one hour using eight gallons of gas, less than $4 worth.

The third colleague was Ethan Signer. He and I took responsibility for special projects that could create new opportunities for the organization. Ethan was a pioneer in the emerging field of molecular biology, and although he was only my age, his brilliant scientific work had earned him a professorship at the Massachusetts Institute of Technology, one of the youngest in the history of the school's biology department. Like me, he had an affinity for the counterculture and the new music. Ethan was also a wizard on the mandolin and other stringed instruments. A few years earlier, he had played backup for Bob Dylan and Richard Fariña.

Ethan and I were determined to continue the attack on the American Association for the Advancement of Science (AAAS). Having first put Science for the People on the political map the previous winter by organizing protests at its convention in Chicago, we were confident we could expand our reach at its upcoming Christmas-break convention in Philadelphia. This time we would have more members, various projects under way, and growing sympathy within the scientific community. Once the Science for the People board agreed to the action, I was put in charge of organizing it. I flew down to Philadelphia several times in the Cessna to arrange for living quarters and office space to use during the weeks leading up to the convention. I also made contact with local antiwar activists for help setting up protest actions.

Ethan and I also wanted to send a Science for the People delegation to China. The United States and China were bitter enemies. Neither recognized the other or had any official diplomatic contact. Chinese scientists claimed that under their communist regime science was done to benefit people, not to generate profit. Did they have anything to teach us? With signs of a coming diplomatic thaw, it might be the right time to promote a visit by a delegation of radical U.S. scientists. Ethan had visited China the year before, one of the only American scientists to do so since the 1949 revolution, so he was known to its government. A delegation of radical scientists would draw media coverage and put our critique of American science before a larger audience.

We wrote to the Chinese embassy in Ottawa, the Canadian capital, and were invited to meet with the ambassador. We drove up in a winter blizzard and, through an interpreter, offered to organize a delegation of U.S. scientists with sympathies similar to ours. After the delegation returned, they would speak and write publicly about their observations. The ambassador was intrigued and promised to contact the Foreign Ministry in Beijing with a positive recommendation.

Shortly after we returned to Boston, Science for the People was asked to send two of its members to Paris in late November for a conference of European antiwar organizations. Ethan and I were chosen. North Vietnamese officials and members of the Vietnamese diplomatic missions headquartered in France would also attend. North Viet Nam and the National Liberation Front (NLF) of South Viet Nam had large embassies in Paris because France was neutral in the war. Paris was also the site of periodic negotiations with the American and South Vietnamese governments. In past years, several dozen American antiwar leaders had met with the Vietnamese in Paris, and a handful had traveled to North Viet Nam to represent the antiwar movement there. Leaving for Paris with Ethan, I looked forward to such quasi-diplomatic experience myself.

Paris was familiar terrain, but I had no time to enjoy it. Every hour at the conference was scheduled, but the agenda was narrower than I had thought. The European groups present all sponsored public campaigns to purchase medical supplies for the Vietnamese. Their fund-raising drives were a visible expression of opposition to the war, and their donors had an opportunity to alleviate the suffering it caused. Many of the Vietnamese at the conference were health officials; others were diplomats who helped coordinate this medical relief work.

These campaigns were a revelation to me. Public fund-raising drives were under way in a dozen European countries. No one was doing it in the United States because we were a party to the war and it was assumed there were laws to prevent it. The Europeans did not send money. Rather, they used the money to purchase medical supplies they then shipped to North Viet Nam and the NLF, thus neutralizing any criticism that the funds might be diverted for weapons instead of medicine. The enthusiastic Europeans had organized door-to-door appeals, staged benefit concerts, raised money on university campuses, and solicited large contributions from wealthy individuals, foundations, and socialist political parties. The purpose of the Paris conference was to coordinate these efforts across Europe instead of having separate campaigns in each country.

Cora Weiss was among the dozen or so Americans representing other organizations at the conference. A stylish woman about ten years my senior, Cora was wealthy in her own right and the wife of Peter Weiss, a prominent progressive attorney in New York. She had used her wealth and social connections to become the doyenne of the New York antiwar movement and one of its most effective fund-raisers. Cora was also a superb organizer, as I would soon discover. She had come to the conference with a plan. Unlike me, she knew of the medical aid work in Europe and had already organized a small committee of Americans, including several prominent physicians, to consider launching a similar effort in the United States. I thought her plan was brilliant. It was just what the American antiwar movement needed to broaden and enlarge its support.

I became obsessed with the idea. Given widespread opposition to the war, I was sure Americans would donate money for medical assistance to civilians in areas controlled by North Viet Nam and the NLF. It was a basic humanitarian gesture, but such a donation would also be sharply confrontational. No one had ever raised money to assist an enemy population in a time of war. It would give Americans a way to protest without risk of arrest or job loss. The more I thought about it, the more excited I became. For Americans to give concrete support to a country the Nixon administration considered *its* enemy would powerfully state that Viet Nam was not *our* enemy. Donors would have an opportunity to defy the government, not destructively, but by engaging in a purely humanitarian act. I told Cora I wanted to help, and she invited me to join her committee. I then spent hours questioning the Europeans at the conference about their structures and organizing methods.

Later, Vietnamese officials and diplomats hosted a special dinner for the Americans. Speaking through interpreters, they told me what others had learned previously, namely, that the Vietnamese bore no grudge against us or the American people, only the American government, and that they saw our work in the antiwar movement as crucial to their survival. They treated us respectfully and made no attempt to direct or control our actions; they only expressed their gratitude. I was buoyed by what I observed and returned to Boston confident that a new tactic had finally been found that could expand the reach and effectiveness of the antiwar movement.

Nixon and Kissinger had reduced troop levels in Viet Nam to 139,000, which suggested to many that the war was winding down. It was not. In early December, Nixon ordered five days of intense bombing just south of Hanoi. Angry protests took place across the country, the most dramatic by VVAW. Its members seized the South Vietnamese consulate in San Francisco. In quick succession VVAW activists then occupied the Lincoln Memorial in Washington, D.C., the Lyndon Baines Johnson Library in Austin, and the Betsy Ross House in Philadelphia. In their most audacious act, they seized the Statue of Liberty, held it for two days, and got extensive national and international attention.

Cora's committee was not meeting again until January, so back from Paris I shifted my attention to the upcoming AAAS convention. Three weeks before it started, I moved down to Philadelphia. Taking off in the little Cessna on a clear moonless night, I climbed into the blackness and flew west of New York City to avoid the airliner traffic. Banking south toward Philadelphia, I descended over all the twinkling lights to a small airport northeast of the city. On a previous trip I had befriended Debbie Frazer, an activist with a Quaker background, and she had invited me to stay in a large apartment she shared with three others near the University of Pennsylvania. Her roommates thought I was an odd character—the flying organizer—but they liked our plans for the AAAS convention and went out of their way to help me.

We intended to be more substantive and less confrontational than in Chicago, but not to lose our radical edge. Before the convention we printed several thousand copies of the manifesto I had co-authored the previous year. The twenty-two-page pamphlet had a plain cover with the word "Censored" stamped diagonally across it.

After Chicago, the four co-authors had revised the manifesto and submitted it to *Science*, the flagship publication of the AAAS and the nation's most prestigious scientific journal. Acceptance was a long shot, but we thought we could generate controversy by trying. Much to our surprise, the three scientists chosen for peer review all recommended publication. One said, "The readers I think will be somewhat surprised that the authors deal with real change and program rather than disruption and confrontation." Another said that our article was "an important position in the debate over the objectives and public responsibilities of science which *Science* magazine has been encouraging for several years."

So far so good, but the conservative editor of *Science* was determined not to publish our article. He sent it to four more referees, all conservatives, hoping to get a 4–3 decision. A closet supporter of ours inside the AAAS sent us copies of the correspondence. Two of the four conservatives advised in favor of publication because they assumed it would expose our faulty thinking. The editor, faced with a 5–2 vote, violated accepted practice and rejected our paper. By claiming it had been "censored" out of the pages of *Science*, we played on the predictable curiosity that word provokes.

Our posture inside the convention did not depend on confrontation, but we were aggressive when necessary, and we collaborated with antiwar activists on the outside who protested scientific support for the war. Hundreds of peaceful protesters, organized by Debbie's friends in the Philadelphia antiwar movement and by local Quaker peace activists, greeted scientists as they streamed into and out of the various convention hotels. Near one a large hand-held banner read, "300 more killed today by U.S. bombs," while next to it demonstrators played dead lying on the sidewalk. I stood nearby gauging the reaction of passing scientists.

Inside the convention we sponsored many of our own panel discussions. One presented data proving that the aerial bombardment in Viet

Nam was the most massive in world history. Another reviewed rampant pollution and pesticide use and called for a radical environmental movement. A third discussed criminal behavior and civil liberties, a fourth, dehumanization in the workplace, to name but a few. We also held nightly meetings to plan the next day's events.

Our focus on a more substantive critique of science confounded our opponents and increased our credibility. However, we did not entirely give up confrontation. For example, Bart and I went to a session in which a psychologist described research on how companies could extract more labor from employees without increasing their wages. We interrupted his talk with pointed questions about why such research was never reversed, why psychologists and other social scientists had failed to help workers get more pay and benefits from employers. The psychologist refused to debate our points, so we refused to allow him to present his.

There were moments of high drama and passion. William Bundy, a principal architect of the war in Viet Nam, was scheduled to speak. He had been in the CIA, had served Johnson in the State Department, and had co-authored the phony Gulf of Tonkin Resolution. Left out in the cold by Nixon, he was politely critical of the new air war strategy. I couldn't wait to get my proverbial hands on him. In my view Bundy and his brother, McGeorge, also a Johnson foreign policy adviser, were war criminals. Many activists went to confront him, and we were in no mood to be cordial. We insisted that before he spoke, we be allowed to question him about his role in the war. The chairman of the session refused, so we refused to allow Bundy to begin. The petulant chairman then adjourned the session and stomped off. We challenged Bundy to stay and debate the war. He agreed. We then rearranged the two hundred chairs into a series of concentric circles, unwilling to look up to him standing on a stage above us.

For the next two hours, we peppered Bundy with pointed questions in an angry and heated exchange. We had studied the war for years, criticized it in writing and in speeches, and debated it with knowledgeable opponents. We knew as much about Viet Nam as Bundy did—with one exception. He had the advantage of having seen secret intelligence reports, and we had the advantage of never having seen those reports, since they were so often wrong or based on distorted analyses designed to serve political masters in Washington. At one point, Bundy used the Nazis in an inept analogy to the situation in Viet Nam. One of the activists with us was a Holocaust survivor who had vivid memories of imprisonment in concentration camps until age eight. He rose to protest Bundy's analogy, at first sputtering furiously but eventually using his own experience in the camps to eloquently counter Bundy's argument.

Daniel Patrick Moynihan, one of the twenty vice presidents of the AAAS and a former counselor to Nixon (and later a U.S. senator from New York), was so angry about our treatment of Bundy that he canceled a speech scheduled later that day and left the convention. Another vice president, Barry Commoner, one of the godfathers of environmental science, criticized Moynihan and argued that our political dissent had promoted an interesting and healthy dialogue. By the end of the day, both the current and the past presidents of the AAAS endorsed Commoner's position. Their endorsement signaled our success. If nothing else, we were part of the debate.

A speech by Hubert Humphrey then generated even more controversy. Antiwar activists detested him. As a U.S. senator from Minnesota he had fought racial discrimination and been a leading liberal, but as vice president he had bowed to Johnson on the war. Many of us had also started as liberals and been radicalized by the war, so we resented liberals who accepted the war as a necessary evil in order to protect their positions in society. Humphrey had become a distasteful symbol of moral cowardice. Before he took the podium, we hung harsh homemade posters on the curtain behind him and insisted they remain there while he spoke.

The former vice president gave a lackluster speech interrupted by boos and catcalls. An activist near the front threw a rotten tomato at him and claimed, as the police escorted him from the hall, that he had missed on purpose. When Humphrey took questions after the speech, the first came from Margaret Mead, the famous anthropologist whose microphone I had commandeered at the Chicago convention. She asked about the intense bombing Nixon had ordered over Viet Nam and also over Laos and Cambodia, the two other countries in Indochina. Humphrey condemned the bombing, called for a complete halt, and claimed to now oppose the war.

His position was a complete surprise, not only to us, but also to the reporters in the room. One of our people, pushing him to be more specific, asked if he would back a three-point program to end the war: condemn the bombing; support a cutoff of U.S. aid to the puppet regime in South Viet Nam; and withdraw from Indochina. Amazingly, Humphrey agreed. I was sitting next to John Froines. We turned to each other in shock. Humphrey was one of the Democratic candidates running for president. The first primary was only two months away in February, and Humphrey had just staked out an entirely new position on the war.

John and I realized how important this could be, so we wrote down the statement Humphrey had just agreed to, word for word. I raised my hand. Humphrey eventually called on me, and I asked if he would sign a written statement attesting to his earlier remarks. Perhaps he failed to realize that we had the statement already prepared, or he was simply too embarrassed to refuse, but whatever the reason he said he would. John and I marched up to the podium and handed him the paper we had just drawn up. He read it, signed it, and gave it back.

The next day, Humphrey's new position on the war received widespread news coverage. He was now on record in complete opposition to Nixon's strategy in Viet Nam. In the *New York Times* article that described how John and I had gotten Humphrey to sign the statement, we got a respectful "Dr." before each of our names. Elsewhere we were referred to as "screaming demonstrators" and "the anti-everything movement."

When it was over, our work at the AAAS convention had given Science for the People increased credibility and visibility. Feeling good about our success, a few of us hosted a party. We had been smart at the convention, but we did something stupid at the party. A hundred people were squeezed into an apartment, and a couple dozen of us who felt very exuberant dropped acid. At first, the LSD enhanced our joy and relief. I embraced the others, and we all danced together as the chemicals in my brain projected a dazzling multicolored light show on an empty white wall across the room. Soon, however, our exhaustion and the crowded apartment turned our "trip" into an unpleasant experience. I retreated to a dark bedroom and waited for the drug to wear off. Two days later, my head clear, I flew the little Cessna back to Boston.

Cora Weiss convened her medical assistance committee in January, and we all reported our experiences in Paris. After some debate, the committee split into two factions. The prestigious physicians present opposed public fund-raising drives, preferring to keep a low profile. They wanted to collect donated medicines and supplies from colleagues and hospitals using their own influence and personal networks.

I had a different idea. I advocated the broadest possible public fund-raising, to be followed by open shipments of medical goods to the North Vietnamese. I argued that tens of thousands of Americans could be organized to donate. That could recast war opposition as a humanitarian response to official violence. Average Americans would have a chance to both oppose the war peacefully and make clear that they did not consider the Vietnamese their enemy. Neither should we fear government prosecution. The authorities would suffer greater political loss by criminalizing medical relief work than they would gain by attacking us.

My remarks made the physicians nervous, and understandably so, given that they might be subject to professional sanctions beyond the criminal charges we could all face. They were courageous people, having already jeopardized their careers and academic appointments by joining the committee, but our goals differed, and we were at an impasse. Unable to agree on a strategy, we tabled a final decision for another meeting a month later.

After the AAAS convention, I worked on the Science for Viet Nam projects and with Ethan recruited scientists for a possible China trip. We were especially interested in those willing to publicize their experiences after they returned, so I was happy to see Bart Meyers sign on. I also became romantically involved with Marilyn Webb, one of my housemates. She had temporarily moved to Vermont to teach at Goddard College, and I flew up to visit her several times. On those trips I had a chance to reconsider how I felt about revolutionary politics.

What I had suggested to Cora's committee was a strategy for building the antiwar movement. It was not a strategy for making a revolution. I thought Karl Marx's analysis of capitalism was sound, but realized he had little to say about overthrowing capitalism in a modern nation. Writing in the nineteenth century, Marx knew nothing of surveillance technology capable of neutralizing secret organizing, or of advertising and mass communication techniques able to cloud people's minds. He had not anticipated the home mortgages and pension funds through which ordinary workers are given a stake in maintaining the economic status quo. If, as I had come to suspect, revolution was not possible in the United States, why were some of us still calling ourselves revolutionaries?

Bitter as I was about the suffering caused by capitalism, the reality of American society could not be ignored. Capitalism was here to stay. Revolution, I realized, was an inappropriate offensive strategy; people who thought as I did lacked the resources to do anything but play defense. Even if the resource problem were overcome, we had no credible revolutionary strategy, nor did I see a way to create one. After much soul-searching, I finally understood that it would not fall to my generation to make a revolution. We could do little more than resist, or make trouble for, the worst aspects of capitalism. I had no choice but to accept that limitation. The overthrow of capitalism was well beyond our reach. If I based my own work on such a fantasy, I would be doomed to fail and would accomplish nothing.

My thinking left me with two fundamental political and moral responsibilities. The first was to help find creative and forceful ways to keep progressive values alive for a future when others might have an opportunity to more fully realize them. The second was to help prevent whatever abuses I could by throwing monkey wrenches into the machinery of oppression. Living up to those responsibilities could still be a path to personal fulfillment and a happy life. If I couldn't be a revolutionary, I'd be a troublemaker.

CHAPTER 16

THE FBI AND THE CIA HAD SPIED ON ANTIWAR ACTIVISTS AND USED UNDERCOVER agents to infiltrate our organizations for many years. Our overheated revolutionary rhetoric was only their most recent excuse. They tapped our phones, read our mail, followed our travels, and did whatever they could to sabotage our work. Years later, after passage of the Freedom of Information Act, many of us obtained heavily redacted files they had maintained on us. The surveillance outlined in my file began in Chicago during the 1966 sit-in.

Those of us who had attracted press attention or were in leadership positions routinely assumed that our movements and communications were monitored, and not just by the feds. Police departments in New York, Los Angeles, and Chicago had "red squads" that did the same. None of this was legal, and vast sums of taxpayer money were wasted in the effort. Undercover provocateurs often advocated violence to discredit the naive activists who accepted their advice and to justify the use of force against them. These official provocateurs also instigated factional disputes, disrupted meetings, falsified documents, and stole money.

We employed various countermeasures against them. Anyone advocating violence was assumed to be a police agent and isolated. When we had to discuss confidential information, we did it in a noisy restaurant or a car with the radio volume turned up to thwart bugs. When we had to make plans over the telephone, we assumed our home and office phones were tapped and talked pay phone to pay phone. I always carried the numbers of several pay telephones near my home or office. When I traveled, I picked up the numbers of a few pay phones close to wherever I stayed. We would ask people to return our calls from a pay phone on their end to a pay phone on ours because the police could not tap into the lines fast enough to monitor our conversations.

As a result, when Ethan Signer asked me to meet him at a noisy bar in Cambridge, I knew something was up. Neither of us spent much time in bars. Sitting opposite him, I immediately saw the excitement on his face. An anonymous scientist had contacted him. The pharmaceutical company where the scientist was employed had just developed a new form of penicillin that did not require refrigeration. I looked quizzically at Ethan, not understanding why this news required a confidential meeting.

Ethan explained the battlefield implications. Helicopters rescuing wounded American soldiers were equipped with small refrigerators to preserve their antibiotics. The Vietnamese they fought against did not have portable refrigerators, and many died from infections that could be prevented by quick access to fresh antibiotics. The anonymous scientist knew that thousands of lives could be saved if Vietnamese medics on the ground carried a broad-spectrum antibiotic that did not require refrigeration. He knew of Ethan's involvement in the antiwar movement and offered to steal a sample of the new antibiotic if Ethan could deliver it to the right people in Viet Nam. An unlimited amount could be cultured from the sample.

Unlike the medical relief proposed by Cora's committee, which would benefit civilians, this would aid the Vietnamese military. Was it the right thing to do? On the one hand, it might prolong the war by saving the lives of enemy troops; on the other, helping the Vietnamese survive the American war was precisely our objective. The new antibiotic would not directly jeopardize American troops, since the beneficiaries were already wounded and at least temporarily out of action. We had to consider the legal implications, too. At best, we would be receiving and transporting stolen goods; at worst, passing them to an enemy in a time of war.

It didn't take long to decide that the chance to save so many lives outweighed our reservations and fears. But we had to be smart about what we did. We agreed that Ethan should not make the delivery to the Vietnamese. There was a small chance that the offer was a setup designed to entrap him. It was also possible that the FBI knew of the pharmaceutical scientist's plans and was simply waiting for him to move. If Ethan kept my identity from the scientist and I made the handoff, we would have some protection. We had both met several Vietnamese health officials in Paris two months earlier. If I went to Paris on some pretext and delivered the goods to them without being observed, we could escape detection even if it was a setup. It was a good plan. Ethan told the scientist he could arrange delivery.

The pretext for a Paris trip came easily. My father, Sid, was about to celebrate his eightieth birthday. We had been close during my childhood, but because of civil rights and Viet Nam we had drifted apart. Previously, we had argued intensely about the war. He was a successful immigrant. The United States had saved him from the Nazis, who had killed one of his sisters and other members of his family. As a result, he was unquestioningly patriotic. Before I was born, he had spent a lot of time in the South as a traveling salesman and had picked up racist attitudes toward African Americans, another arena of passionate dispute between us. When my sister, Robin, married a black man, she felt unable to reveal it to him. I had stood by her side at the wedding. However, more recently, Sid had come to see the war as a mistake. And for a man his age, he was also making a valiant effort to overcome his racism and befriend my sister's husband and his family. I wanted to recognize these changes and do something special for him. An overseas trip fit the bill.

After fleeing Vienna in 1910, Sid had never been back to Europe. I called him in Chicago, and because I wanted the FBI to listen, I used the telephone at home in Somerville. I told him that in honor of his eightieth birthday I wanted to take him to Europe and Israel, a country he had always wanted to see. We would spend a few days each in London, Paris, and Vienna, and then a week in Israel. He was thrilled and grateful, his voice breaking as he thanked me, not only for the trip and the recognition of his birthday, but also because we would be traveling together for the first time in years. I was glad to make him happy, but hopefully it also looked like harmless tourism to the FBI.

Meanwhile, Cora's fledgling medical aid committee was about to meet. I wanted to create an activist organization that would play a prominent role in the national antiwar movement. Knowing that the physicians on the committee opposed that approach in favor of quiet work behind the scenes, I visited several to address their concerns. I wanted to inspire them with the magnitude of what I thought could be accomplished and assure them that we could walk the line between being reckless and being prudently defiant. When the meeting finally convened, we agreed to open a small office in a church basement and hire a member of the committee, Hilda Schwartz, to start raising money. We called the new organization Medical Aid for Indochina since we intended to send medical supplies to Laos and Cambodia as well as Viet Nam.

During this period, our large communal home in Somerville often served as a guesthouse for visiting antiwar leaders. They came because of John Froines, but their visits gave me a chance to develop new friendships, too. Leaders of Vietnam Veterans Against the War (VVAW) were among them. John Kerry, one of the founders, was a local guy I knew, but he had become more cautious as he prepared to run for Congress later that year. Other VVAW leaders who were angrier and more aggressive emerged to speak for the organization.

Ron Kovic was one. A Vietnamese bullet had left him paralyzed from the chest down. He negotiated his way around our furniture in his wheelchair, but he never let his injury slow him down or dampen his determination to stop the war. Later he would write *Born on the Fourth of July*, a moving book eventually made into one of the most powerful antiwar films Hollywood ever produced. In 1972, he was among the angriest of the vets and could project his anger in speeches and media interviews to effectively mobilize others against the war.

Bobby Muller, also a founder of VVAW, was another wheelchair-bound visitor. A determined organizer and a passionate speaker, Bobby had been wounded in combat as a Marine Corps officer. He, too, was paralyzed as a result of a spinal cord injury. Six years later, he would start a new service organization, Vietnam Veterans of America, and in 1997 a group he helped start shared the Nobel Peace Prize for a worldwide campaign to ban land mines.

Several times, the antiwar movement's new celebrity couple also stayed with us. The internationally known movie star Jane Fonda was in a relationship with Tom Hayden, one of the Chicago Seven defendants. She was widely visible as a militant and highly controversial antiwar spokesperson, and he remained one of the movement's strategic leaders. They attracted a great deal of media attention, but both were serious organizers and relentless in their efforts to build the movement. They used their celebrity to recruit people, raise money, and inject an antiwar message into the frequent coverage they received.

I shared an unspoken bond with these new friends and with others who worked as antiwar organizers. Many of us had given up secure roles in society or promising mainstream careers to oppose the war. Even Jane, despite the Academy Award she would win in April for her role in *Klute*, could no longer get work in Hollywood. The bond that united us was a simple one: we all had made a solemn pledge to ourselves to continue work against the war until it was over, no matter how long that took. It wasn't a public pledge, but if you had made it to yourself, you could recognize others who had by their focus and determination.

In early March, the pharmaceutical scientist gave Ethan two sealed but unlabeled test tubes containing the precious cultures. Earlier, we had quietly raised the money needed for the Paris trip. Sid and I rendezvoused in New York and flew together to London. I had no special interest in London but thought it would help Sid if the first foreign country he visited was English speaking. Also, I didn't want to go directly to Paris. I had tried to mislead the FBI by making frequent calls to Sid from my home or office to discuss the upcoming trip, but I had no idea if it had worked. We spent two pleasant days sightseeing, then left for Paris, where we settled into a modest but comfortable hotel just off the Luxembourg Gardens.

Late in the afternoon on our second day, I encouraged Sid to deal with his jet lag by taking a long nap. As he dozed off, I left a note, took the two sealed test tubes, and walked to the Métro station. I wanted to be as cautious as possible because Ethan's liberty was at stake as well as mine, and extra caution cost nothing. I changed trains and direction several times on the Métro, boarding cars just before the doors closed, hoping to throw off any tails. When I felt secure, I took a commuter train to the sub-urb where North Viet Nam maintained its embassy.

As a walk-in, uninvited and unexpected, I knew I would be treated with suspicion. At the locked gate I used my limited French to explain to the guards that I was from the American antiwar movement and had something for the ambassador. After a short wait, an obviously apprehen-sive but apparently low-level functionary came to greet me. We exchanged the usual pleasantries. I suggested he locate someone on the embassy staff who had attended the medical assistance conference a few months earlier and could vouch for me. The right person was soon found, and I was rec-ognized as an American friend. The suspicion disappeared.

The ambassador was away and unable to return, so I was ushered into the office of his second-in-command. Also present was a representative of the National Liberation Front of South Viet Nam and two interpreters. I told them about the formation of Medical Aid for Indochina, and that we intended to function as the European assistance groups did, but with the further edge of doing it from within the United States. I made it clear that Cora had already informed her contacts in Hanoi of our plans.

I then took the two test tubes out of my pocket and laid them on the table between us. Speaking slowly for the interpreters, I explained what was inside. The tone and demeanor of my hosts abruptly changed. They were soon on the edge of their chairs writing down everything I said. They understood the immense significance of the viscous cream-colored fluid in the glass tubes lying between us. I explained that this was not a gift from our new organization but a private matter to remain confidential. They understood. A courier was scheduled to leave the next day for North Viet Nam. The test tubes would be put in his diplomatic pouch and immedi-ately delivered to the minister of health in Hanoi.

Everyone around the table was excited and happy. The embassy offi-cials insisted on hosting a celebratory dinner for me that evening or the next day. I thanked them for their kindness, but having already explained the legal jeopardy I might be in, I told them I preferred to quietly slip back into the role of a tourist to reduce the possibility of surveillance or inter-ference from my government. They accepted my reasoning but insisted on plying me with small gifts, souvenir jewelry, and books.

I left the embassy sporting a big smile. Having completed one good deed, I felt it was time for another. I had shown Sid around London and Paris, cities he had never seen. He was about to show me around Vienna, which I had never seen. I didn't tell him about the test tubes. I wasn't sure he would approve, and even if he did, I knew his concern for my safety would outweigh any satisfaction he might feel. Sid expected Vienna to be a high point of our trip and very enthusiastically described the places he planned to show me. After a childhood in Hungary, he had been sent to Vienna to attend a *gymnasium*, an elite high school. Following his graduation in 1910, he was drafted into the Austro-Hungarian army, no place for a Jew, so like his older half brothers and sisters, he fled to America.

Being a draft dodger with no passport, Sid crossed into Germany buried in a hay wagon. He was jailed briefly in Munich, but a contact there got him out. Traveling on to Hamburg, Sid bought a steerage ticket and arrived at Ellis Island with no money, no visa, and no English. He was jailed again. Ten days later, a half brother who lived in New Jersey vouched for him. Sid studied English intensively for six months and then hit the road in 1911 as a traveling salesman. Two years later, he was rich. In later decades he made and lost several fortunes, often quite colorfully, even though at the end of his life he had little beyond his monthly Social Security check. He had been a daring and audacious man, and I respected him for it.

We arrived in Vienna after dark. Sid was enthusiastic about the sights we would see the next day. I warned him that sixty-two years had passed, and that Vienna had suffered through two world wars and evolved from a Renaissance capital into a modern city. In the morning, we took a cab to the Ringstrasse, in Sid's memory a grand boulevard lined with the mansions of the rich. Confusion clouded his face as we inched through traffic on an inner-city street lined instead with gas stations, auto repair facilities, and broken-down rooming houses. So it was at other once beautiful landmarks buried under graffiti or in disrepair. It would take an archaeological dig to unearth what Sid remembered. I tried to convince him that his confusion was natural. He was a time traveler who had left nineteenth-century Vienna with an emperor on the throne and returned after three-quarters of the twentieth century had passed. But he was disoriented and my words didn't help. I suggested we fly to Israel that afternoon, and he readily agreed.

We arrived at night, and I contacted two old friends. One was a pharmacist I had been friendly with in elementary school who had moved to Israel. The other was an Israeli scientist I knew as a graduate student in the UC Sleep Lab who had become a professor at the Hebrew University of Jerusalem. For the next week, they took turns showing Sid sites I had already seen, so I occasionally left them to do some political exploring. Israel was a vexing problem for the American left. Initially supportive, many of us were outraged at how the Israelis treated the Palestinians they had displaced. Our public criticism of Israel led to a predictable overreaction, and we were erroneously perceived to be in agreement with Arab extremists who advocated the destruction of the young country.

Israel depended upon financial assistance from American Jews, but was also the recipient of a vastly disproportionate share of American foreign aid. Meanwhile, the surrounding Arab states, many of which had wealthy and oppressive regimes, refused to give substantial financial

Israel, March 1972. I am standing on the left; in the middle is Pessach Ben-Horin, my former colleague at the UC Sleep Lab; and on the right is my eighty-year-old father, Sid Zimmerman. *Author's collection*

support to the Palestinians, in part because they feared the rise of a politically progressive Palestinian state would inspire democracy movements in
their own countries. Given the tinderbox of Middle East politics, and its
relevance to us on the left, I wanted to use a little of my time in Israel to
learn more.

I visited some dissident organizations and met with activists who supported Palestinian rights. I learned there was also widespread discrimination against dark-skinned Jews who had recently emigrated from Arab
countries, particularly Yemen and Morocco. Some had formed the Israeli
Black Panther Party, modeled after its namesake in the United States.
They told me they suffered because of their dark skin and lack of European manners and education. Confined to urban slums and dead-end
jobs, they were treated as second-class citizens in a country that made
much of its commitment to democracy. Looking around, I saw other problems. Since I was last there, Israel had been overtaken by consumerism
and had lost its commitment to socialist values. On one rural kibbutz I
had visited previously, I saw a bridal store displaying white gowns that
could not have been more grotesquely out of place.

Sid had a distant cousin, Joseph, who was one of the patriarchs of a
kibbutz. Neither of us had ever met him, but he invited us to visit. Over
dinner in his family's cottage Joseph asked about the American antiwar
movement, aware that some of us were critical of Israel. He was in his
mid-fifties, short, squarely built, with the piercing eyes and hard look of
experienced leadership. Speaking respectfully, I explained my reservations about his country and described my visits to the Israeli dissidents. He
did not respond, but after dinner asked Sid and me to join him on the
porch for a brandy.

Joseph then told us his remarkable personal history. It began in Austria, where he had been an idealistic teenager in the mid-1930s. He joined
the communist youth movement and with his comrades staged street
demonstrations against the emerging Nazi Party and charity drives for its
Jewish victims. When the German Nazis came to power, annexed Austria,
and invaded Poland, Joseph said good-bye to his family and went underground. Like Arcadius Kahan, the dean who had fired me at the Univer-

sity of Chicago, Joseph's band of partisans lived in the forests. And like Kahan, he joined the communists rather than the Zionists.

Through 1940 and 1941, Joseph's partisans ambushed German intelligence patrols, blew up supply depots, and sabotaged railroad tracks and bridges. They also suffered many losses and defeats, but as compatriots were killed or wounded, others came from the cities to replace them. They were constantly in danger, and late in 1941 they were captured and sent to a concentration camp. The Nazis had not yet embarked on their "final solution," the extermination of the Jewish people. Instead, they seized Jewish property and forced their victims into the camps.

Most of the camp inmates were physically timid, but Joseph and the other partisans, all in their late teens and early twenties, trained the more senior inmates to fight. When the thaws came in the spring of 1942, they led an uprising and mass escape. Despite the stereotype of docile Jews being led to slaughter, theirs was not the only such escape. But few of the escapees were sufficiently fit to survive as guerrilla fighters. Most were recaptured. Not Joseph. He kept fighting through the spring and summer. By the fall, networks that supplied the partisans with food, firearms, and recruits could no longer operate. The concentration camps had become extermination camps, and the partisans had to disband.

Joseph made his way on foot and at night to Hungary, which was not yet under direct German control. The Nazis, satisfied with Hungary's right-wing regime, allowed them to run their own internal affairs, which left Hungary an island within the European continent, then primarily under Nazi domination. In late 1942, the Hungarians were not yet deporting Jews. Joseph tried to contact his family in Austria, but learned they had all been deported to an unknown destination and their property confiscated.

He enrolled in nursing school and studied for over a year before Nazi tanks rolled into Budapest in 1944 and took direct control. They stuffed the Hungarian Jews into cattle cars and sent them all to death camps. Joseph didn't go. He organized a band of fighters and again escaped into the woods. His group was not equipped to operate offensively, but they did engage in sabotage and occasionally assisted Allied intelligence operatives working behind German lines. They could not survive the next winter. Before it ended, the Nazis captured Joseph again.

It was early 1945, and he was sent to Auschwitz, the infamous death camp. Days before he was to be killed, the Soviet army liberated the camp. Weak and emaciated, he took weeks to recover. When he could, he moved east toward the Soviet Union. He had been a communist and had fought with the communists, so he decided to begin life anew in the world's only communist country. When the Germans surrendered a few months later, Joseph learned that his entire family had been killed, even his beloved little sister Edith.

Joseph made it to the Soviet Union and was put into a "displaced persons" camp. Most "DP camps" helped refugees locate lost relatives, find jobs, or be placed back into society. Joseph sat in the Soviet DP camp for nine months before his first placement interview. A friend advised him to claim he was Hungarian and not reveal that he was Jewish. Outraged, he replied that they were in the Soviet Union, a workers' state, which did not discriminate against Jews or anyone else. He had training as a nurse, and Russia had untold numbers of war injured. He would be given a medical job and be treated with respect whether he was a Jew or not.

At the placement interview, Joseph's Jewish heritage and medical skills were duly noted. Weeks went by, then months, and as others left the DP camp to start new lives, Joseph remained. He was told to be patient. One day he realized that most of the others still in the camp were also Jews. His decision to fight with the communists instead of the Zionists had been a mistake. There would be no life for him in the Soviet Union, nor in Europe, where Nazism had killed everyone he had ever loved. Zionists were gathering Jewish refugees and pioneers in the British protectorate of Palestine. That was an alternative, but it was impossible to get to Palestine from the Soviet Union. His only hope lay in Amsterdam, where the Zionists in Europe were headquartered. It was not impossible to get to Amsterdam. He could walk.

Joseph's DP camp was in the Ukraine. One night he slipped over the fence and started west. It was fifteen hundred miles to Amsterdam. He walked through postwar devastation, lived off charity, and slept in fields or bombed-out buildings. Disgusted by everything European, he moved in a daze. It took him nine months, but he walked across the entire European continent.

He reached Amsterdam in 1947. The Zionists gave him a passport, clothing, and a train ticket to Marseilles. In the French port, other Zionists gave him a boat ticket . . . to Nicaragua. It was part of a game the Zionists were forced to play to retain permission to operate on French soil. The French were allied with the British, who controlled Palestine and had promised the Arabs that no more Jews would be allowed to emigrate there. To back up their promise, the British navy blocked all sea-lanes leading to Palestine.

As soon as Joseph's ship sailed outside of French territorial waters, instead of turning west to Nicaragua, it turned east and ran the British blockade. There were other such ships, old scows purchased with American money and crewed by Jewish war veterans. During the war, boatloads of European Jews had been refused entry to U.S. ports. Some returned to Europe, where their passengers were killed, which was why the Jewish heroes running these postwar "Exodus" operations no longer relied on other people's ships or played by other people's rules.

Joseph's ship made it past the British blockade. The passengers were off-loaded onto a Palestinian beach at night and were met by Zionists who took them to hideaways. Within days, Joseph was placed on a kibbutz. Five weeks later, on a Saturday off, he took a stroll around a nearby town and was stopped by a British patrol. Having no papers, he was arrested and sent to a DP camp on the island of Cyprus, a nearby British colony. This DP camp was actually a jail, since the British had to prevent its Jewish inmates from returning to Palestine.

Miraculously, among thousands of Jewish prisoners, Joseph found Edith, his little sister. She too had a remarkable story of survival, but the rest of their family, and all their aunts, uncles, and first cousins, were gone. Joseph and his sister remained imprisoned for the next nine months. In May 1948, the underground Jewish army in Palestine declared independence from Britain. Worldwide sympathy over the Holocaust left the British no choice; they packed up and left. The State of Israel was officially established. Five surrounding Arab countries invaded, determined, in their own words, to drive the Israelis into the sea. It was a short but bloody war, and after a few months of intense fighting Israel prevailed.

In May, the inmates of the DP camp all left for the new country. Joseph and his sister joined others to start a kibbutz of their own. Over the next few years, they carved prosperity out of the desert with irrigation, modern farming, and financial assistance from American Jews. Joseph married and had a son. In the following years, he achieved the personal fulfillment that had been stolen from him by the Nazis. More children were born, and his kibbutz thrived, with hundreds of families, thousands of acres, and a few small factories.

Joseph was not quite at the end of his story, but I saw his mood change dramatically. After the initial war against the Arabs in 1948, two wars followed, the Suez War in 1956 and the Six-Day War in 1967. Five years earlier, Joseph's firstborn son had served in the Six-Day War. He paused in a futile attempt to master his emotions, and then revealed that the boy had been killed in combat. His story was over, and he leaned toward me. The fierce resolve in his eyes pinned me to my chair, and the quiet statement he made was said with as much conviction as any I had ever heard. "We will never leave this land. We have paid for it with our blood."

Joseph had not tried to answer my critique of Israel with reason or history. His tale was the most eloquent argument he could have made, but it was not until the next day that I fully understood its power. I told Joseph's story to my professor friend with the same awe and amazement I had felt upon first hearing it myself. He wasn't impressed, which surprised me. Disappointed, I asked why the story had not made as deep an impression on him as it had on me. His answer was chilling. The story is not extraordinary, he said. On the contrary, it is commonplace. It's a story that could be told by tens of thousands of Israelis. It is not, he said, simply Joseph's story, but the story of Joseph's people.

No doubt Joseph would agree. He had told me his history to justify the history of his nation and to claim for it the same right to exist as any other. Despite promises made and broken by imperial diplomats in decades past, despite the complex and turbulent history of the local real estate, the suffering endured in the Holocaust, the gathering of the Jewish tribes in Israel, and the remarkable harvests of plenty reclaimed from desert sands all made it clear to me that Israel was here to stay. The Palestinians had been grievously wronged and, at a minimum, deserved equal rights, fair payment for lost property, and an independent state. It seemed to me that the Israelis, given the suffering and oppression in their own history, should be the first to understand why and, being in power, should bear full responsibility for repairing the damage.

Yet after my evening with Joseph, I felt unable to side with either the Palestinians or the Israelis. The intractable conflict carried too much pain and history to be subject to glib solutions. In past months, I had grappled with the problems of fighting capitalist abuse and realized that lofty ideals were not always relevant. Morality and legal precedent were important, but they had limited meaning when considered apart from real conditions on the ground. It was clear to me that as much injustice as capitalism had produced, as much as had come about because of the State of Israel, both would endure. I needed to focus less on what should be and work instead for what could be. I had to stop waiting for perfect but unattainable solutions because holding out for them could prevent achieving the imperfect solutions actually within reach.

It was time to go home. The pride I had felt in the small courageous act I had performed for the Vietnamese in Paris paled alongside the courage and sacrifice of my cousin Joseph. Humbled by the comparison, I was glad to have lived in less interesting times, and happy that a man like Joseph was part of my personal heritage.

CHAPTER 17

AS I RETURNED FROM ISRAEL, UNITS OF THE NORTH VIETNAMESE ARMY AND THE
National Liberation Front launched a military offensive against South
Viet Nam. Nixon reacted with predictable rage. On April 4, 1972, he told
an aide, "The bastards have never been bombed like they're going to be
bombed this time." Increasingly paranoid, he assumed the North had
attacked in order to undermine his reelection in November, rather than
because of the opening left by the gradual withdrawal of U.S. ground
forces.

Nixon and Kissinger ordered 105 B-52 bombers transferred from
America's nuclear strike force to the operational theater in Indochina.
When refitted for conventional ordnance, these aircraft could each drop
108 bombs containing five hundred pounds of explosives. In mid-April,
when the redeployment was complete, the B-52s attacked residential
areas surrounding Hanoi and Haiphong, the two biggest cities in North
Viet Nam. Civilians were the targets. Nixon wanted to terrorize them in
hopes they would turn against their government.

Daniel Ellsberg, who had revealed the secret Pentagon Papers,
revealed more. In 1968, as an aide to Kissinger, Ellsberg became aware of
options being considered for escalating the war in order to force a North
Vietnamese surrender. He warned that the next escalation could be the
mining of the harbor at Haiphong. Many of us had previously assumed
that Nixon and Kissinger were also considering bombing the dikes that

protected North Viet Nam's rice fields from annual flooding, and, as a last resort, a nuclear attack. When Nixon and Kissinger ordered the B-52s to start bombing the suburbs of Hanoi and Haiphong, Ellsberg sounded the alarm about the harbor, but we knew that further escalations would also be on the table.

Antiwar activists responded angrily. The escalation of the bombing, given widespread criticism of the war, was a shock. Many of us feared that Nixon was increasingly out of control. By April 17, demonstrations, some accompanied by property damage and minor violence, had shut down colleges across the country. At the University of Maryland, National Guard troops occupied the campus. The National Student Association, once the recipient of surreptitious funding from the CIA and never a hotbed of activism, sponsored over 150 campus strikes, some at elite universities like Harvard, Stanford, and Princeton. Protests continued for a week.

On April 22, fifty thousand marched in New York. Demonstrators then went beyond marches. Quaker peace activists and Viet Nam veterans used small boats in New Jersey to keep a Navy munitions ship from departing for Viet Nam. A group of women blocked the entrance to an Air Force base in Massachusetts. Vets blocked the entrance to a Connecticut submarine base. Students stoned the LBJ Library in Austin. Nuns dressed in white sheets played dead on the ground outside St. Patrick's Cathedral in New York City. A Boston alternative newsweekly published the front-page headline "Enemy Bombs Hanoi." Nixon, ever sensitive to his public image and the upcoming election, withdrew another twenty thousand ground troops from Viet Nam.

We in the antiwar movement knew what the White House and the Pentagon did not, that nothing could force the Vietnamese to surrender. If we were right, Nixon's escalation had made further escalations inevitable. Bombs would kill thousands, famine would be used as a military tactic, and a nuclear holocaust would follow. Vietnamese military action could not prevent these devastating escalations. They could only be stopped if we in the antiwar movement made it politically impossible for Nixon to order them. It was a moment of truth for us, because it was obviously our responsibility to mobilize and prevent the coming catastrophe.

I asked myself what I could do, and I realized that building Medical Aid for Indochina (MAI) was more strategic than continuing to work for Science for the People. I liked my work, but Science for the People was firmly established. New recruits were joining, circulation of the magazine was up, and competent people were at work in the Boston headquarters. Friends encouraged me to take the lead in turning MAI into a national presence. I felt ready to meet the challenge, and I made the switch. Initially, there was no money to pay me even a subsistence salary, but I set up a desk in MAI's small office and went to work. Bart Meyers, despite having two kids to support, offered me a small monthly stipend. Before I could turn him down, money started to trickle in and enough was found to keep me going.

MAI lacked seed money for newspaper ads or fund-raising concerts and testimonial dinners, so we had to build it from the ground up. I called antiwar organizers across the country to announce our existence and explain the simple program we offered: use MAI to encourage a humanitarian stand against the war, and we will use the money raised to purchase and deliver medicines and medical equipment to North Viet Nam and the NLF in South Viet Nam. This constructive tactic should draw new people into action and help everyone make a powerful statement against the war. I found a receptive audience. Activists in churches and mainstream institutions immediately sponsored small local events to raise money for MAI. Some also launched door-to-door drives or put collection cans in local stores. Word about us spread quickly within antiwar movement circles but did not extend beyond them.

On May 8, after the United States and South Viet Nam had walked out of peace negotiations in Paris, Nixon made his next move. For the first time, he ordered the military to bomb the suburbs of Hanoi and Haiphong and mine the port of Haiphong. Ellsberg's warning about the harbor rang in our ears, and we knew further escalation would come. World and national opinion condemned Nixon's action. The *Washington Post* said that he had "lost touch with the real world" and was recklessly placing the nation's other foreign policy objectives at risk.

In response to the urban bombing and the mining of the harbor, a wave of violent protests swept across the United States. In Santa Barbara, students blocked three miles of Highway 101 and set it on fire with gaso-line. In Colorado, the road between Denver and Boulder was blocked. In Chicago, demonstrators shut down a major freeway during rush hour. At UCLA, massive arrests included the all-American basketball star Bill Wal-ton. In Berkeley, protesters overturned cars, broke bank windows, and started numerous fires. Elsewhere students attacked corporate offices and firebombed ROTC facilities.

Nixon was playing with fire. If a Soviet ship hit one of the U.S. mines in the harbor at Haiphong, the Cold War might suddenly become hot. Many of us in the antiwar movement were especially anxious when North Viet Nam announced that one of its dike systems had been bombed. The Nixon administration denied it, but we found the Vietnamese more cred-ible. We were all petrified that in his frustration Nixon would order a nuclear strike, and if he had already ordered the dikes hit, that would be next. I wondered what more I could do. The answer came in a phone call from Cora Weiss.

Years before, she had organized a group that delivered mail to and from the American pilots held as prisoners of war in North Viet Nam. They bundled the mail and delivered it to Hanoi in exchange for a return bundle from the POWs. As a result, Cora had experience in North Viet Nam and was acquainted with officials there. She used her access to pass messages back and forth between those officials and leaders of the Ameri-can antiwar movement.

This time the message was for me. The government of North Viet Nam had invited me to come to Hanoi to learn about its medical needs and the available shipping options for MAI's assistance program. I was asked to travel with three others, leave in ten days, and stay in North Viet Nam from May 20 through May 28. Our four-person delegation would be asked to inspect and film bomb damage so that after returning we could deliver eyewitness testimony that civilians were the intended targets. To fortify our case, I would be permitted to shoot color motion picture film, the first American allowed to do so.

Most people would have run from an invitation to a war. Not me. I was thrilled. I knew it was dangerous, and I had concerns for my safety, especially with the intensified bombing. But the war was, and for years had been, the central focus of my life. I could not be ambivalent about the opportunity to see it firsthand, and to meet some of the people we in the antiwar movement had been trying so desperately to save. The trip would dramatically boost MAI's prospects and give me experience I could use to lead it more effectively. I knew the Vietnamese would do everything they could to protect us, so I told Cora I would accept the invitation.

With so little time before departure, we had to quickly raise travel money. The father of a friend of mine was an old-timer at CBS News. Palmer Williams had been there since the days of Edward R. Murrow. I put Cora in touch with him. His team was very excited about getting color footage from North Viet Nam shot by an American. They struck a deal with Cora in which we gave them first refusal rights to buy our footage and they gave us an advance that covered most of the travel expenses for the four-person delegation.

Next, I needed a movie camera. Walter Teller, the documentary film-maker I had befriended in Boston two years before, introduced me to Ricky Leacock, an MIT film professor. A new kind of film, Super 8, had just been developed, and Leacock was the first to design an ultralight 8mm camera that could be synchronized with audiotape. When he heard what I needed and why, he offered me his new rig. Under his direction and Walter's, I got a crash course in how to be a cameraman.

Ethan Signer helped me prepare for the medical aspects of the trip. After a lengthy visit to Hanoi with other distinguished American scientists the year before, he had kept up an active correspondence with health and science officials there. He gave me the names of people who could answer questions about surgical equipment and pharmaceuticals needed in Hanoi, as well as others who could suggest secure shipping routes.

In the midst of these preparations, I called Sid in Chicago to tell him about the upcoming trip. He was not at home. I called the hotel where he worked as a part-time desk clerk, but he had not come in. When I asked why, I was told that his wife had just died. That was the manner in which I learned of my mother's death. I was saddened by the news, but ambiva-lent, too. My mother had spent four years lying in a nursing home bed unable to move, her hands burning with intractable neuropathic pain. My father visited every day but could do nothing for her. When I visited, she often asked me to help her die. Unfortunately for her, I lacked the moral clarity and courage to do so. Twenty-two years later I atoned for my mistake by helping to pass an Oregon ballot initiative that created the nation's first law permitting physicians to help terminal patients commit suicide.

I immediately flew to Chicago. When I arrived, I found that my sister, Robin Napier, had already seen to the funeral arrangements. Our little family of three grieved together, but in a very real sense we had mourned my mother's passing long before. Both my sister and my father encouraged me to go to North Viet Nam as planned. I stayed with them for two days after the funeral and returned to Boston.

Cora and Ethan explained that our host in Hanoi would be Tran Trong Quat, a former army colonel who was the executive director of the Commission for Solidarity with the American People. He would take us around the country, as he had Ethan and other American visitors. Ethan gave me packets of antimalarial agents and antibiotics for delivery to the North Vietnamese and to representatives in Hanoi of the Pathet Lao, the revolutionary forces fighting in Laos. Cora gave me a few letters to deliver, one regarding an upcoming visit by the author and psychiatrist Robert Jay Lifton and the Nobel laureate Salvador Luria, and another from Noam Chomsky. She told us that our tickets for the last leg of the trip between Vientiane, the capital of Laos, and Hanoi on Aeroflot, the Russian airline, should not be shown to customs officials along the way. In Laos, she advised us to be wary of a particular individual at the U.S. embassy who was a covert CIA agent. Finally, she handed me a large packet of mail to deliver to the POWs.

On May 17, I met the three others in my delegation. Marge Tabankin was the president of the National Student Association. Under her leadership it had renounced past associations with the CIA and actively opposed the war. Father Paul Mayer, a Catholic priest, was active in the nonviolent resistance championed by the antiwar priests Dan and Phil Berrigan. The Reverend Robert Lecky helped lead Clergy and Laity Concerned About Vietnam, a nondenominational coalition of pacifist and church organizations. We got acquainted, had a final briefing from Cora, and took off that night for London.

At Heathrow, we boarded a British Airways 747 to Bangkok with stops in Frankfurt and Bahrain. The flight was long, but I was too excited to read or sleep. Like my companions, I was both buoyant and nervously apprehensive. It was my first trip to Asia and my first time in a war. I had never been bombed, never traveled as the guest of a foreign government, and never been required to play a diplomatic role. Like the others, I wanted to be diligent gathering evidence of civilian bombing. I also had to set up good communication and coordination with North Vietnamese health authorities, and I had an added responsibility to guarantee that dollars spent on their behalf brought them maximum benefit. My head was swimming. Four weeks earlier I had been in Paris, then Israel with my father. Two weeks later my mother died. Suddenly I was sitting on an airplane high over Saudi Arabia en route to the Far East.

The big 747 jumbo jets had entered service only two years before, and I was curious about them. Somewhere over India I asked to visit the cockpit. This was before skyjacking and locked cockpit doors. When I got up front, the captain was in the cabin greeting passengers, and the first officer was reading a magazine with his feet up on the instrument panel. He and the navigator showed me around while the autopilot flew the plane. In the thirty minutes I was there, the only work the pilots performed was to call in one position report. The computers did the flying. It was a marvel. Those guys worked less flying a 747 than I did flying my little Cessna.

In Bangkok, the four of us connected to a smaller plane that arrived in Vientiane, Laos, after dark on May 19. The next morning, we strolled around. There was no mistaking we were in Asia. Only two million people lived in Laos, and the capital, Vientiane, was but a small town. Banana, coconut, papaya, and flamboyant trees were visible everywhere rising over a carpet of tropical vegetation and simple houses sitting on stilts. We wandered through an open market overflowing with produce, meat, and friendly people. They moved slowly and with ease. Their round faces were soft and gentle, like their movements.

But something was amiss. At the edge of town, amid the tropical plants and ornate Buddhist shrines, young Laotian men were incongruously dressed in combat fatigues while jeeps and tanks rumbled around them. North Viet Nam had used bordering Laos as a corridor to supply the South, and in response the United States, also ignoring Laotian sovereignty, had dropped thousands of tons of bombs. The bombs failed to cut off the supply lines, but they devastated the peasant culture and killed thousands of civilians, especially in the area known as the Plain of Jars. A Laotian resistance movement, the Pathet Lao, took up arms to resist the United States and build a socialist society. In response, the CIA armed and trained the Hmong and other mountain tribes living on the border to fight the Pathet Lao. They were the combat troops we saw in Vientiane. The United States had created a vortex of war in the region and was sucking an ever-larger portion of Indochina into it.

Late that morning a Russian airliner flew us to Hanoi. Walking off the plane, we were amazed to be in Viet Nam. Two young men ushered us through the crowded terminal into a reception room. I felt like a clumsy giant. Of only average height in the United States, I towered over the crowd in the terminal the way a seven-footer would at home. Our hosts apologized for the small size of our reception by referring to "inconvenient conditions" caused by the bombing. Passport formalities over, we piled into Russian-made cars for a fast trip into Hanoi. We passed rice fields, orchards, and an occasional small village. Closer to the city, we came to commercial and industrial areas. Much was camouflaged. Farm machinery parked on the side of the road was painted maroon or brown and covered with straw mats. Large mounds in the pastures had stairways leading to underground bunkers.

There was little vehicular traffic, but I saw much that was emblematic of rural Asia. Bicycle rickshaws hugged the road. Pedestrians with peaked straw hats wore black pajamas or loose-fitting blue pants and khaki shirts. They walked briskly, dodging an occasional water buffalo pulling a two-wheeled cart. Streets and sidewalks were clean. The people appeared relaxed and quick to smile at strangers in a passing government vehicle. Near a railroad switching yard, our drivers sped up. It was a potential bomb target. At the famous Red River Bridge leading into the city, I remembered a recent U.S. claim that bombs had completely destroyed it. Yet there it was, perfectly intact save for a small section under repair.

We crossed the river on a temporary pontoon bridge. Air raid sirens sounded. Our driver confirmed that an attack was under way. People on the street calmly walked to the one-person shelters buried in the sidewalk. These primitive shelters were four-foot lengths of concrete pipe, three feet in diameter, buried in an upright position. They were holes in the ground without covers, and every street was lined with them, usually ten to twenty feet apart. They did not provide protection from a direct hit, but one person could get below street level and be protected from blast waves and flying debris. A minute after I heard the first siren, the streets were clear.

Our driver couldn't decide whether to make a run for our hotel, where there would be a deep underground air raid shelter, or stop and have us get into the concrete pipes. He was not afraid. He kept telling us in sign language that the planes were coming, but he did it laughingly. Still, we were the only ones left on the street. The driver finally stopped near a row of empty holes, but as I reached for the door handle to bail out, he sped off. A minute later we pulled up to the hotel, a grand old colonial building on a street corner in downtown Hanoi.

A delegation in civilian clothes and helmets anxiously awaited our arrival. They moved us through the lobby, past an ornate bar, and down to the underground air raid shelter. It was a narrow tunnel thirty feet long and six feet wide with a bench on either side. Russians, Indians, and Vietnamese were already there. The four of us climbed in with our interpreter, a frail-looking young man named Quoc. A woman stood at one end of the tunnel with a first-aid case strapped over her shoulder. She was the hotel bartender.

With Quoc's help, we joked and traded stories with the others in the shelter, but beneath the forced good humor I was uncomfortable. The other foreigners present were from countries helping Viet Nam. Mine was bombing it. Above us, my countrymen were killing people, and I felt ashamed. Surely, I thought, the others in the shelter must resent the four of us sitting among them while American bombs fell outside. Previous American visitors to Hanoi had encouraged us not to feel shame but to take pride in the antiwar movement we represented. Good advice, but difficult to act upon with the sound of bombs exploding in the background.

We could feel the shock waves and hear the dull thuds that penetrated and shook the shelter. Each bomb knocked a little more dust off the low ceiling. It lasted forty-five minutes. The odds of a direct hit were small, but

I knew that if we suffered one, the tunnel would not save us. I was afraid during that first attack, but I controlled my fear. The Vietnamese thought the brunt of the raid was about four miles away. I imagined the horror of being under bombs so massive that we could feel them at that distance. One bomb exploded much closer, which meant that the planes were also attacking within the city limits.

When the all clear sounded, the civil defense wardens protecting us metamorphosed into hotel clerks, waiters, and drivers. It was hard to feel fear around them. They were too calm and organized. Each did his or her job smoothly and tried to normalize what for us was outrageously abnormal. Easy with their laughter, they exuded a long familiarity with the ghastly bombing. We registered at the hotel desk and were brought to large rooms with high ceilings. Mine had a tile floor, a fan hanging overhead, and mosquito netting over the bed—a typical tropical accommodation prior to air-conditioning. Five minutes later, the sirens warned of another air raid. In seconds a civil defense warden was at my door urging me to follow him to the shelter. This time I felt no shame. Only anger.

That afternoon we met our host, Colonel Tran Trong Quat, executive director of the Commission for Solidarity with the American People. He was about fifty-five and had a trim build, close-cropped hair, and the demeanor of a military commander. Present were other members of the commission. Quat asked us to undertake two tasks. First, witness and film bomb damage to civilian targets. Second, advise members of the solidarity commission about political conditions in the United States and what they might expect from the antiwar movement in the coming months. Quat stressed they wanted our advice as political comrades, not just witnesses who could tell their story in the United States, which was how they viewed a delegation of physicians expected the following week.

We would spend two of our eight days outside Hanoi, visiting other cities and villages. Conditions would be primitive. Meetings had been arranged for Marge with student groups, for Paul and Bob with religious leaders, and for me with officials at the Health Ministry. Quat assured us that we were free to go anywhere, see anything, and talk to anyone. However, there were limitations on what we could film, particularly military installations and anti-aircraft guns. We were also asked not to film the wounded or people entering bomb shelters. Such events are facts, Quat said, but can be used to support lies, namely, that the bombs frightened their people or that their resistance could be broken because of their injuries.

The government's rule against color filming was in place because they developed all footage before it left the country and had no facilities for developing color film. The solidarity commission had obtained permission for me to take undeveloped color film out of the country for the first time. They were prepared to trust our judgment but requested we ask permission before filming anything that might compromise their security. Also, Quat was adamant that we remain inside air raid shelters during bombing runs.

I told him that to demonstrate civilians were being targeted, we had to film in a civilian area, see the response to the air raid sirens, and, however briefly, see the planes dropping bombs, even if we had to take some risks to get the footage. Our hosts were very protective of our physical safety; an American killed or injured during a visit was not in their best interests. I knew the air raid sirens sounded when the carrier-based planes made landfall sixty to eighty miles from Hanoi. I told Quat that if these attack aircraft flew at six hundred miles per hour and were detected sixty miles away, we still had six minutes to film before the first bombs fell. I asked him to allow us that time. As a former military man, he seemed to appreciate my calculation and said he would try.

We spent the afternoon with the solidarity commission discussing political conditions in the United States. After dinner we strolled through downtown Hanoi. I was surprised at how rapidly it changed after dark. Trucks in camouflage paint filled the streets bringing in food and other goods. Camouflaged public buses, a tempting target during the day, were out in large numbers at night. Despite the tumult, the streets and sidewalks were swept clean. The sights and sounds were strange. So were the customs. There were no locks on the hotel room doors because, we were told, there was no crime. We could not tip our waiters, because extra pay violated socialist principles. There were no taxis because nobody could afford one. Strangest of all, there were no children; they had been evacuated to the countryside when the bombing started.

The next morning I was awakened at dawn. The mosquito net above me rippled in the breeze as the ceiling fan blew humid tropical air across my room. It felt like a 1940s Humphrey Bogart movie, but I quickly snapped out of my reverie. By 7:30 a.m., I sat with the other three Americans in a meeting of the Commission of Inquiry into U.S. War Crimes. Its executive director, Colonel Ha Van Lau, had been second-in-command under Le Duc Tho at the peace negotiations in Paris. He and his aides presented detailed analyses of U.S. attacks on civilians. Surprisingly, they kept meticulous records of the dates, times, and exact locations of these attacks, complete with maps, lists of ordnance dropped, types of aircraft deployed, and the number and type of casualties suffered.

Fittingly, Colonel Lau's presentation was interrupted by an air raid. We donned steel helmets and rushed to an underground shelter. Random pedestrians who had been near Lau's building had also come into the shelter. Quoc, our interpreter, explained we were visiting Americans. I half expected to be lynched. Instead, they smiled and waved their greetings. As the shelter shook from the American bombs, one rose to speak. I anticipated an angry tirade, but he said that while he and his countrymen held the U.S. government in contempt, they bore no grudge against the American people, especially those trying to stop the war. His speech could not have been rehearsed. The man had merely been walking by the building at the time of the air raid. That meant the government had educated its citizens about the distinction the man had made, something I had never known my government to do.

Back in Lau's conference room we saw photographs and maps that detailed the bombing of schools, hospitals, churches, and villages. We were then ushered into the adjacent War Crimes Museum housing unexploded American bombs ranging in size from 250 to 3,000 pounds. There were also antipersonnel cluster bombs. Packed into large canisters, these little football-sized bombs scatter over a large area, hit the ground, and blow up, spewing sharp metal fragments in all directions. The fragments are too small to damage buildings, guns, or other hard targets; their only purpose is to penetrate human flesh. The bombs are designed to injure rather than kill, in order to further tie up overburdened medical resources and personnel. Honeywell, also a supplier of napalm and land mines, manufactured many of the antipersonnel bombs we saw.

While looking at these bombs, we were interrupted by another air raid. In the shelter I marveled at the Vietnamese effort to document attacks on civilians, but I understood its purpose. Guerrilla warfare involved political as well as military struggle, so information was crucial. Unlike in conventional warfare, guerrillas don't have to win on the battlefield; they just have to stay on it long enough and not lose. If they can survive while a more powerful enemy runs out of resources or loses its will to continue fighting, they win in the end. George Washington discovered this principle fighting against a far stronger British army and used it to eventually win American independence.

Since the United States had military superiority, the Vietnamese were forced to rely on political factors as well as military prowess. Worldwide opinion and domestic political opposition had limited the extent to which the United States could deploy its superior force. Potential political outrage had limited Nixon's ability to use nuclear weapons or bomb the dikes. Politics had already severely limited the draft and led to fewer soldiers on the battlefield and mutinies among those already there. The meticulous collection of information and evidence helped the Vietnamese build worldwide and American political opposition to the war, which was critical to their survival.

We had lunch that day with Colonel Quat. He had obtained permission for me to film during an attack. Our meal was interrupted by another air raid, but I could not get to the camera fast enough. The air raids, while still frightening, had become somewhat routine. We spent the afternoon with Quat and the solidarity commission discussing the upcoming Republican and Democratic conventions, the pending presidential election, what impact it might have on the war, and the plans of various antiwar groups. They asked how they could more effectively counter Nixon's claims that the POWs they held were being tortured. I suggested they allow us to interview them on film.

We had come with two proposals from American antiwar leaders. A "Hostages for Peace" plan called for American volunteers to live in various locations with civilians in North Viet Nam. If the United States continued to bomb, it would have to kill its own citizens. Quat expressed his appreciation for Americans willing to share the fate of the Vietnamese, but did not believe Nixon would care. He suggested that a delegation of such volunteers could be invited to Viet Nam for a visit, but they would be welcomed as friends, not as hostages.

Under the other proposal, Americans would sail a "Peace Ship" through the mines and into Haiphong harbor. Quat claimed that a passage had been cleared but that a large ship would be in danger. He promised to refer the question and get back to us. Other, less ambitious projects were also evaluated. The Vietnamese had thought a great deal about the factors that limited Nixon's power. They understood that he was not a dictator free to do as he pleased.

That evening as it got dark, Quat and several members of the solidarity commission took the four of us on a walking tour of Hanoi. There were few air raids after 6:00 p.m. We strolled through a park with a lake and an outdoor restaurant. There was a small zoo and a circus under tents that had shut down when the bombing started. The park had water lily gardens, flowering trees, and thick bushes sculpted into half-life-sized elephants. Leaving the park, we saw that the crowded streets had come alive with nighttime traffic. We passed a department store, a foreign bookstore, a movie theater, and an art gallery. Wherever we went, large crowds of friendly young people questioned us through our interpreters.

The next morning we returned to the war crimes commission and continued our discussion with Colonel Lau. His understanding of strategy was impressive. At one point, I mentioned that Dan Ellsberg's warning about mining the Haiphong harbor had left us concerned about further escalations. Lau said they were prepared for the worst eventualities, including the destruction of the dikes. He leaned back and asked us to turn off our cameras and tape recorders. With a deep sigh he told us they were prepared to lose Hanoi and Haiphong and to fight on for another five to ten years if that was required. I asked if he thought Nixon would use nuclear weapons. He said they were prepared for that, too, but he did not think Nixon could take such a step without producing a backlash that would undermine his other long-term goals. Lau said that the more Nixon escalated the war, the more he would have to reveal his own weakness.

During lunch at the hotel, the sirens went off again. This time we were ready. I checked my watch, grabbed the camera, and ran out the front door. Marge Tabankin was right behind me with the audio gear. We shot two minutes of people moving toward shelters. There was no sign of panic, except from our Vietnamese guides. They kept motioning for us to get back inside, but my watch said there was still time. I heard jet engines getting louder fast. The Vietnamese frantically insisted we get out of the street, but Marge and I stayed put. In the sky to my right, two fighters banked in formation, and I got the shot. We ran back into the hotel, much to the relief of our hosts, and were escorted down to the bomb shelter.

When the raid ended, we bumped into the *New York Times* correspondent Anthony Lewis and finished our lunch with him. He complained that his request to see the heavily bombed city of Nam Dinh had been denied. He also had doubts about conclusions he had drawn in an earlier story he had filed claiming the mines in Haiphong harbor had been defused. He gave us the names of four ships and asked us to see if they were still there. Controversy raged around the world about whether or not the harbor was actually blocked, but I had no intention of passing

May 22, 1972. On a Hanoi street, in a one-person bomb shelter, ready to film an air raid. The camera is the newly designed one given to me by Ricky Leacock at MIT. *Author's collection*

such sensitive information to the *New York Times*, which was read daily in the Pentagon and the White House.

After lunch, we toured a museum and then went back to the hotel to pack. The plan was to leave for Haiphong to inspect war damage as soon as it got dark. Despite the short distance, it was a four-hour drive. The roads were severed in many places by bomb craters. The trip would be dangerous, and we might be exposed to air raids in locations far from protective shelters. But at night, we should be safe.

CHAPTER 18

WE DROVE IN THE DARK TOWARD HAIPHONG. THE UNLIT TWO-LANE HIGHWAY, BARELY used during the day, was a busy thoroughfare at night, just like the streets in Hanoi. Our three-car caravan had to dodge pedestrians and overloaded bicycle rickshaws. Colonel Quat and others from the solidarity commission rode with us, as did Quoc, our interpreter, and several security personnel. In the moonlight, I could see camouflaged trucks, some parked at the roadside, others moving along the highway. There were freight trains rolling and railcars being loaded, but our own progress was slow. Every few miles we had to detour around a bomb crater in the road.

Music on the car radio was interrupted by an announcement that made our Vietnamese friends cheer. Quoc translated. Demonstrators in Washington had blocked an entrance to the Pentagon, chanting, "Ho, Ho, Ho Chi Minh, the NLF is gonna win." President Ho Chi Minh had founded the Vietnamese Communist Party in the 1920s to fight French colonialism. After leading wars for independence against the French, the Japanese, the French again, and finally the United States, Ho had died in 1969 and was revered as the father of his country.

As we approached Haiphong, the devastation visible in the darkness was shocking. Like most Americans, I had seen war only through the cooling lens of a TV camera. I knew the statistics: so many dead, so many bombs dropped. But seeing it in person, driving past dozens of devastated buildings, was far more emotional, even in the dark. I thought about the people who had suffered and died in those buildings, and grieved for strangers I had never known.

After a few hours of sleep in a comfortable guesthouse, we were roused at 4:00 a.m. An hour later, our three-car caravan drove across the flat plains of the Red River delta, past long canals and numberless rice paddies, to the village of Phuc Loc ten kilometers away. We were newly equipped with steel helmets and had traveled in the predawn hours because our caravan was a tempting target for U.S. planes during the day. Phuc Loc was a farming cooperative of several hundred people. There were thatched-roof adobe huts, a village thrashing floor, dirt roads, and a communal water pump. The village sat in the middle of an agricultural area, and as I looked around, I saw nothing resembling a military target.

Quat told us that five weeks earlier, on April 16, 1972, Phuc Loc was carpet bombed by B-52s at 2:30 a.m. The village was a one-kilometer square. The bomb pattern was one kilometer by one-half kilometer. Half the village had been obliterated. Earlier that night, villagers heard bombs exploding in the direction of Haiphong, but few imagined that the planes would attack Phuc Loc. There were 142 bomb craters in the village. We filmed them and several survivors.

Tran Van Thuc, an elderly man, had a family of eighteen before the bombs fell. Ten were killed instantly. The other seven were all wounded. Of those killed, only one body was sufficiently intact to identify. Thuc, in tears, pleaded with us for some explanation. We had none, so we spoke words of sympathy as best we could, and we condemned our countrymen for perpetrating the atrocity. Thuc nodded graciously and expressed admiration for Americans who stood up to their government and defended his people. I smiled outwardly, but inside I seethed with embarrassment and rage.

A thirteen-year-old boy was next. Eight in his family were killed, both parents and six siblings. He carefully described each of them. Our interpreter, Quoc, broke down and had to be replaced. The boy repeatedly said he wanted to grow up quickly so he could join the army and avenge his family. Sixty-six in the village were killed that night, including ten suckling infants.

We left Phuc Loc after the sun came up. As our cars pulled away, I looked again for anything an analyst examining a reconnaissance photo might have mistaken for a military target, a gun emplacement, or an elevated munitions bunker. Nothing. All I saw was rice paddies. Around them, along the canals, young children rode on the backs of water buffalo. They were going out to graze for the day. One little girl read a book on top of her mount. A young shirtless boy lay flat across the back of his massive beast, arms outstretched in the sun. The idyllic pastoral scene was the opposite of what we had just witnessed in the village.

It was broad daylight, but we were told the fighters from the Seventh Fleet aircraft carriers seldom struck before 8:00 a.m., still an hour away. There was time for a short visit to the Vietnamese-Czechoslovakian Friendship Hospital, which had played a critical role during the attack on April 16. As the villagers in Phuc Loc reported, the B-52s bombed the Haiphong suburbs at 2:00 a.m. The bombs fell on factory workers sleeping in their apartment buildings. Simultaneously, low-flying fighters bombed in and around the city. That night 244 civilians were killed and 516 injured. Most of the casualties were treated at the Friendship Hospital.

I filmed doctors on the hospital staff who described being swamped by those casualties. Struggling to save their patients, they were amazed when the B-52s returned at 10:00 a.m. and bombed the hospital. Later that day, at 4:00 p.m., the planes came back and bombed both the hospital and the apartment buildings, apparently in hopes of killing those clearing away debris or looking for survivors. At the hospital I filmed an eight-year-old boy who had been injured at home in the middle of the night and then injured a second time in the hospital when it was bombed the next day. Civilian terror and demoralization were the only possible objectives. The B-52s bombed Haiphong again on May 9, 10, and 18, the last only five days before our visit.

From the hospital we raced back to our guesthouse. Our hosts wanted us inside by 8:00 a.m. They were right. At 8:10 a.m., fighter planes attacked. I heard their engines only seconds after the air raid sirens. Bombs fell on the city but not near us. When the raid ended, we met with the Haiphong War Crimes Commission and the city's mayor, Quang Thao. They claimed that a channel had been cleared through the mines,

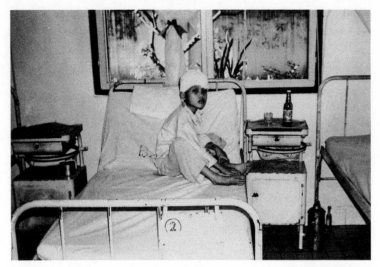

May 23, 1972. Wa Ti Tong, age eight, wounded first in the middle of the night as he slept in his Haiphong apartment and, once again, when the Americans bombed the Vietnamese-Czechoslovakian Friendship Hospital the next morning. *Author's collection*

but only for small vessels, and they took us to the harbor so we could see for ourselves. For security reasons they asked us not to film there. Cargo was moving, but I could not tell how much. In Hanoi we had been told that civilian spotters counted falling bombs and recorded their locations since some had delayed-action fuses and might explode later. Perhaps spotters had counted the falling mines for frogmen to defuse.

At a community house, we filmed two young women. Both were factory workers and members of the district militia. They were assigned to anti-aircraft batteries on April 16. One proudly claimed that hers brought down an American plane. The other did not want to talk about her military exploits, saying instead that she preferred to live in peace with her family. On the night of the sixteenth, as she ran to her gun emplacement, she heard screams from under the rubble of a burning building. She dug into the wreckage and unearthed the bodies of two dead mothers and several of their children. Staying to work with others in the rubble, she discovered the body of one of her close friends, cut completely in two.

We filmed a bombed high school, but almost immediately loudspeakers warned of an impending attack, and we were ordered to take cover fast. We jumped into our cars and drove back to the deep shelter at the guesthouse but had to run across a small park to get to the entrance. I could see three F-4 Phantoms flying in formation directly overhead. One at a time, they banked steeply left. Just as I got to the shelter, their bombs exploded in the distance. Inside, well below ground level, I could still hear the roar of the jets as more bombs shook the ground around us.

I asked to film the attack from the entrance of the bomb shelter. Reluctantly, our security detail agreed. Bob Lecky volunteered to be my soundman and followed me outside. The jets passed directly overhead again; their bombs hit only a few blocks away. The sound was deafening. Anti-aircraft guns on the rooftops around us fired back. Their cannons were even louder than the bombs. I only had tunnel vision looking through the camera's viewfinder and was blind to what was happening immediately around me. With no peripheral vision and explosions ringing in my ears, I was on the edge of panic. The security team added to the chaos by yelling for us to come back inside. I wanted the shot, so I kept the dive-bombing planes in the viewfinder a while longer, then ducked back underground.

That evening, after dinner with Quang Thao, the mayor of Haiphong, we climbed into our vehicles and began the long drive to Nam Dinh, North Viet Nam's third-largest city. A balmy breeze cooled the moist air as we passed oxcarts and bicycle rickshaws on the unlit road. A soldier saluted, thinking no doubt that a caravan like ours must contain high officials. Three times we crossed wide rivers on a barge pushed by a tugboat. Bombs had destroyed all the bridges. Inhaling the fragrant night air on the decks of those barges, I could see palm and banana trees silhouetted against the moonlit sky.

Paul Mayer mentioned that we had not seen a single beggar anywhere in North Viet Nam—no beggars, no prostitutes, no street hustlers, no skinny kids, and yet we were in the midst of a war! We wanted to learn more about average life in North Viet Nam, so at one of the barge crossings we asked Quat to ride with us and answer our questions.

We started with salaries. Quat explained that everyone earned between

60 and 150 *dong* per month, depending upon his or her skill and experience. Workers with both could make more than the president. Physicians
typically earned 100 *dong* per month. Families with more than two kids got
extra money. Rent was a percentage of salary, so two working families
might pay different rents for identical apartments if their incomes differed.
Every factory, hospital, school, government office, and military base had a
day-care center, but people could bring their children to any day-care center they chose. Public transportation was cheap; private transportation was
not. A bicycle cost 200 *dong*. All cars were owned by the state and given to
factories, offices, and schools for distribution to individuals on a shared
part-time basis.

When I asked about the military, I was surprised to learn that despite
the war there was no draft. Males were educated to believe that it was their
duty to serve in the army for at least three years beginning at age eighteen.
In fact, Quat told us, more young men applied to the army than could be
accepted. Those reluctant to serve were not wanted, because they would
undermine morale. Conscientious objectors were respected, but there
were few of them. There were women in the army, too, but not many. I
found much of this admirable, but after my experiences in Israel, I wondered if the communal spirit and shared sacrifice would survive the war.

Sadly, as we listened to Quat on the ride to Nam Dinh, the city itself
was recovering from a devastating attack. Earlier in the day, Nam Dinh
had been mercilessly bombed. Pulling in to the city, I saw smoke rise from
the hulks of buildings and search-and-rescue personnel pick through the
ruins with flashlights. When we arrived at our hotel, I understood the danger we were in. My room had a gaping hole in the ceiling made a few
hours earlier by a bomb. Water and power were out. I recorded the day's
events in my diary using a candle, then lay back to look at the stars visible
through the shattered roof above me.

The next morning we drove through the bombed areas of the city.
Nam Dinh was a center for textile manufacturing. Large factories were
built during the French colonial period and resembled those I had seen
in New England: four-story buildings, over a block long, and made of
red brick. In Nam Dinh they lay in ruins. I walked through the rubble
filming the jumble of twisted pipe, reinforcing rods, and smashed

machinery. Some of it was smoldering, and rescuers were still looking for survivors.

Taking greater risk than we had previously, we left the city in daylight and drove to Bao Ngu, a village severely attacked on May 12, less than two weeks before. It was similar to Phuc Loc, the village we had seen the previous day, and what I saw in Bao Ngu elicited the same searing emotions. Once more, I had to swallow my rage as several mothers told us how antipersonnel bombs had killed their infants. To demonstrate what had happened to their babies, they showed us cooking pots with dozens of perforations made by the bomb's metal fragments. I listened from behind the camera, which felt disrespectful in the face of such anguish. Invariably, I put it down to look them in the eye and then failed to get a critical moment on film.

When our entourage was finally ready to leave, an old woman stopped us. She was very short and bent over, under four feet, thin, shriveled, and without teeth. Her son had been killed. Through our interpreter, Quoc, she insisted on telling us that no one in her village had ever harmed the men in the sky who had bombed them. She was sure that if the American people learned of these crimes, they would do what was necessary to stop them.

Driving back to Nam Dinh, tormented by the scene in Bao Ngu, I saw that our visit had become a topic of local interest. Only a handful of antiwar Americans had ever been to the city. The local newspapers and radio stations were reporting our presence, and since three cars together was an unusual sight during the day, people along the roadside noticed us. When they saw four white faces in the cars, they stopped and applauded. We were getting a heroes' welcome, even though all I felt was shame and embarrassment.

In Nam Dinh we met that afternoon with the local War Crimes Commission and got a detailed report on damage to the province from extensive aerial and naval bombardment. "War crimes" was the right label. After World War II, U.S. officials judged and punished many Nazi and Japanese officers for war crimes comparable to what their younger successors in Washington were then committing in Viet Nam. The use of antipersonnel bombs, the destruction of remote villages, the targeting of civilian housing, the decision to bomb once and then return hours later to bomb the rescue workers and cleanup crews, the attacks on schools and hospitals—what else could such actions be called but "war crimes"?

During the afternoon meeting, we had to take shelter twice. That morning, we had already experienced two air raids while inspecting bomb damage. Each time, we heard the jets before the sirens. After the meeting, we attended a ceremonial dinner where our hosts insisted we join them in repeated toasts. Lubricated by the alcohol, our conversation was very lively. I was amused at how the Vietnamese got us to laugh and discuss superficialities, yet were able to preserve their focus on the serious issues that had brought us together.

We left Nam Dinh at 8:00 p.m. for the ride back to Hanoi on a rural two-lane highway. In the moonlight, I could see rice fields on one side of the road, but on the other a single row of two-room shacks lined the highway. The shacks went on for miles. Kerosene lanterns or candles were visible through their windows. They were temporary quarters for people evacuated from Hanoi. It was an attempt to reduce civilian casualties. If a bomb fell on the single line of houses, fewer people would be hurt than if they were clustered together in a city.

Suddenly people on the roadside shouted at our vehicles. Our drivers put out their headlights. American planes had been heard, their engines distinguishable from the Vietnamese MiGs. We pulled in to a gap between the roadside shacks and got out to listen. Hearing nothing, we drove on but with lights out. Over the radio we learned that Haiphong had just been heavily bombed. We had been fortunate. When we were in Haiphong, Nam Dinh was hit. The next day we were in Nam Dinh, and Haiphong was bombed.

It was a long and tiring drive back to Hanoi. When we finally arrived, I climbed into a hot bath to relax. Minutes later the air raid sirens went off. It was our fourteenth air raid and the first one at night. Hotel guests streamed down to the air raid shelter in pajamas and bathrobes.

In the morning we met with Colonel Quat and Xuan Oanh, a Western-educated and urbane official who traveled frequently in Europe and functioned as a roving ambassador to the worldwide antiwar movement. Both men were tense. Oanh said the U.S. State Department had just declared that no targets in Viet Nam would be off-limits, civilian or military. Quat was postponing a visit by American doctors the following week because of the heightened danger. With sad eyes he admitted they might lose Hanoi, but reminded us that the economic base of North Viet Nam was agricultural and therefore could not be destroyed by bombing. Oanh then announced that following an afternoon meeting with the NLF, we would meet that evening with captured American pilots.

There was another air raid at lunch. Instead of going to the hotel shelter, Bob Lecky, Paul Mayer, and I went outside, climbed into one-person shelters on the street, and filmed the public reaction. That was a mistake. People on the street were so curious about us that our security detail was forced to expose themselves in order to shoo all the bystanders into shelters. Fortunately, the planes did not bomb close to us, but I vowed to stop filming that way. Inside we saw Anthony Lewis from the *Times*. He asked about Haiphong and Nam Dinh, and we shared what we safely thought we could. Lewis was leaving that night. He had gotten a cable from the *Times* urging him to do so because Hanoi was likely to be severely bombed in the next few days.

After that bit of bad news, we went to see the Swedish chargé d'affaires, who was said to be the best informed Westerner in the city. It was a sobering exchange. He, too, thought Hanoi would soon be destroyed, not all at once, but neighborhood by neighborhood as was happening in Haiphong and Nam Dinh. That was a more effective way to terrorize civilians. He asked when we planned to leave. I answered, day after tomorrow, and he shook his head and wished us luck. If the United States hit the runway at the airport, he warned, we would never get out.

In the afternoon we met with Nguyen Phu Soai, head of the delegation from South Viet Nam's Provisional Revolutionary Government (PRG). The PRG was a new umbrella group that brought together the National Liberation Front (NLF) of South Viet Nam and other political opponents of the U.S.-backed puppet regime in Saigon. Soai and his aides briefed us on the devastation in the South. We already knew the casualty statistics, so they detailed the physical damage. Almost 50 percent of their villages had been lost or abandoned since 1961. Herbicides and bulldozers had destroyed over 50 percent of their forested land. Over three million hectares of hardwoods were dead. Two-thirds of their rubber trees were destroyed. Herbicides had reduced their rice production by almost 80 percent, and would poison their land and people for generations to come. It was another litany of war crimes, and I cringed as I heard it.

After dark, we drove to a large building in Hanoi that looked like an old French colonial mansion. It was the site of our rendezvous with eight American POWs. The Vietnamese told us that all eight had signed a letter to Congress condemning Nixon, their commander in chief, for having escalated the bombing. We had no idea that POWs had spoken out against the war, so I was eager to get them on film. A rectangular table covered with a white cloth awaited us. It was surrounded by twelve chairs, four for us, eight for them. In front of each was a teacup and saucer. Half a dozen Vietnamese cameramen and reporters watched from behind the chairs.

I had argued against shaking their hands when we were first introduced. Their letter to Congress was welcome, but we had seen too much of the suffering they had caused to think of them as anything but repentant war criminals. After a few minutes, they walked into the room in single file. They wore striped uniforms made from alternating light and dark maroon cloth. They appeared tall but were not. I had grown accustomed to the shorter Vietnamese. One had his arm in a cast, another a heavily bandaged neck wound. Both had recently been shot down.

When we were all seated, we went around the table and introduced ourselves. The POWs gave us name, rank, service branch, and the month and year of their capture: Captain James D. Cutter, USAF, February 1972; Lieutenant (junior grade) Charles Bernard, USN, December 1971; Lieutenant Colonel Edison Miller, USMC, October 1967; Commander Walter E. Wilbur, USN, June 1968; Lieutenant Commander David Hoffman, USN, December 1971; Captain Kenneth J. Frazier, USAF, February 1972; Captain Edwin A. Hawley, USAF, February 1972; Captain Lynn Guenther, USAF, December 1971.

Six of them had been shot down in the past six months. Miller had been there almost five years, Wilbur four. Hoffman was their spokesperson. He repeated the essence of their letter to Congress so I could get it on film. "We, as a group of Americans detained here, were shocked and struck by the futility of the action that was taken in the bombing raids against Hanoi and Haiphong on April 16 and in the subsequent raids that have taken place. Despite what the pilots are told, and what the majority of the American public seems ready to accept, we know, and I'm sure you have seen and know, that civilian targets are in fact being hit with civilian casualties, both injured and killed, and there can be no reason or excuse for that."

That statement was a bombshell. I couldn't wait to show the footage back in the States. I pressed the other POWs about the care they had received. All eight seemed well fed and in good health, and they all agreed that their medical care had been adequate. Frazier, whose arm was in a cast, responded, "Medical care has been very good. My injuries were treated promptly . . . plus we have a doctor that comes around regularly to check on our health."

This directly contradicted statements Nixon regularly made about ongoing torture. We learned that in the first years of the war, some POWs had been tortured, especially by the villagers they had just bombed, but also by their jailers. However, systematic mistreatment of prisoners ended in the late 1960s on orders from Ho Chi Minh. During the 1970s, it did not occur. Nevertheless, a few POWs, most notably Senator John McCain, the 2008 Republican presidential nominee, allowed the public to think that they had been tortured throughout the entirety of their captivity. That made for a heroic narrative, always helpful in an election, but like other such narratives, it could be amply embellished to achieve other purposes.

Lieutenant Colonel Edison Miller, the Marine fighter pilot who had been there the longest, was also the angriest. In discussing how the war might end, he said, "We're aware of President Nixon's trip to Peking [now Beijing], and now currently in Moscow, and of course he could go to the moon, although I suppose that's too much to hope for, but he's not going to find peace except through talking to the Vietnamese people through their delegation in Paris."

At times, the pathos in the room became almost comically absurd, as when Lieutenant Commander Hoffman, of all people, said to us: "The bombing puts us in very real, very imminent personal danger every time it takes place. I don't know how to describe the feeling of being bombed. I don't think there are words to transmit it to the American people to make them understand that . . . The bombing has been demonstrated to be ineffective. It is not going to stop the Vietnamese will to fight, nor their will to continue . . . The bombings only make it more likely that we're going to have to stay here much, much longer."

I believed the POWs were speaking sincerely. So did my colleagues. They were like any other eight men off the streets of America, seven white and one black, caught in a web of forces they could not control. They, too, were victims. Imprisoned in Asia, in striped suits, the regretful murderers of innocent people, they might be in Viet Nam for many years to come. Earlier, they had uncritically embraced that blind American confidence that whomever or wherever we kill, god is always on our side, so they never questioned their orders, never sought to understand the war, and in the end volunteered to fly the instruments of death. Meanwhile, Nixon pretended that his escalation would get them home faster, effectively turning them into cover behind which he could hide the fact that he was waging a war he knew could not be won.

Outside, getting back into our cars, I saw the POWs climb into two enclosed pickup trucks. There were no windows. The Vietnamese did not want them to see the location of their prison, nor did they want the people on the street to see who was in the trucks. I was surprised to feel sad. The POWs themselves were sad enough, but somehow they added a dimension of tragedy and victimization to everything else I had seen in Viet Nam. I was surprised that I could feel any sympathy for them, surprised that along with my disdain I still felt myself to be a countryman of theirs, and glad that in the end I did shake their hands.

I was fully aware that these prisoners were making statements they knew their captors wanted to hear. Much later, after their eventual release, several who wanted to remain in the military recanted the statements that I filmed and claimed they were made under coercion, threats of either lost privileges or physical abuse, although none claimed that physical abuse was actually ever administered. Others in the group stood by what they had said and insisted there had been no coercion. Based on what I saw and what still exists on film, I am doubtful that any of their statements were made under duress.

The next morning, we were roused early to film damage from a dev-astating attack on a residential neighborhood in Hanoi. We crossed the river on a pedestrian pontoon bridge. Cars waited on the opposite side. The neighborhood we were driven to was unrecognizable. The rubble went on for blocks. There were no structures that had withstood the blasts, none. I saw a few lonesome figures picking through the wrecked houses looking for lost possessions. It was difficult to reconcile the more sympa-thetic feelings I had toward the pilots with the ruined neighborhood I saw that morning.

When we walked back across the pontoon bridge, it had become very crowded. People looked nervously at the sky, aware that we were all trapped on a prime target. Some smiled at the four of us and seemed to know who we were. There was an instant of surprise and curiosity when they saw our white faces, then a smile of recognition and a slight nod or bow. Many of these people were dressed alike, the men in khaki pants and blue shirts, the women in white blouses and black pants. We in the West express individuality through differences in dress and appearance. On that bridge there were none of those differences. Yet our Vietnamese hosts had very different personalities and no difficulty expressing them. I won-dered if the Vietnamese were able to be more expressive of their individu-ality because they were not preoccupied with the competition and envy that in the West are provoked by differences in outward appearance.

Riding back from the bridge, Quoc made a surprising announce-ment. The following evening, despite the bombing, a state-sponsored the-ater group was opening a production of the Arthur Miller play *All My Sons*. Written in 1947, the play revolved around corruption in military procurement and was generally critical of middle-class life in America. It was the third play by Arthur Miller the Vietnamese had translated and produced. The government also had professional touring companies that performed theater, dance, music, and puppetry in all the provinces and cities. And there were numerous amateur groups that performed through-out the country.

It was my last full day in Hanoi, and I was to spend it at the Ministry of Health. When I arrived at their headquarters, the vice minister of health, Dr. Nguyen Van Tin, greeted me with the head of the ministry's foreign affairs department, Dr. Nguyen Van Dong. After initial pleasantries, they were effusive in thanking me for the vials of antibiotic I had delivered to their embassy in Paris. They both smiled broadly as they told me their scientists had started large-scale manufacturing of the new strain and would soon have millions of doses available. Nodding gravely, they said that thousands of lives would be saved, perhaps tens of thousands.

I spent several hours with the two physicians and their aides poring over lists of surgical equipment, pharmaceuticals, and other medical goods in short supply in Hanoi but readily available in the States. We prioritized the long list using two criteria. First and foremost was the urgency of the medical need. How many lives could be saved? How much suffering could be alleviated? Were alternatives available elsewhere? Second was the weight and size of the material, since virtually all of it would move by air. Strained relations between the United States and the U.S.S.R. made shipping through Moscow difficult. Trade relations with China did not yet exist, because Nixon's first visit had taken place only three months before. The best routes were through commercial shippers in Hong Kong and Singapore. Both ports regularly dispatched cargo and passenger planes to North Viet Nam. The lists of medical supplies and shipping routes were exactly what I needed to expand Medical Aid for Indochina.

Interestingly, the Health Ministry officials told me that while their needs were great, they thought it better for MAI to raise small amounts of money from a large number of Americans rather than seek a few large donations from the rich, even if it meant less money overall. Any activity that would broaden opposition to the war in the United States was as important as medical supplies. Small contributions from Americans of modest means would help accomplish that, and be more meaningful in Viet Nam. I took these statements as evidence of how effectively the entire society had been integrated into the political strategy of the government.

Next, I was given a tour of the Bach Mai Hospital. With eleven hundred beds, it was the largest and most modern civilian facility in the country. Rather than occupying a single large building, the hospital was more like a campus with several smaller ones. It would not have measured up to a first-rate hospital in the United States, but I was surprised to see sophisticated equipment, orderly procedures, and good hygiene. I met several physicians who showed me around and introduced me to colleagues and patients. I did not expect to see a hospital as up-to-date and efficient as Bach Mai in an underdeveloped country, let alone one forced to devote most of its resources to war.

The doctors at Bach Mai said their national health system had two goals: prevention and medical self-reliance. On prevention, frequent campaigns about hygiene taught people the relationship between cleanliness and health. The entire population was inoculated against common communicable diseases, and health care was free to everyone. I questioned their emphasis on prevention in a time of war but was told that only by limiting the resources needed to cure disease could they muster what was necessary to treat so many wounded.

On self-reliance, they manufactured their own vaccines. They proudly showed me a lab where they had just produced the Sabin-formula polio vaccine. This work was scattered around the country in small operations to prevent a bombing attack from incapacitating them. Doctors and nurses were also decentralized. Many had lost their lives in the systematic attacks the United States had directed against hospitals. Clinics were decentralized for the same reason. Also, dispersing their medical staff gave them first responders close to any emergency. The doctors I met were an inspiration. I was determined to develop MAI into the kind of organization they deserved.

That evening was our last in Hanoi. Quat and our other hosts from the solidarity commission treated us to a formal banquet. An elaborate ladder of flowers was laid out over a long table covered with a white cloth. Various Vietnamese delicacies were placed inside the ladder. Not surprisingly, the dinner was interrupted by an air raid. We heard bombs exploding in the distance and the Vietnamese MiGs flying up to meet the Americans, but we saw nothing. Back at dinner, Colonel Quat had consumed enough alcohol to finally respond to questions about his personal life. I was amazed to learn he could trace his family's lineage back to the thirteenth century, all in one village some distance from Hanoi. He explained that village heritage is precious to every Vietnamese, and that he had recently spent five days in his ancestral village walking through the bamboo groves he had played in as a child.

I was taken aback. I said, "Quat, you're a soldier in the middle of a war. How can you take five days off just to relive scenes from your childhood? I'm only an organizer in an antiwar movement, and I never take that much time off." Quat laughed and then replied quite simply: "We have had to fight for our independence and freedom continuously for over thirty years. Without periodic rest and spiritual renewal, how could we go on?" Young as I was, I had never considered working for one goal over a lifetime. Quat's words stayed with me for many years.

The next day, May 28, we left Viet Nam, but not before one final appointment. At the studios of Radio Hanoi each of us taped a greeting to U.S. military personnel. None of us called for mutinies or advised Americans to disobey orders, nor did we advocate their defeat. However, we all described in detail the systematic bombing of civilian targets we had personally observed, including hospitals, schools, churches, villages, and residential housing. I said that Vietnamese morale, as we had experienced it, was high and likely to remain so, that North Viet Nam was a unified and well-organized society, and that there was no realistic hope for a U.S. victory. I acknowledged that many American foot soldiers and some American pilots had refused direct orders to engage in combat, but I and the others were careful not to advocate such action.

A crowded Russian DC-3 waited to take us back to Vientiane. We had been in North Viet Nam for eight days, survived eighteen air raids, and filmed enough to hopefully make an impact at home. On the long trip back to New York, I worked with the others to prepare for a press conference, and I formulated a plan to vastly expand the work of Medical Aid for Indochina.

CHAPTER 19

JUST BACK FROM NORTH VIET NAM, THE FOUR OF US STOOD BEFORE A CROWD OF reporters and several camera crews. Our arrival at Kennedy Airport on a Monday evening was not a good time to draw the press to an airport conference, so, tired from the long flight back, we opted for a night's sleep and a Tuesday morning press conference in a Manhattan hotel. We didn't mince words. Based on what we had seen in North Viet Nam, we accused President Nixon of intentionally bombing civilians and other war crimes. We substantiated our charges with photos and film clips. The reporters present responded with interest, but the coverage that night on TV and the next morning in the papers was disappointing. We weren't celebrities, which was made clear by the minimal exposure we received. I resolved to do more.

First, I decided to produce a documentary film from the footage I had shot and to find the help I needed to do it. Second, I called Palmer Williams, the producer I knew at CBS News. He had given us travel money as an advance against purchasing any of the film I would shoot. Palmer worked for *60 Minutes*, which ran fifteen-minute segments instead of the thirty-second pieces that appeared on CBS's news programs, so I suggested he consider producing a segment based on the antiwar POWs. Since no one had that story, *60 Minutes* could treat it as an exclusive. Palmer liked the idea. He offered to pay $1,000 a used minute for the footage, offset by our travel advance. Two weeks later, the segment ran using eight minutes of my film, which more than covered the cost of our trip.

The *60 Minutes* piece had a profound effect on the national debate about the POWs, although it was neither sudden nor obvious at the time. Nixon, Kissinger, and others within the administration stopped talking about POW torture. They knew that every time they did, a reporter or columnist was likely to refer to the *60 Minutes* segment, and they did not want to give that segment any more exposure than it had already received. Pro-war groups, like the American Legion and the Veterans of Foreign Wars, condemned the individual POWs in the film as traitors or tried to excuse their statements by claiming they must have been made after extreme torture. I took some pleasure in imagining the rage Nixon and Kissinger must have felt as they watched American POWs attack their policies in front of an audience of millions.

Having discharged my first responsibility, publicizing the civilian bombing, I turned to my second, expanding Medical Aid for Indochina. My priority was to recruit a national network of organizers who could enlist activists in their areas and begin raising money. Bart Meyers took responsibility for New York. My friend Rich Rothstein, an early SDS leader, coordinated MAI's work in Chicago. Rich was later a leading labor organizer, and later still a nationally known public education scholar. Soon I had MAI organizers in half a dozen large cities.

The ease with which I was able to do this reflected an opinion shared by many organizers: protests and demonstrations were no longer effective. MAI's promise that none of the money raised would leave the country, that it would be used instead to buy lifesaving medicines and equipment for shipment abroad, had great appeal and neutralized criticism. The early enthusiasm from organizers was just the beginning. Word spread, and volunteers started support committees on their own. I hired a few people to help with the larger workload and moved MAI's operations into an inexpensive office just off Harvard Square in Cambridge.

With a national network in formation, MAI had to supply the necessary materials. I wrote model fund-raising letters and press releases, brochures describing MAI's work, copy for collection cans, flyers for use at mass events, and a report to MAI's board of directors about our plans. The

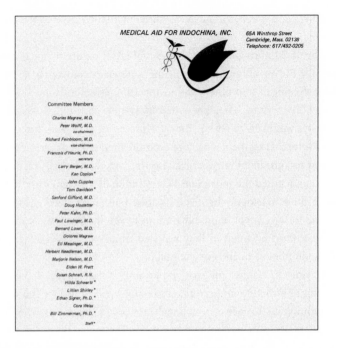

staff found graphic artists to design a logo, stationery, and business cards and to make these materials look attractive and professional.

Taking a bold step, we applied to the Internal Revenue Service for tax-exempt status as an international relief fund. Wealthy donors want a tax deduction for large contributions. In our application, we were careful to emphasize that our medical assistance would go to both sides in the war, although we avoided any indication of how much would go where. Members of our board were familiar with projects in South Viet Nam, Laos, and Cambodia that operated legally and served civilians on both sides of the political lines. We made certain to regularly send some aid to these projects, even though they operated in U.S.-controlled areas, while we reserved the bulk of our assistance for the Health Ministry in Hanoi. We presented a credible case to the IRS, but to the public we always underscored the fact that the vast majority of the aid we sent was to benefit civilians in areas being attacked on Nixon's orders.

While I pursued the expansion of MAI, the civilian-bombing story got traction in the mass media. Led by CBS News and the *New York Times*, and in particular by Anthony Lewis, word about targeting civilians got out. I wrote a front-page story for Boston's alternative newsweekly headlined "Nixon's Six Lies About Viet Nam" and then convinced the *Boston Globe* to print a full page of pictures I had shot in North Viet Nam and a story about my experiences there.

The controversy over targeting civilians energized opponents of the war. Members of Congress, business leaders, and entertainment celebrities criticized the bombing and generated more news coverage. Accusations of war crimes further polarized the debate. Meanwhile, Senator George McGovern of South Dakota emerged as the likely Democratic presidential nominee. A decorated World War II bomber pilot, he had promised immediate withdrawal from Viet Nam.

The civilian bombing also gave new impetus to the antiwar movement. Activists felt responsible for protecting the victims. They pointed to war crimes the United States had committed in World War II, when bombs were used to trigger firestorms that killed tens of thousands of civilians in Dresden and other German cities. The number of civilians killed in the firestorm created over the city of Tokyo was equal to the number killed in each of the two nuclear attacks. Many people believed that Nixon and Kissinger were sufficiently ruthless to repeat these atrocities, which led to a resurgence of protests. Those reluctant to demonstrate sent money instead, which swelled the coffers of antiwar organizations, including MAI.

Our work mushroomed. The many local committees that had sprung up to support MAI were creative and determined, even though in those years grassroots fund-raising was quite primitive. Collection cans were placed in retail stores. Dances and parties were staged on campuses and in neighborhoods to raise money. Lecturers gave us their fees. Performers contributed a portion of their receipts. Bake sales were held. Art was auctioned. Liberal churches and synagogues passed collection plates during services. College kids went door-to-door. In a few places, doctors formed committees to solicit their colleagues, both for cash and for medical supplies. Where large demonstrations did occur, buckets were passed so protesters could throw in spare change for MAI. Eventually, skillful lawyers working on our behalf convinced the IRS to grant us tax-exempt status, which then gave us the ability to solicit large contributions from many wealthy antiwar supporters.

With MAI growing rapidly, I turned back to the footage I had shot in Viet Nam and asked Walter Teller for help. He had produced antiwar documentaries as a member of Newsreel, the left-wing filmmaking collective. Walter enlisted Janet Mendelsohn and Geri Ashur, and the four of us went to work. I wrote a narration, and the others filmed me performing it on camera. We organized the footage into a coherent story, after which Walter, Janet, and Geri did the editing. When they finished, we had a forty-five-minute film. We called it *Village by Village* to describe the strategy of destroying Viet Nam neighborhood by neighborhood and village by village. For the next six months, the film was widely distributed on college campuses and frequently shown by local peace groups.

In June the full range of opposition to the war was on display. Cora Weiss and the renowned folksinger Joan Baez led the Ring Around the Capitol demonstration, in which twenty-five hundred women and children locked hands around the Capitol building in Washington. At the other end of the tactical spectrum, Weatherman had renamed itself the Weather Underground and set off bombs in empty buildings. When their faction of SDS failed to organize a youth rebellion, they had turned to explosives. Their blasts went off at night to avoid casualties, but three of their own had already been killed making bombs in a Greenwich Village town house.

Also in June, five arrests were made in connection with a burglary at the offices of the Democratic National Committee in Washington's Watergate complex. Almost a year would go by before we understood the immense impact this event would have on the war and the nation.

My communal house in Somerville remained a hub of political activity, but a few changes had taken place. Karen Nussbaum replaced one of the women in the house. She was organizing secretarial and clerical workers, one of the first feminists to do so. Her boyfriend, Ira Arlook, who would later lead Citizen Action, the nation's biggest consumer organization, was then a Boston antiwar leader. Marilyn Webb, whom I was still seeing, had accepted a permanent teaching position at Goddard College in Vermont. We were able to spend occasional weekends together thanks to my little Cessna.

In mid-July, the Democratic convention was held in Miami Beach. Progressive delegates forced a rule change that empowered them over the labor unions and big-city political machines. They nominated George McGovern for the presidency, and despite lagging far behind Nixon in the polls, he reiterated his promise of complete withdrawal from Indochina. In future years, the split in the party between the progressive antiwar forces supporting McGovern and the other, more culturally and politically moderate factions crippled the Democrats, who for many years remained torn and unable to forge a coherent identity.

At the same time, Jane Fonda left with three other Americans on a highly publicized trip to North Viet Nam. Their itinerary was almost identical to what mine had been in May, and Colonel Quat brought them to many of the same places. The difference was that Jane's celebrity status commanded widespread press attention. The day after she visited Phuc Loc, on July 20, the Pentagon denied to NBC-TV that they had bombed the village, ignoring the film I had released two months earlier. They also denied dropping antipersonnel bombs on Nam Dinh, again in the face of my footage. I used their denials to once more publicize the evidence I had.

Jane's trip, like mine, ended with a broadcast to U.S. troops over Radio Hanoi. She, too, avoided any call to mutiny or to disobey orders. Like us, she described the extensive civilian bomb damage she had seen. However, earlier in her trip, Vietnamese women at an anti-aircraft battery had invited her to sit in the gunner's position, and a photographer had snapped a picture. Right-wingers squealed about the gun regularly firing on U.S. planes and claimed incorrectly that Jane had advocated mutiny. They accused her of treason, used the picture as "evidence," and demanded she be prosecuted. They called her "Hanoi Jane," a play on "Tokyo Rose," the name given to several Japanese women during World War II who broadcast anti-American messages to U.S. troops in the Pacific. It was based on a lie, but "Hanoi Jane" stuck for many years.

Like other Americans, Jane had carried mail back and forth to North Viet Nam, enabling me to exchange letters with Colonel Quat about the initial work of MAI. Immediately after her delegation returned, another departed for Hanoi that included the former U.S. attorney general Ramsey Clark. They carried another letter from me to Quat and delivered his reply when they returned. Clark had served under Johnson and turned against the war when he was required to prosecute antiwar protesters, among them Dr. Benjamin Spock, America's preeminent pediatrician, and William Sloane Coffin Jr., the nationally known chaplain of Yale University.

Clark's voice was not one the Nixon administration could ignore, as they had that of a mere movie star like Fonda. By then, too many eyewitnesses had seen the civilian bombing, and thanks to the efforts of all of us it gradually became an accepted fact. That put war supporters on the defensive and made them more aggressive. The Veterans of Foreign Wars called for the prosecution of both Clark and Fonda as traitors. Celebrity was a two-edged sword. The lack of it had kept me from more effectively publicizing the civilian bombing, as Clark and Fonda were able to do. On the other hand, not being a celebrity, I was free to continue my work without threats of prosecution.

Our effort to expand MAI paid off over that summer. The timing was right, and medical relief was the perfect tactic to harness the resurgence of opposition that followed the new bombing campaign. Committees raising money for us continued to spring up all over. I worked with the staff in the Cambridge office to recruit more organizers in new cities. We also put together an impressive list of endorsers, which included almost a dozen members of Congress, three Nobel laureates, leading academics like Noam Chomsky, Erik Erikson, and Howard Zinn, famous actors and actresses, religious leaders, lawyers, and physicians. They gave us enhanced credibility with the press and with potential donors.

Our office evolved into a national headquarters. We opened a few satellite offices in other cities with local financial support. I worked into the night to hold it all together, but I was exuberant about the results. We received unsolicited donations in the mail, modest totals from collection cans and door-to-door work, larger amounts collected at public events and by our committees, and occasionally a big check from a wealthy supporter. Twice we arrived in the morning to find a brown paper bag filled with cash hidden between our front door and the screen. One bag contained $5,000, and no indication who had left it. We assumed the donor was an antiwar marijuana dealer reluctant to advertise his generosity. Having neither a way to return the money nor an inclination to do so, we added it to our receipts and credited it anonymously.

Village by Village presented convincing evidence that civilians were intentionally targeted in North Viet Nam, and by early August it had achieved wide circulation. The lone antiwar Republican in the House of Representatives, Pete McCloskey, saw the film and asked me to come to Washington and show it in the Capitol. He would make arrangements and invite his colleagues to the screening. McCloskey, a former Marine

Corps officer, represented Palo Alto, California. He was detested in the White House, but he got his share of press attention.

I screened the film on August 17 in a Capitol auditorium hosted by Senator Ted Kennedy's Subcommittee on Refugees. McCloskey had brought a number of antiwar representatives and senators, but few war supporters showed up. I got acquainted with several representatives, particularly Bella Abzug, Ron Dellums, and Robert Drinan, who had each given consistent and reliable support to the antiwar movement and would continue to do so. McCloskey wanted to give delegates to the upcoming Republican convention in Miami Beach an alternative to Nixon, so he planned to have his name entered into nomination for the presidency. He asked me to come to the convention and show the film. I agreed.

The Republican convention had originally been scheduled for San Diego. Nixon realized that the promise of a week on the beach could draw thousands of California activists and lead to protests that might dwarf those in Chicago four years earlier. Shadowy forces coordinated by the White House and the FBI laid plans for a massive roundup. Years later the details were publicly revealed. Under the label COINTELPRO (FBI-speak for "counterintelligence program"), civil liberties would be suspended and internment camps used to house detained activists. But word about COINTELPRO leaked out and caused widespread protest. To quiet the outrage, Nixon moved the convention to Miami Beach with only three months' notice. That rendered some of the COINTELPRO plans obsolete, but its domestic spying and surveillance aspects continued unabated until Nixon left office.

I arrived in Miami Beach on August 20, but Representative McCloskey told me that the convention was too tightly controlled to show *Village by Village*. It was, he said, an armed camp with enough security to repel a foreign invasion. McCloskey arranged to show the film at a local community center the next day. He invited Republican delegates as well as antiwar protesters to see it, and I agreed to be there to answer questions. I told McCloskey that Fonda was in Miami Beach and had just returned from visiting many of the sites depicted in the film. I recommended we show it to her and invite her to speak as well.

Jane had come to the convention alone. When I found her, she was moving through various protest sites by herself. I thought that was crazy. Pro-war people would have stood in line to spit in her face, and more than a few thought it was their patriotic duty to harm her. We had become acquainted the several times she and Tom Hayden had stayed in our Somerville house. It made sense for us to team up in Miami Beach since we had both been recent eyewitnesses to the civilian bombing in North Viet Nam. We also shared a fear that protests at the convention were going to get out of hand.

Vietnam Veterans Against the War (VVAW) was the most organized presence among the demonstrators in Miami Beach. Many of them had assumed that their sacrifices on the battlefield would earn them a fair hearing from the government. Instead, they had been ignored, and some had reached a point of extreme frustration. I understood their bitterness and rage and knew that a few would be open to calls for violence. McCloskey took Jane and me inside the convention's outer perimeter and showed us the level of force prepared to meet such a challenge. Violence would turn into a bloodbath, which would only help Nixon win reelection.

We screened *Village by Village* in the community center, and both Jane and I spoke to the audience, which was a wild mix of angry vets, peaceful Quakers, irate college students, hippie street kids, and squabbling activists. Sadly, McCloskey was the only Republican in the room. Some vets wanted to shut down the convention. Jane and I sympathized with them but knew that a confrontation could get people killed. But debate was not possible in that audience. Disagreements became shouting matches, and before long most of the vets stormed out.

For the next two days, we went from group to group and meeting to meeting using Jane's celebrity and my movie to educate activists about the bombing and to promote MAI as a new project for the antiwar movement. Fewer than ten thousand protesters had come to Miami Beach, and little planning had been done for them. Jane and I told our friends among the vets about the massive security force waiting to stop any violence. We hoped they could keep others who were spoiling for a fight under control. They couldn't. Brief exchanges of rocks and tear gas broke out on the fringe of the convention. The militant vets met billy clubs with long sticks and iron rods. Firecrackers were thrown. Nevertheless, when the police amassed in force, the vets wisely retreated.

During the two days I spent with Jane in Miami Beach, I got a taste of what it means to be an instantly recognizable celebrity. At a popular Jewish delicatessen, we stopped for lunch and tried to plan our afternoon. A woman interrupted us to praise Jane for her courage. She went on and on. Jane thanked her, but as we returned to our conversation, two more women broke in. Again, Jane responded politely. Soon a line of ten people had formed at our table. Jane was cordial to them all, but we couldn't talk to each other. On the street, it was no different, except that along with kind words from some came hurled insults and vague threats from others. Without her sunglasses and floppy hat, she would have been swamped wherever we went.

The Miami Beach protests were puny in comparison to the massive Republican pro-war presence at the convention and in the surrounding hotels. The VVAW contingent split over differences in tactics and could not function effectively. Jane and I both felt we were not accomplishing enough to justify more time in Miami Beach. A day before the convention ended, we left, she back to Los Angeles and I to Boston. McCloskey got the one vote for president he expected but no more. On the convention's closing day, demonstrators blocked the entrances and were met with a massive police response. A veritable cloud of tear gas hung over the convention and burned the eyes of delegates trying to get in and out. Nixon himself was affected as he entered the hall. Thankfully, no one was killed.

A few weeks before the convention, the antiwar movement achieved one of its most significant and lasting victories: the draft was permanently ended, never to be revived. We celebrated the triumph, even though it came too late to impact the war. Nixon soon withdrew the last American combat troops from Viet Nam, leaving only twenty-seven thousand support troops he promised would be withdrawn by year's end. But the massive and unrelenting air war went on, as did the U.S. funding that kept the South Vietnamese army alive and active.

The switch to an all-volunteer army would severely limit U.S. military power in the years ahead. So, too, would the distaste for war created by the Viet Nam experience. In the 1980s, President Reagan wanted to send

U.S. troops into one war in El Salvador and another in Nicaragua, but political pressure driven by memories of Viet Nam made that impossible. Later, during lengthy U.S. wars in Iraq and Afghanistan, the lack of manpower reduced military options and forced dependence on private contractors. Viet Nam not only changed how we Americans view war; it changed how we wage it.

After the Republican convention, the increased interest in MAI and our determination to develop the organization as rapidly and broadly as possible overwhelmed our operational capacity. I was on the road or in the air much of the time and could no longer aggressively plan for the future, manage the staff, and handle the paperwork. We needed a bigger operation. The MAI board of directors had initially resisted expenditures for salaries and office overhead. By summer's end there was ample evidence that a larger organization could raise far more money for the Vietnamese, as well as help broaden opposition to the war.

We hired Lillian Shirley, an ex-nun active in Catholic antiwar work, to administer MAI's operations. Her boyfriend, Tom Davidson, an experienced organizer among Protestant antiwar groups, came aboard to manage the office, handle legal issues with the government, keep our books, and oversee the shipment of medical material to Hanoi. I was left free to travel, expand the organization, and recruit organizers and local committees in more cities across the country.

Ken Coplon was our next hire. He approached us after turning twenty-one and gaining access to an inheritance of $21,000. Given the egalitarian ethos of the antiwar movement, Ken felt guilty having so much money, so he gave it all away to various left-wing organizations over a long weekend. MAI got $3,000, but Ken also became interested in our operations. Once he had the cleansing poverty he desired, he volunteered to work for us without salary. Ken had graduated from college the previous June with a major in poker playing. He was brash and energetic and seemed ready to do anything. In a few weeks we had the perfect job for him.

Cora Weiss asked Bernie Mazel to visit our office and teach us a new technique he had perfected. Bernie was a pioneer in direct-mail fundraising. He had used it to raise money for CARE, the international relief organization, and to establish the first subscriber list for the *New York*

Review of Books. He offered to oversee a similar program for MAI. Ken immediately saw the potential and offered to work with Bernie. Over the next year, Bernie mentored Ken, and together they raised a great deal of money for MAI. Later, Ken established his own company and raised substantial sums for dozens of progressive organizations.

With the November election looming, Fonda and Hayden organized an antiwar entertainment tour. The previous year, Jane had played in a political vaudeville show that traveled to military bases in the United States and the Pacific to entertain soldiers and sailors, much like the traditional USO shows — but with one critical difference. Instead of performers like Bob Hope who embraced the war, Jane, her friend Donald Sutherland, and other actors performed satirical skits and songs that criticized or made fun of the war, the brass, and the politicians. It was called the FTA show, which in polite company meant Free the Army but on the bases where it played was also understood to mean Fuck the Army. The troops loved these performances and turned out in droves, despite the officers who tried to steer them away. Seeing entertainers who shared their skepticism about the war and took their side against the hated officers moved even more soldiers to protest and resistance.

Jane and Tom organized a civilian version of the tour, called the Indochina Peace Campaign (IPC), to play in the critical electoral states. They hired a resourceful staff that soon had them scheduled in a different city seven nights a week for the seven weeks leading up to the election. The plan was to draw people in with good satirical entertainment, educate them about the war, and use the local press and TV news coverage to spread antiwar messages beyond the in-person audience. I was asked to participate when I could. Daytime screenings of *Village by Village* were made part of the agenda, and MAI was promoted during the shows as a concrete step people could take to oppose the war.

All of us working against the war were frantic about stopping the murderous bombing in Viet Nam and Laos. Once the IPC schedule was set, I thought we could make MAI more publicly visible by sponsoring a coordinated week of activities October 8–14. I wanted to boost morale and show our organizers and volunteers around the country that they were not isolated but part of a national crusade. The enthusiasm was already there. Hundreds of events involved tens of thousands of people in benefit concerts, film screenings, college and church events, neighborhood fund-raising drives, and other appeals for money and support. Everyone associated with MAI helped. Noam Chomsky, quoting from one of our brochures, published a letter in the *New York Review of Books* that said, "Right now it is the U.S. government with its anti-personnel weapons, napalm, and laser-guided bombs that is defining our relationship to the people of Indochina. If we want to define that relationship differently, we'll have to take the initiative. Medical aid is one important way to make a substantive beginning."

Throughout the fall, I promoted MAI and supervised its organizing, but flew out to join the IPC tour for a day or two at a time. Every day meant a different city. Before the evening performances, some of us did interviews on local radio stations, while Jane's celebrity usually got her on daytime television. We showed *Village by Village* and met with local officials to seek their support. But it was the crowds at night, often numbering a thousand or more, that were the high point of the experience and the source of the enthusiasm we all felt as participants.

The events were staged in labor halls, church sanctuaries, and campus auditoriums. Jane was the star of the show, and those who came to see her were not disappointed. Most actors are eloquent only when someone else writes their lines. Jane spoke extemporaneously and could prompt an audience to feel deeply about the war. She typically spent forty-five minutes narrating a slide show of pictures from Viet Nam, some of which she had taken herself. Among the many moving images were miniskirted teenage prostitutes in Saigon who months before had been peasant girls harvesting rice in small villages. They underwent surgery to enlarge their breasts and westernize their eyelids in a desperate attempt to attract the GIs they solicited. It was a side of the war most people had never considered.

After Jane, Tom Hayden gave an analytical speech challenging people to understand the root causes of the war and its complex history. He was a good speaker who did not talk down to his listeners, and he knew as much about the long history of the war as anyone. The other regular was Holly Near, a singer-songwriter with a commanding stage presence who had written several moving and original songs specifically for the IPC tour. Interspersed throughout the evening, others, like me, gave short speeches about specific issues, in my case the civilian bombing and the work of MAI. The IPC tour drew large audiences and good news coverage, but also virulent attacks from local right-wingers, which helped increase our visibility and the size of our crowds.

During the IPC tour and the MAI events, we distributed hundreds of thousands of brochures headlined "Six Million Victims." The title was a sideways reference to the Holocaust, but the brochure described in painstaking detail the one million Vietnamese fatalities during the American phase of the war, the two million Vietnamese injured, and the three million left as homeless refugees. Project Air War, an antiwar research team led by Fred Branfman, authored the brochure. Fred had spent years doing volunteer work in Laos, then returned to Washington to write *Voices from the Plain of Jars*, a moving account of the psychological damage done to Laotian children by the intense American bombardment of their villages.

With the presidential election approaching, progress was made at the peace talks in Paris. Kissinger headed the American delegation, and Le Duc Tho the Vietnamese. Both made secret concessions, of which Kissinger's were far more significant. He agreed to stop all U.S. ground and air operations, to allow the North Vietnamese Army to maintain its large presence in the South, to give the Provisional Revolutionary Government a legal role in South Viet Nam, and to provide U.S. funding for the reconstruction of the country. In return, Le Duc Tho agreed to allow South Viet Nam's president, Nguyen Van Thieu, to remain in office and to release the POWs. Elections to unify the country under a single government would then take place.

Kissinger scheduled a trip to Hanoi in late October to initial an agreement based on these terms, which were still secret. He hoped to be remembered as the negotiator who ended the war, but he had failed to consult with President Thieu before making his concessions to the North. Thieu learned of the secret concessions before Kissinger departed for Hanoi, and denounced the deal. Kissinger flew instead to Saigon to try to turn him around, but Thieu, despite his financial dependence upon the United States, held firm. Kissinger was stuck.

Simultaneously, a rift opened between Kissinger and Nixon. The president believed Kissinger's secret compromises would make him look weak and jeopardize his reelection. Facing opposition from both presidents, Kissinger had to cancel his trip to Hanoi to initial the agreement. The North Vietnamese were furious and in retaliation released the secret terms that had been negotiated. Kissinger, desperate to preserve his role in history, made the fateful public announcement at the end of October: "Peace is at hand." The public rejoiced, but Nixon was furious. According to Seymour Hersh, the investigative reporter, Nixon's pollster told him the announcement would cost him pro-war votes, and that he was likely to lose the election. An hour later, according to the pollster, quoted by Hersh, the president of the United States actually went so far as to call and ask, "What would be the public reaction if we bombed Hanoi?"

Some of this happened in secret, and some was leaked to the press. I could see that negotiations had intensified, and when Kissinger said, "Peace is at hand," I assumed he would not risk such a statement if there were a chance it would backfire. I clung to any hopeful sign, but antiwar activists had been disappointed too often in the past. As the days ticked by after Kissinger's announcement, no further developments took place. Nixon won reelection in a huge landslide, losing Massachusetts but carrying every other state. That sent antiwar activists from optimism to pessimism. Nixon was now unfettered politically and could do as he pleased.

More days passed, but still nothing happened. With American ground combat over, the military front line had shifted to our ships at sea. Fighter planes from Navy aircraft carriers and artillery pieces on other Navy vessels continued the unrelenting attack on Viet Nam. Resistance moved out to sea as well. On one Pacific aircraft carrier, sailors burned the ship's radar. On another, a sailor threw metal parts into the engine and caused severe damage. Both carriers had to be withdrawn from combat operations. On a third, the USS *Kitty Hawk*, a race riot broke out. Scheduled to go home, it was diverted back to Indochina. In November, the USS *Constellation* suffered the first mass mutiny in U.S. naval history just off the California coast. Black sailors staged a sit-down strike and were brought back to port. When the carrier returned for them a few days later, all 144 sailors refused to reboard, raised clenched fists, and sat down on the dock. I saw it all on TV news.

Kissinger finally flew back to Paris to resume negotiations on November 20. He made new demands on the North. They were still outraged about the previous agreement, refused his proposals, and made new demands themselves. Meanwhile, Nixon tried to get Thieu back on board by secretly promising that if he accepted the U.S. position, Nixon would sign the agreement with the North but ignore it and continue to support Thieu's regime in the South, even if he had to resume the bombing to do so. With so many crosscurrents, the negotiations got nowhere. In early December, apprehensive about the survival of the regime in the South, Nixon authorized a massive transfer of military hardware to its government. The South Vietnamese Air Force instantly became the fourth largest in the world.

During this period, MAI thrived. We avoided the disagreements over ideology and tactics that limited the larger antiwar movement. No one had an ideological problem with medical assistance. The IPC tour and our own work had increased MAI's visibility, both inside the movement and in the larger society. Our direct-mail fund-raising, managed by Ken Coplon, returned a significant profit. Our national headquarters buzzed with activity, much of it organized by local coordinators, leaving us barely able to keep up. We were riding a wave of support but kept looking for new opportunities to make trouble for Nixon.

In early December, the Treasury Department gave us one. It sent a letter threatening MAI with federal prosecution for "trading with the enemy." It claimed we were in violation of both the 1799 Logan Act and the 1917 Trading with the Enemy Act. Violations were felonies punishable by large fines and years in prison. I convened the MAI staff and board to discuss our options. We could close down, which all agreed was out of the question. We had started MAI to defy the government. It made no sense to back down after its first threat. We could seek relief in the courts, but that would take too long. We could continue in secret, but that came with other risks and could increase the price we might ultimately have to pay. I thought the best course was defiance, and the others agreed. Instead of running from the threat, we would openly violate both laws and dare the Treasury Department to arrest and prosecute us.

I was willing to bet my freedom we could beat the department in court. So was the MAI staff and board. We knew there was no congressional declaration of war, only the vague Gulf of Tonkin Resolution. How then could North Viet Nam be considered "the enemy"? If we were arrested, we would have to be tried before a jury. I did not believe any jury of twelve would vote unanimously to imprison us for sending medical supplies to anyone. On the other hand, Nixon might be seriously embarrassed if he criminally prosecuted us for simple humanitarian acts, especially if a jury later found us innocent. I knew Nixon was capable of such risk, and I didn't want to go to prison, but with that analysis I felt relatively safe. I also believed that open defiance would generate press coverage, which would rally new supporters and further insulate us against legal harassment.

We purchased medical supplies and arranged to ship them from Kennedy Airport in New York to Hong Kong with transshipment to Hanoi. We distributed a press release that informed reporters about the government's threat and our response to it, and included the date our crates would be shipped along with the airline and flight number. In effect, we invited Treasury agents to come and arrest us, and we invited the press to come and watch. On the evening the plane was to depart, I worried I might have to spend the night in a federal lockup, but there was no response from the government. I watched carefully for a few days, but no Treasury agents appeared. The Nixon administration had made the same calculation we had. The price of stopping us was greater than the price of allowing us to continue. I celebrated with the staff. We had faced down the federal government, and we had prevailed.

Every time we made a shipment to Hanoi after that, we gave the press dates and flight numbers and defied the government to stop us. By refusing to be intimidated, we turned the situation upside down. We didn't have the power of arrest the government had, but when it tried to use that power against us, we sidestepped and deflected it back. Every new shipment gave us another opportunity to demonstrate and publicize the government's inability to stop us. That fired up our supporters and effectively spread the word about our work. We made the government work for us and look foolish at the same time, and we gained valuable experience in manipulating similar situations to our advantage.

CHAPTER 20

PEACE WAS NOT AT HAND. ON DECEMBER 19, I WAS AWAKENED BY A PHONE CALL. THE city of Hanoi was being carpet bombed. An all-out attack began at 8:00 p.m. and continued until 6:30 a.m. These were not the sporadic daytime air raids that took place while I was there, but sustained, repetitive, saturation bombing by B-52s that targeted the central city and lasted the entire night. It was the heaviest aerial assault of the war.

I was sickened, imagining the devastation in Hanoi. Nixon and Kissinger were committing mass murder to improve their negotiating position. The gentle people I had talked to on the streets of Hanoi only six months before were being blown apart in their homes and the bomb shelters where they hid. I wondered if new friends like Quat and Quoc had survived, and was frustrated that after so much work the antiwar movement could not prevent this tragedy. For several days, I was stunned by the magnitude of the destruction. Military officials in Saigon admitted that twenty thousand tons of explosives had been dropped over Hanoi during the first two days—forty million pounds of TNT, the precise explosive equivalent of the atomic bomb dropped on Hiroshima. And it was only the beginning.

Kissinger, after being thwarted in his role as peacemaker, had become bloodthirsty. He convinced Nixon that the North Vietnamese would capitulate if thousands of civilians in their largest cities were murdered by aerial bombardment. Most of our military high command backed him up, as did our foreign policy experts, many of whom he had put in place. They could not have been more willfully ignorant of evidence and experience to the contrary.

They also ignored North Vietnamese military preparations. With help from the U.S.S.R. and China, Hanoi had built capable air defenses, including fighter planes, anti-aircraft batteries with advanced targeting capability, and, most important, surface-to-air missiles. The B-52s had previously used their high cruising altitudes to escape counterattacks. Suddenly they were vulnerable, and several were shot down. A U.S. Air Force spokesman had the audacity to make the absurd complaint that they were up against "the greatest air-defense system in history."

I felt impotent in the face of these attacks. So did my colleagues. Then, on December 23, I heard devastating news. The Bach Mai Hospital in Hanoi was bombed and destroyed. It was the country's largest and most advanced civilian hospital. I had been there on May 27 and remembered the doctors who had given me a lengthy tour. Bombs had damaged the hospital on December 19. Then, between 2:00 a.m. and 4:00 a.m. on

Dr. Art Westing, an MAI supporter, with Dr. Dai, the director of the Bach Mai Hospital, after it was destroyed in the 1972 Christmas bombings. *Author's collection*

December 22, when the staff had little ability to evacuate patients, the Bach Mai Hospital was utterly destroyed in a massive attack that hit most of the buildings on its large campus. I cringed as I thought of the patients I had seen there, and the hospital's precious medical equipment.

The Pentagon denied the attack. It insisted that no civilian targets had been hit and no hospitals in Hanoi destroyed or even damaged. As luck would have it, a four-person American peace delegation was in Hanoi during the bombing. It included the celebrity folksinger Joan Baez; Columbia University law professor Telford Taylor, who held the rank of general as the lead American prosecutor at the Nazi war crimes tribunal in Nuremberg after World War II; Michael Allen, dean of the Berkeley Divinity School at Yale; and activist Barry Romo of VVAW. They were not people who could be ignored, and their testimony eviscerated the Pentagon's credibility.

General Taylor published an op-ed piece in the *New York Times* on Christmas morning. Writing from Hanoi on December 22, he said, "Early this morning, the large Bach Mai Hospital was destroyed. The hospital grounds were torn by huge fresh craters and the buildings that escaped hits were shattered by blasts. Viewed a few hours later, the hospital remains were a terrible scene, with rescue workers carrying patients piggyback, cranes and bulldozers and people using only their hands desperately clearing debris to reach victims said to be still buried in the rubble, and the frantic hospital director running from one building to another."

Michael Allen, writing later in the *Christian Century*, backed up Taylor's view: "We saw Bach Mai Hospital a few hours after it was bombed . . . The hospital's main buildings were gutted hulks. Some walls were left standing, others had collapsed, and there were no roofs at all. At first glance some outlying buildings looked intact, but on closer observation I could see that nothing was left inside." Baez and Romo, interviewed by journalists in Hanoi and upon their return, told exactly the same story. Yet in spite of these eyewitness accounts, the Pentagon continued to insist that the Bach Mai Hospital had not been hit.

Outrage over the denials was matched by the horror of the continuing assault. On December 23, Anthony Lewis wrote in the *New York Times*:

"In the nearly six years of World War II, less than 80,000 tons of bombs fell on the British Isles. Last month alone, the month of November, when American bombing was restricted because of the peace talks, U.S. planes dropped 100,000 tons on Indochina. The total through the Johnson and Nixon administrations is now over seven million tons." With the exception of the firestorms in World War II and the nuclear attacks on Japan, the bombing of North Vietnamese cities during the Christmas holidays in 1972 was the most ruthless and massive aerial assault in history.

We had to keep Bach Mai in the spotlight. That much I knew. Many Americans were outraged that we had bombed a civilian hospital. Pentagon denials were driving the story to the top of the news. The antiwar movement had to keep it there because those denials inevitably fueled suspicions that the Pentagon was telling other lies. If we kept the Bach Mai controversy going, the Pentagon would have to keep lying. We had enough evidence to counter its lies, but we needed a dramatic way to push our evidence into the public debate.

I had resources to help solve this problem, an organization with a national headquarters, full-time offices and staff in cities across the country, and tens of thousands of active supporters. There had to be something I could do. I struggled with the question until I realized the answer was right in front of me. MAI was buying medicines and surgical equipment for Hanoi. Why not buy a hospital? Why not rebuild Bach Mai with American dollars?

It was an audacious idea, which is why I thought it would work. It would keep the controversy alive in the best way possible, with a humanitarian impetus. It would help us reach out to people ambivalent about the war but newly outraged by the bombing of a hospital. And it would limit Nixon's maneuvering room if Americans visibly raised money to rebuild what he had just destroyed. What better way to demonstrate the country was not unified behind him?

Hospital reconstruction was completely in line with MAI's mission. Rebuilding the hospital would mean vastly increasing the scope of our work, but this was the best opportunity we would have to do so, escalating our efforts as the military escalated its. With enthusiastic staff support I brought the idea to the MAI board of directors and our coordinators across the country. They all endorsed the project, and together we mapped out our plans. Ken was confident our newly acquired direct-mail capability could be used to raise money. We called the entertainers who supported us to request they quickly organize small benefit concerts. When we learned that "Bach Mai" means "white blossom" in Vietnamese, we used a white flower on all our printed materials.

Two days later, a financial angel walked into the MAI office. Phil Gerbode, in his late twenties, introduced himself and said he wanted to discuss a large donation. He was looking for a way to use the personal wealth he had inherited to help stop the bombing. I told him about rebuilding Bach Mai. The boldness of the project appealed to him. We agreed the best way to launch it would be a full-page ad in the *New York Times*, an ad that attacked Nixon for destroying the hospital and solicited money to rebuild it. When I told Gerbode it would cost $25,000, he agreed to fund it.

We scheduled a press conference a week later in Washington to formally launch the Bach Mai Hospital Emergency Relief Fund. The ad would appear a day or two after that. We wanted to use the press conference to build interest in the ad. To succeed, we would have to invite the right reporters, find an appropriate location, and recruit at least two well-known spokespeople to stand with us and draw reporters to the story.

Those jobs fell to a new member of our staff, Larry Levin, a slight and physically unassuming man with a courageous history. He had been frustrated by electoral politics in 1970 and had gone to Northern Ireland to work as a reporter. Eventually, he got close enough to the outlawed Irish Republican Army to write extensively about it. When he returned in 1972, he met Tom Hayden just as Tom became interested in his own Irish heritage. Larry, a Jew, helped Hayden, an Irishman, reconnect with his roots, and the two became friends. Tom then hired Larry to do advance work for the IPC tour and function as its press secretary. When the tour ended, I hired Larry to help MAI.

While Larry organized the press conference, Jerry Friedheim, the assistant secretary of defense for public affairs, stated to the *Boston Globe* on December 28, "We have not struck any large 1000-bed civilian hospital. We have no information that indicates that at all." Good news, I thought. Previous Pentagon denials had come from minor functionaries. With a high-ranking assistant secretary drawn into the lie, it would be easier to generate press coverage. I was right. Friedheim, tone-deaf to the controversy swirling around him, insisted that North Viet Nam had falsely claimed the hospital was destroyed for propaganda purposes. Telford Taylor's eyewitness account had been published only three days before. Joan Baez described the horror she had experienced under the bombs every night in Hanoi, but especially on the night of the twenty-second, when Bach Mai was destroyed.

Friedheim was caught with his proverbial pants down. He had no choice but to stick to his story. To contradict him, all we had to do was point reporters to the eyewitnesses who were there. As a result, Bach Mai stayed on the front page. Members of Congress, editorial boards, businesspeople, celebrities, professional associations, and leading academics all condemned the bombing of civilians, and many used the controversy over Bach Mai as their point of departure.

Abruptly, on December 29, it ended. Nixon halted bombing north of the twentieth parallel, ending the threat to Hanoi and Haiphong. Only hours before his announcement the United States bombed another large medical facility in Hanoi, the Mai Huong Hospital. Haiphong's Vietnamese-Czechoslovakian Friendship Hospital, which I had toured in May, had already been destroyed. I was livid and heartbroken remembering the doctors and patients I had seen there. Many other hospitals were hit during the ten-day attack that came to be known as the "Christmas bombing."

If I needed more motivation to rebuild Bach Mai, it came when Joan Baez returned with a letter for me from Colonel Quat. Writing on December 22, he said, "The Bach Mai Hospital you visited once has been completely destroyed this morning. We just came and saw work going on to rescue several dozens of patients and doctors buried under the rubble . . . Several of our committee members have been victims of the bombing, but all of our friends send you their love and greetings." I put Quat's letter down before it made me cry.

A total of fifteen hundred air strikes were made during the Christmas bombing, one-third by B-52s over Hanoi and Haiphong between December 18 and 25. Fifteen of the huge planes were shot down, each with a crew of six. Six more were too damaged to fly. Later it was revealed that some U.S. pilots had declined to fly through the North Vietnamese air defenses, while others refused orders after learning their targets were civilians. Some dumped their bombs at sea or outside the cities. Ground crews sabotaged firing mechanisms or disabled guidance systems. Sadly, these heroic acts were too few to mitigate the massive destruction.

With Larry managing our press conference, I focused on the ad for the *New York Times*. Gerbode suggested I fly to San Francisco to work with Frank Greer and Roger Hickey at Public Media Center, a progressive nonprofit advertising firm that had created effective antiwar TV spots for the "Unsell the War" campaign. After a long day in their shop, we were satisfied we had a well-written and engaging ad. Gerbode said he would also pay to run it in the *San Francisco Chronicle*. I flew back to Boston on a red-eye, and as I deplaned, I saw news coverage of the annual American Association for the Advancement of Science convention. My former colleagues at Science for the People had organized a number of Nobel laureates and leading scientists to sign a statement condemning the bombing.

On January 2, our Washington press conference featured Ramsey Clark, the former attorney general, and Julian Bond, a leader of the southern civil rights movement. We had a sizable turnout. After Clark and Bond spoke, I described my visit to Bach Mai, its role in the Vietnamese health system, the damage that had occurred, and our plans to mount a national campaign to rebuild it. Later that day, the Pentagon finally admitted inflicting minor but accidental damage to Bach Mai during an attack on a nearby petroleum storage area. We fired off an afternoon press release refuting it. The dispute was widely covered, and it kept the controversy alive.

On January 5, our first full-page ad appeared in the *San Francisco Chronicle*. Two days later, it was published in the *New York Times*. The ads stirred up a hornet's nest. Pundits argued back and forth about the appropriateness of our action. Government figures condemned us. It was just what I wanted because I knew the controversy would keep us in the news. Indeed, the public response was huge. The ads were so effective

that some of our wealthy supporters, inspired by what they saw, put up money for a second ad in the *New York Times* and additional ads in the *San Francisco Examiner*, the *Boston Globe*, and the local newspaper in Palo Alto. The $25,000 we paid the *Times* for the first ad returned $50,000 in donations, a better result than any previous antiwar fund-raising ad. The other ads collectively produced almost another $50,000, leaving us with $98,500 to start the rebuilding fund.

The ads also provoked a deluge of support. On January 6, Representative Bella Abzug entered a lengthy description of the Bach Mai Hospital Emergency Relief Fund into the *Congressional Record*. Leonard Bernstein, the eminent conductor, said he would mount a concert two weeks later in Washington's National Cathedral on the eve of Nixon's second inauguration and contribute all the proceeds to the Bach Mai fund. Several Broadway and off-Broadway theaters in New York announced that they too would donate their profits on inauguration eve. By January 11, MAI offices, coordinators, and volunteers around the country had scheduled Bach Mai benefit events in sixty-four cities.

Our timing was perfect. When the public realized that the U.S. military, on Nixon's orders, had destroyed the jewel of the North Vietnamese health system, and rather than take responsibility for its action had denied it in the face of incontestable evidence, in fact repeatedly lying to cover it up, many concluded that rebuilding Bach Mai was the most appropriate moral and political response.

The credibility of the military had been at a low point for years. Most of the press and much of the public assumed they were regularly lied to about the war. During the Bach Mai dispute, Pentagon spokesman Jerry Friedheim became the latest personification of its deceit and a lightning rod for public criticism. When he tried to back away from his more extreme statements, he lost more credibility. First, he definitively claimed there was no damage to Bach Mai, then he asserted it was only a minor facility, and then he admitted that "minor" damage might have been inflicted on what he sarcastically referred to as "a hospital the enemy calls Bach Mai."

Each time Friedheim made another false claim, MAI countered, which kept Bach Mai in the news and promoted skepticism about other military assertions. I was the public spokesman for the Bach Mai fund, so the press often quoted me refuting Friedheim, but the Americans who had been in Hanoi during the bombing were his primary antagonists. On January 18, Friedheim wrote a letter to the editor of the *Boston Globe* in which he claimed to have seen reconnaissance photos that allowed him to say "with certainty" that Bach Mai had not been destroyed. I responded in a letter published several days later calling on him to release the photos, if they existed. The letter gave me another opportunity to describe the destruction at Phuc Loc, which the Pentagon still denied.

On January 19, I flew to Washington to join protesters at Nixon's inauguration. That night Leonard Bernstein's Bach Mai benefit concert in the National Cathedral drew twenty thousand people, more than the building could hold. The next day, I joined a VVAW march from Arlington National Cemetery to the Lincoln Memorial along with thousands of other supporters. Later, tens of thousands of us lined Nixon's inaugural parade to protest. Some held signs, some booed and shouted insults, a few threw projectiles and got arrested. A subsequent antiwar rally drew eighty thousand. The Christmas bombing had provoked a new wave of opposition to the war.

Then, with a suddenness that startled the nation, the American war in Viet Nam came to an end. On January 24, the news I had waited for most of my adult life finally arrived. A peace treaty had been initialed the day before and would be formally signed on January 27. I was elated. The rest of the country, both war supporters and war opponents, rejoiced in the knowledge that America's longest war was finally over. A great weight was lifted off the American psyche.

The Paris Peace Accords, as they came to be known, were essentially identical to the agreement that had been reached the previous October. The United States would cease combat operations in North and South Viet Nam, and the North Vietnamese would release the POWs. Despite their murderous assault on Hanoi and Haiphong and the orgy of destruction unleashed by the Christmas bombing, Nixon and Kissinger had failed to extract any further concessions from Hanoi. They had to accept what opponents of the war had argued all along: to use one of the administration's favored expressions, they could bomb Viet Nam back to the Stone Age and still not force the country to surrender.

Nixon signed the accords because he had run out of options. Once the public understood he was targeting civilians, they turned against him. After failing to wrest further concessions with the Christmas bombing, he knew if he bombed again, the political fallout could prevent him from accomplishing other objectives. The success of the Bach Mai fund meant that escalated bombing would also result in an escalated effort to rebuild whatever he destroyed. MAI had faced down threats of prosecution and demonstrated an ability to organize effectively. Our success would likely be proportional to his escalation. Also, Nixon was increasingly concerned about the Watergate scandal, which had not yet reached the White House but was beginning to cost him political capital.

As we in the antiwar movement celebrated, we took a close look at the Paris Peace Accords and found much that was troubling. During the next sixty days, the twenty-seven thousand U.S. support troops in South Viet Nam would be gradually withdrawn and the POWs in North Viet Nam gradually released. Sixty days was long enough for violations to scuttle the agreement. But most disturbing, the United States was allowed to continue funding the Thieu regime in the South, which meant combat would continue with his troops instead of ours. Thieu was not required to release tens of thousands of political prisoners, some being tortured and held in tiny prison cells called "tiger cages." Among them were the future leaders of the country. In a final flaw, the accords did not stop the savage U.S. bombing in Cambodia. We feared once Nixon had the POWs back and had resolved the Watergate crisis, he and Kissinger were sufficiently ruthless to resume bombing if that became necessary to defend Thieu, regardless of what was in the accords.

It was a bittersweet moment. Those of us in the leadership of the antiwar movement understood these many problems and reluctantly concluded that our struggle had to go on. The "American" war in Viet Nam was over; the war in Viet Nam was not. Yet, despite our concerns, a wave of relief swept the country. It had been eight and a half years since the Gulf of Tonkin Resolution. Over fifty-eight thousand Americans had been killed, as were more than a million Vietnamese. The war had torn apart the United States, politically, socially, and culturally, and left it more polarized than at any time in the past hundred years. Happy it was over, many breathed a collective sigh of relief and expressed the naive hope that these divisions could be healed.

On January 26, the day before the peace accords were signed, I got a telegram from the People's Republic of China inviting Ethan Signer and me to choose and lead a delegation of ten radical American scientists on a four-week scientific tour of China, all in-country expenses paid. Distracted by the intense work I had done for MAI, and no longer directly involved with Science for the People, I had forgotten that our request was still pending. It was an extraordinary opportunity. Only a tiny number of Americans had visited China since the Communist Party takeover in 1949, when diplomatic relations with the United States had been severed.

But we were in the middle of the Bach Mai campaign. If I left to recruit a scientific delegation, and went to China for four weeks, followed by months writing up my observations, the Bach Mai project would suffer. Bart Meyers was the first person I would choose for such a delegation, and since he too was working for Bach Mai, I called to discuss the dilemma. Sorely disappointed, we concluded it would be irresponsible to leave the campaign at such an important juncture. Other scientists affiliated with Science for the People could lead a delegation to China. Ethan, also hard at work for Bach Mai, agreed.

With great reluctance, Ethan and I told the Chinese we would recommend appropriate leadership for the delegation but that developments in Viet Nam prevented us from taking part ourselves. Over the next few weeks, Ethan helped put together an excellent delegation, which soon raised the money necessary to get everyone to China. They toured the country and returned to write *China: Science Walks on Two Legs*, a fascinating book that described what they had seen. I never regretted my decision, but I did envy those who went.

We had organized the Bach Mai fund as a protest against the war. After the peace accords, we transformed it into a symbol of reconciliation. The American and Vietnamese people needed to put the war behind them and build a peaceful future. Rebuilding Bach Mai was a tangible step in that direction. The public responded. Unsolicited contributions arrived, often with moving notes. A Vermont physician and his wife made donations in lieu of gifts to their five brothers and sisters and fourteen nieces and nephews. An eleven-year-old Ohio girl raised money from her classmates and teachers, and wrote, "I do as much in politics as I can for my age. I am very much against bombing, but when I saw a picture of a little boy with napalm all over his face—boy now am I taking action!" Support ran the gamut from innocent children to guilty felons. In January a letter informed us that prisoners in several Massachusetts penitentiaries wanted to donate their meager February salaries to help rebuild Bach Mai.

The *New Yorker* magazine covered Bach Mai on February 10. I was quoted saying, "We now see our role as stimulating people all around the country to organize fund-raising in their schools, churches, hospitals, and places of work . . . This morning, a woman walked in here with thirty-eight hundred dollars in cash. She had raised it from the staff of Massachusetts General Hospital. Everyone there was asked to contribute a day's salary, and about two hundred people participated. We appreciate it more when a lot of people give a little than when a few wealthy people give a lot." That last sentence was obviously borrowed from the Vietnamese doctor who had said the same thing to me in Hanoi. Asked when reconstruction would begin, I explained that Haiphong's Vietnamese-Czechoslovakian Friendship Hospital had been bombed during the Johnson years, rebuilt, and bombed again the previous spring just prior to my visit, then hit a third time during the Christmas bombing. We would not rebuild Bach Mai until we were certain the bombing was over.

The Bach Mai project transformed Medical Aid for Indochina. Widespread interest and financial support allowed us to dramatically expand our operations. In July, we had a four-person staff in Cambridge. By February, our office had expanded into a national headquarters orchestrating the activity of nine other offices with full-time staffs in New York, Chicago, Los Angeles, San Francisco, Detroit, Cleveland, Philadelphia, Pittsburgh, and Minneapolis. Each office coordinated multiple projects and numerous volunteers within its region.

Our growth paid off. We helped the antiwar movement harness the energy of longtime activists as well as appeal to people newly opposed to the war. After the peace accords, we transformed the Bach Mai project into a powerful symbol of postwar reconciliation, and the money we raised saved lives and reduced suffering. On February 12, we did a preliminary accounting. In addition to the $98,500 raised by the newspaper ads, Ken Coplon's direct-mail effort brought in another $78,000 net of costs. We raised $126,500 from scheduled events and benefit concerts. A total of $312,000 came in as unsolicited gifts. We announced a total of $615,000 available for reconstruction, a sum worth several times that amount today, and far more in the less developed economy of North Viet Nam.

The Bach Mai campaign was a strategic and tactical success. Strategically, we had set out to harness the moral outrage provoked by bombing civilians in order to put Nixon on the defensive, limit his ability to use his power, and increase opposition to the war. Tactically, we simply offered Americans a chance to rebuild the damage Nixon had caused and save lives at the same time. It was political jujitsu. Nixon could be resisted but not stopped. Yet when his power was used to kill innocents in a hospital, we redirected a portion of it back against him. The bombing caused horrible damage, but we turned it into a liability for the administration. It is often in moments like this, when defeat seems imminent and an adversary's power is most evident, that such opportunities can be seen and seized upon.

Surprisingly, despite the evidence, the Nixon administration continued to deny they had destroyed Bach Mai. On February 28, in congressional testimony, Dennis Doolin, deputy assistant secretary of defense for Asian affairs, claimed there had been no damage to civilian targets during the Christmas bombing. He said, "That bombing was so precise that the citizens of Hanoi came out to watch the show."

Belligerent and deceitful statements like that were of great concern to leaders of the antiwar movement. U.S. funding still propped up the dictatorial Thieu regime. Nixon was obviously determined to stop South Viet Nam from falling to the North, even if prevented from using U.S. combat forces by the peace accords. We concluded that Congress was the weak link in Nixon's plans. Its members had to approve all future funding for Thieu. That created a strategic opening for the antiwar movement and forced us to look closely at the dynamics of lobbying Congress. Hayden and Fonda had converted the Indochina Peace Campaign (IPC) from a road show into a permanent antiwar educational organization. MAI collaborated with them in sending Larry Levin to Washington. We asked him to figure out how to build an effective antiwar lobbying coalition.

In mid-March, as I nervously watched the implementation of the peace accords, one of the burglars convicted of breaking into the offices of the Democratic National Committee at the Watergate complex in Washington dropped a political bomb. James McCord, a former CIA agent, revealed that it had not been a simple break-in as the other burglars had claimed. Instead, it was political espionage carried out by Nixon's campaign committee, CREEP, the Committee for the Re-election of the President. The press was not yet speculating that Nixon was personally involved, but McCord did state that high officials in the White House had ordered the burglary. I was riveted. So was the nation.

Meanwhile, MAI continued to raise money. Our success led to more ambitious projects. Joan Baez introduced me to her sister, Mimi Fariña, who wanted to organize musicians to support Bach Mai. Mimi and her husband, Richard Fariña, had been popular folksingers until his untimely death in a motorcycle accident in 1966. Like Joan, Mimi was a singer-songwriter and a committed antiwar activist. In mid-February she asked me to fly to San Francisco to meet with musicians she was recruiting for a huge benefit concert. When I walked into the meeting in Marin County, I was introduced to some of the legendary rock stars of the era: Grace Slick of the Jefferson Airplane, Jerry Garcia of the Grateful Dead, Bill Graham, the leading rock promoter in the country, and half a dozen others. They all were enthusiastic about Bach Mai.

In the few hours we spent together, I described Bach Mai and my experiences in Viet Nam and explained what I thought would be the ongoing course of the war. They explained the intricacies of staging a benefit concert. Scheduling was the first problem since most bands were committed months in advance. But the bigger issue was that the artists did not have complete control of their work. The freewheeling spirit of the Summer of Love six years earlier had given way to record companies, booking agents, managers, public relations flacks, lawyers, tax accountants, and business agents. We made big plans that day in Marin County, but on the way home I wondered if all those obstacles could be overcome.

At this point, Watergate began to blow holes in the Nixon administration. The Senate established an aggressive investigative committee. I had great fun watching the finger-pointing climb up the food chain from low-level CIA contract burglars to the upper reaches of government. John Mitchell, the former attorney general, was among those fingered. He had ordered the mass arrests during the Mayday protest two years before and had then resigned to manage Nixon's reelection. The burglary had been carried out on his orders, and two years later, much to my delight, he became the first attorney general to be imprisoned for his crimes. We did not yet know the full extent of the Watergate scandal, but the White House was circling the wagons, which could only be good news for us.

By the end of March, most of the POWs, including those we had interviewed, had flown home, and all U.S. troops were out of Indochina. The peace accords held, in part because of Nixon's diminished political capital. Whatever the reason, antiwar activists breathed a sigh of relief, even though massive bombing continued in Cambodia and a steady stream of military aid funded Thieu's ongoing combat operations in the South. These were new fights we would have to wage, but for the time being we rejoiced. No more Vietnamese would be killed by bullets fired from an American gun or by bombs dropped from an American plane.

Viet Nam had been our country's longest war and its first defeat. Some Americans viewed the war's end as a tragedy that dishonored the nation; others remained angry that we had used superior power to devastate a small country and were relieved our warriors had finally come home. But for all Americans, the war was a long-playing trauma, and its end a cause for celebration. For some antiwar activists, the war had imposed a duty to resist that was now past. They gravitated to other political struggles, of which there were many. Some became organizers for the labor movement, others joined fights for gender, racial, ethnic, or gay and lesbian equality that were just beginning or becoming increasingly intense.

On the other hand, despite the general euphoria, Viet Nam remained engulfed in a war fueled entirely by U.S. money, while the U.S. military still ferociously bombed Cambodia. Both had to be stopped if the war was truly to end. A few determined souls, I among them, resolved to keep organizing until the last gun was silenced. Like others, I had spent much of my adult life challenging the war, and like some had given up a career to do so. I needed the closure, the feeling that all the work and sacrifice had been justified, and the mission accomplished.

Larry Levin recommended that MAI and IPC join the Coalition to Stop Funding the War, which was composed of religious, trade union, and progressive nonprofit groups. The coalition had achieved little while U.S. troops remained in Viet Nam, but Larry thought it could work effectively in a post-peace-accords environment. We followed his advice and asked him to remain in Washington to manage our joint relations with the coalition. MAI continued to promote Bach Mai as a symbol of postwar reconciliation, and Ken's massive direct-mail appeals became the principal way we spread our message and raised additional funds.

Word came from Mimi Fariña that a big rock concert to benefit Bach Mai was too controversial for the corporate players behind the big bands and could not be organized. I was sorry. A Bach Mai concert would have briefly reunited rock music and political protest. Despite becoming highly commercialized, rock music still played an undeniably progressive role in the transformation of American culture. It undercut conventional thinking and encouraged young people to rebel against a conformist world.

Many rock music fans, especially the hippies and dropouts, viewed goal-directed political activists like me with some suspicion. The feeling was mutual. Nevertheless, a sense of shared struggle existed between the activists and the counterculture. We were two sides of the same rebellious coin. The musicians, writers, and artists who created the music questioned American values and promoted a cultural rebellion with political overtones. That rebellion eventually affected the arts, the media, the universities, the military, the churches, and even the government. Over the long arc of the sixties, sex roles changed, parental authority slipped away, and the influence of organized religion declined. As a result, discrimination against women, blacks, Latinos, Native Americans, Puerto Ricans, homosexuals, and the disabled, previously woven into the fabric of American culture, began to unravel.

The resulting upheaval led many of us on both sides of the activist/hippie divide to believe we were on the threshold of dramatic changes in the structure and governance of society. Young people today wonder how so many of us in the sixties took the risks we did, why we sacrificed our careers, our resources, a portion of our own individuality, and occasionally our liberty or personal safety. The reason was simple enough. Whether we were political activists or part of the counterculture, we felt, not just intellectually, but viscerally, that a new social order lay just over the horizon and that within it we would find more liberated and meaningful lives. Whatever our initial motivation, we were swept up, consciously or not, in the hope that a new world was coming. We took the risks we did because we believed, however erroneously, that it would rescue us and provide for our needs.

Of course, that all seems hopelessly naive today. My generation may have had a profound impact on America, but we failed to fundamentally alter the social and political order. Much of our activism was later dissipated by identity politics and meaningless theoretical disputes, and the counterculture we created to oppose corporate domination has since been co-opted by it. More realistic generations followed and can now fight for fundamental change in more practical and less outrageous ways. But no one should look back at the risks we took and judge our actions as either irrational or especially courageous. They were neither. We did what we did because it made sense in the context of our time, just as other actions make sense in other times.

CHAPTER 21

SURPRISINGLY, IN THE MONTHS FOLLOWING THE PARIS PEACE ACCORDS, VIET NAM AND Watergate were not at the top of the news. The biggest story came from the desolate plains of South Dakota. On February 27, 1973, Native American protesters seized the historic village of Wounded Knee on the Pine Ridge Indian Reservation, just south of the Badlands. They demanded that Washington end reservation corruption and respect Sioux treaty rights. They came with guns and said they would fire on lawmen who tried to dislodge them. It was high drama—the first armed confrontation on U.S. soil in the twentieth century—and public opinion sided with the Indians.

Wounded Knee was no ordinary village. For the past two years, Dee Brown's *Bury My Heart at Wounded Knee* had been a national best seller. It chronicled in vivid and horrifying detail the white conquest of the Indian West, describing it as a long and murderous assault on Native Americans. The last massacre occurred in 1890 next to the Wounded Knee Creek. Over three hundred Sioux, mostly women and children, were disarmed there by the Seventh Cavalry and shot dead with rapid-fire Hotchkiss guns.

It was revenge for Custer's last stand. Fourteen years earlier, in 1876, that same Seventh Cavalry, under General George Armstrong Custer, had been famously defeated at the Little Bighorn River by Indians under the leadership of the Sioux chiefs Crazy Horse and Sitting Bull. Later,

Crazy Horse was captured and murdered in a Nebraska fort. His family buried his heart and bones at an undisclosed location along the Wounded Knee Creek (the literal meaning of Brown's book title). By coincidence, in 1890 the last massacre of the Indian Wars took place at the same location (the metaphoric meaning of the title).

Antidiscrimination activism was on the rise among numerous ethnic groups, including Native Americans. In 1969, Indians seized the abandoned prison on Alcatraz Island to remind the nation that they still claimed rights awarded them under treaties signed in the nineteenth century, treaties that had never been officially altered. A provision in many of these broken treaties allowed the Indians to reclaim land seized by the government and later abandoned. Invoking that right, militant Indians held Alcatraz for eighteen months. During that time, the American Indian Movement (AIM) was organized, and in 1972 it seized and briefly held the Washington headquarters of the Bureau of Indian Affairs (BIA). AIM supported the Sioux at Wounded Knee to draw attention to deplorable conditions on American Indian reservations. The Pine Ridge Reservation in particular was the single poorest county in the country and, like many other reservations, was so remote that this extreme poverty went largely unnoticed.

The federal government was stymied. Brown's book and the earlier AIM protests had won public sympathy for the Indians. The armed seizure of Wounded Knee forced the public to choose sides, and despite the guns they chose the Indians. With the Watergate scandal looming, the Nixon administration could ill afford more public outrage provoked by a second massacre on that same blood-soaked ground. In effect, Wounded Knee was surrounded by a protective shield of collective guilt. Unwilling to risk an attack, the government laid siege, hoping to starve out the Indian protesters.

The standoff went on for weeks. Hundreds of FBI agents and U.S. marshals built bunkers and surrounded Wounded Knee. They had armored personnel carriers, machine guns, and helicopters. The Indians inside moved on horseback, wore feathers, and put their hair in braids. Fruitless negotiations were held in a tepee just outside the village. These colorful scenes riveted national and world attention. Every day, newspapers featured the story on their front pages. Every night, TV stations led their news with dramatic footage. Camera crews from Japan, Germany, France, England, and a dozen other countries were on the scene.

On April 3, I walked into the MAI office and found a message from an acquaintance in New York asking me to do a pay-phone-to-pay-phone call. After we connected, I learned he had just come out of Wounded Knee. I knew that Indians from around the country had gone there to help, but was surprised that non-Indians had as well. Swearing me to secrecy, he revealed that the 450 or so Indians in the village were desperately short of food and within days of having to surrender.

I didn't need to hear more. If food was the problem, I understood why I was being called. A lawyer with the Indians knew I was a pilot. Three weeks before, another pilot had landed a single-engine Cessna on a road inside Wounded Knee, unloaded, and successfully taken off. The Indians wanted me to be next. It was asking a lot, given the risk of gunfire, arrest, and losing my pilot's license, but the challenge of finding a way around those risks appealed to me. I said I would give him an answer in the morning.

I hung up and called Bob Talbot, my friend and former flight instructor in Chicago. He was skeptical. If the FBI had been caught napping by the first pilot, Bob thought they would have countermeasures in place for the next. He also reminded me that I could not haul much more than five hundred pounds of food. Not enough to justify flying into gunfire or serving time in jail. The next morning, before I had time to turn down the request, I saw news reports that a deal had just been reached at Wounded Knee. My services were no longer needed. On April 5, five weeks after it started, a formal truce was signed next to the tepee outside the village.

I was both disappointed and relieved. But the possibility of getting involved had aroused my curiosity. I had read Dee Brown's book the year before, so I gathered news articles and found materials written inside the occupied village.

The protesters wanted the government to compensate the Western tribes for broken treaties. One gave the Sioux ownership of their sacred Black Hills and all of western South Dakota. After that treaty was ratified,

Custer recklessly announced in 1876 that gold had been discovered in the Black Hills. Whites poured in and illegally seized Indian land, which is why Custer paid for his sins at the Little Bighorn. The treaties remain legally valid to the present day. Since compensation for tribal losses would cost billions, the government refused to take the treaties seriously. The Indians could not have been more serious about them.

Ending reservation corruption was the other demand at Wounded Knee. Pine Ridge is home to the Oglala band of the Lakota nation, called Sioux by whites. The tribal chairman, Dick Wilson, doled out government jobs to loyalists, who then voted for him, much like a big-city political machine. He controlled the tribal police but also commanded an armed vigilante group, dubbed the goon squad, to physically intimidate opponents. He and his men worked closely with the surrounding white ranchers and had adopted white customs, crew cuts, and Christianity.

The tribe, however, was split. Many Oglalas still lived within the traditional tribal culture and looked to the old chiefs, medicine men, and respected elder women for leadership, not the tribal government. They spoke the tribal language and observed ancient rituals. Years before, these traditional people had resisted demands by the BIA to govern themselves by electing a tribal chairman and a tribal council, but to no avail.

For months prior to the seizure, traditional leaders had protested Wilson's ballot box fraud and control of the tribal courts. Their protests were ignored. Wilson, his tribal police force, and his goon squad unleashed a reign of terror, beating opponents when they caught them in town and attacking others in their isolated rural shacks, not unlike the white cops I had seen a decade earlier in Mississippi who sided with racists attacking black protesters. In response, the tribal elders asked AIM to come to the reservation to assist them. Frustrated by Wilson's continued violence, the elders advised their people to gather at the mass grave in Wounded Knee where the victims of the 1890 massacre were buried. It was holy ground, and the spirits of the dead would protect them there. That led to the seizure of the village.

These nineteenth-century events seemed like ancient history to me but were vivid and recent to the Oglalas. Their Lakota Nation had been the last free people on the High Plains. An eighty-six-year-old survivor of the 1890 massacre, only three at the time, still lived on the reservation. Some protesters had ancestors who were victims of the massacre, and some elders were children or grandchildren of the few survivors. The fight at Wounded Knee went to the heart of our identity as a nation, and the more I learned, the more I wished I had been able to help.

Roughly 450 people were in Wounded Knee, about 50 militants from AIM, another 50–100 members of other tribes there to help, and the rest residents of Pine Ridge. It was a three-way battle between the traditional people inside and the feds and goons outside. The goons fought to protect their privileges under the corrupt tribal government, and while the feds exercised some restraint, they did not. The goons frequently got between Wounded Knee and the federal forces and shot at both sides to provoke firefights, of which there were many.

When the feds cut off supplies, AIM organized backpack trains to infiltrate their lines at night. Indians drove to Wounded Knee from around the country with carloads of food. Young people hiked in at night with forty-pound backpacks. Elders and children guided them through the steep ravines that cut across the deeply eroded terrain. They had to dodge goons and federal patrols over ten miles of prairie. Gradually, the feds discovered the backpack trails, parked armored personnel carriers (APCs) across them, and deployed attack dogs. The backpack trains, which had often included thirty to forty people, dwindled to a trickle, and food supplies rapidly ran out.

As I learned of these circumstances, I watched for the end of the occupation. Nothing happened. Instead, the Indian and the government negotiators each complained to the press that the other side had failed to abide by the terms of the April 5 truce. On Monday, April 9, it was clear that the truce had broken down and the occupation would continue. The next day, Michael Falk, an acquaintance from Newsreel, the antiwar documentary film collective, called the MAI office and asked to see me. He had just returned from Wounded Knee.

Michael and a friend had hiked in with backpacks guided by an Oglala woman. Several times they were nearly exposed by flares and had to drop to the ground. A patrol passed so close that they heard the marshals whispering. They stayed a day and hiked out that night. On the trail, they were arrested but released in the morning. Michael checked in at the AIM support operation in nearby Rapid City and returned to Boston. He had a message for me: we need you.

I wanted to help, but I told Michael I would not fly a suicide mission. It was too risky to land on a road like the last pilot. We needed a different plan, one the feds could not anticipate, and one that could deliver a greater payload. We struggled with various ideas, but nothing seemed workable. Then it hit me. Why land at all? Why not deliver the food by parachute? The FBI would not have a contingency plan for parachutes. I got very excited as I realized that if landing was no longer necessary, we didn't have to use a small plane. We could use a big one, even a DC-3 capable of hauling two or three tons. Circling high, out of rifle range, we could figure the winds and drop parachutes all day.

I had a weakness for audacious ideas and was quickly swept up by this one. Two or three tons of food would break the siege and put the Indians in a commanding position. That was trouble it would be fun to make. I told Michael I would organize the flight, but I wanted to keep it confidential, even from the Indians. Spies and infiltrators would be all around them. I'd work with my own people and show up unannounced. The Indians wouldn't know food was coming until it arrived.

There was a lot to do, right away. We had to raise money that afternoon and the next morning. I had to quickly find a parachute rigger, an airplane, and a pilot (I was not yet qualified to fly twin-engine aircraft). But why not try? It was a realistic plan. Michael agreed to raise money. I called Bob Talbot in Chicago.

Skeptical as he had been before, he thought this plan could work. He knew of a DC-3 for rent and said he would consider flying it. That was all I needed to hear. I was happy to use my knowledge of aviation to break the FBI siege, but I also realized we could create a national catharsis for the Indians since most Americans would applaud our action. We might even take a film crew along in exchange for a promise to protect our identities. Viewers would cheer as the parachutes floated down. I knew I was getting ahead of myself, and that the whole project might be more than I could handle, but I was very excited and suddenly very determined.

I gathered the MAI staff, laid out my plan, and said I was taking a few days off. If others wanted to help, they could volunteer free time since this was not an MAI project. They were flabbergasted, especially by having to start immediately, given the urgent need for food in Wounded Knee, but they all wanted to help. Larry Levin, up from Washington, said he would call wealthy antiwar supporters in New York. Ken Coplon volunteered to do the same in Boston. We would need $5,000 by the next day. I told them to say the money was for enough food to break the FBI siege but not that we were flying it in or using parachutes.

Ken was nervous about so many people knowing our plans, but I thought we had to take the risk. If we got arrested, we would be charged with bringing food to starving Indians. What jury would convict us? Ken countered that the government would not charge us with bringing food. They would say we dropped guns and ammunition. He was right. I asked Larry to find a credible newspaper reporter to go with us in exchange for an exclusive. He could testify to the content of what we dropped.

As the meeting broke up, I half jokingly asked if anyone knew a left-wing parachute rigger. It was an absurd question for people with no connection to aviation, and I expected only laughter in response. Instead, Lillian Shirley turned to Tom Davidson and reminded him that he had known a skydiver in college in North Dakota. Tom had not seen the sky-diver in five years but offered to track him down.

I called Palmer Williams, the 60 Minutes producer who had bought my POW footage, and arranged to see him the next morning in New York. Over the next two hours, Michael raised $500. A rich friend of his in New York offered to give us more if I met with her in person. Ken and Larry got generous commitments from others in Boston and New York. Tom found his skydiver friend in Albuquerque. He had the skills we needed, over six hundred jumps and plenty of rigging experience, but he knew a Chippewa Indian in North Dakota who would be even better. If he failed to find the Chippewa, he would consider joining us himself.

I went home to pack a bag and on the way stopped at Charlotte Weissberg's apartment. I asked her to draft a statement to go with the food we dropped. I wanted our action to express solidarity between the antiwar movement, still fighting U.S. aggression in Indochina, and Native Americans, fighting more long-standing U.S. aggression at home. I promised to call her for the statement later. I also asked Charlotte to line up a good criminal lawyer in case we needed one. By 7:00 that night Larry and I were on the air shuttle taking off for New York. Ken stayed in Boston to collect donations the next day.

At an early breakfast, Michael's friend offered to contribute $1,300. At 9:00 a.m., she and Larry left to get the cash. I went to CBS-TV, but to my surprise Palmer was not interested. CBS was on top of the Wounded Knee story, and its one correspondent who might be willing to join the airdrop was marooned in Beirut. Palmer recommended someone at ABC-TV since it was being routinely scooped by CBS on the story. I made my proposal to ABC an hour later, and it immediately committed a film crew pending approval by its corporate lawyers.

Meanwhile, Larry had worked the phones and gotten more commitments from antiwar donors—lawyers, physicians, professors, artists, and children of the wealthy. Because of past work, they trusted us without asking too many questions. Ken secured $2,000 from Ping Ferry and Carol Bernstein, wealthy donors who had helped fund MAI's direct-mail appeals. We had what we needed. I called Bob and told him to rent the DC-3, then left for Chicago.

Larry stayed in New York to coordinate with ABC, find a print reporter, and gather the New York donations. I asked Ken to wire the Boston money to Chicago, but also to stay put to back us up if we needed help en route to Wounded Knee. Michael offered to bring the $500 he had raised to Chicago at his own expense so he could help me there. Tom's rigger didn't find his Chippewa buddy and was having second thoughts about joining us. He wanted more information. I asked Tom to fly him to Chicago at our expense so we could talk.

Sly picked me up that night at O'Hare. Back in Chicago after fixing his gambling debts, he was older and poorer, but well adjusted to his modest lifestyle. We drove to Ron Chutter's apartment; he too had come back to Chicago. Sly knew some of the underworld characters at the wholesale produce market in Chicago, and before our trip to the Caribbean, Ron had gone to the wholesale food market in Minneapolis every morning to get produce for the grocery store he and his girlfriend, Eddie, had managed. I asked them to buy the first two thousand pounds of food we would need at the Chicago wholesale market early the next morning, hopefully without attracting undue attention.

In the morning I went to Midway Airport to see Bob. He had bought a comfortable house just across the street. Unfortunately, the DC-3 was in the shop, half-dismantled, and would not be available for four days. Bob explained to the owner that federal aviation regulations permit parachute drops from an airplane if the pilot has permission from people on the ground and does not fly through restricted airspace. The feds had not yet established restricted airspace over Wounded Knee, so a parachute drop could be made legally, although other criminal charges might still apply. Bob wanted to wait for the DC-3. I explained we could not. The Indians were close to surrender. Every day counted. I wanted to take off the next morning.

Bob knew three other DC-3s for rent. He called, but two were booked. The owner of the third would not rent it for our mission. Next we tried Beech 18s, a twin-engine cargo plane with half the capacity of a DC-3. Bob found only one. Again, the owner didn't like the mission. Once more, Bob advised waiting for the DC-3. I knew that might be too late. Frustrated and anxious, I struggled to find a solution. Then it came. Whatever we can bring in one big plane, we can bring in a bunch of small ones. I told Bob that if we didn't find a DC-3 or Beech 18 by 6:00 p.m., we'd rent single-engine planes and find more pilots to fly them.

I went to the terminal to meet Michael, who had flown in from Boston. He gave me $500. We looked for Jim Stewart, the parachute rigger. Passengers deplaning from Albuquerque included a tall, lanky man in jeans with a red nylon shoulder bag that looked like a parachute pack. We introduced ourselves. When he peppered me with questions about Wounded Knee, I asked Michael, who had been there a week before, to talk to him while I called New York.

Larry had hailed a cab that morning and asked the driver to make multiple stops. For the next four hours, he went in and out of apartment buildings and offices. Each time he emerged, the increasingly astonished driver saw him stuff more cash into an envelope, like an upscale dope dealer or a bookie's collections man. When it was over, he had another $2,650. That was the good news. The bad news was that ABC lawyers had nixed network participation in the airdrop. There would be no film crew, and Larry had still not found a print reporter to fly with us. I asked him to fly to Chicago that night.

Michael convinced Jim to join us. They rented a car and left to buy parachutes, which Jim said would be available at Army surplus stores. I went to the Western Union office to get the money Ken had wired from Boston, then returned to Bob's to meet his wife, Cindy, and beg for permission to use their house as a staging area. She, too, had followed the Wounded Knee story and despite her conservative politics was eager to help.

Ron and Sly arrived with a ton of food. Cindy directed her two teenage stepsons to carry it down to their basement. There were sacks of flour, rice, beans, onions, and carrots and large quantities of margarine, cheese, fruit, canned ham, and more. Hours later, Jim and Michael showed up with parachutes, duffel bags, and heavy webbing. Jim told us to pack a hundred pounds of food into each duffel bag and sew the webbing into cargo nets big enough to hold two duffels. If we attached the parachutes directly to the bags, rather than the cargo nets, the opening

Preparing the duffel bags of food for the Wounded Knee airlift. Inset: the finished bags, ready to be loaded onto the planes. *Photos by Richard Bresden / Author's collection*

shock would tear them apart. Ten parachutes could then deliver the ton of food. If we found a DC-3, we'd get more.

Bob made a valiant attempt, but at 6:00 p.m. we were forced to change plans. No big planes were available, so Bob arranged to rent three single-engine Piper Cherokee Sixes. They were six-seat aircraft powered by big three-hundred-horsepower engines. With the four back-seats out, we would have room up front for a pilot and a man to handle the cargo, and we'd still be able to haul seven hundred pounds. Bob then pulled the rug out from under me. With four kids and a mortgage, he could not jeopardize his community college teaching job. I had to fly one of the planes, and we had to find pilots for the other two. Jim Stewart overheard us and revealed that he had a private pilot's license and could fly one.

Bob then invited two pilots he knew to come to his house and discuss an "unusual" job. Jim set up an assembly line in Bob's basement, employing Cindy, their four kids, Ron, Sly, and Michael to sew together cargo nets and pack food into duffel bags. The two pilots arrived, both in their late twenties, one white, the other black. We went into a bedroom, and I asked what they thought about Wounded Knee. They both expressed sympathy for the Indians. I told them friends in another city were organizing an airlift and needed pilots. They were cagey, realizing the mission wasn't entirely legal. We danced around until I became more confident they were willing to consider such work. Then I told them the truth.

The white guy laughed sarcastically; let me get this straight, he said, chuckling, you want me to fly into a war zone, break an FBI siege, maybe get shot or arrested, risk losing my pilot's license, and for that I get paid nothing. Yes, I said, nodding, that's right. He nodded back, got up, and walked out. Meanwhile, the black guy stayed put. We looked at each other. After a minute, he said, nobody ever dropped food on blacks fighting for civil rights. Yes, I replied, I know. He thought for a moment, looked up, and said, okay, count me in. We shook hands. His name was Bill Wright, and he was a master pilot, with instrument, instructor, and airline transport ratings and several thousand hours in the air.

When I got down to the basement, I saw unhappy faces. Sewing the thick webbing into cargo nets was taking too long. Jim worried we wouldn't finish. Bob and I started to help just as Larry walked in off the plane from New York. He handed me a wad of cash and introduced Tom Oliphant, the young Washington correspondent for the *Boston Globe*. Tall and slender with shoulder-length hair, Tom wore his signature business suit, bow tie, and beat-up running shoes.

I thanked him for the good pieces he had written about the war. He complimented my work at Medical Aid for Indochina. Then I laid out the ground rules. I told him he could see and write about anything that happened on the airlift but not reveal our names, our donors, organizations with which we were affiliated, or any locations we passed through, including our Chicago staging ground. He agreed. I took him at his word because his future access to stories like ours would depend on it. He apologetically asked if we planned to drop weapons. I said no, but we wanted him to verify every item we did drop. Finally, Tom sheepishly said he would have to remain an unbiased observer rather than a participant. He could do nothing to help us, only watch and report what he saw. I asked if that included sewing cargo nets, and he, embarrassed, said yes.

Everyone but Tom focused on the cargo nets, but as the night wore on, progress was slow. Bob left and returned later with an older woman and her two adult daughters. He had asked his neighbors to help sew. They smiled incongruously at the radical conspiracy gathered in the basement. This was, after all, Chicago's white working-class Southwest Side, not far from where I had marched with Martin Luther King in 1966. I expected the women to be uncomfortable, but instead they sat down next to Jim and quickly learned what to do. They had sewing machines and more daughters at home, so they took webbing to make cargo nets there.

I was furious, took Bob aside, and asked why he thought these women could be trusted. Who are they, I barked, the local revolutionaries? Bob said, I don't know what their politics are. They're just neighbors, Mr. and Mrs. Average American. He drives a fuel truck and has a second job. They've got six kids. I went over there, told them what we were doing, and said that if they wanted to help, they'd have to keep it quiet since some people disagreed with us. The older woman said, sure, we want to help. They'd been following the Wounded Knee story, and she said, what worthier cause is there than the Indians? My anger melted away. I was so alienated from these conservative communities that I was surprised to find such sympathy.

Midnight came and went. It was clear we would not finish before dawn. Everyone kept busy, and in the middle of the jumbled lines and piles of food some kind of order prevailed. The neighbor women walked happily into the chaos from time to time to check a detail or excitedly chat with Bob about the project, often with teenage granddaughters in tow. Bob's basement overflowed with community spirit. His neighbors had unwittingly joined an antigovernment conspiracy, yet they were enjoying themselves and were happy to be part of it.

I walked out into the cold night air to take a break, wondering what motivated them. They were conservative people, yet they understood that countless crimes had been committed against the Indians. Wounded Knee had become a potent symbol. Because of it, the country was alive with Indian ghosts. They galloped across the land on bridges of collective guilt, their power sudden and immense, at once unexpected and inescapable. America watched, spellbound, as eighty-three years later the ghosts emerged from the morning mists of South Dakota on the very spot of the last shameful massacre. It made me appreciate the inherent goodness of our people and how an appeal to relieve human suffering often overcomes ideological differences.

As we worked on the cargo nets, I asked Jim Stewart what he did in Albuquerque. Until the previous week, he had been a fifth-grade teacher. He complained to his principal that Indian and Chicano kids were being mistreated. The principal replied that his contract would not be renewed. Fed up with the school, Jim quit. Before finding that teaching job, he had considered living with his wife in a mountain cabin and killing deer for the winter. Like me, he had once wanted to fly fighters, but when he learned the truth about Viet Nam, he got himself thrown out of Air Force pilot training. Back home, his wife was pregnant and he needed work. They were thinking about starting a wilderness survival program for kids.

Daybreak came and we finally finished. There was room for another 150 pounds of food, so Ron and Michael went back to the wholesale market. Charlotte called with a draft message to put in the duffel bags. She had also found a lawyer in New York willing to stand by. Larry wrote up cards for everyone with the lawyer's phone number. Jim and I left with Bob to take instruction in one of the rented planes. Neither of us had ever before flown a plane as big or as powerful.

I went first. Bob put me through the paces: blind flight, slow flight, steep turns, stalls, and emergency landings. When he was done, he went so far as to pull the key out of the ignition, which killed the engine and forced me to do a dead-stick landing on a grass strip. Once down, Jim and I switched places, and Bob did it all over again with him. He pushed us as hard as he could to make us ready for whatever might happen at Wounded Knee. When we were done, Jim went back to Bob's house to supervise packing the parachutes. Bob and I got the other two airplanes.

When we returned, the whole crew was on Bob's front lawn with all the multicolored parachutes stretched out on the grass. Larry ran up to me sputtering about secrecy and how this scene would blow our cover. Jim explained that with insufficient room in the basement to fold the chutes, he had no choice. At that moment, three of Bob's students showed up to help. Our secret airlift had become a neighborhood event. We had to get out of there fast.

Each plane needed a man to push out the cargo, so Bob asked two of his students to join the airlift. One was a wildly energetic character with long curly black hair and a bushy beard. Short and thin, he looked like an electrified hippie. Snake, as he wanted to be called, was a skydiver and a Viet Nam vet and seemed, despite his looks, to know what he was doing. The other guy was his opposite. Barely twenty years old, John Adelman was short, a little pudgy, and straight as they come. He was a forklift oper-ator at a Sears warehouse. When Bob offered him a chance to join the crew, John said, what the hell, you can't go through life just working at Sears . . . if you're going to get in trouble, you might as well get in trouble for doing something good. Once more, I was surprised at how otherwise conservative people were willing to take risks for the Indians.

I told Snake to handle cargo in Bill Wright's plane, John to do the same for Jim, and Larry to fly with me. On the way west, Jim could train the three of them to secure rip cords and handle the cargo nets. Tom, the reporter, could switch planes and have a chance to observe us all. The three pilots left Bob's house to get the planes. We taxied them to a quiet

Going over our plan one more time before takeoff. From left to right: Bob Talbot,
Bill Wright, John Adelman, an unidentified helper, me, and Larry Levin.
Richard Bresden/Author's collection

corner of the airport. The others drove cars stuffed with cargo to meet us
and load up, which took a lot longer than planned. By the time the planes
were ready it was almost 5:00 p.m.

Larry grabbed me and said it would be dark soon. None of us have
slept, why go now? I countered that there wasn't much holding the crew
together. If we delayed, some might have second thoughts. Besides, I said,
every third person in the neighborhood knows what we're doing. If we
don't leave now, we won't be able to. Larry reluctantly agreed. We gathered the crew. With two Bills, we decided to call Bill Wright "Billy." I told
everyone I would take charge of operational and financial decisions, but
that Billy, as the most experienced pilot, would be the air boss. Decisions
involving safety of flight would be his.

In the rush, we had neglected to get aerial navigation charts for the
flight west. We called around but found none. We gave the one chart we
had to Billy. Jim and I agreed to fly behind and to the side of his plane and
follow him to Council Bluffs on the Iowa-Nebraska border. We had no
experience with formation flying, and knew it was more dangerous in the
dark, so we promised to stay well clear of each other. Council Bluffs was

halfway to Wounded Knee, the weather was good all the way, and the terrain was flat. We could radio each other during the three-hour flight, but if we lost sight of the other planes and got separated, the two planes without charts would be unable to find airports or each other in the dark.

We strapped in and started the engines. Midway tower cleared our takeoff, and with wheels up we turned west just as the sun slid below the horizon. The three planes flew a wide V formation with Billy in front. We slowly climbed to forty-five hundred feet. The urban landscape below merged into suburban sprawl and then farmland. Twilight faded to darkness. Each of our planes had a red rotating beacon on its tail. When it was too dark to see the other planes, I watched the red beacons and tried to keep a half mile distant from each.

Larry's face was bathed in a red glow from the instrument panel. There was no moon, only inky blackness and a few twinkling farmhouse lights. After thirty minutes of staring at the blinking red lights on the other two planes, I dozed off. Larry pushed me awake. Billy had slept the night before. Jim could nap because John was a student pilot and knew enough to keep their plane straight and level. I had to stay awake, since Larry was not yet able to do that. I made needless conversation on the radio and taught Larry the rudiments of straight and level flight. Eventually, I could close my eyes for a minute or two. He held the controls and woke me if the distance or angle from the red lights on the other planes changed.

When we finally arrived at Council Bluffs, I followed Billy's plane through the carpet of city lights and found the airport. We landed, tied down the planes, and got a cab to a motel and restaurant. Most of us had not eaten all day. Billy telephoned for weather and learned that a snowstorm would pass through overnight. By morning it should be clear all the way to Wounded Knee. We planned to fly into Wyoming, wait until shortly before sunset, and make the drop coming in from the west. We hoped the feds would focus their search west of Wounded Knee while we flew back east.

The weather had other plans. That night, the snowstorm stalled over Council Bluffs. In the morning, it was low overcast all the way west, making a drop impossible. If we ducked under it and diverted north, there was decent weather in eastern South Dakota. Seven scruffy guys, one black, flying three airplanes stuffed with cargo might draw unwelcome attention there, but we thought it important to get closer to Wounded Knee and agreed to accept the risk. At the airport, as I cranked up my engine, I heard Billy radio that his was too cold to start. Jim and I shut down. We convinced a mechanic to drive his car onto the tarmac and boost Billy's battery with jumper cables. His engine started and the little three-plane squadron got back in the air.

We tracked Interstate 29 low along the Missouri River. When the river swung west, we followed the highway north into blue skies. Billy radioed for us to practice formation flying, which would be necessary over Wounded Knee. We had selected a half-V formation with each plane behind and to the right of the one ahead. Pilots sit on the left, so this allowed the pilot of a trailing plane to easily see the plane in front. In an emergency, either of the two forward aircraft could peel off to the left and be clear of any trailing aircraft. Since the cargo doors were also on the left, parachutes would not float back into the other planes.

Formation flying requires a delicate touch. As we maneuvered the planes closer together, we looked like drunken birds, unpredictably gaining or losing altitude relative to the other aircraft. After thirty minutes, we were able to fly a hundred yards apart and maintain constant separation. Then it was fun. We practiced peeling off and reentering the formation as we all turned northwest. With more practice, we achieved a forty-yard separation, the distance we would use at Wounded Knee. Towering cumulus clouds appeared in the distance, so Billy radioed for weather. A snowstorm was about to hit Huron, South Dakota, our planned destination. We pushed up the throttles, raced in, and touched down just ahead of the storm.

Billy and I strolled into the airport weather station, and two friendly meteorologists offered us coffee. I knew they would have questions, so we gradually let them discover we were rich rock musicians on a big-time camping trip to the southern Rockies. A local dentist had flown in just ahead of us. He offered a ride to a good motel in town and we accepted, but once on Main Street I saw how much we stood out. We had too much hair, and we were racially integrated. To lower our profile, we split into three groups and ate separately.

Later, we returned to the airport in a rental car to attach the rip cords to the parachutes. Billy and I maneuvered the night weatherman away from the window that faced our planes while Jim supervised the others working outside. The weather forecast was a disaster: snow all the next day. As the weatherman spoke to me, Billy got behind him and pointed to the bulletin board, then came around in front so I could swing back and read what he had pointed to. It was a government bulletin declaring a restricted flying zone above Wounded Knee. We could not make the parachute drop legally.

The weatherman, making casual conversation, said his son lived in the southern Rockies and a lot of planes there smuggled marijuana up from Mexico. Billy and I smiled. He thought we were dope runners. With that on his mind, our real mission would never occur to him. But his talk took an ugly turn. He ridiculed "those damn Indians" at Wounded Knee for living off the government. For ten minutes, he railed against Indian women purposely getting pregnant to collect welfare and Indian men who would rather drink than work. Finally, Larry came in for water, which was the signal that the work outside was done. On the ride back, Billy laughed and said, that dude would've said all the same shit about "niggers" if I wasn't sitting there beside him.

Curious, I asked Billy about his background. He had grown up on Chicago's South Side, across town from where I had. He graduated from high school with street smarts, but seeing only limited opportunities, he joined the Army. Unfortunately, it was 1965. Trained as a "combat engineer," he and other young black men were assigned to rudimentary construction work in South Viet Nam. They expressed their hatred of the war by sabotaging bulldozers and other heavy equipment. Billy was court-martialed, not for sabotage, but for intervening when another enlisted man assaulted an older Vietnamese woman who had mistakenly wandered into their compound. Out of the Army, he trained as a pilot, but being black made him ineligible for airline work. He flew charters and did instruction instead, took his flying very seriously, and was able to earn enough to climb into the middle class. As we drove on, I realized how much I had come to like him.

Back at our motel, the snow worried me. It was the end of the second day of what was supposed to be a two-day trip, and Billy and John were regularly employed. Concerned about their jobs, I called a meeting. Billy instantly confirmed my earlier impression. Look, man, he said, the job is gone. I might as well do what I'm doing now and do it right. When you commit yourself to something, you're supposed to do it. I don't care when we do this, but this is a job I want to see done. This is the kind of thing that should've happened years ago when people were fighting for civil rights in the South.

John agreed, about the job if not the politics. Billy and I told the crew about the new restricted zone over Wounded Knee. It took less than a minute to go around the room. No one gave a damn what the government called the airspace over the reservation. We were going in.

CHAPTER 22

LARRY WOKE ME EARLY. HE WAS FRANTIC. SOME IN THE CREW WANTED TO TURN BACK. I stumbled out of the motel room. It was mid-April, but a blanket of falling snow covered Huron. In the next room, they all spoke at once. They had seen a priest on TV who had come out of Wounded Knee. He claimed the goon squad was using .50-caliber machine guns against the Indians.

Jim was calm but forceful. He knew it was very difficult to hit a moving airplane with a rifle, but machine guns were different. Snake was having an emotional breakdown. He had become acquainted with .50-caliber machine guns in Viet Nam and did not want to encounter them again. Larry argued the priest was wrong. The FBI and U.S. marshals would not allow civilian use of machine guns, and while they no doubt had their own, they would never use them against unarmed aircraft. I knew Larry was right, but I had to restore everyone's confidence.

Okay, I said, we need reliable information, so let's go get some. We can't make the drop in this snow, so we'll take one of the planes, fly to Rapid City, and make contact with the AIM support people there. Billy is instrument rated, so we can fly on top of the weather. He can take the other two pilots and we'll all be back tonight. We'll interview people just out of Wounded Knee and get the truth about the machine guns. That seemed to satisfy everyone.

Billy's plane lifted off Huron and was immediately engulfed in thick clouds. Jim flew under Billy's supervision, getting a lesson in instrument

flying on the way west. I'd get mine on the way back. Ice quickly accumulated on our wings. We were cleared to six thousand feet, and just as we
got there, we broke out into sunshine. The ice melted away as we
skimmed along the nearly flat tops of the billowy white clouds beneath us.
It was breathtaking.

An hour later, the clouds disappeared. The terrain below had
changed from the checkerboard farmland of the Midwest to the desolate
High Plains. The land was hilly and eroded, the roads no longer parallel
or crossing at right angles. Billy pointed out the difficulty in telling one
town from another and worried we might drop the food on the wrong
place. At Rapid City, we were sequenced to land behind a Frontier Air-
lines jet. Jim taxied to the transient parking area, and we tied up the
plane. It was the closest commercial airport to Wounded Knee, so we
walked into a passenger terminal packed with marshals and FBI agents.
We assumed AIM's phones were tapped, so instead of calling we took a
cab to their address.

It wasn't an office; it was a suburban tract house. I wondered why until
I realized how much easier it is to secure a stand-alone structure than
one office in a larger building. Inside, people worked the phones, lawyers
interviewed recent arrestees, and people stockpiled food and backpack
gear. I warned Jim and Billy about infiltrators and told them to guard what
they said. Michael had given me the name of a Washington paralegal who
was coordinating the operation. She was next door with well-known leaders of the black civil rights movement meeting with increasingly well-
known leaders of the American Indian Movement. We waited patiently.

When Rita arrived, I asked her to come to a pay phone to call
Michael so he could verify our identities for each other. Once trust was
established, we told Rita we were flying food into Wounded Knee. She
was thrilled. She assumed we had one airplane and would land in the village. I thought it best to leave her with that impression. The truth would
be a welcome surprise. She confirmed that the goons had no machine
guns, and casually mentioned that a white guy in the house had flown in
with the pilot who had landed in Wounded Knee weeks before. We asked
her to bring him to the lawn so we could talk and not be overheard.

His name was Oliver. Before we told him our plans, he told us that he had been in Wounded Knee several times and the goons definitely did not have automatic weapons. We also learned that Oliver had served on a medical evacuation helicopter in Viet Nam. That got our attention. He not only had flown into Wounded Knee but could recognize landmarks from the air, a more difficult task than people imagine. I looked at Billy and Jim. They knew what I was thinking and nodded in silent agreement. I told Oliver we were flying into Wounded Knee in the morning and wanted him to come as a spotter. We were, however, concerned about security and had to insist on certain conditions. He would have to leave with us immediately: no phone calls, no last-minute goodbyes, just right into Rita's car and out to the airport. He let out a happy hoot and said he had a packed bag in the house and would be back in ten seconds. He was. Billy, Jim, and I agreed to say nothing more until we were airborne.

On the way to the airport, Oliver talked incessantly. We liked what he had to say about the machine guns, but the food shortage in Wounded Knee was extreme. People were subsisting on rice and salt. On his last trip a few days before, Oliver had joined a warriors' society ritual, dancing around a fire, chanting, and beating drums. The medicine men told the warriors that an airplane was coming with food and asked them to pray to the Great Spirit to protect the plane on its journey. Oliver said the medicine men had their holiest objects, talismans handed down from grandfathers a hundred years ago, and had used them to ask the Great Spirit to guide the fliers.

I was moved by his description, and as I took the pilot's seat to get my instrument flight instruction from Billy, Jim sat with Oliver in the back and told him about our plans. He was taken aback. Three airplanes. Parachutes. A ton of food. Jim said we needed him to guide us over the last ten miles. After the drop we would take him to a distant airport and give him airfare back to Rapid City. Oliver was inspired by the scope of the project. In a burst of excitement, he told Jim that after this drop he could get us a load of M16s in another state for a second drop.

My eyes met Billy's. Less than an hour after meeting us, Oliver had just suggested we conspire to transport a cache of illegal automatic weapons across state lines to Wounded Knee. Oliver was either very naive and stupid or an FBI plant. Either way, we had to keep him from making any phone calls until after the drop.

We were short on fuel, so I made a night landing in Pierre, the state capital. Billy got the gas, while I called Huron to explain the situation with Oliver and ask for a car to meet us at the airport. We had a smooth flight back through dark but clear skies. At the motel, I called together a briefing. We would take off a few hours later at 3:00 a.m. and make the drop at dawn. We trusted Oliver on the weaponry at Wounded Knee. His ass was on the line as much as ours. I also realized we could trust him to spot the parachute drop. If he were a police or FBI agent instead of an overeager and stupid militant, and he wanted to entrap us into making a second drop with weapons so we could be arrested and put away for a very long time, he could only do that if he helped make the first drop a success.

Map of the Pine Ridge Reservation, including Wounded Knee.

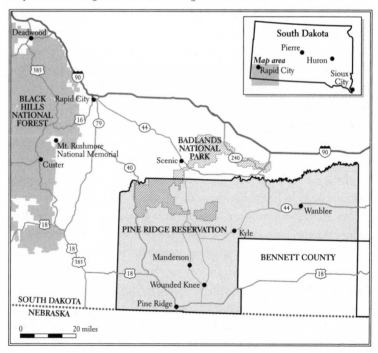

I went over our plans. The area controlled by the Indians was small, so to make the drop accurately, we would have to risk some rifle fire and go in low. Flying at five hundred feet, Jim calculated, we would have only forty seconds over Wounded Knee. We planned to arrive at 5:06 a.m., the moment of dawn. There would be ample light, but the feds and goons might still be asleep. As we escaped to the east, anyone shooting at us would have to aim into the sun.

I asked Jim to review what could go wrong with the parachutes. A chute could fail to open or a cargo bag break apart in flight, he said, but both were very unlikely. What if a rip cord failed to separate from the parachute? I asked. He laughed, then said, forget that, it's a million to one. I persisted. Well, he answered, you'd be flying with two hundred pounds of food hanging from your tail. Billy looked up and said, not for long. He explained that the plane would gradually slow to sixty-three miles per hour. At that speed in a Cherokee, the wings would stall—that is, they would lose sufficient lift to keep flying. In a normal stall, the heavy engine in the nose causes the plane to fall nose first, so it picks up enough airspeed to become flyable again. But with a weight hanging from the rear, the plane would stall tail first, which was inevitably fatal. Every head turned toward Jim. It never happens, he protested. I didn't care. We had to plan for everything to go wrong that could go wrong. Jim agreed to tape a hook knife to the bulkhead next to each cargo door. The knife could be grabbed quickly, hooked under a rip cord, and pulled up to cut it free.

Tom Oliphant asked to speak. He said he was inspired by our determination and was tired of merely observing. He wanted to help. He was bigger than Larry and thought he could do better handling cargo on my airplane. Larry welcomed the help. We all cheered Tom, shook his hand, and congratulated him on his new status as a member of the crew. We had lived and worked with him for three days and liked his easygoing but professional style.

We drove to the airport sleepless but ready to fly. In the dark, we had at first failed to see all the ice covering our airplanes. The snow had melted, and when temperatures dropped after dark, the snowmelt froze into a thick coat of ice. We had to chip it all off by hand. The painstaking process took an hour and a half. Our fingertips were frozen. Worse, it was 4:30 a.m., too late to make the drop at dawn. Billy wanted to go in anyway. The weather was good, and we could still arrive by 6:30 a.m. Jim disagreed; more feds and goons would be awake and ready to shoot at us. We weighed the alternatives and decided to go.

Jim and I started our engines. Billy's plane stayed dark. I saw him running toward me on the tarmac and knew the cold had killed his battery again. With no car available for a jump start, Jim and I "hand propped" Billy's plane, spinning the propeller by hand as if we were cranking an old car engine, except we had to guard against the prop taking our heads off once the engine caught. Despite our efforts, the big three-hundred-horsepower engine would not start. We had to wait until 8:00 a.m. for a mechanic.

We discussed flying in at sunset, but Oliver thought there would be too many feds and goons ready to shoot at us. We had to postpone the drop until the next morning, but we were afraid we had outlived our welcome in Huron. Suspicion was likely to increase at the motel and the airport. Rapid City had been easy to get into and out of despite the heavy concentration of federal forces, so Billy suggested we spend the day there, "under all those federal noses." It would take only forty-five minutes to fly from Rapid City to Wounded Knee, and the morning forecast called for perfect weather. At 9:00 a.m., Billy's plane was ready. We all got airborne, climbed to sixty-five hundred feet, and leveled off, prepared for a smooth flight to Rapid City.

No such luck. Billy had a problem. He radioed that his alternator warning light was on and his engine was surging. Jim and I throttled back and banked away on either side to give him room to maneuver. We had seen a Piper dealer in Pierre the night before, and since we were nearby, Billy wanted to get his plane checked out there. We flew behind him in case his engine quit and followed him into Pierre. He landed first and taxied in. Jim and I parked nearby.

Pierre had been quiet the night before, but on Monday morning it was a busy state capital hub, and it had another unexpected surprise for us. The federal court in Pierre was hearing a request that morning for a restraining order to prevent further blockades of food into Wounded Knee. Not knowing that, we casually strolled into the terminal for coffee and met a throng of federal lawmen in town to oppose the order. It was the perfect moment not to arrive. We broke into three groups and drifted back outside. I took off right away. Jim soon followed. Billy got his plane repaired and came later. In Rapid City, I rented a car and motel rooms and picked up the others as they arrived. We planned to stay out of sight and keep Oliver from calling anyone.

With the crew tucked into motel rooms and Oliver under surveillance, Larry and I left. We had other work to do. Larry called Ken in Boston and told him to contact the wire services and major newspapers at 7:30 a.m. eastern time, 5:30 a.m. in Wounded Knee, and give them a list of our cargo and a copy of the message in the food bags. We hoped publicity about the airdrop would lead more people to criticize the feds for having used starvation as a tactic. If we aborted the drop, Larry would call Ken back and let him know in time.

I assumed the phone at the AIM headquarters was tapped, which meant I could use it to create a false trail for the FBI to follow after the airdrop. I went to see Rita. She was delighted to help. I told her to use her tapped phone to call the airport in Lusk, Wyoming, at 6:15 a.m. and ask for the pilot of a Cherokee that had just flown in. Lusk was a hundred miles in the wrong direction, west, while we planned to flee east after the drop. An hour later, she was to do the same at Casper, a hundred miles farther west, and an hour after that, again in Riverton, another hundred miles in the wrong direction. I assumed the FBI would be furious when a ton of food came floating past their roadblocks and in their anger would jump at the first lead that came along.

Everyone was ready at 2:30 a.m., and the weather was as good as predicted. Larry drove to the airport alone as a decoy. He got in one of the planes and waited. Nothing happened, so he assumed the planes were not being watched and came back for the rest of us. The airport was deserted. We removed the cargo doors on the planes, stowed them aft, and armed ourselves against the cold with heavy gloves and stocking caps.

We huddled in the dark for a final briefing. The plan was to fly thirty minutes south to the Angostura Reservoir, a large body of water easily identified from the air. The planes would circle the reservoir single file with Billy in the lead and me in the rear until Billy radioed it was 4:44 a.m.

The open cargo door on one of the planes. We flew with these doors removed to allow the duffel bags and parachutes to be pushed out during flight. *Photo by George Lindblade/Author's collection*

We would then turn east and descend to treetop level to avoid radar. Wounded Knee was twenty-two minutes away over open prairie. When we arrived at 5:06 a.m., the sun would be just over the horizon. Ten minutes out, Billy would fall back to the number two position. Jim would lead the climb to five hundred feet, and Oliver, flying with Jim, would guide him to the actual drop zone.

The wind over Wounded Knee was from the southwest at ten knots. Our parachutes would drift north and east. Jim said the chutes would open at 350 feet and descend at 20 feet per second for 17.5 seconds. If we flew along the west and south edges of Wounded Knee, the horizontal drift would carry the chutes into the village. We would have only forty seconds to unload the cargo, so Jim would radio us the second we hit the drop zone. Otherwise, we would keep radio silence. If one of us failed to drop all of his cargo, he would have to make a second pass or fly home with food. After the drop, the three planes would flee east, northeast, and southeast, respectively, then adjust their course for a direct flight to Chicago.

Before we broke up, Tom said he had been inspired by our actions and considered the airlift a noble endeavor. His remarks were followed by an uncomfortable silence until Billy said that even though we had endured more hassles than expected, he was thrilled we were about to make the drop. He confided that this was probably the most important thing he had ever done. As his statement sank in, Jim said he felt the same way. Heads nodded. We were ready. Billy swung his arm with a flourish and joked that he finally had a chance to use a favorite line from the movies: Gentlemen, synchronize your watches, it is now three forty-six. We all laughed, but Jim and I quietly set our watches to Billy's time.

Airborne out of Rapid City, I flew past Jim's plane in the darkness, pulled abreast of Billy's, and rocked my wings. It was the signal that all three planes were flying and together. With the rear cargo doors off, it was far below freezing inside the planes. The wind rushed past at 140 miles per hour, so the noise was deafening. First light incongruously revealed the faces of four dead presidents carved into the sacred Black Hills of the Sioux. Two Mount Rushmore heads, Washington and Roosevelt, had personally killed Indians in battle, while under the orders of a third, Jefferson, many more had died.

The cargo handlers went to work. We took off with the cargo flush against the front seats to keep the airplane's center of gravity as forward as possible. Once we were airborne, the heavy bags had to be moved aft. The cargo nets each weighed two hundred pounds, too heavy to lift and throw out. Instead, one-third of their bulk had to stick out the door into the passing airstream so the inboard end could be lifted and the cargo tumbled out quickly. Each plane had three cargo nets, except Jim with four. By placing two side by side in the open doorway, and one or two more on top, we hoped to make it all happen in forty seconds. The most difficult task was getting the upper cargo nets on top of the lower ones.

Larry climbed out of the co-pilot's seat to help Tom. While they worked on our cargo, we arrived at the reservoir. Billy banked into a circular path around it, and Jim and I followed. It was 4:35 a.m. — nine minutes to go. Larry and Tom got the cargo nets in position, and Larry returned to his seat beside me. Each cargo net had a parachute pack and an attached rip cord. Tom had to attach the other end of the yellow rip cords to the floor bolts that normally held the rear seat belts. With the seats gone, we created a static line system with these bolts. As the cargo fell, the rip cords affixed to the seat belt bolts would pull out the parachutes and open them.

Billy's voice came over the radio: the time is 4:44, acknowledge. We did. Billy led us to an easterly heading as we all throttled back into a gradual descent. Relief and satisfaction washed over me as I realized the food would actually be delivered. I swung around in my seat to double-check Tom's work. It was not quite right. I told him that the upper cargo net had to stick out past the lower ones or he would be unable to tumble it out of the airplane. Tom went to work while I maneuvered the airplane into the half-V formation we had rehearsed for the drop. The three planes were 150 yards apart and descending. I moved the throttle back and forth to narrow the gap between my plane and Jim's. It was all going as planned.

Suddenly there was a sharp noise, like a gunshot. The plane shook violently, as though it had been hit. The control wheel came out of my hands, and the nose of the airplane shot upward into a very steep climb. Instinctively, I pushed the controls forward to get the plane back to level flight. I could not. On the edge of panic, I whipped around in my seat. Tom was moaning in the back and staring out the open doorway. The cargo net on top was no longer there. Tom had pushed it too far, and it had fallen out of the plane. I swung back around to fight the controls, stupidly thinking I understood the problem.

I didn't. The missing cargo net did not explain why the plane was pointed up so steeply or why I couldn't get it back down. I turned around again, choking down my fear and searching for some clue. There it was. Amid the tangle of cargo and rip cords, a perfectly straight yellow line pointed directly toward the open rear doorway. Horrified, my eyes followed as it went down outside the aircraft. It was a rip cord, and it was stretched taut because a very heavy object was hanging from it. That was why we were pointed up so sharply. The rip cord had not detached when the cargo net fell out of the plane. We were flying with a two-hundred-pound weight hanging from the tail. It was exactly the fatal scenario Billy had described two nights before in Huron.

I looked at the airspeed indicator: 110 and dropping. With the plane pointed up at such a high angle, the climb was too steep for the engine. The plane was slowing down, rapidly. If our airspeed fell to 63, we would slip into a tail-down stall, and there would be nothing I could do. We would die. I shouted back to Tom, the bags are hanging out there, get the knife off the wall and cut the rip cord, fast. The cargo net was still attached to the rip cord, so I assumed the parachute would be, too. Fully or partially open, it would create enormous braking drag, further slowing us down. I was frantic. I spun the trim tab forward for maximum nose-down flight, dropped the first notch of flaps to get more lift at the slower speed, and pushed the throttle all the way open. But I still could not push the control wheel forward and get the plane level.

Airspeed was down to 100. I whipped around to check Tom's progress. He was frozen in panic and had not moved. Larry saw it the same instant I did. He dived out of the co-pilot's seat, crawled over the third cargo net, and grabbed the hook knife taped to the wall. He wasn't wearing a safety line, and with the airplane pointed up so steeply, he was in danger of falling out the rear doorway, but he didn't hesitate. The cargo net in the doorway blocked his access to the rip cord, so he thrust the blade in Tom's face and yelled at him to take it and cut the rip cord. Tom snapped out of his trance, grabbed the knife, and started cutting the thick yellow line.

My eyes were riveted on the airspeed indicator, the gauge of our life or death. Eighty-seven. Tom knew nothing about the stall speed or the extreme urgency of what he was doing. A chilling fear started to drag me under. Barely this side of a panic, I could only yell to Tom, cut it, cut it, or we're going to die. The airspeed kept dropping: 85, 82, 78. Cut it, Tom, I shouted, cut it. We were seconds from death. Tom still struggled with the rip cord. I was soaked with fear, eyes locked on the airspeed indicator: 75, 74, 73. It was too late, I knew it: 72, 71. Suddenly the nose dropped. Tom had cut through the rip cord. The cargo net and its trailing parachute fell away, and I regained control of the airplane.

I reset the controls to recover precious airspeed. The other two planes were below and a half mile ahead, so I adjusted our rate of descent to catch up. We still had more than four hundred pounds of food aboard.

Larry and Tom, knowing little of stall speeds and aerodynamics, had no idea how close we had come. But they had seen my panic, and they deserved an explanation. When they heard it, Larry tried to comfort Tom, who blamed himself for the near disaster. I asked them both to get the remaining cargo organized. We were less than twenty minutes from Wounded Knee.

While they worked, I continued to line up in the formation. Since I was last, neither Billy nor Jim knew what had happened to us, nor could I tell them without violating radio silence so close to the drop zone. The other two planes were already aligned, so I maneuvered in to form the half V. A measure of calm returned as I saw that the airplane was responding normally.

We were flying straight, but it suddenly dawned on me that I was holding the control wheel turned far to the left. The plane should be rolling into a steeply banked left turn. It wasn't. When I moved the wheel farther to the left or back to the right, the plane dutifully banked in one direction or the other. Perplexed more than afraid, I checked the instruments and flight controls in a methodical search for the problem, but I found nothing. With no place else to look, I turned to check the back, and my glance drifted out the open rear doorway. What I saw so horrified me that for a moment I dismissed it as impossible and looked away. Then a new eruption of panic forced my eyes back out the door. Part of the tail was missing.

The left horizontal tail fin ended in a stump of bare and twisted metal. The outboard two feet were gone. The horizontal tail keeps an airplane level. The rear portion, the elevators, allow pilots to go up and down. Clearly, the cargo net had hit the tail as it exited the airplane, ripping off the outboard section. The part of the tail that remained was rippled from the impact. I knew there would be more damage I could not see, and feared the impact might have been strong enough to weaken the structural supports that held the entire tail assembly to the fuselage. Without a tail, airplanes like the Cherokee nose over and dive straight into the ground.

I had to land. I looked for a straight section of highway and started to execute the emergency landing checklist, praying the tail would stay on for another sixty seconds. As I descended, my fear subsided, and I was able to weigh our options more logically. The plane was responding to my control inputs. The air was smooth. If we kept a constant speed and there was no turbulence, pressure on the tail would be minimized, and we might be able to fly a while longer. A lot of food was still on board. We had nursed it across a thousand miles and committed ourselves, utterly, to its delivery. To successfully land on a road, the tail would have to stay on for another minute. If it stayed on for another fourteen minutes, we could get to Wounded Knee. I was too stressed to fly the plane and explain everything to Larry and Tom, even though I owed them a full explanation. I had to decide, and I decided to fly on.

I undid my preparations for the forced landing and eased the plane back to its number three position in the formation. We descended to fifty feet above the ground. I was scared to death. I knew the tail could bend off at any time. I was short with Larry and Tom, who had no idea of the danger we were in. Ten minutes out, Billy slipped back to the number two position and Jim took the lead. Larry climbed into the rear to help Tom with the cargo. Manderson, a reservation town, passed under our left wing. Marshals and FBI agents slept there, and the roar of our three three-hundred-horsepower engines would certainly wake them. But we were too low to be seen, and Wounded Knee was only four minutes away. It was too late for anyone to stop us.

Jim's plane rose out of the formation on its way up to five hundred feet. Billy followed. I gently started my climb. My concentration was fixed on the engine and flight controls. I made last-minute adjustments to the fuel flow and propeller speed and was so completely absorbed in flying the plane and maintaining my position in the formation that I lost my fear. The ground dropped away, and a tiny white speck in the distance gradually grew into the outline of a hilltop church three miles ahead. It was the Sacred Heart Catholic Church, built by tactless missionaries next to the mass grave of the 1890 massacre victims.

We reached five hundred feet two miles from the church, which sat in the middle of the drop zone. I could see sandbagged federal bunkers and APCs that blocked the four roads into the village. Satellite bunkers and reinforced trenches were visible everywhere. More APCs sat in the surrounding hills looking down on Wounded Knee. Inside the village, make-shift bunkers and trenches faced outward. We had indeed flown into a war zone, and for the first time we began to scan the ground for shooters. We expected to be shot at by frustrated feds and goons rousing themselves from sleep, but we also knew that we would be unable to hear any gunfire over the noise of our engines and the roar of the air passing the open doorways of our aircraft. I would have preferred to hear the shots, since it was far more unnerving not to know if there were bullets coming at us or not. In fact, shots were fired as we passed over the northwest perimeter of Wounded Knee and later as we made our escape, but we only learned of them hours later.

I looked at my watch: 5:06 a.m. Ahead in Wounded Knee, no one was visible. A single column of smoke rose from the center of the village. Expecting us to land one plane on a road, the Indians had kept a smoking fire burning to show us the wind. It confirmed the light southwesterly breeze in the forecast.

Jim flew past a roadblock and banked right to set up our run along the west and south perimeter of the village. Billy and I followed. The radio crackled with Jim's voice: go, go, go, go. Tom and Larry toppled the first cargo net out of the airplane, then the second. I banked left as we flew past the church. We had done it. Tom lay on the floor looking out the open rear doorway at the parachutes. Larry and I watched through the side windows. We saw a magnificent trail of billowing parachutes floating grace-fully to the ground. One of Jim's had failed to open, but five others formed a multicolored line across the sky. Together they rode the southwest wind toward the center of the village and hit, almost simultaneously, exactly on target.

Instantly, fifty people erupted from the village. They ran to the para-chutes, collapsed the canopies, and detached the duffel bags from the cargo nets. More people came. They were running around in wild pande-monium. Some jumped up and down and waved their jackets at us. Oth-ers danced and hugged anyone within reach. What a moment! I could feel their joy! But we still had a problem. I banked to the right, thinking about our tail, and fled to the southeast.

Billy delivered two cargo nets successfully, but as he lost altitude on his way out of the drop zone, he saw a marshal on the road impotently shaking a fist at him. Billy could see that Snake was exhausted from the effort with the first two cargo nets and would have a hard time getting the third in position by himself. If he made another pass, he doubted Snake would be ready in time, and the frustrated marshal might be waiting for him with a rifle or a machine gun. Having completed two-thirds of his mission, Billy decided against further risk. He put a hill between himself and the guns at Wounded Knee and made his escape to the east.

Jim saw one of his first two parachutes fail to open. Realizing John could not get the two remaining cargo nets in position in time, he sent Oliver back to help. With twice as much food as he had effectively delivered still aboard his plane, Jim felt he had no choice but to make a second pass. Not knowing about the shots that had already been fired at us, but anticipating them nonetheless, he rolled into a steep right turn, lost altitude, and flew into a shallow valley south of Wounded Knee. He kept below the ridgeline with the village on the other side. Invisible to potential shooters, he worked his way back west, made a climbing right turn, and popped over the ridge perfectly aligned with the drop zone. John and Oliver tumbled out the two remaining cargo nets and watched them float down and land on target. Jim got a brief glimpse of the celebrating Indians, banked left, and fled to the northeast.

Of the ten cargo nets we had come with, seven reached the besieged Indians—about fifteen hundred pounds of food. Later, Dennis Banks, a founder of AIM and the war chief inside the village, described the scene on the ground:

> We got to a point where there was just no food at all. We began to send out the old people. One morning, I suddenly heard this noise . . . People said they could hear planes coming in and we should get ready for a gas attack. Then some people said it wasn't the Army because we heard a few shots from up in the direction that the engine noise was coming from. They figured it must be somebody else because the feds wouldn't shoot at their own planes.
>
> I ran outside to a bunker. When I looked up, I saw that these three planes were coming in and they were flying at such a low level

that I realized it couldn't be the military, it couldn't be an attack, it was for us, it couldn't be anything else but a drop for us . . . These bundles were coming down and everyone went running over to get them. People began hollering and screaming. Jeez, they were grabbing each other and screaming up and down and crying . . . The airlift was like a new beginning for us, like a rebirth of Wounded Knee.

Meanwhile, I was flying a crippled airplane. After the drop, I descended to two hundred feet to get below radar and escape the FBI helicopter if they got it airborne in time to chase us. I kept my speed down to reduce stress on the tail. More than anything, I wanted to land on a road and get out of that airplane, but that would mean arrest and prosecution. We had to choose between safety and escape. Safety meant landing on a road. Escape meant flying two more hours to get out of South Dakota, where Wounded Knee was on everyone's mind. I didn't think my nerves could take it. Yet the air was smooth. A high overcast prevented direct sunlight from hitting the ground and generating the warm air masses called thermals that rise upward and cause turbulence. If the cloud cover remained and the air stayed smooth, we might have a chance.

I told Larry and Tom about the tail. They were stunned, then nervous and fearful. I explained the forces acting on the plane and the nature of the danger we were in, but they couldn't understand the aerodynamics and they knew it. Tom asked what I would do if I were alone. It was the right question. Two images flashed through my mind. In one, I saw the crew of the airlift in handcuffs. In the other, I saw our plane nose-dive into the ground. I looked at Tom and nervously said I would stay low and fly on. If the air became turbulent or the plane got the slightest bit harder to control, I would land wherever we were, airport or not. Tom and Larry looked at each other and nodded their agreement.

I flew east along Highway 18 parallel to the border between South Dakota and Nebraska. We passed several small country airports. If we had to land fast, I could go down on the highway if not one of these airstrips. I was scared, but I had to keep my fear from causing panic in the others. The missing rear door could only be reattached from the outside, so I was stuck with the noise and cold, which made it harder to stay calm. I kept twisting around in my seat to look at the fractured tail assembly. Every minute seemed like an hour. I checked off landmarks on the chart as we passed them, constantly calculating and recalculating the time and distance remaining. After an hour, the terrain became flatter as the High Plains gave way to the Mississippi basin. I descended with the land, staying five hundred feet over the ground—high enough to avoid attracting attention but low enough to land quickly if I had to.

Meanwhile, Jim and Billy had each landed at small country airports to replace their rear doors. Billy and Snake had a leisurely flight back to Chicago. Jim flew to Omaha and gave Oliver airfare back to Rapid City. Oliver asked where he was headed next, but Jim demurred. We never saw Oliver again. Jim and John flew back to Chicago but, like Billy, didn't go to Midway. Both flew into suburban Hinsdale Airport. Bob had told us earlier that FBI agents were making inquiries at Midway and might be waiting for us there, so he met the two planes at Hinsdale and had his flight students ferry them back to Midway. Bob drove Billy, John, and Snake to their cars and Jim to the airline terminal for the next flight home to Albuquerque.

I had kept radio silence, so the other two planes knew nothing of our predicament. They enjoyed triumphal flights back to Chicago, while we flew in mortal danger. Having already suffered panic, I found the prolonged fear even more difficult to endure. Minute after endless minute, I sat behind the controls thinking we were going to die. After two excruciating hours of subfreezing temperatures and howling noise, we finally reached the confluence of the Missouri and Niobrara rivers, thirty minutes from Iowa. But instead of relief, my fear only increased. I realized I had been staring thoughtlessly at a narrow band of blue sky above the horizon in front of me. Somewhere ahead, the high overcast clouds ended and warm sunshine would start to bounce thermals off the ground below. It was suicidal to fly that airplane into turbulence.

I set a course for the commercial airport at Sioux City, Iowa, thinking that maintenance facilities there would allow us to repair the airplane in a few days and return to Chicago. The band of blue sky on the horizon got wider. We had thirty miles to go, fifteen minutes' flying time. Five minutes later, the amount of blue sky had increased and the actual border of the overcast became visible. Two minutes later, we flew out from under it into bright sunshine, still eight minutes from the airport.

The first thermal hit, but caused only a ripple. Nevertheless, the little jolt to the control wheel sent shivers down my back and nightmare visions into my brain. Thirty seconds later it got worse. It did not matter how close we were. The game was up. We had to land. I pulled back on the throttle for a gradual descent. With Larry's help I had continuously monitored the nearest airport as we flew along. A small airstrip sat three miles directly in front of us. I made a slight course correction and headed directly for it.

The turbulence increased. A strong gust pushed the airplane's nose below the angle of a normal descent. I moved the control wheel back slightly. Nothing happened. I pulled the wheel back farther. Still nothing. Finally, with the control wheel back so far it hit the stops, the nose inched back up. Under normal circumstances, a similar control wheel deflection would have looped the plane over on its back. Turbulence bounced us all over the sky. I was losing control. The airstrip was two miles ahead. Another gust pushed the nose down. I pulled the control wheel all the way back to the stops but could not get the plane out of a steepening dive. It was over. I was out of options. Suddenly another gust pushed the nose back up, and I saw the airstrip in front of me. If I made it, I would have to land in the wrong direction, with a tailwind instead of a headwind. I didn't care; nor did I slow down to land. Getting to that runway in the next minute was the only way I could save our lives.

Another big gust hit and pushed the nose down. Again, I pulled the wheel back to the stops but was unable to return the plane to level flight. This time, there was no rescuing wind gust. We were going down and I couldn't stop it. Unable to pull the control wheel back any farther, I pushed it forward and milked it back and forth. It was all I could do. By first pushing and then pulling back, I tried to raise the nose a little each time. It worked, but the turbulence got worse. The nose was pushed up and down, and the wings rocked from left to right. I fought back with the control wheel, but it felt more like riding a rodeo horse than flying an airplane. Half the time the plane was completely out of my control. I was tense but fully alert, and I had no fear, only a cold, calculating focus on getting to that runway.

We were a half mile away, then a quarter. Normal landing airspeed is 75. We were going 100. I did not slow down. The tailwind meant we would hit at 110. It was going to be a controlled crash. The runway was narrow and not very long. As we approached, I saw it was gravel, which meant braking problems. We passed over the apron, and the landing gear slammed onto the loose gravel. I killed the throttle, stayed off the toe brakes, and cautiously pumped the hand brake. The plane was going too fast. It ran off the end of the runway. Thankfully, there were no obstacles, and the grass slowed us down enough for me to finally stop the plane. We were safe. Every muscle in my body went limp. There was nothing more to do, no more fear squeezing my mind into a knot of concentration. I closed my eyes and tried to compose myself.

Larry and Tom jumped out and reattached the rear door. I taxied to a lone hangar where two men were working on an airplane, cut the engine, and climbed out. They looked at our plane and asked what had happened. I told them we hit a bird. Was it big and brown? one asked. Yes, I said. You fellas musta hit an American eagle. There's lots of 'em around

The damaged tail of the aircraft I flew during the airlift showing the outboard portion of the left horizontal stabilizer, which had been ripped off. *Photo by George Lindblade / Author's collection*

now. I grinned and nodded. Yeah, we hit an American eagle, all right, a really big one, too.

We all walked around the plane to inspect the damage. It was worse than I had thought. I knew part of the tail was gone, but where the fuselage tapers down to a narrow cone just ahead of the tail assembly, a rip in the metal went from the top of the fuselage cone all the way around and past the bottom. We had been flying with the entire tail assembly only barely attached. Horrified, I saw it was already bent three inches to the right. One of the mechanics looked at the damage and said the tail could not possibly have stayed on much longer. He glanced up at me, scratched his jaw, and said, you three fellas shouldn't be alive. I can't see how this airplane here could've possibly been flyin'. I stared at the tail, feeling a little faint.

We had landed in South Sioux City, Nebraska. I arranged to store the plane at the little airfield, and one of the mechanics drove us across the Missouri River to the airport I had tried to reach in Sioux City, Iowa. They had scheduled service to Chicago. I called Bob back at Midway and told him about the damaged plane and its location. I asked him to tell the owner that we would cover the deductible on his insurance policy, but the insurers would have to get the plane repaired at the little South Sioux City airport. With two hours to wait for a flight to Chicago, Tom found a quiet corner and wrote his story for the *Boston Globe*. Ken had already contacted several reporters, so Larry followed up. One by one, he called the Associated Press, the *Washington Post*, the *Los Angeles Times*, and the *New York Times* and set up anonymous interviews with a pilot from the Wounded Knee airlift.

During my interview with the *New York Times*, the reporter gave me devastating news. The parachute that failed to open landed between Wounded Knee and the federal bunkers, in no-man's-land. Two hours after the drop, a few Indians left their bunkers to get what could be salvaged. The FBI and marshals, furious about the successful drop, opened fire. The Indians shot back, which set off a huge firefight. The feds then fired tens of thousands of rounds into Wounded Knee using rifles and the heavy machine guns we feared might be used against us. Several people took refuge in the church next to the mass grave site. A machine-gun bullet tore through the wall and into the back of Frank Clearwater's head. He was an Indian man from North Carolina who had driven a carload of food to Rapid City and had hiked into the village with his wife, Morningstar, only the night before. He was the first fatality at Wounded Knee.

Larry and I went into a tailspin. We blamed ourselves for Clearwater's death. The airdrop had led to the firefight, and since we were responsible for the airdrop, we were also responsible for Clearwater dying. Was a man's life worth what we had accomplished? Tom saw us intensely absorbed. Unaware of the news, and not wanting to disturb us, he filed his story with the *Globe* without clearing it with us first. That would prove to be a costly mistake.

On the airline flight to Chicago, we told Tom about Clearwater. At a scheduled stop in Davenport, we sent a telegram to Rita in Rapid City with a request that she convey our condolences to the people in Wounded Knee. After finally arriving at O'Hare, we said good-bye to Tom, who immediately flew back to Washington. I checked in with Bob. He reported that the others had made it back safely and dispersed, but that the FBI was snooping around Midway asking questions about us. It was late afternoon and we had not slept, so I told Bob I would meet him in the morning with the money to pay the aircraft rental charges. Still distraught about the death, Larry and I went to a friend's apartment and slept for twelve hours.

Early the next morning, Ken called from Boston to read us the news coverage. Stories were in all the major newspapers. They reported that antiwar activists had organized and carried out the airdrop to support the Indian movement. Tom had caused us some serious trouble during the drop, but when Ken read us the front-page story in the *New York Times*, we were grateful to have had him along. Spokesmen for the Justice Department claimed we had dropped "leather cases," implying that our cargo had been guns and ammunition, just as we feared.

However, our gratitude to Tom ended abruptly when Ken read us his front-page story in the *Boston Globe*. At the end of the otherwise accurate account, Tom described a crash landing "near Sioux City, Iowa." In his rush to file the story, and in reaction to the extreme anxiety we had all experienced, he had forgotten his promise not to mention any of the places we passed through. There were only a few airports in the Sioux City area. The FBI would see Tom's story and quickly inspect them all. When they found the plane I had been flying, they would easily trace the tail number to Midway. We had no time to spare.

We raced down to Bob's house. He told us that FBI agents were already at Midway and were more aggressive than they had been previously. Two planes had been returned, and Bob had told the owner about the third. I gave Bob enough cash to cover the three rentals and the deductible, but just as I did, the owner called him from the airport. Two FBI agents had just left his office headed for Bob's house. They had my name and Billy's. Larry and I grabbed our stuff. Bob hustled us out his back door as the two agents knocked on the front door. We went straight to O'Hare and got on the next flight to Boston. The FBI would get us eventually, but we wanted friends and lawyers nearby to help.

Larry and I were confident we could beat the feds in court. Our greater concerns were the impact of the airdrop at Wounded Knee and Frank Clearwater's death. Sadly, his was not the last fatality. Nine days after the drop, the feds killed Buddy Lamont. He had served with the Army in Viet Nam. Two of his great-grandparents were buried with the 1890 massacre victims.

But the airlift did achieve its purpose. It destroyed the government's strategy at Wounded Knee. The public applauded our effort, and the Indians renewed their commitment to remain until their demands were met. Simultaneously, the unraveling Watergate scandal put more pressure on Nixon to resolve the conflict. The Justice Department blamed us for their failure and filed criminal charges against us that reflected their anger. But with the Indians able to hold out, the government had to give up. On May 8, seventy-one days into the takeover and twenty-one days after the airlift, the government finally capitulated and granted some portion of the three Indian demands. They offered to send a White House delegation to meet with the traditional chiefs to discuss treaty rights, bypassing Dick Wilson and the tribal government. They authorized an extensive investigation of the operation and finances of Wilson's tribal government and the local office of the Bureau of Indian Affairs, and they committed to protecting people on the Pine Ridge Reservation from unlawful abuses of power by the local authorities.

Despite the victory, some of us in the airlift crew continued to feel remorse about our role in Clearwater's death, and several people who had been inside Wounded Knee during the occupation tried to console us. They gave us their perspective on what had happened. Kevin McKiernan was one. As a progressive freelance radio reporter, he had gone to Wounded Knee to cover the story, but like Tom Oliphant he had been inspired by what he saw and had joined the action he was covering. Later, Kevin became an accomplished journalist and filmmaker. He wrote:

> I remember the morning of April 17, 1973, as if it were yesterday. We were hungry and thought Wounded Knee had been forgotten by the rest of the world. It was about dawn. Three low flying small airplanes flew in formation wing-to-wing from the northern end of the village. The silky parachutes floated to earth. Men, women and children ran to the welcome bundles. Federal gunmen opened up from the hills and from a helicopter overhead, firing their machine guns . . . Frank Clearwater sat up near his mattress for his first morning in Wounded Knee. A sniper round blew the back of his head off. People fought back all day and ate the food that evening. The idea of the drop was as important to us as what it contained.

Months later I visited the reservation and met Gladys Bissonette, one of the traditional elders. She had helped spark the protests against the tribal chairman's corruption and had joined in the decision to seize Wounded Knee. I asked her if the people inside thought that the airdrop had caused Frank Clearwater's death, and she finally laid my qualms to rest.

"Oh, no! Oh, no!" she said. "That was the FBI and the federal marshals who were responsible for that. They wanted to starve us out, and they intended to keep us from getting any food. But then this airlift come and got all that food to us. We knew that this was why they shot at us,

because we had gotten that food. We had gotten some help from somewhere, and that's what they didn't want. They didn't want us to get help
from anywhere. You mustn't blame people that come and do some good
on account of some others who do something evil right afterward. Why,
then nobody could do anything to change this government."

CHAPTER 23

LARRY AND I WAITED FOR THE FBI AT THE MEDICAL AID FOR INDOCHINA OFFICE IN Cambridge. It was a Thursday, the day after we eluded them in Chicago. Charlotte had lined up John Flym, a professor at Boston's Northeastern University Law School, to represent us. The day passed but agents failed to show up, so Larry flew back to his office at the Coalition to Stop Funding the War in Washington. By lunchtime Friday, they had still not come, so I called him to say that maybe they never would. As usual, I spoke too soon.

Late Friday afternoon, two men arrived. They had crew cuts and wore the signature beige raincoats of the FBI. They asked to speak to me. I insisted Ken Coplon join us as a witness. When the four of us sat down, I turned on a tape recorder. They didn't like that. The FBI does not conduct recorded interviews, they said. I knew that and was only playing with them. I told them to produce a warrant or get out. They left.

Early the next morning, I awoke to simultaneous pounding on the front and rear doors of my house in Somerville. It sounded like an arrest just from the knocking. Outside the front door, three agents flashed badges and drawn guns. I asked to see a warrant. They said it was downtown and that if I did not open the door, they would break it down. It was a beautiful wooden door, so I let them in. They slapped me in handcuffs just as a housemate appeared on the stairs in his pajamas. He waved a tape recorder, said he was Danny Schechter, the News Dissector, and that he was covering the arrest for WBCN-FM.

Before the agents could react, Danny started to mock-interview one of them. His matter-of-fact questions and valid press card confused them, and he quickly turned the otherwise tense scene into a farce. Danny kept at it until they threatened to arrest him for obstructing justice. Meanwhile, the three agents who had "covered the back" joined the three in the house. Two started upstairs to our second floor, but other housemates, Linda Gordon and Ann Froines, also in pajamas, refused to let them pass until a search warrant was produced. The agents tried to shove past them, but Linda and Ann shoved back. The agents retreated. Thousands of listeners throughout the Boston area were delighted that evening when Danny played a tape recording of the entire episode on his news program.

I was detained for several hours at FBI headquarters and brought before a federal judge. With Flym's help, the judge released me on my own recognizance. I had to give up my passport and agree not to leave Massachusetts without his permission. Leaving the courtroom, John listed the charges. I was stunned. Three federal felonies: interference with federal officers in the lawful performance of their duty; interstate travel to aid, abet, or incite a riot; and conspiracy to commit offenses against the United States. Each carried a five-year prison sentence. The last two were the same charges filed against the Chicago Seven after the 1968 Democratic convention. Apparently, bringing food to hungry Indians was a more serious offense.

Years later, a high-ranking government official told Tom Oliphant that President Nixon had read the New York Times article about the airlift in the White House and had flown into a rage. Battered himself by Watergate, Nixon shouted about the New Left flying a squadron of airplanes in formation, making a precision parachute drop at dawn, defying the FBI, and aiding an armed insurrection on American soil. It's an outrage, he shouted, find them and throw the book at them. Over the next few days, they did exactly that. Bob Talbot, Bill Wright, Jim Stewart, Larry Levin, John Adelman, and Tom Oliphant were all charged as I was. Snake and Oliver were never found.

Because no one outside the airlift crew knew about Tom Oliphant's direct involvement in the drop, his arrest came as a shock. Only once or twice before had a reporter been indicted for the "crime" he had been assigned to cover. With the press hammering Nixon on Watergate, Tom's arrest was seen as a White House counterattack. And, as often happens when the government prosecutes protesters, the arrest backfired and helped us. Charges against the airlift crew would have been a one-day story, but Tom's arrest angered the national press corps. Reporters and columnists rose up with a single voice to condemn the Justice Department for arresting a newsman covering a legitimate story.

Revenge came a week later. Attorney General Richard Kleindienst, who had charged us, was fired along with three high officials in the White House. Their involvement in Watergate could no longer be hidden. Nixon appointed Elliot Richardson to replace Kleindienst, who had himself replaced the disgraced John Mitchell. Richardson was from Boston, knew Tom's boss at the *Globe*, and understood that his arrest was counterproductive. He dropped all charges against Tom. Larry's charges were also dropped for "lack of sufficient evidence." The FBI had hard evidence against the rest of us. We had used Bob's house and connections at Midway. Billy and I had shown our pilot's licenses to rent the planes. Jim had used his real name on a motel register. John had called home from a motel phone instead of a pay phone. Larry was the only one who had been scrupulous about not leaving such evidence behind.

The charges hanging over me were very serious, and I should have been more anxious about them. I wasn't. I was confident no jury would convict us of such crimes given what we actually did. Also, I knew our lawyers would file pretrial motions that would take months to resolve, so there was no immediate threat and no reason to panic. My main concern was to continue building MAI, and I didn't want fear about the future to undermine my work in the present. Money still came in for Bach Mai, but not reliably for our other projects, like rural health-care centers, inoculation programs, and urgent shipments of surgical equipment and medicines. In fact, because of the signing of the peace accords, MAI needed to redefine its work. So did the rest of the antiwar movement.

Over the past decade, the movement's strategy had been based on opposition and resistance. We created opposition to the war by exposing its injustice and brutality. We encouraged resistance to it by focusing on narrow but critical groups: draft-eligible young men, military recruits, and college students able to take greater risks than the population at large. It was a strategy based on making trouble for the institutions prosecuting the war. After the peace accords, we needed a new strategy because peace had come to the United States but not yet to Viet Nam.

The new strategy we developed saw Congress as the weak link in any attempt to continue the war. Ongoing combat by South Vietnamese forces required U.S. funding, which meant Congress could turn off the financial spigot despite what Nixon wanted. The Christmas bombing had reduced support for the war, thanks in part to our efforts. With U.S. troops out of Viet Nam, the public had no appetite for sending them back. Millions still passionately opposed the war. If we organized them to pressure Congress with letters, phone calls, and visits, cutting off funding for the war through grassroots lobbying might be the best way to end it.

On the other hand, we knew it would not be easy to take a movement based on opposition and resistance and redirect it toward work within the system. Alliances would be needed with trade union and religious groups experienced with congressional lobbying. The fragmented antiwar movement would have to be brought back together. Many Viet Nam vets were furious at how the system had treated them and wanted no part of it. Street-fighting protesters were too militant to effectively lobby. Students who had come to believe in the fundamental corruption of the American political system could not easily be asked to participate in it. And we ourselves, as leaders of the movement, had been good at finding creative ways to throw monkey wrenches into the political machinery; it remained to be seen how good we were at working within it.

Despite these misgivings, in the months following the peace accords a strategic focus on Congress emerged as our wisest course. It had been two years since the failed Mayday protest, and leadership within the movement had shifted from big coalitions sponsoring massive protests to smaller, task-oriented groups working on narrower agendas. MAI was one example. Another was the Indochina Peace Campaign, which had evolved into an educational organization that wrote and designed engaging materials about the war for distribution to a growing national network of activists. A third example was the Indochina Resource Center, formed by Fred Branfman and Don Luce in Washington. It researched conditions in Indochina, published authoritative documents, and distributed reliable information to the press. Other groups with professional staffs and specific agendas were also part of this network.

These organizations shared a common perspective. Their leaders were on friendly terms, talked frequently, and met often during the spring to discuss implementation of the new strategy. Along with more mainstream groups, we were all affiliated with the Coalition to Stop Funding the War (CSFW). We knew it would be difficult to sell our congressional strategy to the militants and to convince them to participate in a system they had rejected or from which they were profoundly alienated, but we felt an honest analysis of the situation left us no choice.

We were no longer amateurs. We were in our early thirties and had been organizing against the war for years. Those of us who had once been revolutionaries were prepared to walk the halls of Congress like good liberals begging representatives and senators for support. Our revolutionary objective, to build an egalitarian society free from discrimination with a guaranteed standard of living for all, remained an ultimate goal. But we knew it could not be won through revolution and had no idea how else to achieve it, so we tacitly agreed to put off the larger questions until we had finally stopped the war.

We agreed on three strategic goals: first, to prevent the United States from killing more people in Indochina by stopping the bombing of Cambodia; second, to free the vast number of political prisoners being tortured in South Vietnamese jails; and third, to bring down the corrupt regime in South Viet Nam, which was said to depend on U.S. aid for 90 percent of its budget. These objectives could be achieved through acts of Congress. We were not optimistic, and we knew a great deal would be required of us. We were inexperienced at lobbying and quite possibly unable to lead large numbers of people into such work. Nonetheless, we had a responsibility to provide strategic direction and workable tactics, so we pressed ahead.

Larry Levin left MAI to become the executive director of CSFW. The religious and labor groups within the coalition, more experienced with congressional relations, provided the bulk of the lobbying muscle. But with Larry at the helm, the antiwar organizations were able to shift their tactics toward congressional work, even though we had a steep learning curve. Coalition staff told us which bills to support, which committees had the most leverage, and which representatives and senators were best positioned to advance the bills we wanted to pass.

Members of participating antiwar organizations gradually learned to stage public events in the home districts of representatives and senators to influence their votes. Antiwar activists worked alongside church and union activists to present films and slide shows, distribute pamphlets, and hold campus and church events designed to get voters to write, call, or visit elected officials and lobby for our goals. We knew we would have to unleash a torrent of pressure to be effective, but we thought enough people still cared about Viet Nam to do that.

Watergate helped. The scandal was emasculating the Nixon administration, which had told Congress so many lies about the war that a reservoir of mistrust and anger had accumulated on Capitol Hill. As more scandalous Watergate revelations emerged and more of Nixon's subordinates were fired, the White House lost political influence. Senators and representatives realized that the balance of forces was shifting, and they became more susceptible to pressure from constituents. Members of Congress who had opposed the war submitted good bills and organized support among their colleagues. But we had no illusions. The deck was still stacked against us in Congress and the task ahead truly gargantuan.

For six weeks after my arrest, I worked to advance the congressional strategy both nationally and within MAI's network of supporters. My focus shifted back to the Indians in early June, when the airlift crew was ordered to Deadwood, South Dakota, for our arraignment. I had wanted to fly there in my Cessna, but the first time I went up in it after the airdrop, I got fifty feet off the ground and panicked. I was afraid to fly. I made an immediate landing, sat on the tarmac and talked myself down, then went back up for a short flight. It was months before I felt comfortable in the cockpit and years before I completely overcame my nervousness in turbulence. I had a minor case of post-traumatic stress disorder.

During and after the seizure, the government had arrested hundreds of Indians on various charges. Ken Tilsen, Bruce Ellison, and other lawyers established the Wounded Knee Legal Defense/Offense Committee (WKLDOC) to give them free legal services. The Center for Constitutional Rights (CCR) in New York defended the airlift, initially by providing the services of Bill Kunstler, one of the two Chicago Seven lawyers. When Dennis Banks and Russell Means, the most visible Indian leaders inside Wounded Knee, were arrested and charged with offenses that could lead to their imprisonment for over a hundred years, CCR shifted Kunstler to their defense, and his colleague Mark Amsterdam took our case. Like WKLDOC, CCR was funded by charitable contributions raised from movement supporters.

At the arraignment, the airlift defendants did well: while the heavy charges remained in place, we got off without bail, our passports were returned, and our travel restrictions lifted. Many of the Indians fared worse; some had bail set as high as $100,000. Having come all the way to South Dakota, Larry, Billy, Jim, and I wanted to meet the people we had helped, so we stayed for a week. In Rapid City, we saw the lawyers at WKLDOC. Afterward, we drove to the reservation for a heroes' welcome. Wherever we were introduced as the fliers who had made the food drop, the gratitude was overwhelming and deeply emotional. But on the reservation I saw heartbreaking poverty. The town of Pine Ridge, the administrative center of the reservation, had a few one-story government buildings but otherwise was a jumble of broken-down houses and decrepit trailers. Mangy dogs roamed over junked cars and piles of trash that littered the yards. In the countryside, away from the town, people lived a little better, however deep their poverty.

In Wounded Knee, we paid our respects at the grave site of the 1890 massacre victims and walked through the deserted bunkers and shelters used during the seizure. A dozen miles away, we called at the rural home of Chief Frank Fools Crow, who had gathered a council of Lakota chiefs and headmen from across the West. These old chiefs had rejected elections ordered by the federal government. They derived their authority from tribal members determined to preserve traditional Lakota culture. When we arrived, the solemn group was gathered outside under a freshly built pine canopy reviewing a letter from the White House.

At the home of Oglala Lakota Chief Frank Fools Crow, just after the airlift arraignment at Deadwood in June 1973. From left to right: Jim Stewart, Larry Levin, Chief Fools Crow, me, Bill Wright, and an unidentified Indian elder. *Author's collection*

The Nixon administration had postponed a meeting about treaty rights promised in the settlement that ended the Wounded Knee seizure. The chiefs were angry. Yet they interrupted their council for an hour to greet us. Many of the old ones had deeply furrowed faces and spoke only Lakota. We had to address them through interpreters. They had been teenagers in the first and second decades of the twentieth century and described the reservation in those years as an open range. In later years, white ranchers leased away the best land and forced a culture of individual ownership and barbed-wire fences on the tribe. Many resisted, but the Lakota culture was drained of its vitality, and the Lakota people fell into poverty and alcoholism.

In their council, the old chiefs hammered out an angry response to the White House, at the end of which they said, "Hope is the fountain of youth for all mankind, and we Indian people are the proud owners of the deepest well of hope in the world, but that well is almost dry. We are a people who can maintain our dignity in spite of poverty and other extreme social ills, but even the most dignified people in the world cannot live on hope alone."

We got back to Boston in mid-June, and I found the congressional lobbying campaign doing well. We had assumed that passionate opponents of the war who had tired of demonstrating would participate in large numbers. We were right. More help came from Watergate. The Nixon administration had sent burglars into Dan Ellsberg's psychiatrist's office. Ellsberg was on trial for releasing the Pentagon Papers, and the burglars were looking for material to use against him. Exposed, Nixon tried to influence the judge by offering him the directorship of the FBI. Because of Nixon's interference, the judge had no choice but to dismiss all charges against Ellsberg, further embarrassing the administration.

Outrage over Watergate and Viet Nam permeated the country. We took advantage of it. CSFW coordinated our activity, and antiwar sentiment poured into congressional offices. At times, switchboards were flooded and mailbags stuffed to overflowing. We had done grassroots political organizing for years and knew how to produce such results, but our tools were primitive. We had no personal computers, no e-mail, no Internet, and no social networking Web sites. We used archaic Addressograph and mimeograph machines and distributed material via the mails at significant cost for postage. Antiwar organizations had mailing lists numbering in the tens of thousands, while affiliated labor unions, churches, and social and academic organizations could communicate with hundreds of thousands more.

Elected officials, nervous that Watergate had spawned increasing discontent with government, soon got nervous about their own survival in office. It was the best possible environment in which to lobby for change, and despite our inexperience we achieved our first success. In the last days of June, Congress forced Nixon to accept a complete bombing halt over Cambodia beginning August 15. It was extraordinary: our first strategic objective already achieved! We knew we had activated only a portion of the Americans opposed to the war and hoped that the Cambodian victory would inspire others to join us.

The fight shifted immediately to military assistance for South Viet Nam, and to the political prisoners being tortured in its jails. Cutting U.S. military assistance meant the South Vietnamese army would have fewer bullets, vehicles, and other supplies. Once, as militant protesters, we had shouted, "One side's right, one side's wrong. Victory to the Viet Cong." Now, as grassroots lobbyists, we pushed for the same objective. The political prisoners were critical as well, for reasons of justice and humanity, but also because many potential leaders of a postwar Viet Nam were among them and were needed to rebuild the country.

Senators Kennedy and Fulbright introduced a bill to substantially cut Nixon's request for $1.6 billion in military aid for South Viet Nam. Their bill became the main goal of our lobbying. The political prisoners also got attention when a congressional aide traveled to South Viet Nam and obtained photographic evidence that many were kept in "tiger cages" so small an adult could not stand upright. We knew Americans would not like paying for torture, so we publicized stories about individual victims and endorsed a bill sponsored by Senator James Abourezk to prohibit American dollars from funding torture or harsh imprisonment. The young aide who got the "tiger cages" pictures was Tom Harkin, later an Iowa congressman and senator himself.

In June, I received a letter from Colonel Quat in Hanoi. He wrote, "We got the news that you have been arrested for supplying food for the people at Wounded Knee. We heard that now you are free on bail but facing a possible 15 years sentence. It is obvious that the people who want to indict you are the same who took the lands from the Indians, who massacred the Vietnamese people and who are responsible for the Watergate scandal. Their reactionary actions could be only checked by the struggle and we hope that you will succeed. Receive our best wishes of courage, good luck and good health."

Throughout July, as Quat implied, I had to bounce back and forth between Indochina and Wounded Knee, but my nervousness about the shift to a congressional strategy had ended. We had not convinced all elements of the antiwar movement to join us, but enough had to give us a fighting chance . . . and our first win. Instead of having to argue for the strategy's value, I had time to advance it, especially within MAI. We had tens of thousands of antiwar supporters who received Ken Coplon's periodic direct-mail appeals. We added requests to lobby for specific bills and timed the mailings to match the legislative calendar.

As Ken and I watched the overburdened lawyers at WKLDOC, we realized we could also use our direct-mail skills to raise money for them. I felt responsible for covering legal expenses for the airlift crew, since I had gotten them arrested. Mark Amsterdam's work at CCR would benefit them all, but a few wanted lawyers they knew personally, and I agreed to cover their fees from money we raised. I continued to be confident and cavalier about my own charges, but I fully understood that others with families, jobs, mortgages, and pilot's licenses to protect were worried. It also infuriated me that the government had brought such severe criminal charges against the Indian leadership and had systematically violated the agreement that ended the occupation, in essence turning it into yet another broken treaty.

Ken and I told the WKLDOC lawyers we would raise the initial seed money for a direct-mail campaign, write the letters, manage the logistics, record the receipts, and give a portion of the net proceeds to the other airlift lawyers but save most of the money we raised for them. We took no fee for the work. Our mailings were an instant success. Public sympathy for the Indians remained high. Over the following year, we delivered thousands of dollars to the airlift lawyers and tens of thousands to WKLDOC, which then developed its own direct-mail team.

During the summer, Mark Amsterdam pursued our case vigorously. His strategy was to bury federal prosecutors under a blizzard of pretrial motions, hoping they would dismiss the case or drop charges because we were not worth the work they had to do to respond. He filed motions to change the venue, to dismiss because the grand jury had excluded Indians, to reveal spies in the defense camp, to recuse the judge for bias against Indians, to show the basis for the conspiracy charge, to declare the riot statute unconstitutional, and to demand copies of the grand jury minutes. Mark did the heavy lifting, but I had to check the facts and history.

In North Viet Nam the previous year, I had learned two lessons from Colonel Quat. As I watched him maintain meaningful relations with people from across the political spectrum, pacifists to revolutionaries to just plain Democrats, I saw how he skillfully avoided sectarian arguments and looked beneath outward differences to find the ideas that brought people together. I drew on that lesson as I became more involved with the diverse coalition lobbying Congress to end the war.

Quat's second lesson was the importance of short work breaks for physical and spiritual renewal, so when Mimi Fariña called to invite me to join her for a weekend in Santa Barbara, where she and Hoyt Axton had a nightclub gig, I agreed. Mimi loved California and had tried to convince me to move there. I was skeptical, thinking that it was too far from the epicenter of American politics. Yet I felt myself at a personal turning point. Antiwar work was in a new phase. MAI had been at the cutting edge during the shooting war when we sent aid to "the enemy," but was no longer as confrontational. The focal point of struggle against the war was in Congress, and I began to think the time might soon come for me to leave MAI and work more directly on lobbying.

I enjoyed the weekend and the especially lush environment around Santa Barbara. When it was over, Mimi drove me to Santa Monica to visit Hayden and Fonda at the Indochina Peace Campaign office. Tom and Jane seemed quite able to do political work in California—and they lived close to the beach surrounded by palm trees and bougainvillea. It was the antithesis of the gritty urban environments in Chicago, New York, and Boston I had lived in. We discussed how to better coordinate our lobbying work, but I couldn't fail to notice how much more pleasant their working conditions were compared with mine.

I returned to Boston in August concerned about the future of MAI. From ten offices, we were down to five, some only part-time. After the adoption of the Paris Peace Accords some activists had drifted to other political issues, publicity became harder to generate, and fund-raising was an uphill battle. Yet we had to keep attention focused on the U.S.-financed ground war in Viet Nam. Helping victims of the war reminded the public that it was still going on. So, while MAI was no longer at the cutting edge of the antiwar effort, it remained an established and successful organization with an important role to play. To insure that everyone involved with MAI shared the same assumptions about its continuing urgency and how it fit into the larger antiwar strategy, I scheduled a national MAI conference to be held in Pittsburgh in late September. The MAI staff created new materials, including a moving slide show, and put a renewed emphasis on assisting rural health facilities in the embattled regions in South Viet Nam.

During the late summer and early fall, the political prisoners in South Viet Nam became a central focus for the antiwar movement. Estimates of their number varied from 100,000 to 400,000. Activists coordinated by the Indochina Resource Center made model tiger cages. They were set up in public places around the country with photo exhibits of the prisoners. Meanwhile, IPC distributed thousands of plastic bracelets embossed with prisoners' names. MAI supported both efforts and the ongoing campaign for Senator Abourezk's bill to cut off funding for the South Vietnamese police and prison system, although it was more difficult to lobby on that issue than it had been for the August 15 Cambodian bombing cutoff.

In September, IPC brought more attention to the political prisoners in South Viet Nam by sponsoring a monthlong speaking tour for Hayden, Fonda, and Jean-Pierre Debris, a French activist who had been arrested in Saigon and had spent two years in a South Vietnamese prison. Debris described the plight of the prisoners in graphic detail and from firsthand experience. MAI activists helped recruit audiences for these appearances and assisted IPC.

The movement's grassroots lobbying capability was gradually improving. We organized delegations to visit congressional offices, bought local radio spots, billboards, and newspaper ads, used political donors to try to convince senators and representatives to oppose the war, and generally applied all the community-organizing tactics we knew. To broaden the base of participation in this effort, IPC called for a national conference in Dayton in late October. MAI co-sponsored the event, and a variety of religious, pacifist, and women's groups were invited.

The MAI conference in late September refocused our organizers and our network on the importance of continued medical relief work. A month later, the IPC event in Dayton built additional support for the grassroots lobbying campaign. Lobbying was still a new and unfamiliar tactic to many of us, but the determination displayed in Dayton was inspiring. The War Powers Act had been introduced in Congress, and the possibility of its passage, with the limitations on presidential war-making authority it contained, increased our motivation and our optimism.

I went to Chicago after the Dayton conference to see my family and to rendezvous with Marilyn Webb, who was writing a magazine piece about our old friend Rennie Davis. An appeal of the Chicago Seven contempt citations was being heard, and Rennie would be there with some of the other defendants. Rennie, a hero of the antiwar movement, had suffered a mental breakdown and had morphed into the zombielike disciple of an East Indian mystic, the guru Maharaj Ji. To make matters worse, the guru was only fifteen years old. It was preposterous, but Rennie had succumbed, and the little guru was drawing huge crowds of young people. Marilyn was writing about this strange phenomenon. So was a student I had known at Brooklyn College, Robert Greenfield, who by coincidence was in Chicago researching his book *The Spiritual Supermarket.*

When Tom Hayden arrived from Dayton to join the other Chicago Seven defendants, the four of us pondered Rennie's bizarre metamorphosis. Tom and I tried to be sympathetic, but thought the extreme pressure and stress Rennie had worked under for so many years had broken his mind. Marilyn felt that intense political work of that kind had left a spiritual void in all our lives, and that Rennie was looking for the transcendent experiences we all required. Robert was less interested in Rennie but fascinated by the fact that so many lost young souls were in pursuit of East Indian mysticism. Later, he and Marilyn attended an enormous rally in the Houston Astrodome sponsored by the little guru and agreed he was just another charlatan.

Robert, Marilyn, and I sat through the Chicago Seven contempt appeal. A federal judge had been brought in from Maine to officiate. Prosecutors lost most of the contempt citations, but did win two each against Abbie Hoffman, Jerry Rubin, and Bill Kunstler, and seven against Dave Dellinger. Because Judge Julius Hoffman had acted so outrageously during the original trial, in consideration of "judicial error, judicial or prosecutorial misconduct, and judicial or prosecutorial provocation" no sentences were imposed.

On November 7, 1973, the antiwar movement's congressional lobbying strategy achieved a second momentous victory only months after having stopped the bombing of Cambodia. Congress had passed the historic War Powers Act only to have it vetoed by Nixon. On the seventh, thanks to thousands of phone calls, telegrams, letters, and visits to congressional offices around the country and in Washington, Congress overrode the veto. The new law forced the president to provide official notice to Congress within forty-eight hours of U.S. military forces being deployed overseas. If Congress failed to approve the deployment, those forces had to be withdrawn within sixty days.

The War Powers Act had a profound impact over the next year in that it limited Nixon's ability to respond to the deteriorating military situation in South Viet Nam. Many years later, in the 1980s, the law effectively prevented President Reagan from making ill-advised U.S. military deployments in Central America. Later still, it forced both Bush presidents to seek congressional approval before their respective invasions of Iraq. Unfortunately, when it came to Iraq, members of Congress were too weak and compliant in the face of presidential popularity to use the powers they had.

In quick succession, other lobbying victories followed. A month later, after all the "tiger cage" demonstrations, prisoner bracelets, photo exhibits, and publicity we generated about the political prisoners in South Viet Nam, and all the voter contacts with Congress that resulted, legislation passed blocking further U.S.-sponsored training of police forces in South Viet Nam and all other countries. Congress also removed all funds for Thieu's police and prison system from South Viet Nam's economic aid package. We had lobbied hard for this legislation, and it was widely understood to be a victory for the antiwar movement.

Our most important success at the end of 1973 received the least attention. All of our lobbying, no matter what else was advocated, emphasized the urgent need to cut military assistance to South Viet Nam. We knew we lacked the strength to block these funds entirely, so we urged elected officials to substantially cut the budget rather than try to kill it. Our strategy worked. Nixon had asked for $1.6 billion. The final appropriation was $1.1 billion, almost one-third less. We regretted that so much money would allow Thieu to continue the war, but we knew that a one-third reduction over the next year would have a crippling impact on his offensive capability. Also, this large budget cut would help us work for further cuts later.

Surveying the gains we made in 1973, starting with the peace accords and culminating in these legislative triumphs, I understood that we had won significant victories not with protests and defiance but with focused work inside the established political system. I knew that revolutionary social or political transformation could not be achieved by such work, that the system had no capacity to transform itself, but neither did I see a strategy for achieving the transformation I thought was needed. Until I did, I was reluctant to walk away from the potential for incremental but important change exemplified by our legislative achievements.

Years later, we discovered that during this same period Nixon planned to violate the peace accords and renew the U.S. bombardment of South Viet Nam in order to protect the embattled Thieu regime. Those plans became more difficult to execute as his political power was sapped by Watergate and the common but still unproven assumption that he had been personally involved. He had lost more political capital with Vice President Spiro Agnew's resignation on the heels of corruption charges. But Nixon had won a second term, was therefore free from the usual political constraints, and was pigheaded enough to bomb if he chose to, at least for sixty days under the new War Powers Act. What stopped him was money.

Nixon could not spend money on military operations that Congress had not appropriated. If he went outside the law and bombed Viet Nam in spite of the peace accords, he risked his presidency. We had turned Congress into an antiwar battleground and had revealed the significant antiwar sentiment within it. A resumption of the bombing would create an angry backlash. Nixon could not risk that when the possibility of a Watergate-related impeachment still hung over him. Without our work in 1973, it is likely Nixon would have bombed South Viet Nam and destroyed the peace. In retrospect, our skill and good luck in taking advantage of Watergate may have saved the peace and insured the future viability of Viet Nam.

CHAPTER 24

JUST BEFORE THE LEGISLATIVE VICTORIES IN THE FALL OF 1973, I WAS OFFERED A CON-tract to write a book about the Wounded Knee airlift. It wasn't much, a $2,000 advance from Swallow Press, a tiny publishing house in Chicago, but I accepted it. I was tired, and a little confused. For two years, since the start of MAI, I had worked at an exhausting pace. While pleased with what I had accomplished, I was uncertain about what to do next. The easy choice would be to stay at MAI and continue living in Somerville. The harder choice would be to find a more direct way to work against U.S. war funding in Indochina. I preferred the harder choice, and I thought taking three or four months off to work on a book might provide a good transition.

I was outraged by the deplorable conditions on Indian reservations and wanted to expose them in hopes they could be improved. The seizure of Wounded Knee had taught Americans more about their Indian neighbors than any single event in the twentieth century. It was the right time to push the envelope. Wounded Knee had also electrified the Indian population, unleashing a new wave of Indian militancy and civil rights activity and awakening a cultural heritage and spirit of resistance that could enrich the lives of thousands of Indians. That process deserved to be helped along.

Leaving MAI for a few months was not a problem. The staff had matured and could carry on without me, especially at a time of gradually diminishing medical relief work. On the congressional front, we had just won significant victories and would not have to fight major new battles for a few months. I would be back in harness by then.

Given the small size of the advance, I decided to live in Mexico. It was cheap and warm and would allow me to escape another winter. Having grown up in Chicago, I did not have a positive relationship with cold weather. I bought an old VW camper to travel cheaply and asked Bob Talbot to find a buyer for my airplane, which he did at, of all places, Midway Airport. I got $4,500 for N5460B. The Cessna 172 had served me well, and with only a $500 loss over two and a half years I had gotten my money's worth.

I bought a stack of gold coins with the money, put them in an empty coffee can, sealed it thoroughly, and buried it under a big tree on a friend's farm in western Massachusetts. I faced serious criminal charges, and while optimistic about the outcome I could not be sure what would happen. Also, the president was a madman. He had already demonstrated a willingness to round up people like me with the COINTELPRO program prior to the 1972 Republican convention. It was not inconceivable that if faced with impeachment, he would declare martial law. It seemed prudent to have a little escape money hidden away.

As winter began, I loaded the VW camper and headed west. I had an appointment in Minneapolis with Dennis Banks, a founder of the American Indian Movement and the most influential leader and war chief inside Wounded Knee. Banks greeted me like an old friend. His straight black hair was twisted into long braids tied at the bottom with rawhide and bright green cloth. Obviously proud of his Indian blood, he was a lean and sturdy thirty-six-year-old. Banks introduced me to other leaders of AIM, which had been founded in Minneapolis and was headquartered there. I interviewed each over the next several days.

Dennis was not what white society would call a "good Indian." In fact, he was an ex-con. The Bureau of Indian Affairs had taken him from his parents as a small child and sent him to an Indian school four hundred miles away. He got home eleven years later, worked for a short time, joined the Air Force, and spent three years in Japan. Leaving the military, he did community work in Minneapolis for four years, but found no opportunity for advancement. He fell into drinking and petty crime and served three short terms in prison. During the last one, he knew he had to change or die. He refused prison work and got the solitary confinement he craved. For nine months, he read voraciously, first about Indian history, then more broadly. He said this to me: "Sitting in that jail cell [in 1967] I began to understand there was a hell of a movement going on that I wasn't part of, the antiwar movement, the Black Panther movement, the civil rights movement, the SDS. It was inside the jug there that I thought there has to be an Indian movement, too. Otherwise, it will pass us by. And realizing then what was really going on, I made a commitment that there would be an Indian movement."

Dennis never went back to prison. In 1968, he helped launch AIM. As an eloquent and charismatic speaker, he repeatedly traveled the country organizing new chapters on reservations and in the Indian ghettos in Minneapolis, Denver, Chicago, and other cities. His leadership inside Wounded Knee had earned him a federal indictment that could send him back to prison for 180 years. I didn't know it then, but after a nine-month trial the following year the judge would dismiss all charges against Banks and his co-defendant, Russell Means, ruling that FBI agents had violated innumerable laws during their investigations and were guilty of "misconduct."

Dennis explained the early history of AIM and the complex events at Pine Ridge that had led to the seizure of Wounded Knee. He got me material published by various Indian sources I never would have found on my own. I left Minneapolis with a carton of papers and a stack of tape cassettes and headed west to the reservation. Dennis and I remained friends and saw each other for many years after that first visit.

When I got to the Pine Ridge Indian Reservation, I was in real danger. The tribal chairman, Dick Wilson, and his goon squad were no longer constrained by the presence of reporters. They had unleashed a reign of terror after Wounded Knee in which residents who had supported the seizure were beaten and raped. Then the guns came out. In July, two men were shot; one died a few weeks later. In August, a well was poisoned. In September, a man and his daughter were fired upon, and the girl lost an eye. In November, an AIM supporter was beaten to death. A week later, a sniper gunned down another, and five days later a fifteen-year-old AIM supporter was found in a ditch with a bullet through his heart. I arrived at the height of this violence, a lone white man on a reservation polarized between warring Indian factions.

The most sensational of the killings was that of Pedro Bissonette, twenty-nine, who had actively opposed Wilson's corruption. A natural leader and prominent figure during the seizure, Bissonette was stopped on a desolate road by two tribal cops and shot dead. They claimed he had gone for a gun, but autopsy evidence indicated seven bullet holes made at point-blank range. Two thousand people came to his three-day wake. Wilson barred Banks, a Chippewa, from setting foot on the Sioux reservation, so the funeral procession detoured to the edge of reservation land, where Banks, standing just over the line, spent a few minutes gazing at the body of his fallen comrade.

Wilson had been livid at the success of the airdrop. If he knew I was on the reservation, I could be his next victim. In Minneapolis, Dennis had suggested I talk to Bissonette's aunt, Gladys, who could give me clear and reliable information. I called on her first, and she greeted me with warmth and gratitude for the airlift. I spent long hours with Gladys talking into a tape recorder, then spoke to others she recommended. I conducted these interviews during the day and as inconspicuously as possible, but I drove two hours to the relative safety of Rapid City for the night.

Gladys Bissonette was in her fifties, somewhat overweight, but very spry and energetic. Deeply cut lines swept across her weather-beaten face, reflective of the harsh conditions she had lived through. She looked the same as other older women I saw on the reservation, but inside her not so unusual exterior burned intelligence and determination that were very unusual. She had been a tribal leader before and during the occupation, and her understanding of the social and political forces at play was detailed and insightful.

She was born Gladys Spotted Bear, and her grandfather was a young man in the time of Sitting Bull and Crazy Horse. At seven, over the objections of her parents, Gladys was sent to the Holy Rosary Mission School and taught to be a Catholic. The nuns beat her when she spoke Lakota, as they did the other Indian children. Nine months of the year, she lived and worked at the school and was forced to speak in English and pray in Latin. During that period, despite the harsh winters, most reservation Indians still lived in tents or simple shacks. There were no doctors or medical help, so Gladys watched a few of her playmates die of curable diseases.

Married, she became Gladys Bissonette. After growing up near Wounded Knee, she moved into the town of Pine Ridge hoping for an easier life. It never came. When I saw her in 1973, 60 percent of the reservation workforce had no employment, not even part-time. Only 9 percent of the homes had electricity, and only 5 percent had running water. A few people still lived in chicken coops and abandoned automobiles. Infant mortality was four times the national average, and overall life expectancy only 44.5 years. The Pine Ridge Reservation was an internal colony, comparable to exploited areas in the Third World, a red, white, and blue version of apartheid.

Gladys and a few other older women had organized the first protests against Wilson's corruption and had stood up to the threats and intimidation that followed. They often shamed male relatives and neighbors into more courageous acts than they would have taken on their own. When the protests proved ineffective, Gladys pushed to bring AIM to the reservation and take over Wounded Knee. My interviews with her and a dozen others she introduced me to filled another stack of tape cassettes. But during these interviews, Gladys frequently warned me to leave the reservation because my life was in danger. Indeed, it had been a frightening place to work, and after several days, when I had the material I wanted, I was happy to be on my way.

With the tape recordings of Gladys and Dennis, I could personalize an account of reservation life and chronicle the rise of Indian militancy. Adding in the other interviews and the archive of material from Minneapolis, I had what I needed to start writing. I pointed the VW camper south toward Mexico, feeling exhilarated. For the next few months, I would be free from schedules, phones, meetings, and obligations. Alone, in a place where I had little knowledge of the language, my time and routine would be mine to control. After the intense pressure and stress of the previous years, I was more than ready to embrace the solitude, at least temporarily.

I crossed the Rio Grande at El Paso, drove through Juárez and into the desert, headed for the Yucatán and the island of Cozumel. Caribbean beaches still haunted my imagination. On the eastern Caribbean islands I had roamed in 1969, relations between whites and blacks were not always comfortable. Cozumel, the western Caribbean island that Charlotte and I had visited in 1965, was populated by Mayan Indians. Never having been enslaved or economically exploited by Europeans or North Americans (although the Mexican elite had more than made up for that), Mayans harbored no resentment toward whites. Cozumel was not yet developed. Cancún did not yet exist. The entire east coast of the Yucatán Peninsula was underpopulated and free from commercial tourism. I hoped my book would make a difference, but whether it did or not, writing it on a warm Caribbean beach would at least be good for my own body and soul.

In the Yucatán, I revisited the ancient Mayan ruin sites at Uxmal and Chichén Itzá I had seen with Charlotte. Afterward, I drove to Puerto Juárez, a village on the unsettled eastern coast that in the future would become Cancún. Down the coast there was a Mexican naval installation at Puerto Morelos with a pier used by commercial fishermen. I paid one a small sum to hoist my VW onto his boat with a crane and lash it across the bow for the four-hour crossing to Cozumel.

The island had retained the peacefulness and simplicity I had experienced in 1965. The few tourists were serious scuba divers drawn to Palancar Reef, the spectacular underwater garden first popularized by Jacques Cousteau. I rented an unfurnished house on the edge of the island's one small town. The house was a one-story cinder-block construction divided into four rooms. A similar house sat on the left. However, my neighbors to the right were an extended family of Mayan Indians living in a large thatched-roof hut. Their walls were made of dried sticks tied together. Their primary language was a regional dialect of Mayan. The older ones understood little Spanish, so my conversation with them was limited to smiles and waves.

The town had six blocks of paved streets, but the street in front of my house was unpaved and very rough. I bought a couple of chairs and made a desk from a door and cinder blocks, but there was no need for a bed. Two of the four rooms had sturdy hooks about five feet off the floor that were used for hammocks. Like many tropical people, the Mayans slept off the ground to protect themselves from snakes, scorpions, and other crawling threats. Daytime, the hammocks were put away, allowing what had been a bedroom at night to serve another purpose during the day. I had to learn to sleep diagonally across a wide hammock in a more or less horizontal position, but once I did, I slept comfortably.

Thus began one of the most tranquil and relaxing times of my life. Typically, my day started with a stroll to the public market for a stack of fresh corn tortillas, some butter and lime, and whatever fresh fruit was available that day. I then wrote for two or three hours. Just before lunch, I climbed into the VW, drove to a sand beach that stretched for miles, and ran as far as I could. I had just stopped smoking, and the running kept me away from cigarettes. After lunch, there was more writing, and at mid-afternoon, the highlight of my day: a trip to a spot where coral reefs were within swimming distance of the shore.

In those years, the waters teemed with fish, and I was going after my dinner. I had snorkeling gear and a speargun and spent many idyllic hours floating over the beautiful coral gardens in pursuit of one good meal or another. I rarely came back empty-handed and occasionally even found a lobster. On a day of bad luck, a little restaurant served as a backup. After dinner, I strolled in the zocalo, the square plaza in the center of town. Occasionally, a band played, but every night I enjoyed watching the little kids run around and the bigger boys and girls edge up to each other in the usual courting rituals. Afterward, I wrote for another hour or two before climbing into my hammock for the night. The days ran into each other, and I often lost track of time, although frequent letters from home kept me apprised of events there.

I had a few visitors, among them my old friend Scott Van Leuven. We had drifted apart, but when we got into the ocean to spearfish together, it felt like old times. We killed a large barracuda, gutted it on the beach, and gave it to the Mayan family living in the hut next door. They fed the head to a feral cat. A lethal disease, ciguatera, was poisoning some of the fish, and the cat was a convenient way to test for it. Later, we shared a great meal, but as usual the conversation was limited to smiles, gestures, nods, and waves.

The months passed. I picked up a little Spanish, celebrated my thirty-third birthday, and lived my simple life as a writer. It was a serene time and I enjoyed it immensely, but after several months monotony crept in and ate away at my contentment. I finished a first draft of the book in the spring, said good-bye to a few new friends, and got my VW camper back on the mainland.

I made the long drive through Mexico and the southeastern states to Washington. Larry Levin had good news. More groups had joined the antiwar lobbying effort, and a broader coalition had formed, now called the United Campaign. In March, while I was in Cozumel, Nixon had requested $474 million to supplement the December appropriation of $1.1 billion for the Thieu regime in South Viet Nam. It was roughly the same amount our lobbying had cut from his original request of $1.6 billion. Nixon was trying to undo his congressional defeat. Tens of thousands associated with the United Campaign rose up in anger and lobbied against his request. It was defeated in the House of Representatives. Nixon then requested another $1.6 billion for South Viet Nam for the coming year. The United Campaign was prepared to make opposition to that demand its main task over the next few months. There was plenty of work still to be done.

Once back at my desk in the MAI office, I saw that changes had taken place. MAI continued to raise substantial sums for the Bach Mai Hospital Emergency Relief Fund, and while the staff had more difficulty bringing in money for MAI's other projects, the organization remained viable and effective, at least financially. Yet it was losing its political edge, focusing instead on postwar reconciliation and humanitarian relief for war wounded. The antiwar movement's strategic imperative was to cut funding for the Thieu regime. MAI encouraged its donors to lobby their representatives and senators to that end, but the organization's main concern had to be raising money and finding new donors, not finding new people to lobby Congress. War raged on in Indochina, so MAI's work continued to be meaningful, but it had gradually moved from the strategic center to the sidelines. I didn't want to be on the sidelines.

I mulled over what to do and, among others, talked to Tom Hayden. He invited me to move to Los Angeles and join Jane Fonda and him in the leadership of the Indochina Peace Campaign. IPC was at the center of the lobbying effort and was providing much of the printed material and analysis that was driving it, along with a lot of the strategic leadership. I would not have considered his offer earlier, but after enjoying California so much the year before, and missing the last winter in Cozumel, I thought winter-free Southern California sounded pretty good. I discussed the move with friends, and in June called Tom and agreed to come.

It was difficult saying good-bye to housemates and co-workers with whom I had shared so much, and hard to contemplate moving to an unknown city where I had only two friends. But finding the most effective way to help stop the war was what I most wanted, and with that in mind I knew it was time to move on. I sold the VW camper and bought an old VW sedan, dark red with a sunroof. With my worldly goods thrown on the backseat, I set off driving west once again. This time I took it easy, avoided the interstate highways, and crossed the entire country on back roads. A lot had changed. The culture of the sixties had burst out of the urban areas and college campuses and swept through the little cities and small towns. I saw it in how people dressed and acted, and I heard it in their conversations. After an interesting trip, I arrived in Los Angeles on the Fourth of July 1974.

CHAPTER 25

THE INDOCHINA PEACE CAMPAIGN OCCUPIED A TWO-STORY ART DECO BUILDING A block from the beach at the far south end of Santa Monica. Tom, Jane, and four others worked in it full-time. Jack Nicholl and Carol Kurtz, long-time friends of Tom's from the Berkeley antiwar movement, and their young son lived in a Santa Monica beach house with Jane and Tom, their infant son, and Jane's daughter from a previous marriage. Paul Ryder and Susan Wind (now Early) were younger and shared an apartment a mile away in Venice with Susan's young son. I moved in with them and laughingly gave friends back east my very California address: corner of Speedway and Horizon.

Speedway is an alley that runs behind the Venice boardwalk and is only a few steps from the beach. And what a beach! The Easterner in me was shocked to discover that a two-block section at the base of Horizon had been designated clothing optional. On any sunny weekend day, there were hundreds of naked people sunbathing or frolicking in the water, even though the beach was at the edge of a densely populated urban neighborhood. Ah, California! (The nude beach survived less than a year before the authorities ran out of patience.)

Despite the pleasant surroundings, people at IPC worked with the same intensity and dedication I was used to back east. They, too, were troublemakers who had devoted years to the cause and were determined to go on as long as necessary. And they were 100 percent focused on the congressional strategy. Starting with their tour in 1972, IPC had built a large network of activists and a chapter structure in about forty cities. The chapters sponsored leafleting, door-to-door work, teach-ins, visits to the district offices of representatives and senators, film screenings, and educational speakers, all designed to get more people to call or write elected officials in Washington.

The IPC staff issued news releases in response to breaking events, but their primary mission was to produce educational materials about Viet Nam, Laos, and Cambodia, the three countries of Indochina. The staff also published a biweekly newspaper, *Focal Point*. A huge effort was required to publish the paper, but we had to supplement the limited and often distorted information activists got in the press. The paper became the glue that held our national network together. Its name expressed our view that Indochina was the "focal point" of a worldwide struggle between economic imperialism and national liberation movements, another reason the war was so important to us.

After we had cut Nixon's request for $1.6 billion in assistance to South Viet Nam for the current year to $1.1 billion, he requested another $1.6 billion for the coming year. The goal of IPC and the United Campaign was to make an even deeper cut in that request. Again, we didn't feel we had enough strength to block it all, but Nixon was losing support because of Watergate and we were optimistic. We had good reason. Two of the three strategic goals we had set for ourselves the year before had been achieved. We had stopped the bombing of Cambodia and defunded Thieu's prison system. If we succeeded in our final goal, cutting money for military operations in South Viet Nam, we knew the war could not be sustained.

Our intense work during July and early August led to another dramatic success. The House voted on August 6 to cut Nixon's new request from $1.6 billion to $700 million. The Senate would later concur. It was a watershed victory. Having cut a third from South Viet Nam's current budget, the antiwar movement succeeded in cutting more than half from the next. The big cut would limit Thieu's ability to wage war. He would have less of what he needed most: fuel, guns, and ammunition.

The August 6 vote soon became a watershed of another sort. Nixon had lobbied hard for the full $1.6 billion. His stinging defeat in the House, coupled with articles of impeachment voted out of the House Judiciary Committee only two weeks before, finally convinced him his time was up. On August 9, Richard Nixon became the first American president to resign in disgrace. House opposition was too great for him to withstand an impeachment proceeding. I watched the footage as his helicopter lifted off the South Lawn at the White House, and cheered wildly with the rest of the IPC staff. I felt enormous satisfaction. For six years, Nixon had been the embodiment of everything I had fought against. Seeing him slink away in shame and dishonor vindicated my decision to stay committed to antiwar work.

We cheered, too, because Nixon was the second president we in the antiwar movement had driven from office. He was undone because of his paranoia about us. Disturbed by massive demonstrations during his first term, he became convinced of conspiracies between the antiwar movement, his critics in the press, his opponents in Congress, and the North Vietnamese. The more he failed to uncover such conspiracies, the more reckless he became. At the Watergate headquarters of the Democratic Party, Nixon actually hoped to find evidence tying Senator George McGovern, his 1972 presidential opponent, to an illegal plot.

Nixon's fundamental error was in not believing that opposition to the war had become a genuine mass movement, that it had radiated from a small core of protesters to an eventual embrace by Americans in every corner of society. The two burglaries Nixon authorized at Watergate and at Dan Ellsberg's psychiatrist's office, burglaries that eventually brought him down, were motivated by his paranoia over antiwar opponents. Enormous power, overarching authority, hubris, and arrogance: the saga had all the elements of a Greek tragedy, but the simple truth is that if the antiwar movement had not been there, Nixon most certainly would have served out his full second term. Knowing I had played even a minuscule role in that outcome was all the reward I needed.

However, while it lifted our hearts, Nixon's resignation had little impact on our work. Vice President Gerald Ford assumed office and vowed to continue Nixon's foreign and domestic policies. We vowed to oppose him. But the August 6 legislation that cut military aid to South

Viet Nam contained an unrelated provision that was of special interest to me. It was a ban on additional money for the development of binary nerve gas. Binary nerve gas was what had driven me out of scientific research. The scientist at Fort Detrick who had asked Bart Meyers for a copy of his research report was developing a binary nerve gas for the Army. ("Binary" meant it became lethal only when its two components were combined in the field.) Nerve gas had driven the two of us out of scientific research, and on August 6 we rejoiced as the House bill very properly drove nerve gas out of science.

Shortly after the passage of that landmark legislation, members of the Justice Department contacted Mark Amsterdam, my attorney in the Wounded Knee case, and offered to drop all criminal charges if the airlift defendants pleaded guilty to violating three federal air regulations and paid a $500 fine for each. Instead of fifteen years, they offered fines of only $1,500, no prison time, and no criminal record. It was a great victory, but their offer made it clear that they lacked confidence in their own case.

Their problem was obvious. If prosecutors claimed we dropped guns, which would effectively bias jurors against us, we had eyewitness testimony to the contrary from Tom Oliphant, who watched the bags being packed, and from Bob Talbot's neighbors in Chicago who had helped. On the other hand, if prosecutors admitted we had dropped only food, we simply didn't believe any jury would send us to prison. Apparently, prosecutors didn't either.

Ours was not the only Wounded Knee trial still pending, but it was one of the easiest to win. If we kept it alive, the government would have fewer legal resources to devote to the other Wounded Knee defendants. Also, two of the airdrop crew, Bob Talbot and Bill Wright, were professional pilots. If they pleaded guilty to violations of federal air regulations, their careers would significantly suffer. I was not in a compromising mood. I told Mark to reject the offer and challenge them to take us to trial.

The news about nerve gas and Wounded Knee was very pleasing. I had taken significant risks over the years: quitting science for politics, bringing stolen antibiotics to the North Vietnamese, defying the Treasury Department when it threatened to prosecute MAI for trading with the enemy, and flying the airlift to help the Indians. Each had entailed a calculated and reasonable risk, but was a gamble nonetheless. After returning from Mississippi in 1963, I had posed for myself a choice between a life that was predictably safe and secure and one that was unpredictable, not safe or secure, but more stirring and perhaps more consequential. Twelve years later, I was confident I had chosen well.

I didn't know at the time that only a week hence I would be forced to consider that calculus once more. After winning the August 6 vote, the IPC staff prepared to escalate our efforts. We assumed the balance of forces was shifting in our direction, and we were determined to take maximum advantage. As a start, we invited activists across the country to a rustic lodge in the mountains east of Los Angeles for a weeklong organizer training session in late August. There, along with skilled friends from other organizations, we taught the classes. We had spent years as organizers ourselves, often under the most trying conditions, and we wanted to pass on what we knew so others could expand our work.

Tom left the mountain retreat a day early and returned to Santa Monica. The next morning, he called and asked me to come back to deal with a situation that could not be discussed over the phone. He said he would pick me up on a street corner in Santa Monica later that afternoon. At the appointed hour, Tom's light blue VW pulled up, and I squeezed into the backseat. An attractive woman sat next to him. She was dark haired, casually dressed, and about my age. Tom introduced me to Joan Andersson, whose name I recognized. She was a founder of the Bar Sinister, one of the original law collectives working to assist activists and other clients unable to afford more traditional lawyers. She was a frequent public speaker and had recently defended Latino activists falsely accused of setting fires in a hotel after Governor Ronald Reagan gave a speech there condemning bilingual education.

Tom turned up the radio, standard practice to foil microphones that might be planted in the car. We were well aware that he and Jane were subjects of intense FBI and L.A. police red squad surveillance. With the radio blaring, Tom told me that Huey Newton, chairman and co-founder of the Black Panther Party, had skipped bail on a trumped-up murder charge in Oakland and was trying to get to Cuba, where he would be safe from extradition to the United States.

Huey had sought help from a famous friend in Hollywood, Bert Schneider, who was hiding him in his Mexican beach house. Bert had produced *Easy Rider*, a breakthrough countercultural film in 1969, and had just finished a feature documentary, *Hearts and Minds*, which was not yet released but promised to be a devastating attack on the war in Viet Nam (it won an Academy Award the following spring). The only way to get a fugitive to Cuba was to smuggle him in, and the quickest way to do that was by private plane. Bert needed a pilot. He didn't know me, but he had heard about my flight into Wounded Knee, so he called Jane to find me, and she asked Tom to set up a meeting. The airlift had made me the go-to pilot in left-wing America, but the price of that notoriety was to be first in line for missions like this.

Tom made it clear that he and Jane were too closely watched to participate in any attempt to help Huey, and in any case did not want to jeopardize our antiwar work by getting involved. I, too, was ambivalent, but pointed out that before anyone even considered flying Huey to Cuba, advance arrangements would have to be made with the Cuban military. Otherwise, an aircraft intruding in the country's airspace would likely be shot down. Tom gestured toward Joan. She had contacts with the Cubans and would try to get permission. Since Tom did not want to be involved, I asked her to walk with me on the nearby beach and talk it over.

I was skeptical. Here was a risk that not only stretched the limits of personal safety but also put me on very ambiguous moral and legal grounds. Was it justified? Now, in the context of my present work? Ever? Huey Newton was an important national and international symbol of the fight for equal rights. He had achieved celebrity status as a determined leader. The Panthers were the most militant part of the civil rights movement, so I felt it especially important he and his image be protected. But my priority was to stop the war, and I was unwilling to be diverted from that goal even if the personal risk could be minimized and I came to believe it was the right thing to do.

Joan had worked with and defended the Panthers, and as we strolled on the sand, she reminded me of all that the FBI and police departments in Oakland, Los Angeles, and elsewhere had done to sabotage and undermine them, including shootings, false imprisonments, forgeries, theft, and undercover provocateurs. Her arguments had an impact. Once more, I was confronted with the "good German" dilemma: How far do you go to resist your own government when it acts illegally or immorally?

But before struggling with the answer, I had to find out if a flight was feasible at all. Joan chaired the international committee of the National Lawyers Guild, a progressive bar association, and had spent time with Cuban officials in Havana. I told her I would not even consider flying into Cuban airspace unless I had permission from Fidel Castro himself. Joan blanched at my audacity but understood it was justified. She offered to go to New York and launch such a request through diplomats she could approach at the Cuban mission to the United Nations.

Joan was as curious about me as I was about her, so we kept walking on the beach long after dark. We tried to grapple with the moral and legal ambiguities that came with Huey's flight, but we had no ambivalence about his intended destination. Like most people on the left, we considered Castro a revolutionary hero who had overcome U.S. sabotage to feed and house his people, erase Cuban illiteracy, create the single best medical system in the Third World, and end the economic oppression previously endemic to Cuba.

As we walked, it was hard not to notice that Joan was a brilliant and beautiful woman with a fierce integrity and obvious personal courage. She had a buoyant and open personality and a ready smile. It was a warm and balmy night. The deserted beach was illuminated by a full moon reflected in the rippling waves. Our conversation drifted away from résumés and politics. We talked about ourselves, got better acquainted, and thoroughly enjoyed each other's company.

Early the next morning I met Bert Schneider. He was tall and wiry, about forty, with wavy blond hair and movie-star good looks, but he was very nervous and understood he might be in well over his head. He had gotten Huey over the border and down to his beach house on the Pacific coast, but that was still a long way from Cuba. I told him that Joan was ready to go to New York to find out if the Cubans would accept an incoming flight, but she needed her expenses covered. He promised to provide whatever money was necessary.

That afternoon Joan boarded the last flight to New York. I had been impressed by Bert's daring in helping Huey, and told her so. His liberty and a lucrative movie career were on the line. Previously, he had been an outspoken supporter of the antiwar and civil rights movements, so I thought we had a responsibility to protect him, as well as Huey. In New York, Joan contacted a Cuban diplomat at the UN and arranged a secret rendezvous in Central Park. She was advised that the Cuban government welcomed refugees from American injustice, like Huey, but would do nothing to assist them. If Huey arrived in Cuba, he would be accepted, but they would not alter their air defense procedures to accommodate his entry.

I explained to Bert that there was no way to fly Huey into Cuba without serious risk of fatalities, including Huey's. The only way to get him there safely was by boat. Bert understood. Over the next two weeks, he and his friends found a sailboat captain who smuggled Huey onto the island. He stayed for three years. In 1977, with a new Democratic administration in office, Huey thought he could get a fair trial and returned. He was right. Later that year, he was acquitted of all charges, and in 1980 he earned a Ph.D. But throughout those years, the FBI kept up its illegal campaign against the Black Panther Party, instigating devastating splits within it, some of which became violent. The party was forced to dissolve, and in 1989, Huey was murdered on an Oakland street not far from where they had first organized.

In September, my co-workers on the IPC staff and the rest of the national antiwar movement continued to build on our August successes. The House vote that had cut aid to South Viet Nam to $700 million energized our supporters, and the successful organizers' school helped expand our activist network. But we had no desire to rest on our laurels. We seized the opportunity to expand our lobbying strength and worked at it meticulously. We knew we had become players in a great drama, which was confirmed on September 21, 1974, in a *New York Times* article. David Shipler, writing from Saigon on the effect of the budget cuts, said: "The reduction in military aid has already prompted Government forces to retreat from some isolated outposts that would have been defended vigorously a few months ago. The army has stopped firing most of the artillery shells it used to lob randomly into Communist-held areas. This week the Saigon military command announced the curtailment of air force flights to conserve fuel and ammunition . . . According to military men, however, the cuts are not deep enough to cause Saigon's quick defeat." Not yet, they weren't. But this news was music to our ears. It was the outcome we had worked for, and we were determined not to let up.

We in IPC collaborated with the other organizations in the United Campaign to promote the International Week of Concern in late September and early October. Lectures and teach-ins were held in locations across the country protesting further military aid for South Viet Nam and Cambodia. Displays of tiger cages were set up and occupied by protesters playing the role of South Vietnamese political prisoners. Thousands of voters visited their representatives and senators in Washington or in their district offices, and tens of thousands more wrote or called to voice their opinions. Our momentum continued to grow, and we kept the pressure on.

During that fall period, I stole a little time to work on the airlift book. Much to my surprise, despite so much happening around me, I was also falling in love with Joan Andersson and spending time with her. There was much to feel good about, but all of us in IPC were upset by intense criticism from people on the far left. They argued that by participating in the system, that is, by lobbying Congress, we were leading people astray instead of building support for more fundamental change.

Some of this criticism came from old friends who had migrated further left, and because it was couched in harsh and uncompromising political rhetoric, it often took the form of hurtful personal attacks. These people clung to outmoded revolutionary organizations isolated from the working class they hoped to organize. With no revolution on the horizon, these Maoists, Stalinists, Marxist-Leninists, Trotskyists, and anarchists descended into a swamp of sectarian bickering, each claiming they represented the true path.

I had no trouble rejecting such ultraleft sectarianism. However, criticism also came from nonsectarian friends still committed to revolutionary goals and ideologically opposed to attempts to reform the political system from within. However mistaken I considered them, when they called me a counterrevolutionary and claimed I had sold out, it hurt, and it led me to a new wariness about the role of ideology in social movements.

The New Left had both helped and been inspired by the civil rights movement in the early 1960s, and to a great extent had spawned the anti-war movement in the mid-1960s. The New Left came into existence because young activists rejected the rigid ideology that had limited the thinking of people in the old left, and limited what their organizations, like the Communist Party USA and the Congress of Industrial Organizations, could do to build support. Throwing off those ideological blinders led to our initial success. Unfortunately, allowing those blinders to be put back in place a decade later led to our ultimate failure.

America will forever be in debt to the New Left for sparking movements against war, racism, environmental degradation, and ethnic and gender discrimination. However, we failed to forge those protest movements into a unified political force with a positive and credible agenda for fundamental change. That failure was provoked in part by impatient activists who looked for shortcuts in foreign ideologies like Maoism. There was no fit to American realities, and by the end of 1974 their strategic capitulation had trapped them in ideological straitjackets. Ironically, the New Left, born of a desire to overcome ideological rigidity, collapsed on its deathbed, a victim of the same disease.

I had moved in the opposite direction. I saw no practical path to revolutionary change despite believing such change was needed. Instead of surrendering or tilting perpetually at windmills, instead of my letting the perfect become the enemy of the good, I decided to work for lesser goals that could actually be achieved. Our lobbying success convinced me that it was wrong not to pursue incremental change within the existing political system if more fundamental change was not possible. For me, it was simply a matter of weighing real political achievement against merely being politically correct.

CHAPTER 26

ON DECEMBER 6, 1974, THE NORTH VIETNAMESE ARMY (NVA) AND THE NATIONAL LIBER-
ation Front (NLF) of South Viet Nam launched an offensive in South
Viet Nam's mountainous Central Highlands, most aggressively in the
province of Phuoc Long. By December 18, their forces had cut off
the provincial capital, Phuoc Binh, which could no longer be supplied
except by helicopter. Simultaneously, a number of district capitals, the
equivalent of our county seats, fell to their forces in other parts of the
country. The NVA and NLF had captured the strategic initiative in
the war. No doubt, the cutbacks for South Viet Nam's military had played
a role.

We applauded this development, but at the same time realized that
conservatives would use the heightened military activity and the threat to
the Thieu regime as an excuse to build support for increasing U.S. military aid. We wanted to head off that possibility, so we suggested to the
other antiwar groups in the United Campaign that we co-host a national
gathering in Washington the weekend of January 25–26. It would be the
second anniversary of the Paris Peace Accords, signed on January 27,
1973, an ideal time for voters to come to the Capitol and remind members of Congress that their constituents wanted peace.

We enlisted prestigious antiwar clergymen as co-sponsors and called
the gathering the Assembly to Save the Peace Agreement. We were determined to recruit as many citizen lobbyists as possible, provide them with

training, education, and entertainment over the weekend, and on Monday, January 27, the actual anniversary, and Tuesday coordinate their visits to the offices of representatives and senators in the Capitol.

The IPC staff put me in charge of organizing the assembly. We expected thousands to attend rather than the hundreds of thousands who had come to protest in years past, so the planning and organizational work was not difficult. I spent four weeks in Washington and received competent help from people who had worked on past demonstrations, most notably Gail Pressberg. Together we obtained a hall for a large audience, got police permits for a march to the White House, found meeting rooms where state delegations could discuss their joint presentations to elected officials, located rooms for the press to conduct interviews with our spokespeople, recruited musicians, and wrote and printed the instructions and directions that would allow events to flow smoothly.

On Saturday, January 25, the citizen lobbyists recruited by the United Campaign organizations descended on Washington. We had arranged to house some in space volunteered by local residents, and we had organized a full set of activities and training sessions over the weekend, including seminars and lectures on the history of the war, the provisions of the peace accords, and the current state of affairs in Viet Nam and Cambodia. Our lobbyists had to be prepared to debate fine points of policy with elected officials and congressional staff on Monday.

Sunday evening we gathered everyone at the New York Avenue Presbyterian Church. It was only two blocks from the White House grounds, and in the other direction only four blocks from Mount Vernon Square, the area my delegation from Illinois had blocked during the Mayday protests. We recruited Senator George McGovern to give the keynote address. He was passionate about ending combat in Indochina and happy to speak to so receptive an audience. An appearance by a national figure of his stature helped motivate many of those present.

After other short speeches, Joan Baez walked onto the stage with her guitar. She sang for a long time because the audience loved her and would not let her stop. Her voice, so extraordinary when she was a young folksinger, had grown even stronger. At thirty-four, she was a politically sophisticated woman, confident in her pacifism, and accomplished in motivating activists with her performances. When the assembly ended, we lined up for a candlelight march to the White House. With three thousand participants, our line snaked around the grounds close enough for President Ford to see us.

When Monday came, our people swarmed over the Capitol. Its corridors and the adjacent Senate and House office buildings were crowded with citizens wearing antiwar buttons, carrying signs, and distributing literature. Delegations of dozens could be seen entering or leaving the offices of any representative or senator not immovably for or against us. Our people all made it clear they were registered voters. They had a big impact but in a manner entirely different from the militant mass demonstrations of the past.

Our earlier concerns about conservatives using the new offensive in Viet Nam as an excuse to increase aid were justified. A week before the assembly, President Ford announced that the deteriorating military situation in Indochina required him to ask Congress for emergency assistance. He waited until the day after the anniversary of the peace accords, then requested an additional $300 million in military aid for South Viet Nam and $222 million more in military assistance for Cambodia. Leading senators and representatives, even some who had been pro-war, gave him a lukewarm reception, but that was no guarantee they would actually vote against the requests. We had to spool our lobbying campaign back up to full strength because the fight against Ford's request would be decisive in stopping the war.

I stayed in Washington for the rest of the week to assist Larry Levin, still at the helm of the Coalition to Stop Funding the War. His group had coordinated the citizen lobbying on Monday and Tuesday and now had to build a new campaign to defeat Ford's request. Many activists who had come to Washington to lobby also stayed. Late Tuesday night, the Weather Underground set off a bomb in the State Department. It detonated in a men's room on the third floor, injuring only the toilets. The bombers wanted to help the situation but as usual only made it worse. Our strategy was to show members of Congress that mainstream American voters had joined forces with the antiwar movement. Bombing the State Department sent the opposite message.

Back in Santa Monica, the IPC staff joined the other organizations in the United Campaign to push hard for the defeat of Ford's supplemental request. The assembly in Washington had convinced new people to join us, given us new organizing contacts, and expanded our network into new geographic areas. Collectively, we had gained credibility with members of Congress who had not previously been allies. But while our message enjoyed a new receptiveness on Capitol Hill, we feared Ford's request would be difficult to defeat given phony conservative rhetoric about the need to save a loyal "friend" like President Thieu.

That made February a busy month, but at the end of it I received a welcome gift. Several weeks before, President Ford had appointed Edward Levi, the president of the University of Chicago, as his new attorney general. Levi and I had negotiated the end of the 1966 sit-in at the UC Administration Building. With him as attorney general, we had a new relationship, since he was in charge of the criminal case still pending against five airlift defendants, including me. His unequivocal response came on February 27, two years to the day after Indians on the Pine Ridge Reservation first seized Wounded Knee. All charges against us were dropped. No reason was given, but perhaps a more level-headed administration than Nixon's had become embarrassed by our indictment, and indeed by the entire federal involvement at Wounded Knee. But I doubt that the date was an accident. Nor do I doubt that Attorney General Levi recognized my name among the defendants. There is some value in winning an opponent's respect.

It was an important victory, more for the other defendants than for me. In later years, with no criminal records, three of them were able to pursue careers from which they otherwise would have been excluded. With racial barriers down, Bill Wright got a job flying midsized jets for Comair, Delta Air Lines' regional carrier. He worked his way up to captain and flew until mandatory retirement at age sixty. Bob Talbot moved from the political right to the political left. He flew very dangerous missions in the mountains of Guatemala for Maryknoll missionaries, then piloted DC-8 jets between the United States and Europe for Flying Tigers. They fired him for trying to organize a union. He got another job flying international cargo but died of a heart attack at fifty-nine. Jim Stewart went back to school, earned a Ph.D. in physics, and became a longtime professor at Western Washington University. His research there focuses on how to better train science teachers for the public schools.

I had little time to celebrate the Wounded Knee victory because in early March fighting dramatically escalated in Viet Nam. NVA and NLF forces gathered in very large numbers around the city of Ban Me Thuot, another provincial capital in South Viet Nam's Central Highlands. On March 10, they launched a massive assault against the city. The next day, it fell when fully half of the four thousand defenders surrendered or deserted their posts.

On March 13, two days later, President Thieu made a fateful decision. He abandoned three provinces in the Central Highlands: Darlac, of which Ban Me Thuot was the capital, Pleiku, and Kontum. These three provinces constituted 16 percent of the geographic area of the entire country. Those civilians still loyal to the government began a chaotic migration toward Saigon. The roads were hopelessly clogged as swarms of people fled with whatever they could carry. Cars could not get through the throngs and were abandoned. Those throngs were swollen with army deserters who had shed their uniforms to avoid being shot by soldiers still loyal to the government. The NVA and the NLF took quick advantage of the chaos and attacked small cities and military outposts throughout the country.

Our lobbying had become a critical factor, and we knew it. If Ford got his emergency funding, Thieu would hang on and the war would continue. If he didn't, there was a chance the NVA and the NLF could eventually march all the way to Saigon. Every morning I scanned the papers the way Americans devoured battle maps during World War II, and every day there was news. On March 19, the coastal city of Quang Tri fell. It was South Viet Nam's northernmost city, above Hue and Da Nang. Five days later, another coastal city, Tam Ky, just south of Hue and Da Nang, also fell. On March 25, the ancient city of Hue, the precolonial capital of Viet Nam, was captured. The State Department had to airlift forty thousand people out of Da Nang to locations farther south.

The war was at an obvious turning point, and nobody saw it more clearly than troops in the South Vietnamese army. Their remaining units in the northern provinces all broke ranks and deserted. Where thousands had been on the roads fleeing with their possessions, the new collapse of South Vietnamese authority on the northern coast forced hundreds of thousands to become refugees and jam the roads as they too fled south.

It was a disaster. Ford ordered the chief of staff of the U.S. Army to fly to Saigon the morning after Hue was lost to assess the rapidly deteriorating military options and make recommendations to Congress about additional funding. It was too late. Congress brought Ford's request for emergency military aid to a vote. This was the moment of truth, and before the day ended, the additional $522 million in military assistance for South Viet Nam and Cambodia, crucial to their survival, was defeated. We had won! It was the single most important victory since we had launched the congressional strategy two years before.

Five days later, on March 30, Da Nang was captured when a hundred thousand South Vietnamese army troops surrendered after being abandoned by their officers. At the same time, equally decisive military action took place in Cambodia. The rebel forces of the Khmer Rouge slowly moved toward and then encircled the capital city of Phnom Penh, still under the control of General Lon Nol, the military dictator loyal to the United States.

The defeat of the $522 million in supplemental military aid was decisive, and those of us who had pushed the lobbying strategy deserved most of the credit for it. With that vote, the United States lost control of the war. Our lobbying campaign had put war supporters on the defensive and effectively focused antiwar opinion on the Congress, where it did the most good. The next, and hopefully the last, phase of the war would be determined by events on the battlefield. I assumed that President Thieu and General Lon Nol would concentrate what was left of their respective armies around their capitals and dig in for a lengthy rearguard action. That could mean more work for us in that it would likely lead to desperate requests for financial help from Congress, which we had to be prepared to oppose.

My analysis may have been logical, but I could not have been more wrong about the timing of events. On April 1, General Lon Nol was forced to flee Cambodia in fear for his life. The Khmer Rouge gained control of both banks of the Mekong River, which meant the United States could only supply the capital city of Phnom Penh by helicopter. The Khmer Rouge then obtained rockets capable of bringing down the helicopters, and supplies rapidly dwindled. In Viet Nam, only a week later, a very large NVA force attacked the city of Xuan Loc. I found that amazing since Xuan Loc was only thirty-eight miles from Saigon.

Throughout the first half of April, along with everyone else in the antiwar movement, I was transfixed by the news from Indochina. On April 13, helicopters evacuated all personnel from the U.S. embassy in Phnom Penh. That could only mean that U.S. leaders thought the city was about to fall. We watched, mesmerized, for four days until, on April 17, the Khmer Rouge marched triumphantly into Phnom Penh. The war in Cambodia was over.

We celebrated, not knowing the horror that was to come. Our opposition to U.S. support for the brutal military dictatorship of Lon Nol failed to consider the possibility that his opponents could be far worse. They were. The leaders of the Khmer Rouge suffered from extreme ideological rigidity and were convinced they could erase all traces of "Western" corruption by forcing their entire population, professionals and skilled workers included, out of the cities and into collective farms. The war provoked by the United States had so brutalized these previously peaceful people that extreme violence became commonplace. Over the next three years, close to two million Cambodians died. The horror only came to an end when the new Vietnamese government, appalled at the killings across its border, toppled the Khmer Rouge and installed a government in Phnom Penh that has survived to this day.

After the abrupt collapse of the Lon Nol regime, attention shifted back to Viet Nam. There too the long years of military stalemate were coming to an amazingly rapid conclusion. On April 21, Graham Martin, the U.S. ambassador to South Viet Nam, met with President Thieu. Dispensing with the sham that Thieu was the legitimate leader of an allied nation, Martin exercised his authority as the American proconsul and ordered Thieu to resign. Furious, Thieu made a bitter speech attacking the United States. He then consoled himself by fleeing to Taiwan with hundreds of millions of dollars stolen from the aid the United States had given to South Viet Nam. The next day, Xuan Loc, the city thirty-eight miles from Saigon, fell after a two-week battle.

These clear-cut victories were astonishing after so many years of battlefield stalemate. Previously, the war had its decisive battles and large-scale offensives but had always returned to an equilibrium in which both sides traded gains and losses. This was different. On April 23, we were shocked at the news that a hundred thousand NVA soldiers were advancing on Saigon itself. President Ford spoke that same day at Tulane University. Recognizing that Congress had tied his hands by refusing more military aid, he said that Viet Nam was "a war that is finished as far as America is concerned."

The final blow came sooner than I had thought possible. By April 27, Saigon had been encircled. South Vietnamese army officers fled, leaving thirty thousand troops leaderless and marooned. The NVA fired rockets into downtown Saigon, the first time in the long course of the war. The city disintegrated into chaos as all civil authority disappeared. Widespread looting took place. The next day, a South Vietnamese general took over the presidency and called for a cease-fire. He was ignored. By then, we at IPC had given up our work and were spending all of our time monitoring the news. Our job was done. The Vietnamese were about to end the war.

On April 29, the NVA shelled Tan Son Nhut Air Base outside Saigon. Years before, this massive military facility had been the busiest airport in the world. After the shelling, civilians tore down the fences and looted whatever they could carry away. Ford ordered the immediate helicopter evacuation of all Americans and their closest Vietnamese associates. No one in the military had expected the collapse to come so soon or so abruptly, so the evacuation fell into chaos. At Tan Son Nhut, panicked South Vietnamese fearful of the NVA swarmed over the departing helicopters. They clung to the landing skids, preventing the choppers from taking off. Some got airborne, and those holding on lost their grips and fell to their deaths.

The Americans moved the evacuation to the embassy. Armed Marines held off thousands of desperate Saigon residents trying to flee the country. Helicopters rotated into the compound one at a time, loaded up, and took off for three aircraft carriers standing by in coastal waters. South Vietnamese pilots with access to helicopters stole them and flew to the carriers with friends and family, then refused to leave. There was no room for new arrivals to land, so helicopters were pushed over the side. In eighteen hours, a thousand Americans and seven thousand South Vietnamese were flown out of Saigon. Many times that number of Vietnamese, who had been employed by the Americans and promised evacuation, were left behind.

At 8:35 a.m. on April 30, 1975, the last ten Marines left the embassy, finally ending, in shame and in chaos, the long and tragic American presence in Viet Nam. That morning a Dutch photographer snapped a picture of a long line of Vietnamese civilians climbing up a ladder to the narrow roof of a building where a lone helicopter prepared to lift off. There were many dozens in the line but room for only ten on the chopper. It was widely believed to be a picture of the last helicopter to leave the American embassy, and as such it came to be the defining photo of the American defeat. In fact, it was the roof of a nearby apartment building.

NVA and NLF forces encountered no resistance as they poured into Saigon. Their trucks and tanks streamed down the boulevards, while soldiers rode on top waving flags and brandishing weapons. On the sidewalks, many cheered, while others looked on wondering what to expect. By 11:00 a.m., the red, blue, and gold flag of the Provisional Revolutionary Government of South Viet Nam flew above the presidential palace acknowledging the unconditional surrender of South Viet Nam. America's most tragic and destructive foreign intervention was over. The Vietnamese people, who had fought for their independence against the French, the Japanese, the French again, and finally the Americans, were a free and unified country for the first time since the nineteenth century. Ho Chi Minh's vision, born under colonial rule in the 1920s, was finally realized.

I didn't know what to feel: elation, triumph, anger, sadness, loss. I felt them all. It had been a ten-year odyssey. When it started, I wanted only to stop an unjust war and avoid becoming a good German. By the time it ended, I had rejected my own country and helped an enemy I had grown to respect. The sacrifices along the way had been well worth the result, and the victory was also mine to embrace. I briefly felt myself atop the tanks rolling down the streets of Saigon, but my triumphal thoughts dissolved into remorse at all that had been lost and destroyed.

In 1964, when they launched the American war, the CIA and the State Department lived in a fog of anticommunist hysteria. It took them eleven years to understand the obvious. Viet Nam had a two-thousand-year history of subjugation by, and warfare with, China and would never willingly become its vassal. Competent intelligence work should have easily revealed that the Vietnamese were fighting for national independence, not an economic ideology. They repeatedly stated they would fight for their freedom for as long as it took and to the last man. Since they had been doing exactly that more or less continuously since the 1930s, the evidence was compelling enough to take them at their word. I had been a mere student in 1964, but like so many others I had simply gone to the library, where this information was readily available.

Naive as we were at the time, we did our homework. One of our bitterest opponents, Johnson's defense secretary, Robert McNamara, admitted long after the war that U.S. policy makers had made two fundamental errors in Viet Nam. First, they failed to study and understand the "enemy." Second, they relied on advanced technological weapons ill suited for fighting a sophisticated guerrilla force. Activists had understood both points almost from the beginning. Arrogant policy makers like McNamara had never even tried. Instead, they thoughtlessly sent a generation of American youth to war and provoked the bitter and paralyzing divisions that continue to cripple our nation.

Stopping the war was the moral and political crusade that defined my early life and the life of my generation. When it ended, I felt exhilarated. I had stood for what was right and good, been ridiculed, rejected, and punished for it, but utterly vindicated in the end. I also felt great sadness. Over fifty thousand young Americans died because of the conceits of power-mad advisers like McNamara and Kissinger and the two presidents who empowered them. At the time, we thought they had also killed a million Vietnamese — later we learned it was more. This cataclysm, with all the lost limbs, maimed bodies and minds, injuries, illnesses, birth defects, and displacements, had been for nothing.

I was proud to have resisted. At the beginning, we were a tiny band of protesters, a handful, but we stood our ground despite the hostility of almost everyone around us. We nurtured that tiny band into the largest antiwar movement in the history of the world, and on the morning of April 30, 1975, we prevailed. Until the Tet Offensive in 1968, we had been unsure of the outcome. After Tet, we knew that history had reached a turning point. Europeans had pushed west since 1492, first across the Atlantic, then as Americans across the new continent, and finally as imperialists into the Pacific to seize the Philippines and annex Hawaii. Two more wars gave us an economic stake in Japan and Korea, and then Johnson took the next step — into Viet Nam. But in 1968 that nearly five-hundred-year western hegemonic thrust was finally turned back. Viet Nam came to foreshadow our future. It was our first war of choice; it would not be our last.

With the lobbying campaign, the antiwar movement finally found a way to end the combat, but that was not our only triumph. Two other major achievements, of equal importance, kept the United States from winning the war and destroying Viet Nam. First, we prevented numerous escalations in military tactics, including the use of famine as a weapon, but, most important, we stopped the United States from deploying nuclear weapons. Second, we undermined political support for the war, eventually turning a majority of the country against it. As a result, the Pentagon lost the ability to draft new recruits, while combatants in the field became so disillusioned that many mutinied, making further ground combat operations impossible.

Our third major achievement, the lobbying campaign, blocked the funding Nixon needed to continue the war after the peace accords had been signed, a tactic he was prepared to execute through proxies in Saigon and Phnom Penh. Ambassador Graham Martin had often lobbied in favor of military assistance to Thieu, which put him at loggerheads with us. After the war, Martin admitted that the Assembly to Save the Peace Agreement, which became the last mass protest against the war, had been "very effective." In testimony before Congress, he described our work against military funding for South Viet Nam and Cambodia as a "beautifully orchestrated campaign," concluding that "the negative decision was made inevitable by one of the best propaganda and pressure organizations the world has ever seen." No doubt there was self-serving exaggeration in that comment, but Martin's subsequent testimony indicated his remarks had been sincere.

Despite the internal disunity and ideological extremes present during its final phase, the antiwar movement was one of the most powerful grassroots movements in the history of the country. Unable to stop the war in its early stages, we did make it possible for the Vietnamese, fighting for their independence as our forefathers had, to win it. We helped give them a new nation. And we helped create new limits on the extension of American military power that severely curtailed reactionary U.S. influence, particularly in Central America, for years to come. Not bad for a movement fashioned out of a ragtag army of protesting kids.

However, having built the antiwar movement, we knew the time had come to close it down. The Coalition to Stop Funding the War shut its doors. So did IPC. Several million dollars had been raised for the Bach Mai Hospital, but other nations had also raised money for Bach Mai, so the American funds were used to rebuild the hospital's ear, nose, and throat wing, while contributions from other countries were used to reconstruct the other wings. MAI folded itself into a larger coalition called Friendshipment, which continued to send aid to war-torn areas in Indochina. A few groups in the United Campaign kept up their advocacy for postwar reconstruction and diplomatic relations between the former enemies.

It was hard for me to shift gears after so many years of single-minded focus on the war, but I had no choice. During the extended sixties, I and my friends and associates had led lives of intensity and excitement. We were at the forefront of national and international politics, and we were intoxicated by our involvement. We believed that not only were we living in history; we were actually having an impact upon it. The future would be different, yet I had to find a way to maintain my involvement and enthusiasm no matter what I did. I still had an interest in science but no desire to return to scientific work. I had become a political person. And while I expected life to be less exuberant than in the past, I was hooked on the great adventure of social change and wanted to do more with the political skills I had acquired. Yet I had not expected the war to end as abruptly as it did. So, like others around me, I had a new question to answer: What do I do now?

CHAPTER 27

MY DECISION ABOUT WHAT TO DO AFTER THE WAR SET ME ON A COURSE I HAVE used to navigate across the years from that day to this. After Saigon fell, Tom Hayden resolved to run against John Tunney, the first-term junior senator from California, in the 1976 Democratic primary. He asked me to manage his campaign. Neither of us had any electoral experience, but lobbying Congress had convinced us that the left could at least aspire to political power.

Despite my wartime political experience, I felt ill equipped to advance the postwar political work I thought was needed. I knew a good deal about foreign affairs and national security issues, but relatively little about domestic policy. I knew how Americans felt about Viet Nam, but not their views on jobs or health care or taxes. I was familiar with leaders like Ho Chi Minh and Che Guevara, but these were foreign heroes for whom most Americans had no sympathy.

To be politically effective, I had to reconnect with my own people and my own country. Nothing would force that more effectively than trying to win an election. In it we would have to address the issues of greatest concern to voters, rather than the issues of greatest concern to us. We would have to communicate effectively and with a broader cross section of society. If we were serious about alleviating the discrimination and financial insecurity that still distorted the lives of too many Americans, sooner or later we would have to master the electoral game.

Jane provided the initial money, and Joan left the Bar Sinister to join us. We four were the first of what would become a large staff. We knew we had only a small chance, but the twin traumas of Viet Nam and Watergate had fueled demands to reform government. A well-known antiwar activist like Tom could do well with the liberal voters in a Democratic primary. Win or lose, we could use the campaign to seed a new political organization in California. It made sense to me. I liked fighting against long odds and working behind the scenes on projects of real import. Politics had lit up my life and I wanted more.

But not everyone agreed. The others on the IPC staff worried that a candidate campaign would be corrupted by money, that compromises in principle would be required, and that too much attention would land on one individual. They felt a new political movement should be built from the ground up, not the top down. Our IPC friends moved to Washington to work for a new nonprofit organization lobbying to improve U.S. foreign policy.

We launched the Senate campaign a full year before the June 1976 primary, but we were amateurs. We had never worn suits and ties as adults. We had never thought deeply about domestic issues. Nevertheless, Jane was a news magnet and brought us extensive coverage. She and Tom were irresistible to the press: a beautiful rebel movie star and a real-life rebel who had been a strategic leader and a street-fighting Chicago Seven defendant. It was an unusual situation, but one we could orchestrate to give Tom's candidacy more visibility and financial support.

Over the first three months, I built a large campaign organization by hiring a few Democratic Party operatives and many veterans of the antiwar movement. Larry Levin and Fred Branfman held senior positions. Ken Coplon, by then running his own company, managed our direct-mail fund-raising. Dick Flacks, after surviving the attack at the University of Chicago and joining the faculty at the University of California, Santa Barbara, coordinated the campaign there with his wife, Mickey. Flacks developed our policy positions with Derek Shearer, who had been the managing editor of the alternative Boston newsweekly that ran the headline "Enemy Bombs Hanoi" after Nixon escalated the war in April 1972.

Numerous other antiwar activists whose skill and competence had been tested during the war were also hired.

Jane ran through her savings and quickly learned to be an effective fund-raiser. She recruited some of the country's best-known actors and rock musicians to help. At one typically star-studded fund-raising event in Orange County, I was pleased to renew my acquaintance with Lieutenant Colonel Edison Miller, the most outspoken of the POWs I had filmed in Hanoi.

Yet despite all the attention, we remained stagnant in the polls, stuck at 15 percent to Tunney's 55 percent. In January, after six months of campaigning, we tried to increase our support by publishing *Make the Future Ours*, a book-length issues platform prepared by Branfman, Flacks, and Shearer. We were ahead of our time. We advocated universal health care and ending dependence on foreign oil by shifting to solar energy. We called for gay rights, green jobs, publicly funded child care, and increased veterans' benefits. It sounds eerily familiar to the issues in the 2008 presidential campaign, but we had pushed for many of the same reforms thirty-two years earlier, in 1976.

We still didn't move in the polls, but we did open a deep fissure in the California Democratic Party, which was controlled by pro-business moderates. The party's grassroots activists, labor union members, and minority groups were its backbone, but they had little influence and felt excluded. Progressive leaders within the party grew frustrated, and the bravest among them stepped forward to endorse Tom. Most prominent were Cesar Chavez, founder and head of the United Farm Workers, and Ron Dellums, Oakland's charismatic black congressman who had been one of our most reliable antiwar allies.

Yet despite such support, we were not getting through to voters. The methods we had used to organize the antiwar movement were not working in the context of an electoral campaign. A successful movement can be built with a relatively small portion of the population, even as little as 1 percent, if they are aggressive and their message resonates with a larger number, as our antiwar message had. An election required 50 percent support, a very different task.

We had to try other methods, so I hired Peter Hart, a Washington poll-ster, to help us develop a message strategy with which to produce thirty-second TV spots. We made several, but then vigorously debated when to put them on the air. Given our 15 percent to 55 percent deficit, I wanted to air the spots in early April, two months before the election, in hopes that a bump would also allow us to raise more money. The Democratic operatives on our staff argued that voters did not pay attention that early and our money would be wasted. In 1976, it was unheard of to advertise that far in advance of an election.

Being new to electoral politics, I wasn't bound by conventional wis-dom. We had always been risk takers, and this seemed like the time to take another. I spent every cent we had and bought two weeks of TV time in early April. It was a make-or-break gamble. When new polling numbers came out a week after the advertising, I was startled to see that Tom's sup-port had more than doubled from 15 percent to 33 percent. How, I asked myself, could we have worked for ten long months building a huge, multi-faceted campaign organization that had recruited thousands of volunteers and reached tens of thousands of voters only to see no movement whatso-ever in the polls, and then with a mere two weeks of TV advertising double our support? The results contradicted everything I knew about political organizing.

I quickly reassessed what we were doing. There were then 6.4 million registered Democrats in California. I realized that even if our campaign organization was able to contact a thousand new voters a day, simple arithmetic revealed that it would take sixty-four hundred days to reach all of them, and only once. That was eighteen years! Television ratings indi-cated that our two weeks of advertising had already delivered multiple messages to 95 percent of those 6.4 million Democratic voters. I knew it cost thousands of dollars to buy one TV spot shown one time in one city, but when I took those spot costs and divided them by the number of viewers each spot reached, I realized that on a per capita basis (the price of delivering one message to one viewer) the cost was only a frac-tion of a cent, less than printing leaflets and having volunteers pass them out free.

That was a revelation. Television advertising wasn't expensive; it was cheap, provided you needed to reach voters across a broad geographic area. TV spots could also deliver a message to almost all voters simultaneously, and then change or modify it instantly, if necessary. And while thirty seconds was very brief, the messages were effective. Moving images married to voices, music, and sound effects allowed producers to create dramatic emotional content that resonated more powerfully than the rational and logical messages better suited to print media.

I understood that TV advertising was destined to play the dominant role in American political campaigns, and I resolved to learn more. But TV came with problems. Television advertising was manipulative, precisely because of its potential to elicit emotional responses, and it was too often used to distort the truth. Most people on the left wanted nothing to do with it. As a campaign manager, I didn't have that luxury. It had become obvious what would happen if Tunney advertised and we did not.

Our jump in the polls brought more support. Two well-known media consultants volunteered to assist us. Sid Galanty had directed TV spots for Hubert Humphrey in the 1968 presidential race. Later, he and his partner, Gary Horowitz, made the TV spots that elected Tom Bradley, an African American, mayor of Los Angeles in 1973. Our new advertising team was complete when Jack Fiman, a time buyer, joined us and offered his expertise.

More money came in because of Tom's rapid rise in the polls, but Jane had another ace up her sleeve. The movie studios had blackballed her after her trip to Hanoi four years before, but with the war over they said she might be able to reestablish herself as a leading actress if she began with a light comedy. She agreed to star in *Fun with Dick and Jane,* and Columbia Pictures gave her a $200,000 advance. She gave me the money to pay for more advertising.

Sid, Gary, and Jack created a convincing advertising campaign that used Jane's father, Henry Fonda, as an on-camera spokesperson. But we weren't working in a vacuum. Tunney mounted a TV campaign, too, and his corporate backers assembled a budget that dwarfed ours. We were able to buy TV spots the last ten days before the election, but Tunney was on the air far longer. When I saw how much airtime he had, I had no doubt we were flying into a headwind.

We had grown to twenty-six offices. Over four thousand volunteers went door-to-door, and in the last eight days they distributed 1.25 million pieces of campaign literature. I planned an election night rally in a hotel ballroom, but Bobby Kennedy weighed on me. Exactly eight years before at an election night rally in an L.A. hotel ballroom following the 1968 California Democratic primary he had been assassinated. In the unlikely event that Tom won, I didn't want him to become the next progressive leader gunned down as his potential was first realized. I bought him a Kevlar vest, insisted he wear it under his suit, and then carefully secured the ballroom.

Tunney won 53.8 percent of the vote, Tom got 36.7 percent, and seven minor candidates split the rest. We licked our wounds but were widely congratulated for doing as well as we did. Articles appeared saying we represented a new force that had emerged from the radical movements of the sixties to claim a place in mainstream politics. We appreciated all the good wishes. But we knew our experience had been unique because of the celebrity status and resources Jane had brought to the campaign,

Tom Hayden and I share a moment on the podium at the end of his U.S. Senate campaign. Jane Fonda is on the right. *Photo Star Black*

and therefore it could not serve as a model for others. Yet we had moved the movement forward. We had understood the mechanics of elections, learned to use language voters could understand, and laid the groundwork for a new political organization.

Personally, the campaign had given me what I came for. I had found my way back to America, not to embrace its past mistakes, but to work within it for positive change. I had learned about domestic policy, message development, canvassing, polling, and other techniques essential to electoral work. Most important, I had come to understand the power of political advertising. I could see that if the left remained quarantined in a small corner of protest, relying only on grassroots techniques, it would be unable to advance. I wondered if the new skills I had acquired could help lift that quarantine, but before I had time to think, I was back in action.

Cesar Chavez called. The United Farm Workers (UFW) had gathered signatures to place an initiative on the November ballot that would guarantee their right to organize. They needed help with advertising, so Cesar asked me to pull together the team that had produced Tom's and be his media consultant for the Proposition 14 campaign. Agribusiness had amassed a multimillion-dollar TV effort using spots designed to elicit anti-Mexican racism. Despite Cesar's popularity, Proposition 14 fell behind.

My media team developed a script for a TV spot that convincingly undercut the agribusiness commercials. We brought it to Cesar's campaign manager, Marshall Ganz, the UFW director of organizing and a veteran of SNCC and the southern civil rights movement. Marshall authorized us to film the script.

Just before we started, the governor showed up. Jerry Brown wanted to be in the Proposition 14 commercials. I told him that was a mistake. I didn't think a politician, no matter how popular, could overcome the emotional spots being advanced by agribusiness. We needed memorable visual images and an emotional appeal of our own, not talking heads. Brown's entourage made it clear that he planned to raise much of the money the UFW would use to buy airtime, so I was overruled. Chavez and Ganz had little choice. Besides, Jerry had won his last race and I had lost mine. On Election Day, Proposition 14 went down two to one. Jerry

Brown got a badly needed lesson in humility; Chavez and Ganz learned what emotional TV advertising could do.

I returned to work on a master plan for the Campaign for Economic Democracy (CED), the new organization we were forming out of Tom's Senate campaign. Proposition 14 had shown me the potential of the ballot initiative: an organization could write its own law and campaign for it. I wanted to use ballot initiatives to build CED. Tom disagreed. He wanted the organization to advance public policy goals and try to elect members to ever higher offices. When Derek Shearer's then wife, Ruth Yannatta (now Goldway), declared for a state assembly seat and asked me to do her advertising, I decided to leave CED to Tom and start my own political consulting company.

I had come to see politics differently than I had in the sixties. Then, we had to protest, first against civil rights abuses and later against the war, sexism, ethnic discrimination, a polluted environment, and a host of other ills. Protest was defensive; it followed the agenda of our opponents. I wanted to be offensive and work for progressive change. I thought I could help do that by adding an electoral capacity to the left's otherwise limited political arsenal.

I called the new company Loudspeaker. Sid Galanty and Jack Fiman joined me when there was work but otherwise maintained their own businesses. We were only able to get a few local campaigns in 1978. Joan and I had been living together for the past three years, so we survived on her salary as an attorney for the California Agricultural Labor Relations Board. The book I started in Cozumel, *Airlift to Wounded Knee*, was published but achieved only modest success, except on Indian reservations, where, much to my satisfaction, it was widely read by young people.

In September 1978, Joan gave birth to our son, Nico, and we both luxuriated in what for us were the new and intense pleasures of parenting. As his first year passed, she decided to be a full-time mom, and I supported her decision. By June 1980, Loudspeaker's growing reputation led to bigger clients. We served as media consultants for two California initiative campaigns that had opponents with multimillion-dollar budgets, winning one against the real estate industry and losing the other to big oil. We were also awarded a CLIO, the Oscar of advertising, for a dramatic TV spot that stopped the construction of a nuclear waste dump in New Mexico.

I had wanted to straddle activism and electoral politics, and so far I was succeeding. We had tried to capture new tax revenue to expand public transportation in our campaign against big oil, and though we lost, I felt I was learning to operate offensively. In stopping the nuclear waste dump, which was defensive, I had used TV producing skills acquired in electoral work to be a more effective protester.

Once more, not everyone agreed with me. I wrote and spoke publicly, urging activists to get involved in elections, but I was often criticized by publications and leaders on the left for drawing people into a flawed system unable to deliver real reform. I was attacked even more vigorously for insisting that progressives master and use advertising, particularly on TV.

Fortunately, our initiative work in the June 1980 primary was noticed. Stanley Weiss, a self-made industrialist with a remarkably adventurous spirit, was trying to build the Citizens Party by running the environmental scientist Barry Commoner for president in November. Stanley thought I was the right guy to manage the campaign. By the time it ended, we both swore never to involve ourselves in another third-party effort, but we became friends. Stanley urged me to form an expanded political consulting firm and offered to help finance it. He and three other progressive funders gave us a large loan, and with it we launched Zimmerman, Galanty & Fiman (ZGF) in 1981.

But as we acquired these new resources, Ronald Reagan was inaugurated. His victory in 1980 had been fueled by large numbers of white working-class voters, especially males, who had switched their allegiance to the Republicans. It became clear that a new conservative era had begun. There would be more to protest, and offensive success would be less likely. As Sun Tzu advised over two thousand years ago, "One defends when his strength is inadequate; he attacks when it is abundant." Our strength was not abundant.

The most critical issue we had to protest was Reagan's belligerence toward the U.S.S.R., which had rekindled our fear of nuclear war. As a result, ZGF agreed to manage a 1982 California ballot initiative advocating a nuclear weapons freeze. Elsewhere, our advertising skills were more in demand as Reagan's victory energized progressive organizations and increased both their fund-raising capability and their desire to protest his policies.

The degree to which we had been put on the defensive was further revealed as the boundaries of the coming culture wars emerged. Greed seemed to be the new Republican ideology. "Big government" was denigrated as conservatives tried to roll back Johnson-era reforms. Sixties activists dug in for the long haul and with other progressives unable to contest for power found roles in which they could express or promote their points of view. Some took jobs as teachers, others as labor organizers, social workers, community college instructors, public defenders, environmentalists, consumer advocates, clinic doctors, journalists, community organizers, or antidiscrimination activists. They built the bridges on which the legacy of the sixties was carried forward.

One offensive action still possible was to prepare for a post-Reagan era by electing more progressives to office. In 1982, ZGF was able to do that. We won gubernatorial primary and general election races for Toney Anaya, a crusading former attorney general in New Mexico. We won congressional primary and general elections for Lane Evans, a progressive thirty-one-year-old running in a conservative rural Illinois district that had not sent a Democrat to Washington since the Great Depression. Once in office, he amassed the highest anti-Reagan voting record in the Congress. And in California, despite Reagan sending his defense secretary to campaign against us, we won the ballot initiative advocating a nuclear weapons freeze.

That year, we also helped Tom Hayden win a state assembly seat after he had spent several years building the Campaign for Economic Democracy. The organization's grand design was never realized, but it advocated effectively for solar energy and other progressive change, and it trained many young activists who became leaders in government and in public interest work. Tom served for ten years in the assembly and another eight in the state senate. Jane Fonda resurrected her movie career and in the late 1970s and early 1980s made a string of successful films with progressive social and political themes.

In 1982, ZGF also began to work with Jane on a project entirely foreign to our past experience but which succeeded beyond our wildest dreams. Jane acquired an interest in diet and exercise, opened a fitness studio, and developed new workout routines for women. The newly invented home videocassette players allowed exercises to be taped so women could work out at home. Jane asked Sid Galanty to film the routines and offered ZGF a portion of the profits. Her *Workout* video became a worldwide sensation and the largest-selling videotape ever. It sparked a new American interest in exercise and fitness. We filmed six more versions, and used the profits to repay the loan that Stanley Weiss had organized for us.

Our electoral success led to a big break. Immediately after the November 1982 election, Marilyn Katz, a friend and former antiwar leader, brought me to Chicago to meet Harold Washington, a black congressman running for mayor in early 1983. The city had never had an African American mayor. I signed on as Washington's media consultant and happily went to work fighting the storied Chicago political machine that had controlled the city during my childhood and student years. But the vote in Chicago quickly became one of the most bitter and racially polarized elections in modern American history. For example, once, while I was walking on a downtown Chicago street, an elderly matron spit on me when she saw the Washington button on my coat. The incident was typical of the bigotry and racial polarization consuming the city. National reporters flocked to Chicago to report on the rapidly escalating conflict.

ZGF asked Daniel Dixon, a high-level advertising copywriter, to help us. We won the Democratic primary, but ten days before the general election, polling by Patrick Caddell and Paul Maslin revealed that Washington's Republican opponent, who had vigorously fanned the racist flames, had pulled ahead and would win. According to conventional wisdom, political campaigns did not deal with racial prejudice directly, so we broke the rules once again. Against the advice of everyone but the pollsters, Dan helped us craft highly emotional TV spots that shamed Chicago for its racism. We got the spots on the air only six days before the election, and they caused a sensation. Washington won with 51.7 percent, and post-election polling confirmed that our spots had done it. Years later, in analyzing how we had turned the city's racism back in Washington's favor, Kathleen Hall Jamieson, a campaign communications authority, wrote, "There is not a more powerful instance of 'reframing' that I know of in the modern history of televised campaigning."

Washington's victory raised our star in the small world of political consulting. Dan Dixon joined us, the company became Zimmerman, Galanty, Fiman & Dixon (ZGFD), and we took our place among the country's leading Democratic media consultants. We helped many candidates over the next two cycles. Most memorably, in 1984, we made TV spots for Gary Hart's presidential campaign and almost succeeded in winning the Democratic nomination. In Texas we made TV spots that won a U.S. Senate primary for Lloyd Doggett. In that campaign, I worked closely with an unknown Louisiana lawyer trying to save his declining reputation as a campaign manager; his name was James Carville. I was with him when he gave a young college graduate, Paul Begala, his first job in politics. After we lost the general election, the two teamed up to win several tough campaigns, which led to their management of Bill Clinton in 1992 and later fame as news commentators.

Despite the limitations of the Reagan era, our offensive work helped elect more progressives than I had thought possible. But I also remained committed to defensive protest since I was determined to make as much trouble as possible for Reagan's conservative agenda. ZGFD did free work for underfunded environmental and labor groups, civil rights and feminist organizations, and others trying to limit the conservative thrusts. They were compelling causes, but antiwar activism had seeped into my DNA, so when Reagan began to consider separate U.S. military interventions in El Salvador and Nicaragua, I got more deeply involved.

In El Salvador, an armed revolution was under way against a repressive regime supported by the United States. Our military advisers were already on the scene. Joan and I founded Medical Aid for El Salvador (MAES) based on the model of Medical Aid for Indochina. We were joined by a new friend, the actor Edward Asner, who took a public leadership role. Ed was the star of *Lou Grant*, a top-rated TV sitcom, but lost the program because of his courageous support for MAES.

Elsewhere in Central America, a forty-year dictatorial dynasty that had ruled Nicaragua and been supported by the United States fell to Sandinista revolutionaries in 1979. Reagan claimed they were a security threat, ordered the CIA to arm and train a counterrevolutionary force of mercenaries, and went to war against them. As the contra war dragged on, I saw a way to stop it in 1986. The last House vote to fund the contras had passed by a margin of fewer than two dozen. Another vote would come up in 1987. If it was lost, Reagan could only continue the war with U.S. troops. But 1988 was a presidential election year, and I was certain he would not commit the military and risk a political backlash that could hurt the Republican nominee. It was an ideal time to mount an intensive multifaceted lobbying campaign to block congressional funding and leave Reagan with no alternative.

I teamed up with Chuck Blitz, a brilliantly insightful but unsung strategist and fund-raiser. Together we assembled a team of specialists and launched Countdown '87, targeting twenty members of the House wavering on contra aid. Marge Tabankin, my traveling companion in Hanoi and President Jimmy Carter's head of VISTA, helped Chuck raise close to $1 million from a network of young progressives with inherited wealth. Community organizers trained by the United Farm Workers coordinated door-to-door work in the congressional districts. David Fenton, a sixties activist with press experience, handled our news operation. Rosa DeLauro, an experienced Washington operative, managed the overall effort. Stanley Greenberg did the polling and focus-group research, which I used to craft the radio and TV spots. In April 1987, the House voted 215–213 to cut off funding, and the contra war came to an end.

This project was but one of hundreds happening across the country during those years. Nodes of activism coalesced around individuals, committees, labor unions, progressive elected officials, or friendship networks to accomplish limited but specific goals. In the process, new funding sources were developed, young activists were trained, new alliances were forged, and isolated progressives were put in touch with others. These nodes of activism radiated out to others and inspired more action as they demonstrated the value of collective work.

Through this process, citizen activism was nurtured and survived, and new leadership developed. In the case of Countdown '87, Rosa DeLauro became a long-serving congresswoman and Democratic leader. Stan Greenberg, whom she married, polled for Bill Clinton in 1992, and later for Nelson Mandela and other national and international figures. Marge Tabankin led the Hollywood Women's Political Committee, which raised millions for progressive candidates. David Fenton started a successful progressive press relations firm. These leaders trained and inspired others, and in this way, both over and under the radar, the progressive movement remained alive and was even able to expand.

We also succeeded in El Salvador. In 1992, the UN brokered a truce and created a coalition government. American troops never intervened. Medical Aid for El Salvador, led by our executive director, Mario Velasquez, raised over $5 million primarily through a direct-mail campaign skillfully managed by Ken Coplon. We delivered medical services, trained barefoot doctors, built rural health clinics, brought injured children to the United States for medical care, and created a state-of-the-art prosthetics clinic to assist victims of land mines. One of our employees, frustrated at fitting prosthetic legs, decided to do something about the land mines. She quit to start a project of her own. Five years later, Jody Williams shared the Nobel Peace Prize for organizing an international treaty to ban the manufacture and use of land mines.

But in early 1987, despite our success, I grew dissatisfied with what I was doing. My desire to use elections to offensively advance progressive ideals had been foiled by Reagan and the rise of conservatism. We managed to get a few progressives elected to high public office, but given the committee structure in Congress, the country had to wait years for them to build the seniority necessary to accomplish meaningful goals. And with a conservative in the White House, no progressive laws would be signed in any case.

Three years before, Joan had given birth to our daughter, Emma. With her arrival, the great happiness we had experienced as Nico's parents increased manyfold. We had given Nico my last name, so we thought it fair to give Emma Joan's. Our family became the Zimmerman boys and the Andersson girls and has remained exceptionally close and loving ever since. But early in 1987, Joan told me I was in danger of failing as a father.

With Joan Andersson and our infant son, Nico, in 1979. *Author's collection*

Nico was eight, Emma three, and I was traveling so much that I was rarely available when they needed me. Being a good father meant more to me than success as a political consultant.

It was time to take another big risk. I had remained intrigued by ballot initiatives and thought they might provide a way for progressives to achieve more offensive success. Because of the expense involved in getting them on the ballot, initiatives had been used primarily by corporate and wealthy interests. If I could get the funding to do a progressive initiative and deliver a dramatic win, it might be possible to get the money to do more. After six years of Reagan, I burned with a desire to work offensively and roll back some of the losses we had suffered at the hands of conservatives. I knew I would have to stay involved in defensive protest, but a political career meant little to me if nothing positive could be achieved. With some trepidation, I decided to disband ZGFD, focus on California ballot initiatives, and avoid the excessive travel that had deprived my children of an attentive father.

I was also ready with an idea. Auto insurance rates were sky-high in California, and a fight against the insurance industry could unite people across political lines. With an initiative we could bring down premiums, regulate the industry, and put it under the control of an elected insurance commissioner. Chuck Blitz offered to help raise the seed money. I called Ralph Nader, not yet the victim of the narcissism and bad judgment that led him to run for president and eventually empower his corporate enemies by throwing the 2000 presidential election to George W. Bush. Ralph had an aide in Los Angeles write the initiative, and later I trained him to be the spokesperson for the campaign. Proposition 103, on the November 1988 ballot, provoked the most lopsided initiative battle in history. At least $99 million was spent against us, while the campaign I managed had only $2 million. But we won in a dramatic upset. Twenty years later, a national consumer group estimated that since its passage, Proposition 103 had saved California customers $62 billion, about $3 billion per year. That was the offensive action I wanted.

Chuck introduced me to Pacy Markman, one of Madison Avenue's leading advertising copywriters. He had run the Coca-Cola account at twenty-eight, created the ads that launched Miller Lite beer, and won a remarkable sixteen CLIO awards during an extraordinary career. After years of being involved in progressive politics on a part-time basis, he was ready to jump from commercial to political advertising. We formed Zimmerman & Markman (Z&M) in January 1991 to focus on public interest advertising and ballot initiatives, and thanks to Pacy's talent we immediately had the ability to produce advertising significantly more dramatic and emotional than our competitors.

By then, many progressives who had once been critical came to me for advice, at least about advertising and elections. Yet they remained skeptical about initiatives. Because of the large sums of money required, initiatives had often been a tool of private interest groups working against the public interest. Many progressives felt that despite an occasional initiative win we would always be at a financial disadvantage. I pushed back, arguing that initiatives were an arena of political struggle we could ill afford to abandon. If large-scale fund-raising was required, it was our responsibility to master the necessary techniques.

For the next twenty years, Pacy and I worked for a few candidates, assisted many protesters, and did a lot of public interest advertising for groups like the American Civil Liberties Union and the Natural Resources

Defense Council. However, we concentrated the bulk of our energy on a long string of ballot initiatives that more than satisfied my desire to act offensively despite the conservative era in which we were marooned.

In Oregon in 1994, we won an initiative that created the nation's first physician-assisted suicide law, an advance that has already spread to Washington State. Four years later, in Arizona, we did the advertising for an initiative that established public funding for qualified candidates in state elections, paving the way for a reform that ultimately will be essential to progressive change: getting private money out of politics. In 2004, we managed one of our most satisfying efforts, the Proposition 63 campaign in California. Through it, we imposed a 1 percent surtax on annual income over $1 million. The resulting revenue, over $1 billion a year, pays for community mental health programs that target the homeless mentally ill and at-risk children, two populations often last in line when legislators fund social programs.

As we fought these many battles, Pacy and I joined another offensive effort to change the nation's harmful and ineffective drug laws. Using ballot initiatives, we passed laws that had no chance of being enacted any other way. With the assistance of my capable and exceptionally thorough deputy, Dave Fratello, we wrote, managed, and created the advertising for seventeen ballot initiatives in ten states between 1996 and 2008. Thirteen of the seventeen were successful. Ethan Nadelmann, founder and head of the Drug Policy Alliance, organized the funding for this national effort from George Soros and other philanthropists.

Our initial success was California Proposition 215, the nation's first medical marijuana law, in 1996. Over the next four years we won medical marijuana initiatives in Alaska, Washington, Oregon, Nevada, Colorado, and Maine, helping to alleviate the pain and suffering of hundreds of thousands of patients. In 2000, we won our most significant drug reform victory, California Proposition 36. It ended incarceration for nonviolent drug possession and offered state-sponsored treatment instead. Since then, Proposition 36 has freed thirty-five thousand people a year from jail and saved the state hundreds of millions of dollars.

As Z&M worked on these and other initiatives, MoveOn.org, a new progressive online organization, asked us in late 2002 to create advertising opposing the coming invasion of Iraq. They had 300,000 members and thought that if the advertising was good enough, they could get their members to pay for it. It worked. The dramatic TV spots we made for MoveOn.org, and the nationally coordinated actions they sponsored before and after the invasion, rapidly increased their membership and thrust them into the leadership of the movement against the Iraq war. At the same time, the leaders of MoveOn.org developed new techniques for Internet-based political organizing. Once again, I was protesting a U.S. war, and when it continued through the summer of 2003, we realized that the only way to stop it was to defeat President Bush in 2004.

With Wes Boyd, MoveOn.org's co-founder, I managed the group's 2004 independent presidential effort, which raised and spent $23 million on TV advertising in critical electoral college states. Stan Greenberg's firm did the polling and media testing. Z&M's hard-hitting TV spots attacked Bush's war policies and his domestic economic stewardship. We called him a "MisLeader," and the label soon entered the political lexicon. Wes and I anticipated Ohio swinging the outcome and ran anti-Bush TV spots there starting eleven months before the election. It wasn't enough. John Kerry, a Viet Nam vet and former antiwar activist himself, lost Ohio, which allowed Bush to win reelection.

In 2006, we worked with Eli Pariser, MoveOn.org's executive director, to beat back the skepticism of Democratic leaders who thought they could not win enough seats to regain control of the House. We produced and aired dramatic TV spots in April 2006 in the districts of eight Republican incumbents thought to be too strong to beat. Polling after our spots ran indicated that these incumbents were vulnerable. Washington Democratic leaders enlarged their field of play and in November won control not only of the House but unexpectedly of the Senate as well.

In 2007 and 2008, MoveOn.org endorsed Barack Obama in the primary and campaigned for his victory. Its membership had soared past five million. Z&M produced advertising that attacked Bush, the Republicans, and John McCain once he won the nomination. By the summer of 2008, the Obama campaign had raised unprecedented sums of money and had put together the largest, most sophisticated, and most efficient grassroots organization in history. Its ability to do so was in no small measure the result of pioneering online organizing work, and Internet tools and techniques, that MoveOn.org had helped develop over the previous six years.

Unlike our antiwar movement in the sixties, the movement against the war in Iraq learned to work within the mainstream, avoid extremist tactics and rhetoric, raise money at the grass roots, and find messaging that united young and old, rich and poor, students and workers. They, we, were able to fight on many fronts and use all the tools of political campaigning to both defensively protest the war and run sophisticated offensive electoral campaigns that captured the Congress in 2006 and helped win the presidency itself in 2008. Along the way, we had the privilege of being present at the birth of the online citizen activism destined to shape the next century.

MANY VETERANS OF THE SIXTIES JOINED BARACK OBAMA'S 2008 PRESIDENTIAL campaign. We felt a distant echo from our past in the remarkable burst of citizen activism that Obama unleashed. I felt great personal closure. My son, Nico, four years a lawyer, spent two months running the Obama campaign's election protection operation in a three-county area northeast of Cleveland. Working under him for the last ten days were his mother, Joan, a member of Yale Law School's class of 1968, and his sister, Emma, forty years behind her mother as a member of that same school's class of 2008. That our family's combined legal skills helped protect the integrity of the vote for Barack Obama in Ohio, four years after Republican-sponsored voting irregularities there had deprived my own campaigning of a victory in 2004, was a special delight.

The progressive activism that brought Barack Obama to power in 2008 captured the spirit of the sixties. We have yet to see if his victory becomes the enduring legacy of those turbulent times. In 2011, a new wave of global citizen activism, fed in part by Occupy Wall Street, strengthened my belief in the links between the sixties and the present. Conservative pundits deny such ties. They see the sixties as a brief histori-cal detour that debased our culture and had little effect on the ongoing political life of the nation. Their analysis is wrong.

The astonishing fifteen years between 1960 and 1975 broke sharply with the past and became a pivot between a pale, orderly, and conformist

period in U.S. history and the more frenzied, multicolored, often preposterous times that followed. Those years laid the tracks that shaped the evolution of our society, our culture, and our politics. Simultaneously, and
paradoxically, they also provoked an era of deep conservatism. Today, that
conservative era may finally be fading, despite the anger and outrage visible as it declines. If a more progressive period is now to follow, the sixties
will have shaped them both.

The post-sixties conservative era was instigated in part by the antiwar
movement. Our forceful tactics, the radically different lifestyle championed
by the hippies, and the humiliating defeat in Viet Nam inflamed conservatives and led to Republican electoral success. At the start of the Viet Nam
war, most of the protesters were just kids. We lacked resources and experience. We were cut off by the McCarthy era from an older generation that
might have provided some guidance. We had no base of support or access to
even limited financing, as the civil rights movement had. Because we were
opposed by the entire social order, we utilized tactics that were unusually
vigorous and creative, but also were often repugnant to those outside the
movement. We had no choice; we did what we had to do.

Early antiwar protesters, based on the college campuses, were by def-
inition middle-class. Working-class kids were working, or accepting what
they saw as the inevitability of being drafted; they did not protest until
later. Early protesters like me became alienated from society and rejected
middle-class culture. Working-class people, struggling to achieve that status, saw us as strange, subversive, and unpatriotic. As the culture of the sixties evolved, they came to deeply resent us. Despite being lifelong
Democrats, many voted for Richard Nixon in 1968, and more than a few
for George Wallace, the racist third-party candidate.

These conservative trends broadened in the late 1970s, until white
working-class anger, driven by the widening cultural antagonisms, swept
Ronald Reagan into office in 1980. A straight line can be drawn from the
hard hats of the labor movement who beat up antiwar protesters to the so-
called Reagan Democrats who switched parties in 1980 to vote Republican.

But as these white working-class voters moved right politically, many
of their children moved left culturally. Their young men grew long hair,
dressed unconventionally, and with their sisters and girlfriends embraced

the sixties culture of "sex, drugs, and rock and roll" that years before had swept through the college campuses. Some rejected church attendance, sexual abstinence, and blind patriotism, hallmarks of their parents' generation, and fell victim to the same generational warfare in the 1970s and 1980s that had roiled middle-class families in the 1960s. Later, after Reagan's conservative movement failed to deliver the prosperity his empty nostalgia for the 1950s had promised, many in the older generation moved even farther right because of these conflicts.

However, while antiwar activists bear some responsibility for provoking the conservative era that followed the sixties, we also provoked a lot more. As our opponents gained strength in the late 1970s and 1980s, the progressive ideas unleashed earlier found expression in a host of new political organizations, some led by people described earlier in this book. With agendas based on core values advanced during the sixties, powerful groups sprang up in support of abortion, feminism, gay rights, nuclear disarmament, the environment, immigrants, human rights, urban planning, alternative energy, and the disabled.

The dreams of the sixties were part of the great tradition of American progressivism and continued to flourish in the shadow of the conservative era that followed. Far from being irrelevant, as right-wing commentators would have us believe, the ideals of the sixties held on with the tenacity of tidal barnacles, allowing wave after wave of conservative dogma to wash over them but never relinquishing their hold on America's hearts and minds.

During the 1970s and beyond, progressive leaders built new organizations and won some electoral victories, but it was the more numerous political troublemakers working at the grassroots level who kept the ideals of the sixties alive: the union member who put in extra time to protest a labor grievance; the mom who tried to improve the local schools after her kids were asleep; the public defender who stayed late because she knew her client was innocent. While the ideology of greed and self-centered consumption was championed by the dominant conservative culture, such people embraced more humane values and lived their lives accordingly.

The sixties had taught them not to turn away from injustice, not to accept the status quo because it's the way things are. Millions came to see

themselves as part of the fight for a better world, not a common perception before the sixties. Our society has been so thoroughly affected by this
spirit that we've even invented a new career track, "public interest," to
help young people embrace the fight for justice as a central aspect of their
lives. Those public interest jobs are another invention of the sixties, and
thanks to them we now have troublemakers everywhere.

Even deeper factors connect us to the sixties. Those years altered our
language and the very categories of thought we now use to interact politically. For example, the word "activist" was rarely used before the sixties. It
was invented to describe civil rights workers and antiwar advocates who
weren't satisfied to merely voice their opinions but instead provoked
"actions" to further them. Before us, those who led political action were
called "organizers," with the assumption that they were professionals. We
invented a new role and "organized" political action as unpaid citizen volunteers. How different politics would now be without activists.

Yet "activist" and "public interest" are not the only new words and
concepts introduced in the sixties. Starting with the term "military-
industrial complex" first uttered in January 1961, here are some of the
words we use today to think about politics, all of which first emerged in the
sixties: affirmative action, abortion rights, sexual liberation, environmental-
ism, consumer protection, nuclear disarmament, the silent majority, the
moral majority, the religious right, youth culture, the establishment, political polarization, gender equality, minority rights, gay rights, the war on
drugs, sexism, feminism, identity politics, investigative reporter, corporate
responsibility, community organizer. The list is not exhaustive.

The very word "antiwar," so common today, did not exist before the
sixties, when one had to spell it "anti-war." The sixties utterly reorganized
our thinking about war. Now we can no longer draft people into the military. Because of Viet Nam, our citizens won't permit it. In the 1980s,
memories of Viet Nam were so raw that a few veterans of the antiwar
movement were able to join with a new generation of activists to stop U.S.
military interventions in El Salvador and Nicaragua despite President
Reagan's desire to commit our troops there.

In fact, opposition to war has so evolved it is now a culture unto itself.
In 1990, the first President Bush had significant opposition simply in

sending American troops to retake Kuwait after the Iraqi invasion. A decade later, when his misguided son launched a war of aggression against Iraq, a new antiwar movement materialized almost instantly and in numbers that had taken us years to organize after the start of the war in Viet Nam. Building opposition to war was no longer necessary. The debacle in Viet Nam and the protest against it had created permanent opposition to war.

The sixties even altered how we see ourselves. Hard as it may be to remember, before the sixties most Americans wanted to be like everyone else. The man in the gray flannel suit and the stay-at-home housewife were the white middle-class ideals, while various ethnic groups were more concerned with blending in and assimilating than with the preservation of their own heritage. Many Americans were uncomfortable or even anxious if they thought others saw them as "different." The sixties turned that upside down, as Americans now take pleasure in trumpeting their differences.

My generation transformed America. A nation dominated by blind patriotism and unthinking conformity became a people quick to protest and quick to embrace the popular mantra to question authority, two attributes now fundamental to our political life. The sixties wove both into our national character. We may have failed to spark the political revolution we once sought, but we provoked a revolution in the thinking of human beings everywhere. The world will never be the same because of who we were and what we did.

In 1964, at the start of the Viet Nam antiwar movement, we were tiny clusters of young people armed with nothing more than the moral clarity to see through government lies and the courage to risk taking action. In 2003, initial protests against the war in Iraq drew hundreds of thousands of Americans of all ages and stations linked to each other through the Internet. Within months we numbered in the millions. That explosive growth occurred because leadership stepped into the breach, and with so many participants, the extreme militancy of the sixties was no longer required. As a result, this new antiwar movement reached deeper into America than ours had. In fact, it was not a protest movement at all. With such widespread participation, it was an opposition movement ready to fight for political power. How times had changed.

When this new movement started in 2003, the nonprofit space in our economy had mushroomed since the sixties. Idealistic young people were employed in public interest jobs throughout the country. Activism, a willingness to stand up to authority, and the habits of collective action had become commonplace. The Iraq antiwar movement soon motivated its own presidential candidate and provided the critical resources that allowed Democrats to win the Congress in 2006 and the White House in 2008. What a sweet irony it will be if four decades of conservative ascendancy that began as a disapproving reaction to the militant tactics of the Viet Nam antiwar movement finally end because of political victories of the Iraq antiwar movement.

But progressive action, like any force of nature, leads to reaction. The fight to end the era of conservative ascendancy is not over. Tea Party activism, fueled by billionaire backers and right-wing media outlets, sprang up with remarkable speed in response to President Obama's 2008 election and allowed Republicans to retake the House of Representatives in 2010. When they then gridlocked the government and prevented Obama from addressing the economic pain caused by the Great Recession, Occupy Wall Street activism sprang up with equal speed on the other side, reminding us that politics is dynamic and change is never one-dimensional.

The question we now face is not whether America is on the threshold of a new progressive era—it is—but rather whether we can use the legacy of the sixties and the new activism unleashed in 2011 by Occupy Wall Street to push ourselves off the threshold into a full embrace of progressive ideals. I am convinced that citizen activism is now the only way to do that. But as I learned in the sixties, activists are not revolutionaries, even though their objective might be a revolutionary transformation of society. Activists achieve incremental gains, not massive and immediate upheavals. If those gains are sufficiently widespread, transformations can occur even when the activists themselves are unaware of how their work combines with that of others to affect the overall sweep of history. Here's an example.

Harold Washington's successful 1983 campaign to become the first black mayor of Chicago was organized and managed by veteran activists from the Chicago Area Friends of SNCC and the housing and education struggles that followed the civil rights movement. The three leading consultants who assisted them, the press secretary, the pollster, and I, the media consultant, were all veterans of the antiwar movement.

That's not surprising. However, Washington's victory affected African American life in the city, especially on the South Side, which was his base. Blacks were newly optimistic about electoral politics. The excitement was palpable, as people previously excluded from politics saw new possibilities. In the midst of the excitement, a twenty-four-year-old black kid with a funny African name arrived on the South Side to take a job as a community organizer. The optimism around him did not go unnoticed as Barack Obama weighed his own political future.

Just before that Election Day in 1983, the twenty-eight-year-old *Chicago Tribune* reporter covering the Washington campaign invited me to lunch. He had interviewed me frequently in previous months, so we were well acquainted. In the restaurant he leaned across the table and in a confidential tone told me that he was tired of doing what he did and wanted to do what I did instead. He asked for my advice about how to become a political media consultant, and I gladly gave it. The following year, he quit the *Tribune* and soon established himself as the leading political consultant in Chicago. His name: David Axelrod.

History is a mysterious companion: it never reveals the long-term consequences of your actions. Had Barack Obama not been inspired by Harold Washington's win, had David Axelrod not left the *Tribune* to become a political consultant ready to befriend him and guide his career, and had MoveOn.org not helped develop the Internet organizing and fund-raising tools that Obama and Axelrod would use to wage a brilliantly successful campaign twenty-five years after Harold Washington was first elected, American history would be different. I had no idea that the small role I played in those three events, alongside hundreds of others whose contributions were as important as mine, would then combine with myriad other acts and circumstances and coincidences, each essential to the final outcome, to win the presidency in 2008.

That victory may yet signal a fundamental shift in American politics. We'll see. But it occurred not only because random coincidences in the lives of Obama and Axelrod connected them to political turmoil decades earlier but also because they knew the intense commitment of the millions who fueled their remarkable 2008 campaign, regardless of their age or level of awareness, was inspired in part by the cauldron of sixties politics and the high level of citizen commitment and participation the sixties first introduced to America. The decision Obama and Axelrod made to hold their election night victory celebration in Chicago's Grant Park exactly forty years after the disastrous riots on the same ground at the 1968 Democratic convention was no accident. Ask them.

But Obama's victory has proven once again that winning the presidency is not enough. Presidents cannot enact progressive reform by fiat. They must govern from the middle, the inevitable result of a two-party system that holds elections at preset intervals. Such elections can only be mere oscillations between center-right and center-left governments, as all candidates must strive to capture the moderate middle that determines electoral outcomes. During the long decades in which conservative ideology has dominated, we had Democratic Congresses and Democratic presidents. It was the dominant ideology that was conservative, not every elected official. No doubt we will have Republican Congresses and presidents even if our people now gradually (for that's all it can be) move to the left.

Worse, perhaps, than the electoral setback in 2010, the Supreme Court's *Citizens United* decision means that right-wing billionaires, polluting corporations, and Wall Street financiers are now free to provide massive financial support to conservative candidates. But this setback does not change the fundamental equation. Big money has always manipulated conservative activists like the Tea Party into undermining their own economic self-interest. And we, as progressives, have always used the power of an aroused citizenry to resist their agenda and expand our rights.

In 2011, Occupy Wall Street aroused our citizenry. For the first time in almost one hundred years, the lop-sided distribution of our income and wealth was elevated to the center of political debate, an enormous and potentially far-reaching accomplishment. Occupy Wall Street's message, that our nation is divided into "the 99%" and "the 1%," is a critical first step that will animate the class-consciousness needed to correct our obscene economic inequality.

Occupy Wall Street achieved a second triumph. It created an "Occupy" franchise that allowed activists across the country to organize related protests anywhere and everywhere. Under this universal banner activists began to address a broad spectrum of issues and institutions. Hopefully, these actions will proliferate. The task going forward is to forge them into a coherent national crusade capable of achieving a progressive transformation.

As a lifelong activist and a professional political strategist, I know that there are many pitfalls that await the building of such a crusade. Therefore it seems fitting to me to end this book by erecting a few warning signs (♦) for future activists who will build on the Occupy events of 2011 and carry forward the battles for core values that we fought in the sixties.

♦ **STAY A FRANCHISE; DON'T OPEN A STORE.** Don't take a position on every issue. Don't try to be all things to all people. Stay on message. You are nimble and creative because you are not tied down. Resist the temptation to institutionalize yourselves by becoming an organization or prematurely launching a political party. That will drown your spirit in internal affairs and fund-raising. Other progressive organizations are available to play this role. We need you to stay a wild card, able to act quickly and without warning.

♦ **NEVER LOSE THE MEME OF 1% VS. 99%.** It exposes the ultimate weaknesses of our society and our enemies. Don't allow those weaknesses to be papered over. A constant emphasis on how we are all part of the 99% keeps our side together and can reunite us after disagreements. Your focus should be on those with extreme wealth who do not pay their fair share, ultimately the nub of many other problems. That will allow you to recruit unlikely allies. And don't let anyone label this class warfare; it isn't. Our demand is only that the 1% pay their fair share.

♦ **DON'T BASH BIG GOVERNMENT.** It's a Republican trap. In the years after the sixties, conservatives made exaggerated complaints about government waste and inefficiency. These distortions undermined public confidence in Washington, which then allowed the Republicans to dismantle government regulations on finance put in place after the Great Depression. That deregulation brought on the Great Recession of 2008. Remember, it is unchecked bureaucracy that is wasteful and inefficient, not government in and of itself.

♦ **GOVERNMENT SHOULD BE OUR TOOL, NOT THEIRS.** Without stronger financial regulation than was previously in place, our standard of living will decline further. Americans now face the iron law of unregulated capitalism: the rich get richer and the poor get poorer. Government is the only means by which working Americans can protect themselves on a capitalist playing field heavily tilted toward the wealthy, the only means by which the 1% can be forced to pay their fair share, the only way to break the power of the oil companies and create a clean energy future.

♦ **UNREGULATED CAPITALISM IS THE FUNDAMENTAL PROBLEM.** A compelling vision of a progressive society will emerge in the course of the struggles still ahead. Meanwhile, you are stuck with market capitalism and you should focus on bringing its worst aspects under control. Occupy Wall Street helped put financial regulation at the center of political debate. Keep it there. If financial regulation remains a central demand of the 99%, you can keep your focus on extreme income differences and effectively isolate the 1%.

♦ **BE THE OWNER, NOT THE REPAIRMAN.** Apologists for the 1% will put you on the defensive by insisting that you tell them exactly how to regulate Wall Street or secure the health-care system. Don't respond. You own the national house. If they built it for you without beds for everyone or a kitchen big enough to feed all the people, they've got to come up with a plan to fix it. Your job is to approve the plan and supervise the construction, not draw up the blueprints.

◆ **BE NICE TO DEMOCRATS.** Democrats are not your allies or even your friends. But you need them. Like Republicans, they depend on big money for campaign contributions, so even if they take complete control of government, they will never enact transformational change on their own. But a popular movement can develop enough power to force elected Democrats to support reform. In the future, you will need elected Democrats to pass your reforms just as the civil rights movement needed them to pass the Civil Rights and Voting Rights Acts.

◆ **DON'T GET SO UPSET ABOUT VOTING FOR DEMOCRATS.** Hold your nose and do it. It's necessary. Republican governments do far more damage than Democratic governments, both to people in poverty and to the rest of us. They spread false consciousness and make it more difficult for us to organize. Stop fussing about Democratic flaws. They are who they are. Real change will only be driven by citizen activism, not elections. So, when an opportunity comes along to put a Democrat into office instead of a Republican, take it, and then go back to movement building.

◆ **STOP WORRYING ABOUT "THE SYSTEM" CORRUPTING YOU.** Debates about working inside or outside the system waste your time. Both are necessary and neither is enough. Most progressive goals can only be achieved with the power of government (taxing the rich, neutralizing the oil companies, etc.), but these goals will not be achieved until rebellious activists force government to accept them. Activism and legislation, while different, are equally essential for progressive reform.

◆ **YOUR MISSION IS TO DESTABALIZE SOCIETY.** Only in times of crisis will those with power relinquish some of it to forestall losing all of it. You need to create these crises. Since transformational reform cannot be achieved by working inside government, a mass movement must first destabilize the political and economic status quo. The demands made by that movement must be based on common sense, so average Americans can support them, but they must also be unattainable within the status quo. That's what makes for a crisis.

♦ **BE MILITANT BUT NONVIOLENT**. The 99% are turned off by violent tactics, but to get their attention you must break through the news cycle by being militant. Take over public land, block access, prevent foreclosures, get arrested. You've got to prove you are serious and are not going away, and you need the press coverage to communicate. But rely on activism. It emerged worldwide in the sixties, but has now spread across the globe and become exponentially more powerful because of the Internet and social media. In 2011, the Arab Spring provoked Occupy Wall Street, which then inspired protests against austerity in the European Commonwealth and a corrupt election in Russia. The genie of citizen activism is out of the bottle. It's not going to be stuffed back in any time soon.

♦ **BE PROMISCUOUS**. Get involved with everyone. Of course racists, homophobes, and their ilk must be isolated, but almost everyone else is a potential friend. Reach out to conservatives, cops, businesspeople. The enemy is that portion of the 1% who aggravate and benefit from the current extremes of economic inequality. They have the government, the money, and the guns. Your only asset is the people. So never let battle lines be drawn that leave you with less than 99% on your side.

♦ **THINK STRATEGICALLY**. Too often we pursue goals because we desire or deserve them rather than because we have the ability to attain them. Strategic thinking means clearly assessing strengths and weaknesses on both sides of a fight before engaging, developing credible plans for organizing the resources needed to complete the tasks you undertake, delineating clear milestones that allow you to realistically measure your success or failure, building new alliances while simultaneously disrupting those of your opponents, and choosing tactics not because they are comfortable or dramatic but because they are most likely to get the job done.

♦ **DREAM UP NEW TACTICS**. Occupations are effective, but you need new ways to engage the 99% you want to represent. Militant actions on your part will always be necessary, but since most of the 99% have neither the time nor the willingness to risk arrest, other tactics must also be employed. I am reminded of 1971 when the antiwar movement had become too militant for the millions of Americans ready to oppose the war. By developing more inclusive tactics like Medical Aid for Indochina and the congressional lobbying done by the Indochina Peace Campaign we gave people a forceful and subversive way to express their opposition to the war without exposing themselves to personal jeopardy. We had to discover new nonviolent ways to mobilize people in the past; now you have to do it for the future.

Those are my warning signs. Here are the strategic demands that make the most sense to me.

Get money out of politics. This is a prerequisite for everything else. Elected officials will not reform themselves. Until we end campaign contributions and lobbying, we will not get the legislation we need. Full public financing of elections can only be won if activists build a force *outside* government and then apply that force *to* government.

Pass a new tax policy. Gilded Age concentrations of wealth undercut a just society. No one can achieve wealth apart from society and its governmental functions, so wealth must be forced to give back a fair share. At a minimum, we need taxes on financial transactions, higher estate taxes, special tax rates for high earners, and a capital gains tax rate equal to the rate on earned income.

Create green jobs. The only way to avoid a climate catastrophe is to break the power of the oil companies. Doing so will allow us to use public investment and legislative incentives to create millions of new jobs through the development of renewable energy sources and through retrofitting, green construction, efficient mass transit, and new technologies.

Cut military expenditures. Our military is too big. It gets us into trouble abroad, and it has the potential to limit liberty at home. Our reliance on nuclear weapons casts a shadow over all humankind. Withdrawal from Afghanistan and drastic cuts in our defense budget will free up billions for more productive purposes. In 2010, our military expenditures were six times those of China, the closest competition. We're not buying added defense, only defense contracts.

These four strategic demands are not a "program." That would require a comprehensive vision of a progressive society. Instead, they are goals around which our work can be organized. They are "strategic" because a progressive society cannot be built without them, and because they can unite the entire progressive spectrum. Each would also make it easier to pursue other important goals, like protecting the environment and supporting minority rights.

Many will shrink from such an ambitious agenda. They don't see what's coming. Look around. Our government is deadlocked. The middle class is disappearing. Our schools don't teach. Poverty, unemployment, and homelessness are rampant. Traffic is gridlocked. The health-care system is bankrupt. Even our planet is losing its ability to sustain us. Our future will be tumultuous, and in tumult there will be ample opportunity to organize dissent.

Remember this: the great movements of the sixties, the civil rights movement, the antiwar movement, the feminist movement, the gay rights movement, all began in an atmosphere of ridicule and hostility. They succeeded because their cause was just, they had the determination to fight for years against seemingly impossible odds, and they invented new tactics with which to educate the public. In each case, minorities worked to win rights from the majority. Now we can work for the majority, the 99%. That's why I refuse to sink into pessimism about the future. None of us can see what might be just over the horizon.

I started this book for my children. During my college years, two pebbles were dropped into my pond, the student demonstration in Paris in 1960, and a friend taking me to visit SNCC in Mississippi in 1963. Those two pebbles sent out the ripples that shaped the rest of my life. I wanted to drop a pebble into my kids' ponds, not an ugly one like colonial war or official racism, but a pebble that might give them a little inspiration, or at least connect them to a time when young people had stood up bravely for what was right and good and true. The sixties I lived through are a fading memory, and my generation is due to exit the historical stage. I thought the lessons of the sixties were too important to our future to allow them to disappear into the past. Once I started writing, I realized I had a message for a larger audience.

The commitment I made to work for justice and equality helped me avoid the alienation that corroded the lives of some of my peers. With others, I worked constructively when we could and made trouble for our enemies when we could not. Our ideals were the beacon toward which we sailed, although we soon realized we would never reach the other shore. It will fall to future generations to create a society fully committed to those ideals. It fell to mine to keep them alive so that someday they can. I hope the fire of our commitment, however bleak the times we lived through, will help inspire future activists to erase the injustice and poverty that need no longer have a place in our world. What I learned along the way is that performing good works, political or otherwise, with no expectation of recognition or reward, was for me the secret to leading an honorable and happy life.

ACKNOWLEDGMENTS

Many people helped me during the writing of this manuscript, but a few deserve special mention. Steve Wasserman, my agent, saw the potential for a readable book buried in the disjointed pages I first sent him. His insightful critique and later support set me on a more productive path. Gerald Howard, my editor at Doubleday and a man of limitless literary knowledge, was the Sherpa who guided me up a mountain of pages and kept me from falling off rhetorical cliffs or becoming entrapped in logical crevasses. Jeff Alexander and Hannah Wood made all my dealings with Doubleday a pleasure rather than a chore.

My wife, partner, and best friend, Joan Andersson, and my dear friend and lifelong colleague, Bart Meyers, both of whom you met earlier in this book, devoted many hours to reading and editing previous drafts. They helped me recall past events and wisely advised me on what to include and what to leave behind. I hope one day to return the favor since they both have their own stories to tell.

My son, Nico Zimmerman, was a discerning critic who mercilessly pressed me to more clearly organize and explain my thoughts. My daughter, Emma Andersson, and my daughter-in-law, Lisa Hageman, gave me the benefit of their judgment and insight, as did Ian Bassin and Alice Radosh.

Dan Ostlund first suggested I write this book, a suggestion I ignored. Nevertheless, his persistence planted the seed that several years later started to sprout. Ethan Signer graciously gave me permission to tell the story of the stolen antibiotic I smuggled to the Vietnamese, a tale neither of us has ever before revealed. Danny Lyon approved the use of two photographs in Chapter 3 that he shot on our 1963 trip to Mississippi; and Kevin McKiernan allowed me to quote from a letter he wrote about his experiences in Wounded Knee.

There is also a list of people too long to include who provided essential help. Some reminded me of past events, helped me verify long-lost dates and times, recalled people I had difficulty remembering, or shared their own stories. Others critiqued my point of view or helped me prepare materials to enhance the distribution of the book. You all know who you are; know too that I am grateful for the time and energy you spent assisting me.

As always, acknowledgments like this must include a declaration that despite the help I did receive, all the statements of fact, opinion, and analysis are entirely my responsibility, and any errors that may have crept into the manuscript are due to my oversight only.

Finally, I want to thank the early leaders of the civil rights and antiwar movements whose courage and determination created a community of principled dissent I was eager to join.